New Canadian Readings

INTERPRETING CANADA'S NORTH

Selected Readings

Edited by
Kenneth S. Coates and William R. Morrison

Copp Clark Pitman Ltd.
A Longman Company
Toronto

ISBN 0-7730-4782-4

Editing: Melanie Sherwood
Design: Kathy Cloutier and Susan Coull
Cover: "Man Hunting at Seal Hole" by Niviaksiak. Reproduced with the
        permission of the West Baffin Eskimo Co-operative Ltd., Cape Dorset,
        NWT, Canada.
Typesetting: Barbara Cholewa and Carol Magee
Printing and binding: Alger Press Limited

Canadian Cataloguing in Publication Data

Main entry under title:

Interpreting Canada's North: Selected Readings

ISBN 0-7730-4782-4

1. Yukon Territory. 2. Northwest Territories.
I. Morrison, William R. (William Robert), 1942-   .
II. Coates, Kenneth, 1956-   .

FC3956.I76 1989   971.9   C89-094677-9
F1090.5.I76 1989

Copp Clark Pitman
2775 Matheson Blvd. East
Mississauga, Ontario
L4W 4P7

Associated Companies:
  Longman Group Ltd., London
  Longman Group Inc., New York
  Longman Cheshire Pty., Melbourne
  Longman Paul Pty., Auckland

Printed and bound in Canada

FOREWORD

New Canadian Readings is an on-going series of inexpensive books intended to bring some of the best recent work by this country's scholars to the attention of students of Canada. Each volume consists of ten or more articles or book sections, carefully selected to present a fully-formed thesis about some critical aspect of Canadian development. Where useful, public documents or even private letters and statistical materials may be used as well to convey a different and fresh perspective.

The authors of the readings selected for inclusion in this volume (and all the others in the series) are all first-rank scholars, those who are doing the hard research that is rapidly changing our understanding of this country. Quite deliberately, the references for each selection have been retained, thus making additional research as easy as possible.

Like the authors of the individual articles, the editors of each volume are also scholars of note, completely up-to-date in their areas of specialization and, as the introductions demonstrate, fully aware of the changing nature of the debates within their professions and genres of research. The list of additional readings provided by the editor of each volume will steer readers to materials that could not be included because of space limitations.

This series will continue into the foreseeable future, and the General Editor is pleased to invite suggestions for additional topics.

J.L. Granatstein
General Editor

CONTENTS

INTRODUCTION

Throughout our history the idea of the North has kept firm hold on the national consciousness, yet until recently the region was little known to most Canadians. Now, after generations of neglect (particularly by the federal government), the country is beginning to accept the implications of the fact that nearly half its land mass lies north of the sixtieth parallel. As the nation struggles to understand this vast and diverse land, northern issues become national issues. This new interest brings much hope—hope for improvement in the lot of the northern native people, and for a reordering of the region's traditional boom and bust economy. But there are matters for concern as well. Has the colonialism of the past finally been set aside? Has the country truly accepted the cultural and social aspirations of northern natives? Will the region's natural resources—an Eldorado for politicians and the business community—sustain continued exploitation?

Nowadays, it is difficult to escape contact with the North. The region's artistic treasures, Inuit carvings and prints, native handicrafts, Ted Harrison's paintings have become symbols of Canadian culture. Books about the North by authors Farley Mowat and Pierre Berton are internationally recognized. Politically, demands by the Yukon and Northwest Territories for greater autonomy, and the debate over native land claims keep Northern affairs in the public eye. Northern defence, particularly the issue of Canadian sovereignty in the Arctic, has attracted renewed interest. The plan for icebreakers specially adapted to the Arctic, for example, represents the federal government's determination to end its own neglect.

The Canadian North increasingly attracts attention from university-based scholars, although the physical, natural, and (more recently) social scientists have been more involved than the humanists. The Association of Canadian Universities for Northern Studies plays a major role in encouraging Arctic and Subarctic research; organizations such as the Arctic Institute of North America at the University of Calgary, the University of Alberta's Boreal Institute, and the centre for Northern Studies at Lakehead University do much to stimulate interest in northern topics. Also, there are encouraging signs that the region will participate in research and study of itself. Arctic College, in the Northwest Territories, has recently added university transfer courses to its offerings. Its western counterpart, Yukon College, now offers a variety of subjects at the university level, and is developing a unique Northern and Native Studies programme, as well as encouraging northern-based research.

Although there are only a few scholars in each discipline actively pursuing northern studies, the northern scholarly community as a whole is a fairly tight-knit group. Lacking a large following within disciplinary boundaries, academics have reached outside their own communities for techniques, insights, and knowledge of other disciplines. The result is researchers who confront new ideas, methodologies, and concepts, and broaden both their perspective and their audience. *Interpreting Canada's North* seeks to continue this multi-disciplinary approach to the study of the region. The sixteen papers in this volume include the work of specialists in geography, anthropology, political science, literature, and history.

It is never an easy task to select items for a book of this sort; other editors might well disagree on the choice of essays, or even on the approach to the subject. This collection, therefore, is personal insofar as it reflects our definition of the North and our sense of some of the most important trends in contemporary northern scholarship. We have selected articles which reflect the diversity of scholarly inquiry into the North, which highlight key issues concerning changes in the North from precontact times to the present, and which utilize different methodologies in an attempt to understand the past. As a unit, they offer the student an interpretive introduction to the major themes of northern Canadian scholarship.

Several qualifications are in order. There are many definitions of the Canadian North. We have arbitrarily limited this collection to works dealing with the Yukon and Northwest Territories. Secondly, although this is an historical reader, it draws on material from several different fields and will, we hope, be of use to students and instructors in other disciplines. A collection of this size must, of course, seek to be representative rather than comprehensive. Finally, we have purposely omitted several key themes or periods in northern Canadian history due to the absence of a suitable article, limitations of space, or availability of published material on these topics. We trust that the articles selected for this volume will answer many questions about the historical evolution of the Canadian North; we are confident that they will excite even more questions, and will encourage further research into the history of this long-neglected region.

The first section, "Images of the Canadian North," deals with the perceptions that outsiders have had of the region. All too often, studies deal with the North's image instead of its reality. The standard, well established popular conception of the North as a cold, forbidding, and inhospitable wilderness has done much to limit the development of the region. Louis-Edmond Hamelin, professor emeritus of Geography at Université Laval, examines both the origins and the nature of these images; students with little experience of the North will no doubt recognize in his analysis some of their own conceptions and misconceptions. I.S. Maclaren of the Department of English, University of Alberta carefully considers the concept of the northern environment held by the early explorers, relates these views to contemporary European ideas, and suggests how these perceptions became so integral to the nation's image of the Arctic.

The second section, "Indians and the Advance of Europe," explores the response of the native population to the arrival of fur traders and missionaries. Shepard Krech III, of the Anthropology Department, Brown University, whose wide-ranging ethnohistorical work on the Athapaskans has done much to revise earlier thinking about these peoples, examines one of the most important questions surrounding early contact. His detailed reconstruction of Kutchin population, and of the impact of diseases on these people underscores the fundamental importance of epidemic illness in the history of the North. Kerry Abel, an historian at Carleton University who also draws on the rich ethnohistorical resources available for the North, examines Dene reaction to the arrival of European missionaries. Other historians have argued that the Indians accepted Christianity because their own spiritual world collapsed. Abel disputes this thesis, instead suggesting that the Dene approached the new world view on their own terms and at their own pace. A.J. Ray, an historical geographer at the University of British Columbia whose research has shaped our understanding of the Canadian fur trade, offers a sweeping analysis of the nature of the northern trade. His study of the Hudson's Bay Company's use of credit, and of the natives' reliance on such assistance, does much to explain the economic history of the North in the early twentieth century.

Articles in the third section, "The Gold Mining Frontier," deal with the social, economic, and political transformation of the Yukon Territory between 1880 and 1910. During the period highlighted by the Klondike gold rush, the North American mining frontier reached into the Yukon basin, disrupted the regional economy and the lives of the native population, and forced the Canadian government to respond to an unexpected assault on its sovereignty. Thomas Stone, an anthropologist at the State University of New York, Potsdam, provides an unusual perspective on a neglected period of Yukon history—the years immediately preceding the gold rush. In this article he explains how the miners, much like the aboriginal peoples, relied on mobility and separation as means of social control. Morris Zaslow, emeritus professor of history at the University of Western Ontario and *honoris causa* dean of historians of the Canadian North, places the gold rush in its international context.

The life of all gold rushes is brief. In the decades following the charge to the Klondike, the regional economy imploded, and most non-natives left the North. Yet change continued, particularly for native people. The articles in the fourth section, "After the Gold Rush," are by William R. Morrison of the centre for Northern Studies, Lakehead University, and Kenneth S. Coates of the History Department, University of Victoria. This period saw the construction of several new boarding schools for northern native people. Coates' essay examines the impact of one such school on the native children of the Yukon and the efforts of the Anglican missionaries to overcome the school's shortcomings. Americans have long played a major role in determining the nature of economic and social development in the North. Morrison assesses the United States' influence on the region, and Canadians' reactions to it. One of the most important social forces in the North is the transiency of its non-native population. The last essay discusses the extent and significance of this phenomenon as illuminated by a dramatic event—the sinking of the *Princess Sophia* in 1918.

The section titled "The Inuit" considers the historical role of this unique and important people. Living in a harsh and inhospitable environment, the Inuit have accommodated themselves brilliantly to their surroundings. They have also proven particularly adept at responding to the advance of Europeans, explorers, whalers, fur traders, and missionaries. Anthropologists J. Smith and E. Burch of the Museum of the American Indian, Smithsonian Institution, offer a detailed examination of relations between the Chipewyan and the Inuit. Their paper comments extensively on the methodological problems involved in such an inquiry, and serves as a reminder that inter-cultural relations in the North extend beyond native-white contact. W.G. Ross, a geographer at Bishop's University, is well known for his work on Arctic whaling. In this essay, he examines the environmental impact of whaling in the Arctic islands region and the Inuit response to this destructive and rapacious industry. Philip Goldring, an historian with Parks Canada, begins his more specific study of Baffin Island examining this age of the whalers, but expands his investigation to consider the twentieth century fur trade. Together, these articles cast light on the many forces of change affecting the Inuit in the era before government involvement in their lives.

"The Modern North," the last section in this book, focuses on the complex and fast-changing society and economy of the North during the post-World War II era. This period was a time of rapid transformation which began with an aggressive expansion of the mining sector and by the bureaucratization of the region. This was also a time of political evolution, native assertiveness, challenges to Canadian sovereignty, and northern mega-projects. The articles in this section explore several aspects of this complex re-ordering of northern life. The importance of government in the development of the modern North is particularly evident in John O'Neil's analysis of the introduction of health care to northern native people. O'Neil, a medical anthropologist with the University of Manitoba, adopts a colonial model in explaining the aboriginal people's complex relationship with northern health care professionals. Michael Asch, an anthropologist at the University of Alberta, examines a key aspect of one of the most important events in the history of the modern North—the Mackenzie Valley Pipeline Inquiry. In his paper, Asch challenges Thomas Berger's economic model, and, drawing on his understanding of Dene economic activity, suggests an alternative plan for regional development. The final paper in the collection, by Frances Abele of Carleton University, School of Public Administration and Social Work, argues that native people and other northerners have reacted to two contradictory tendencies in the Canadian constitutional tradition: liberal individualism and Tory pragmatism; she insists that understanding current northern debates in this way provides grounds for optimism about aboriginal and territorial self-government.

This collection offers, of course, only a starting point for the study of the Canadian North. The articles assembled here, ranging widely over time and across disciplines, represent the multi-directional scholarly effort to comprehend the human history of the region. It is our hope that this volume will bring the North to life, and illustrate the complex working of cultures, technologies, government policies and economic forces in the powerful lands north of 60°.

SECTION 1

IMAGES OF THE CANADIAN NORTH

IMAGES OF THE NORTH*

L.-E. HAMELIN

Several types of documents relate to assorted overall, or specific images of the North. Among them is the oral literature of the indigenous peoples, with a delightful and enigmatic body of stories and legends;[1] the writings of researchers, non-specialized, but widely disseminated; literature such as newspapers; and finally, results of specific objective tests. In spite of the need for the latter, we should not decry images of the North that have emerged from texts based on more traditional approaches. Indeed, these documents may exercise an enormous influence on the thoughts of the northern inhabitant. Thus, Voltaire, speaking to the French of France, referred to the miserable Canadian settler, squatting "in the snow between the bear and the beaver." Present-day texts might still reveal a distant echo of that writer's opinion.[2] The same thing happened around 1900; those who produced the overly enthusiastic bulletins on the Klondike were largely responsible for the paradoxical image of the gold fields that became current. A critical and complete survey of all visions of the North would have to consider northern literature in all its forms, and that in itself would result in a major work. I shall touch on only a very small part of that encyclopedic total.

Among whites, the popular imagination has rarely perceived the North as a whole; it has, rather, regarded only particular and very localized northern situations. The current perceptive totality would include a host of little sectoral tableaux relating, for example, to the Northwest Passage, a particular polar expedition, the Inuit, the RCMP, the cold, and to the Klondike. Moreover, many of these topics would be characterized by inadequate information. Ten centuries after the arrival of the Vikings in North America, we still have not been able to interpret the deceptive appellation of "Vinland." For several centuries, a persistent confusion has prevailed between

* L.-E. Hamelin, *Canadian Nordicity: It's Your North Too* (Montreal: Harvest House, 1979), 1–13.

Hudson Bay and the "frozen sun of the North." Cartier's expression, "the land God gave to Cain," still appeared to have its echo in the scientific literature in 1935.[3] Captain J. Elzear Bernier is considered to be an explorer, but in reality he mainly played a political role in territories that were already discovered. Biologist M.J. Dunbar has spoken about the reputation of Hudson Bay for infertility. This kind of reappraisal would be desirable for the great majority of particular northern situations. It is at the level of specific conditions, rather than at that of the total area, that we find true or erroneous images of the Canadian North. Nonetheless some overviews have been presented.[4]

From what may be established from an incomplete inventory of mirages about the North, two extreme opinions frequently emerge:[5] an over-idealized vision and an excessively pessimistic vision. Whereas these two illusions have usually operated alternately, they have also undergone parallel development—and that has made them even more confused.

The Double Illusion among Non-Indigenous People

The majority of informative or interpretive documents have given rise to two types of conflicting and mutually regulating emotions: mirages and disappointments. Attractive mirages, particularly those fired with the pioneer spirit, are contrasted with disappointments, which have disabused, in particular, those seeking massive, quick profits. These two sentiments have not affected members of the various social classes proportionately; the executives have been, on the whole, more inconsolable over their blighted hopes, and the little man has been more intoxicated by the prospect of intense, if short-lived, illusions of good fortune. Because the misfortunes have become better known than the successes, this mechanism has nourished a generally negative perception of the North.

The list of northern adventures that did not give rise to further development, such as Martin Frobisher's gold rush to Baffin Island four centuries ago, would be a very long one. Much later, miners had been talking about the copper at Chibougamau for fifty years before they began to exploit it. Few of the Klondikers grew rich during the three months that they had judged, a priori, to be long enough to make a pile of gold nuggets. And how many fortunes have disappeared in ill-justified ventures of financing and prospecting?

We can see the same result in the realm of exploration. We remember more readily disasters, such as that of Franklin in the mid-nineteenth century, than successful journeys such as that of Mackenzie in the late eighteenth. And, even in the latter case, the great river Mackenzie discovered did not lead to the Pacific as he had hoped. Polar toponymy reflects the difficulties and disappointments of a host of adventurers.

The North has certainly been the victim of myths based on indifference, if not of repulsion. Explorers and missionaries, who worked during periods that might be described as pretechnical, have left the idea of a harsh land and climate, a view that was not at all unfavourable, to the success of their book sales and the gathering of alms. The anticipated harshness combined to accentuate the physical harshness. It is easy to concur with Vilhjalmur Stefansson's apt comment than in the North, "imaginary problems are more important than real problems."[6] It was, in large measure, natural and historic conditions that created the heroism of the sailors, "men of iron in wooden ships." In our generation, we might consider the reverse!

Settlement also produced an overwhelming amount of negative evidence, although northern settlement has been neither abundant nor always permanent. The great majority of centres in the Northwest Territories have less than five hundred inhabitants; a similar situation prevails in both the Yukon and Nouveau-Québec. Even in the Near North, which is more fully integrated with the communication networks of the south, the population is very scanty. This sparseness would be even greater if the inhabitants had not learned to fulfill a great diversity of functions. In Abitibi (Quebec), most of the settlers who came to practise agriculture in the tradition of North America pioneering now earn their living by totally different means.

Further, human achievements have been difficult and limited. In a nation where yield and profit are the usual measure of things, it is not surprising that an acute feeling of repulsion and disinterest arises and is nourished.

Parallel to this, but working in the opposite direction, there are the prophets, men who are more optimistic than realistic. They have been touched by the magic of the North. They have come from every walk of life and, in their ardent promotions, they have turned their attention to every last little scrap of the immensity of northern Canada. To Curé Labelle, the North[7] was to become the "main highway for French-Canadian nationalism." To cite another case, a certain influential man of politics predicted thirty-one million inhabitants on the two shores of James Bay by the end of this century.[8] Before preliminary operations began for harnessing the Quebec rivers that debouch into James Bay, there were not even five thousand inhabitants in this area.

The enforced opening up of the North associated with the Second World War created a climate of enthusiasm regarding the North. In 1946 Maurice Duplessis, commenting on his own laws on mining development, stated that in Ungava "Providence had already gone three-quarters of the way"; one only had to bend over to pick up the iron scattered on the surface.

After the re-discovery of oil at Prudhoe Bay in 1968, United States capitalists shipped to Alaska all the materials necessary for the imminent construction of pipelines; but several years passed before the first line was built. A similar euphoria presided over the organization of the conferences on *Mid-Canada Development* between 1968 and 1971; up until now, few concrete results have emerged from this project.

What must be clearly recognized is this duality between appeal and disappointment, between means to development and the natural propensity to avoid difficulties. These twin tendencies constantly recur: "There seem to be many visions of the North.... The southern vision (the North is a hinterland to be exploited for the benefit of southern Canada)....The romanticized vision (wilderness must never be touched)....The pessimistic vision (which sees only the problems) and the developmental vision (with natural gas opportunities)."[9]

The entire history of the North revolves around this confrontation, at the same time both clear and confused. Idealists are incessantly attempting to involve southerners in northern adventures; incessantly, people lacking the pioneer spirit, or disappointed investors, put the brake on the northern projects. Apart from the war years, when the northern surge was unnatural, development has coincided with periods when mirages of feasibility dominated. Thus, at any given moment, concepts of good or bad exercise a profound impact on life, financial activity, mobility of the labour force, presence of political forces, and on awareness of certain problems. These mechanisms should not be surprising. Is a country not the fruit of the mind?

In the minds of the whites, a comparable oscillation applies equally with respect to the Amerindians. As far as the Euro-Canadian is concerned, the twin images of the good Indian and the bad Indian have existed side by side. In 1972, responses to a test still gave the Eskimo the status of the "noble savage," with a pure ideology threatened by southern civilization. On the other hand, disagreeable prejudices are more common. The fact that whites are surprised at the technical skills of adults, the intelligence of children, the ease of childbearing on the part of the mothers, constitutes so many manifestations of the preconceived image of the indigenous people.[10] Others have noted that the "learning materials" of the Department of Education of the Northwest Territories had included numerous uncharitable, incorrect, or incomplete allusions to the indigenous peoples, who comprised 54 percent of the school population.

There Are So Many Norths within the North

Although the input is imposing, it does not form a compact mass or organized whole; it consists rather of a whole series of disparate and poorly connected interpretations. This divergence is initially apparent at the individual level. Jim Lotz distinguished among white northerners: "The Developers, the Maintainers, the Innovators, the Old Northern Whites, the Transients, the Outsiders, the Outside Insiders."[11] Each perceives the North differently. In a community in the Eastern Arctic, a study on the perception of ethnic identity revealed three type-portraits of people: "the priest, the Anglican missionary's wife, and the trader." Moreover, it was found that behaviour and gestures were adjusted according to perception of things and individuals. Thus, by custom, only the Eskimo language was used when asking people to wipe their feet before coming in.[12] Administrators coming from the towns of southern

Canada tend to have a distorted view of the North with regard to the environment in which northern residents live. This perceptive dissonance, this distortion, is very obvious particularly with regard to housing and education policies.

On the spatial level, the North is again perceived differently. The majority of inhabitants, even northerners, have great difficulty picturing the North in its geographic immensity; theirs is still a fragmented North. This Balkanization tendency is not at all surprising, given, on the one hand, the lack of any old, strong, unified political structure. Thus the images, on the level of the perceptible North, those to which the individual can develop his own behaviour, have multiplied. There is not one single mental image of the North; a host of partial and often contradictory assessments are found. On the spatial level, they are overlapping or discontinuous; on the chronological level, they display prolongations, adaptations, and even reversals of opinion.

Mentally, a Canada That Is Only Slightly Northern

Despite the importance of the mental aspect in the definition of the North, and the polymorphic nature of that perception, the North has still not penetrated deeply into the comfortable society of southern Canada. Even while resident northerners are on the increase in absolute numbers, the small proportion they represent in the total population is growing slowly. This demographic situation has its equivalent on the level of thought and everyday life. Evidence of this is widespread. Only 7 percent of Canadian stamps carry a northern message and, even then, they often do so in a deceptive manner—for example, by amputating Canada's Far North. At Dorval Airport in Montreal, the large mural devoted to Canada seems to represent only southern Canada. In 1970, W.L. Morton recognized that "no scheme of Canadian historiography yet advanced is wholly satisfactory because none as yet takes account of the occurrence of the North."[13] The Canadian historian most intimate with northern archives is M. Zaslow, and his testimony is just as clear: "Canadians fail to recognize that they are essentially a northern people."[14] The same assertion has been expressed differently by F.K. Hare: "Canadians have not, as a nation, put the North anywhere near the centre of their mythology."[15] Henri Dorion concluded his comments on a text devoted to boundaries (including those of Labrador) by speaking of political ignorance, and by affirming that, "our territorial awareness is not very rigorous."[16] To give another example, some law students, when asked to enumerate Canada's major problems mentioned the North in only 9 percent of cases, and even then it was bracketed along with the cold climate.[17] Finally, to mark the occasion of the Olympic Games in Montreal in 1976, Canada issued a five-dollar coin displaying a map of the country: part of the High Arctic does not appear on the map.

The limited interest Canadians seem to evince regarding their North does not contradict the fact of a large number of characterizations of the North, as such. On the contrary, this apathy expresses rather the determining effect that excessively severe and painful images have produced on people's minds. An inadequacy of accurate knowledge has certainly not favoured the process of perception based on reliable stimuli, and conversely, it has tended to develop images full of distortions. A North that was poorly known at the outset could not avoid becoming the target of illusions and prejudices.

The North—A State of Mind

In a white mining community in Alberta's Middle North, a test has shown that the most significant local factor was neither the cold nor the snow, but the friendly atmosphere; moreover, the principal desire of the inhabitants was a relative decrease in isolation. It was primarily by means of these two psychological terms that these residents defined their own situation most clearly. A traditional monograph on this locality would not have allowed one to pinpoint the deeper thoughts of the local population.[18]

The North is more than an area, it is a passion. The mental configuration which it inspires constitutes a trait as deeply anchored as a European's attachment to the site of a particular hamlet or valley. Félix-Antoine Savard's Gildore[19] is more than just a simple canoeman from Rabasca; like other northerners, his route to the North lay through the "pays d'en haut" and the West. Other adventurers have served their northern apprenticeship in the "King's Posts" of the Quebec North Shore. Throughout history, certain types of people, coming into contact with the various zones of the North, have developed very characteristic attitudes. Could anybody have expressed or embodied better the virtues of liberty and vitality than the *coureur des bois* of the Middle North? For him, as for the logger of yesteryear, and even the moose hunter, the North is like an irresistible itch, which implacably drives the man to mobility. In certain cases, nothing succeeds in stifling the call of the North. Equally, one finds cases of escape into the North, where distance from the daily, monotonous round serves as nourishment, and even renaissance. The North is not simply a thing of wonder, however. Fear, tragedy and bravery all emerge from one of the first novels written by an Eskimo.[20] Northern themes have fed part of Canada's literature.[21]

Perceptions Differ between North and South

To analyse the northern setting by means of tests is to discover, in most instances, a difference between the views expressed by southerners and northerners.

A study of the regions preferred by forty-three second year geography honours students[22] established that the mainland Arctic coast was the least desirable area of Canada; but yet, the design of their mental map did not include the northern part of the Arctic archipelago.[23]   Conversely, the two preferred regions were southern Ontario, and southwestern British Columbia. This kind of differential appreciation of places could have very important consequences for the future development of the nation. The author concludes, "The preferred areas may well plan for sizeable increases in population and pollution; conversely, places which are particularly disliked may well plan on development being even more difficult than usual." If this trend is realized, intra-Canadian disparities are not likely to decrease. In Quebec, the North is again perceived differently from the South; a questionnaire distributed in the spring of 1971 included, among others, two sections relevant to the present topic: "As compared to the Montreal Plain, does the Quebec shore of Hudson Strait appear to you to be a region isolated from the minds of and misunderstood by the people of southern Quebec?" The percentage of positive responses to the two parts of this question were 77 percent and 80 percent respectively.

Clearly resident northerners are strongly aware of the uniqueness of their region, as one of the members of the Northwest Territories Council declared:

> Our laws must harmonize with the land and its people. Unfortunately, Mr. Chairman, the laws that are continuously brought before this Council for enactment have been determined by, and patterned after, the laws which exist in the ten provinces of Canada. They are generally a carbon copy of provincial acts. The people who are in a policy-making capacity and drafting legislation, are people whose experience, primarily, has been in the South. Their understanding of people and life style and society is of the South. This is what they understand. The life styles of the people are vastly different. Housing is a good example. The southern Caucasian society is concerned about good houses, they are concerned about security, they are concerned about worldly possessions, and there is nothing wrong with that, but the northern society is not concerned about these things.
>
> ...The very differences that exist between the North and the South are climatic conditions and the vast distances that we are confronted with. Also we have a great many problems associated with liquor, different concepts of justice, health, work habits, and the skills of the people.[24]

This extract from the official minutes of the Territories demonstrates the rift, which in the minds of northerners, separates the Canadian North from the Canadian South. It is not my intention here to discuss the value of the opinions expressed, nor to consider whether they apply only to Amerindians.

TABLE 1   *Percentage Distribution of Northern Problems as Seen by Northern Students*

Order	Problem perceived	Frequency of mention (percent)
1	Impact of development	18.2
2	Alcoholism	15.2
3	High cost of living	13.7
4	Isolation	12.1
5	Pollution	10.6
6	Cultural changes	9.1
7	Education	9.1
8	Housing	4.5
9	Abuses in welfare allocations	4.5
10	Amerindian land claims	3.0
Total		100.0[25]

On another occasion, fifty school children with twelve years of education, and living in Frobisher Bay, Inuvik, and Yellowknife were asked what, according to their understanding, the problems of the North were. In the interpretation, the reader should be made aware of two points. First, there is the originality of the northern implications of certain words in current usage. The problems of the North, associated with housing, alcoholism, and pollution assume a form and characteristics very different from those in the South. The same is true of cultural changes and development. Seen in their true dimensions, the school children's responses express greater nordicity than is apparent from the terms alone. Moreover, items 4 and 10 are manifestly northern. In the second place, this view of the North is not the back-country view; it reflects, rather, the urban location of educational institutions, and the articulation of a sophisticated system of education. Regionally, it applies particularly to the Mackenzie District, which is waiting for its pipeline, and to the acute social problems of Frobisher Bay.

Northerners, both whites and Amerindians, have a clear awareness of their difficult, misunderstood situation. Consequently, many have been moved to bitterness. "A large proportion of people interviewed expressed dissatisfaction with their present life."[26] This attitude is translated into a desire to move (also among the Indians), into a pessimism with regard to the future, and into a high incidence of suicide. Attitudes of despair are so widespread that the concepts southern planners have applied to northern Canada must be questioned.

This attitude has been clearly exposed by researchers.[27] A test of perception on the economic development of the Northwest Territories sought to find out the degree of causal relations of "big business" with regard to certain parameters. According to table 2, the judgement made by "enlightened" southerners with regard to major economic developments in the North is both significant and harsh. The North is not respected; Amerindians are almost totally ignored; northern public opinion is scarcely listened to at all; the territorial government wields only a limited influence; and ecology, whether cultural or natural, is not a matter of concern. Without any doubt, the South leads the North, flaunting a colonial, centralized, and purely capitalist form.

In conclusion, I believe that I have established the existence of images, especially their multifaceted nature. Hence, a cold region does not consist solely of measurable natural elements, capable of becoming the object of so-called natural and objective knowledge. All the polar components are analysed on their merits or not, by the mind; even the idea of cold becomes an identifying element. The North does not lend itself to a study of "realities"; tests and historical documents allow us to grasp partially the fruits of the cognitive processes themselves. One of the least known fields of northern study concerns the different images evoked by each ethnic group, regarding the same theme, for example, territoriality.

TABLE 2 *In the Territorial North, to What Extent Is Large-Scale Economic Development Influenced Or Determined by ...*

Item	Level of Influence	
	To a greater extent	To a lesser extent
Resident Northerners		x
Northern Native People		x
Federal Politics	x	
Territorial Politics		x
Northern Public Opinion		x
Large Companies	x	
Smaller Economic Activities in the North		x
Non-economic (Cultural)		x
Ecological Considerations		x
Concern for the Post-developmental Era		x
Southern Canada as a Whole	x	
Northern Regional Disparities		x

SOURCE: Based on a perception test, LEH, Toronto, 1974.

A simple concern with the liberal expansion of knowledge prompts some reflection on the attitudes that should be taken regarding the North. Official policy, for example, is a source of much anxiety. If it is true that southerners are not mentally northern-oriented,[28] and that their orientation is erroneous, or at least is different from that of northerners themselves, or that they are constantly torn between aspects of a double illusion, is it not therefore dangerous to permit southern Canadians to make major decisions concerning the country's North and to impose a form of government on northern areas. Moreover, do not the perceptions that the main northern groups hold of their own cultural differences beg that they rise up against the excesses of "homogeneous Canadianization?" Present policies stress legal niceties and engineers' designs, but perception of a "true" reality must also enter the current preoccupations. Knowledge of psychology and the possession of some fellow-feeling may be of great help in understanding the northern people, native and otherwise.[29] Mental images can be found for each of the themes of the North, whether a person is dealing with territoriality, the environment, settlement, politics, peoples, or development.

Notes

1. Three references to illustrate this developing literature: Maurice Métayer, *Tales from the Igloo* (Edmonton: Hurtig, 1972); Marie-Jeanne Basile and G. McNulty, *Atanukana: Légendes montagnaises* (Quebec, 1971); R. Savard, *Carcajou et le sens du monde: Récits Montagnais-Naskapi* (Quebec, 1971).

2. M. Trudel, *L'influence de Voltaire au Canada* (Montreal: Fides, 1945).

3. M. Jefferson, "The Problem of Ecumene: The Case of Canada" *Goegrafiska Annaler* 16 (1934): 146–59.

4. W.C. Wonders, "Our Northward Course," *The Canadian Geographer* 6, 3–4 (1962): 96–105; J.W. Watson, "The Role of Illusion in North American Geography," *The Canadian Geographer* 13, 1 (1969): 10–27; H.L. Sawatsky and W.H. Lehn, *The Cultural Geography of the Arctic Mirage* (Vancouver, 1975), 29–36.

5. The opposition between these two attitudes is expressed even at the level of journalistic literature. See Blair Fraser, ed., "Our Double Image of the North," *Maclean's* 77 17 October 1964). This special issue contains 118 pages on the North. Among the collaborators of this report are Pierre Berton, Doug Wilkinson, G. Hunter, and R. Harrington.

6. V. Stefansson, *The Arctic in Fact and Fable*, Headline Series 51 (New York, 1945).

7. He was referring to the Near North in the western Laurentians, in the second half of the nineteenth century.

8. J.C. Langelier, *Le bassin méridional de la baie d'Hudson* (Quebec: Dussault, 1887).

9. W.P. Wilder, text of conference, Yellowknife, NWT Council, 12 June 1973, 1.

10. Pierrette Désy, "Les Indiens du Nouveau-Québec," *De l'Ethnocide* 10/18, serie 7 (Paris, 1972); Markoosie, *Harpoon of the Hunter* (Montreal: McGill-Queen's Press, 1970).

11. J. Lotz, *Northern Realities* (Toronto: New Press, 1970).

12.   J. Briggs, in *Patrons and Brokers in the Eastern Arctic*, ed R. Paine (St. John's, 1971), 55–73.

13.   W.L. Morton, "The 'North' in Canadian Historiography," *Transactions of the RSC* 4, 8 (1970): 31–40.

14.   M. Zaslow, *The Opening of the Canadian North, 1870–1914* (Toronto: McClelland and Stewart, 1971), xi.

15.   F.K. Hare, Introduction to *The Natural Landscapes of Canada*, by J.B. Bird (Toronto: Wiley, 1972), 1.

16.   Henri Dorion, "Connaissances des frontières canadiennes," *Cahiers de Géographie de Québec* 11 (1962): 147–48.

17.   L.-E. Hamelin, P. Beaubien, and G. Poulin, "Perception du Canada au premier cycle de géographie," *Didactique Géographie* 1, 3 (1972): 1–9.

18.   This is not an isolated example; psychologists have noted a comparable order of priorities among workers wintering in Antarctica. "It may come as a surprise that the bitter temperature, the long polar night and other physical problems of Antarctica living are not the most significant causing human adjustment problems. The physical deprivations and dangers are remarkably well tolerated by almost everyone. The three basic stresses to which members must adjust are: 1) intimacy of an isolated group; 2) sameness of environment; 3) absence of customary sources of satisfaction and gratification," R.E. Strange, "Emotional Aspects of Wintering Over," *Antarctica* 6, 6 (1971): 255.

19.   Hero of *La Dalle-des-Morts* (Montreal: Fides, 1965).

20.   Markoosie, *The Harpoon of the Hunter*.

21.   Jack Warwick, *The Long Journey* (Toronto: University of Toronto Press, 1968).

22.   H.A. Whitney, G.W. Brown, and R. Elliott, "The View from Southern Ontario: Preferred Locations in North America, " Canadian Association of Geographers, *Preconference Publication of Papers* (Waterloo, 1971), 25–32. See also CAG 1975, (Vancouver: Simon Fraser University, 1975), 191–95.

23.   The frequency with which the High Arctic is expunged from United States maps representing Canada seems to surpass the exigencies of scale and to prolong a certain tradition of contesting geopolitically Canadian ownership of the Arctic Islands. Canadian teaching materials, inspired by the USA, do not even prepare students for the existence of a Canadian Extreme North.

24.   L. Trimble, *Official Report of the Council of the Northwest Territories Debates*, Yellowknife 46th sess., 27 January 1972, 780–81.

25.   Gemini North, *Man and Resources: A Survey of Northern Priorities* (Yellowknife, 1972).

26.   AA. Mackinnon and A.H. Neufeld, *Project Mental Health: A Study of Opinion North of 60°* (Saskatoon, 1973).

27.   During the Canadian Association of Geographers Conference in Toronto, May 1974, within the framework of a special session on the development of the Canadian North. The question was: "In the Territorial North, to what extent large-scale development is influenced or determined by...?"

28.   To the question: "What do you think Southerners know about the NWT?" addressed to northerners in the street, 77 percent replied, "nothing,"and 23 percent, "very little," *Yellowknifer* (February 1974).

29.   Arctic Institute of North America (Montreal, Washington, Calgary), "Psychiatric Problems of Man in the Arctic," in *The Arctic Basin,* by J.E. Sater (Centreville, 1969), 215–24.

THE AESTHETIC MAP OF THE NORTH, 1845–1859*

I.S. MACLAREN

From 1818 to 1859 the British Admiralty waged a concerted campaign to discover a Northwest Passage. It was only one of a series of mammoth enterprises on the part of the British nation that were undertaken in order to know the world intimately. During the same period, of course, Charles Darwin sailed in HMS *Beagle* to South America, uncovering evidence that would lead to a new understanding of the history of life on the planet. David Douglas made his herculean trips on the Pacific slope of North America, discovering the mighty sugar pine and thousands of other species. Thomas Huxley sailed in HMS *Rattlesnake* to Australia and explored anatomical oddities that would rend Victorian notions of an harmonious relation between natural processes and moral ends. David Livingstone would shed light on the interior of the earth's darkest continent.

The extraordinary feats of these great British explorers often overshadow the more modest travels of a great number of early nineteenth-century Britons. Tours to Europe had been viewed since Renaissance times as a vital part of any English gentleman's education, but toward the end of the eighteenth century the focus of the Grand Tour shifted slightly from the touring of continental art galleries and historical sites to the description and depiction of Europe's geographical wonders and beauties. Then, in the last decades of the century, continental hostilities kept most English tourists at home; consequently, tours around their own island became fashionable, with numerous guidebooks by such self-proclaimed guides as William Gilpin[1] and William Wordsworth[2] appearing to tell the traveller where to go and what to see.

* *Arctic* 38, 2 (June 1985): 89–103.

By the end of the Napoleonic Wars in 1815, British explorers, like less adventurous British travellers, were well versed not only in astronomical computations for charting landscapes, but also in two important and widely known aesthetic principles used to chart landscapes and seascapes, the Sublime and the Picturesque. Just as the measurements of latitude and longitude told the explorer where he stood relative to Greenwich, so the description of new tracts as more or less sublime or picturesque permitted him to identify the new land relative to those British and European scenes familiar to him and to his readership. The deployment of these aesthetic principles formed a crucial part of geographical discovery in the North from the time of Samuel Hearne's three overland treks (1769–1772). The geographical character of the vast subcontinent was being defined, except in the more prosaic and factual of the post journals kept by fur trade factors, only partially by the environment's own features; it was being defined as well in terms of, if in contrast to, known geography. "The geography of any place," Watson[3] has argued, "results from how we [want to] see it as much as from what may be seen there." Not surprisingly, the discovery of the North entailed a similar process of identification that combined human expectation and fact, illusion and empirical reality.

It has been argued by Gombrich[4] that the visual world can be represented only by known and widely held schemata or modes of perception. In the case of the nineteenth-century British explorer in the Arctic, the known schemata for representing nature in prose and pictures were the Sublime and the Picturesque. They would permit him, figuratively speaking, to draw aesthetic maps of the Arctic that other Britons could read sensibly. Thus, they acted as the Linnaean system for botannical identifications did for the naturalists among the explorers and as the astronomical computations of latitude and longitude did for the astronomers among them. All such systems are, loosely speaking, taxonomies or schemata—in short, metaphors, but metaphors that, because of the authority vested in them by a society, become accepted as the most accurate measurements of the external world.

The Sublime referred to the geography of vastness—vast open space whose dimensions defy definition or even imagination. Open stretches of ocean or prairie, perilous mountain peaks or abysses, thunderstorms or tornadoes—nature in its extreme habits threatening human welfare and inspiring fear and wonder—were regarded as the sublime qualities of the external world. In 1756 Edmund Burke[5] had disseminated the notion of the Sublime among British readers. It had been an item in the aesthetic baggage of travellers to the Swiss and Italian Alps since the mid-sixteenth century. Burke's treatise made an understanding of it an indispensable item.[6]

The Picturesque grew out of the habit of viewing tracts of land as if they were landscape paintings. A prospect or viewing "station," usually set on a moderate rise, looked out over a foreground, a lower middle ground through which a river meandered, and an enclosing background of bluish hills or mountains. A single vanishing point on the horizon encouraged a single, static perspective from each "station"; at the sides of the view, trees in clumps or rows would act as *coulisses* (literally, the wing curtains on the stage of a French theatre) to "frame" the scene and encourage the single perspective. Great variety in elevation, vegetation, and light intensity was sought in the landscape, but the sense of all features harmonizing was never to be sacrificed. The notion of a composed landscape remained paramount.[7] Extreme displays of nature that threatened to burst the bounds of the moderate, composed, framed view had no part in this aesthetic. Indeed, because the foreground usually included signs of, or else seemed to invite, leisurely habitation by humans or domesticated animals, the picturesque landscape usually confirmed the British eighteenth-century belief, disseminated by Newton in science and by Pope and Thomson in poetry, that a basic harmony operated in the relations between man and his world. The seeker after the Picturesque in nature was meant to discover that quintessential harmony.

Because the wild, the desolate, the vast, the sublime geographical features of Europe lie, for the most part, outside England, the Picturesque became England's aesthetic.[8] It was, proclaimed Stendhal, one of the essential aspects of early nineteenth-century England.[9] The Englishman who discovered the Picturesque abroad, therefore, was achieving three purposes: he was affirming England's belief in its own imperial destiny by stamping foreign tracts as English in appearance; he was conducting his travels/explorations in a sufficiently orderly manner to be able to perceive the composed qualities of nature; and, most importantly, he was nourishing his own aesthetic identity as an Englishman, which required sustenance in proportion to his temporal distance from the gentle hill-and-dale topography of his Home Counties or the more rugged but still composed lacustrine beauty of his English Lake District.

Aesthetic Responses to the North up to 1849

During the first two decades of the Admiralty's assault on the Northwest Passage (1818–1837), British explorers naturally discovered countless sublime landscapes, as Loomis has demonstrated.[10] But it would be a mistake to overlook the many picturesque views that they recorded and the function played by them. One instance must suffice for present purposes. Fort Enterprise (Fig. 1) was erected in autumn 1820 on a site chosen in part for aesthetic reasons by John Franklin and the officers of his first overland expedition.[11] Robert Hood, the midshipman who did not survive the tundra crossing in 1821, considered "the beauty of the situation" at Fort Enterprise to have "far exceeded our most sanguine expectations."[12] "We could not have selected," wrote John Richardson to his mother, "a more convenient or beautiful spot. The surrounding country is finely varied by hill and dale and interspersed with

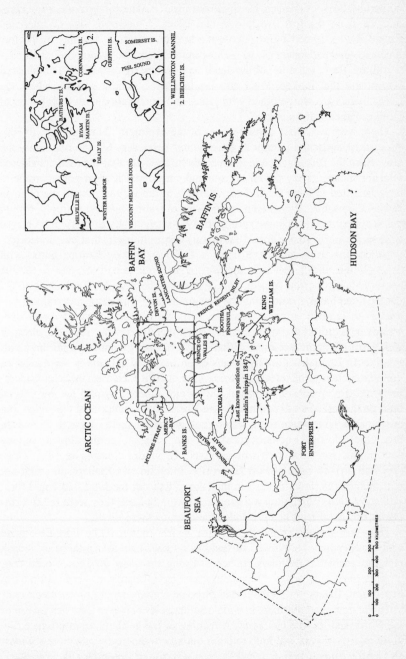

FIG. 1. Modern map of the Canadian North, showing places explored during the search for Franklin. (Courtesy Department of Geography, University of Toronto)

numerous lakes connected by small streams."[13] The picturesque view commanded from the fort overlooked two lakes of moderate size (Winter and Round-Rock), joined by a meandering stream, all set in a valley at the tree line near the headwaters of the Yellowknife River. The completion of the fort permitted the completion of the landscape picture by presenting a humanized foreground that looked down into the lacustrine middle ground, where the river "banks are well-clothed with pines, and ornamented with a profusion of mosses, lichens, and shrubs."[14]

There were two main consequences of the explorers' determination to construct this landscape picture as their winter residence. On the one hand, the view from the fort functioned in an aesthetic capacity that the men considered vital for morale. They prized the site and considered it great good fortune to have been led to it by the Indians. Nothing in the vicinity would match it on aesthetic grounds. Richardson, who wrote to Back while on a supply trip to the Coppermine river in the spring of 1821, aesthetically dismissed the barren land to the north of the fort: "[William] Gilpin himself, that celebrated picturesque hunter, would have made a fruitless journey had he come with us....nowhere did I see anything worthy of your pencil. So much for the country. It is a barren subject, and deserves to be thus briefly dismissed."[15] On the other hand, maintaining the illusion of the Picturesque in terrain as evidently un-English in most respects as is the Subarctic was a habit that, whatever it did to maintain morale, jeopardized from the start the physical welfare of the arctic explorers. What is underscored by making a northern valley into an English valley by means of an imported schema is the danger of not apprehending the terrain's own unique qualities. Had aesthetic considerations not governed site selection, the winter quarters would not have been built on the top of a hill commanding a "beautiful" prospect of the valley, but down at the lake where food, water, fuel, and wind shelter were to be had. In fact, the physical consequences of the site selection almost proved catastrophic for those men who survived the tundra crossing in 1821. Once they had arrived back at Fort Enterprise, Franklin and Richardson could not pull themselves down the hill to the lake to fish out the food that could forestall starvation. When they were rescued by the Indians, they were fed fish immediately. Aesthetics had precluded their saving themselves.

Thus, the search for the Picturesque in the Arctic, if the Fort Enterprise near-disaster may be allowed to stand as a rather extreme instance of a clash between aesthetic and physical needs during the early decades, would continue in the 1850s, when 34 expeditions sailed in search of the third Franklin expedition. Balancing aesthetic and physical welfare would prove precarious, often engaging the mariners in wide discrepancies between their perception of the North and its true character. A reading of the aesthetic map produced by those later voyagers will help to point out where the discrepancy grew widest and narrowest between, to recall Watson's notion of geography, the travellers' expectation of terrain on the one hand, and the North's unique identity on the other.

Searching for Franklin: The 1848 and 1849 Expeditions

The Admiralty had not sponsored an expedition to the North since George Back's nightmare voyage of 1836–1837 when, on 26 May 1845, Franklin sailed out of the Thames, his mission nothing less than the discovery of the Northwest Passage. Sighted by the whaler *Prince of Wales* in Baffin Bay on 26 July, HMS *Erebus*, under Capt. James Fitzjames, and HMS *Terror*, under Francis R.M. Crozier, sailed under Franklin's command into Lancaster Sound, never to be seen again. Arctic sublimity thereby realized its vast potential to swallow whole and intact an entire expedition. Nine years passed before any remains of the starved sojourners were discovered and 13 before Francis L. McClintock and Lieut. W.R. Hobson came across the skeletons of the majority of the 129 sailors strewn across the west and south sides of King William (IV) Island (Fig. 1). The sublimity of the disappearance into a void extends to this day, for only a single paper was ever found to help decode the mystery of the men's fate.[16]

For all the picturesque description of arctic scenes that former voyagers had reaped, the British public still saw the region as the frozen continent and, at least imaginatively and aesthetically, if not scientifically, located it, as Milton had, somewhere on the far side of hell.[17] Franklin had embarked in *Erebus*, named after the son of Chaos, brother of Night, and father by her (Night) of Aesther (Air) and Hermera (Day); in it he sailed into the impenetrable darkness that is the home of Erebus. Thus was the macabre stage upon which the fate of his last quest was played out. History has uncovered the lamentable probability that all Franklin's men were dead before the first search expedition arrived in the Arctic.

In 1848 searches were initiated on three fronts: from the Pacific Ocean via Bering Strait, from the Mackenzie River, and from the Atlantic Ocean via Baffin Bay. Each of these searches produced published accounts, but two are most germane to the present discussion.[18] William Henry James Browne, who sailed with James Clark Ross in HMS *Enterprise* and HMS *Investigator* in 1848, produced a portfolio of *Ten Coloured Views* of Ross's unsuccessful attempt to penetrate past (North) Somerset Island.[19] As well, the case for an artistic response to the North is made in prose by Robert Anstruther Goodsir, who sailed only as far as Baffin Bay in 1849, and whose *An Arctic Voyage* was published in 1850.

Failure to find Franklin did not deter Browne from responding imaginatively to the Arctic. Accompanying Ross through Lancaster Sound, he participated in the sledging expedition from Port Leopold, at the top of (North) Somerset Island, and part way down the island's east coast in the spring of 1849, while Ross explored the west coast down as far as 72°38′N. No published narratives were forthcoming of this frustratingly unavailing

FIG. 2. W.H.J. Browne's "Noon in Mid-Winter. H.M. Ships *Enterprise* and *Investigator* in winter quarters, Port Leopold, North Somerset—Noon in December." (Courtesy Metropolitan Toronto Library Board)

voyage, which escaped from the ice of 28 August 1849 and was back at the Orkney Islands in September, but Browne's ten pictures fill the void admirably.

The conventions of the Sublime—emphasis on vertical or horizontal expanses, the placement of tiny human figures in the picture to intensify the scale of the topography, and the extremities of landscape novelty—structure Browne's views and influence his choice of subject matter; nevertheless, these aesthetic considerations do not impede fulfillment of the pictures' functional roles as documentation of locations reached and phenomena witnessed. Darkness at noon provides him with the opportunity of exhibiting perhaps nature's own most sublime example of *chiaroscuro*—the balance of light and shadow in a picture. Entitled "Noon in Mid-Winter..."(Fig. 2), the scene's moonlight and the slightest hint of sun on the horizon combine with the stars to provide a most uncommon array of lighting over a windswept, desolate landscape. In "The Bivouac (Cape Seppings)..."(Fig. 3), a meal on the ice contributes more novelty to a picture already made sublime by its extreme verticality. A slight echo perhaps of J.M.W. Turner's paintings of cattle feeding beneath Yorkshire cliffs. Browne's work captures the wonderful castellated appearance of the cliffs on the west coast of Prince Regent Inlet (Fig. 1). In both Figures 2 and 3, the horizon is set so low in the vertical layout of the painting as to suggest how slight the purchase is that the travellers, in contrast

FIG. 3. W.H.J. Browne's "The Bivouac (Cape Seppings): The Party, under command of Lieutenants Robinson and Browne, at Dinner on the Ice, after the First Southern Deposit of Provisions, May, 1849. Temperature Forty Degrees." (Courtesy Metropolitan Toronto Library Board)

to Turner's lowing cattle, have on the face of the terrain/ice in the polar realm. The possibility that Franklin's men had encountered difficulty but were managing to survive in such desolate lands seems all but precluded by the sublimity depicted so dramatically by Browne. Finally, the avid reader of exploration narratives would recognize a further sublime aspect of Browne's "Bivouac" picture. It recalls the same coastal cliffs depicted in H.N. Head's sublime picture of the loss of HMS *Fury* in August 1825 when it was crushed by the ice against the coastal cliffs.[20] The same region would also remind the reader of the last winter spent by the crew of John Ross's *Victory* at Somerset House in 1832–1833 prior to a miraculous escape from the jaws that would seize Franklin.[21] In itself, dining on ice in May suggests a precarious activity to the English reader, and with these added echoes and the apparent impossibility of escaping from the ice to accessible land were the dining room floor to break up, the scene depicted by Browne resounds with multiple sublimity.

As if to bear witness to Browne's work, Goodsir, who commanded HMS *Advice* into but not through Baffin Bay in 1849 in search of his brother Harry, who was dead with Franklin, makes an unequivocal declaration of the aesthetic attributes of the North: "I do not think there is any region in the world where the landscape painter could enjoy better studies than in the Arctic regions."[22] Goodsir's own picture-making sensibility is highly developed and is attracted most by the picturesque variety of the ice formations in Baffin Bay:

> All that has been said of the coral reefs of the Southern Seas may well be applied to the icy masses of the Northern; but I must suspect it must be with the accompaniment of such weather as we at this time enjoyed, for a whistling north wind soon drives one to look for the picturesque in the neighbourhood of the cabin stove.[23]

Goodsir's enthusiasm must be tempered by the recognition that because his voyage failed to penetrate Lancaster Sound he did not pass a winter in the North. Nevertheless, his remarks concerning the picturesque properties of icescapes do compare with several made by John Richardson, a veteran of six northern winters, when he wrote from Great Bear Lake in the same summer (1849) that,

> here only, of all the countries I have seen, can I understand the deep blue shades of the ancient Italian masters....The depth of shade which marks out low snowy waves of the lake when the sun is low would surprise a painter brought here for the first time.[24]

While the weather initially induces and latterly curtails Goodsir's celebration of the moving islands' picturesque features in his Baffin Bay scene, the collision of several icebergs awakens simultaneously a captain's concern but also the landscape traveller's eye for the Sublime:

> And hark! the lengthening roar continuous runs
> Athwart the rifted deep: at once it bursts
> And piles a thousand mountains to the clouds.

One might almost think that the poet of the "Seasons" had witnessed such a scene. Great misshapen columns, like those of Stonehenge are not infrequently seen reared on end, on the top of these ramparts, poised so delicately, that a slight touch will send them thundering down on either side.[25]

Just as Thomson had utilized the sublime chaos of the floe in the "Winter" segment of *The Seasons* to depict foreign realms, Goodsir, more than 100 years later, quotes Thomson to embellish his guidebook to the Arctic.[26] Likening slabs of ice to the most primitive but at least familiar architecture, as George Back had done 15 years before him, he also intimates from the allusion that the delicate assembly of the ice fragments appears both chaotic and intentional.[27] The sublime thrill that he experiences derives as much from the positioning of the massive pieces on the brink of annihilation as from their appearance. In short, the associations arising in the mind contemplating the icescape are as powerful as the effect directly on the mind of any of the natural elements.

The indulgence in associationism had long been sanctioned by landscape enthusiasts, since it redounded to a landscape enthusiast's sensitivity to be able to derive a plethora of sensations—emotional and intellectual—from the contemplation of a scene. Not surprisingly, this form of extrapolation tends toward increasingly fanciful responses to landscape during the apogee of nineteenth-century landscape touring. The power of associationism is given free play by Goodsir on several occasions,[28] but perhaps nowhere is it more fancifully displayed than in his aesthetic response to "one of the most beautiful icebergs" encountered by HMS *Advice*:

> It was of immense size. The south side, on which we advanced towards it was almost perpendicular, as if a recent split had taken place; but on rounding the corner and coming abreast of the west side, which we did almost within arm's-length, we found it to be wrought into ledges,—ledge above ledge, each festooned with a fringe of crystal icicles, which here and there reaching the lodge beneath, formed columns slender as those of a saracenic mosque; within them ran a gallery green as emerald. Two or three tiny cascades were tinkling from ledge to ledge, and fell with a soft splash into the water beneath, sending the pearl-like bubbles dancing from them over the smooth surface. All was glancing and glittering beneath a bright sun, and if I had had it in my power I could have stood for hours to gaze at it. Passing the corner, the north side was seen to be cut into two little deep bays with sloping shores, a long point running out between them. The lowest ledge of the west side rounded the corner and inclined down towards the

nearest bay, if so it may be called, and ending in a broad platform. This little bay seemed so snug, and lay so beautifully to the sun, that, unnatural as it may appear, one could not help fancying it,—as a fit site for a pretty cottage.[29]

Goodsir finds himself running the aesthetic gamut on this iceberg. He begins at the sublime south side whose "immense" vertical character suggests to him a recent sublimely cataclysmic rending. He then turns the corner to encounter a picturesque, horizontally ordered western scene and a picturesque cottage dell on the northern side. In fact, he concocts with an impressive aesthetic resourcefulness a landscape tour from a single iceberg. Furthermore, he practises a sort of imaginative sculpting, creating the columns of a mosque in which the ice is magically "green as emerald," as it was in perhaps the most widely known of the period's examples of associationism—Coleridge's *The Rime of the Ancient Mariner,* itself based on exploration narratives.[30] Besides the columns, Goodsir produces a "tinkling" fountain, bays (as if the ice were, indeed, an enchanted mobile island), and a neighbourhood for an English cottage that would ravish picturesque painters such as George Morland or poets such as Wordsworth who wrote in "Tintern Abbey" of

> These plots of cottage-ground, these orchard-tufts,
> Which at this season, with their unripe fruits,
> Are clad in one green hue, and lose themselves
> 'Mid groves and copses.[31]

The subject matter is perhaps so foreign but, for the moment, so innocuous, that Goodsir is capable of transforming it into familiar sights. Although he refrains from composing a complete picture, he does render the berg more art than nature and, in so doing, follows the normal and, for a reader, most effective procedure for identifying an unfamiliar visual phenomenon by means of familiar aesthetic concepts and images: a saracenic mosque or a Lake District cottage brings the sight of the iceberg to life for his reader. Clearly, Goodsir is not transported by his fanciful indulgences—his earlier remark concerning when and where the picturesque can be sought, and his qualification of the bay ("if so it may be called") mark two narrative rudders guiding his associationist voyages—but his scenes are more fanciful than many of the picturesque scenes envisaged by previous arctic explorers. They introduce a trend toward the more fanciful scene in the works of what may be called the second generation of maritime arctic explorers of the nineteenth century—explorers who either were not yet born or were very young when Franklin made his first expedition in 1819. The more fanciful scene may reflect a landscape practice that had passed its prime in England, but also represents one way by which the British mariners could persuade themselves and their nation of the benignity of the Arctic until the Franklin expedition was rescued and while they pressed bravely on in their rescue attempts.

Searching for Franklin: The 1850 and 1851 Expeditions

The trend toward a more fanciful picturesque view of the North continued through the narrative and pictorial works produced by members of 1850 and 1851 search expeditions. During these years Lancaster Sound became the haunt of many British mariners. The Austin expedition of 1850–1851 (one of six expeditions to set sail in 1850) consisted of four ships: HMS *Resolute*, under Sir Horatio T. Austin, who had been first lieutenant on HMS *Fury* when it was wrecked in 1825 during Parry's third voyage; HMS *Assistance*, under Capt. Erasmus Ommanney; and two screw-steamers, the *Pioneer*, under Capt. Sherard Osborn, and the *Intrepid*, under Capt. Bertie Cator. These four ships produced three newspapers among them: the *Aurora Borealis* published aboard the *Assistance* on the 15th of each winter month (November 1850–March 1851) and republished in London under the title *Arctic Miscellanies* in the following year; the *Illustrated Arctic News*, edited by Osborn and George F. McDougall, published at the end of each month on board the *Resolute* (October 1850–March 1851) and republished in facsimile form in London in 1852; and a few issues of a rare paper titled *Minivalis*.

The *Resolute* and *Pioneer* wintered at Griffith Island (Fig. 1), while the *Assistance* and *Intrepid* wintered 28 miles away at Assistance Bay, Beechey Island (Fig. 1:2), at the southeastern extremity of Wellington Channel. There the two ships were joined by the *Lady Franklin* and *Sophia*, under the command of the whaling captain William Penny, by the *Felix* and *Mary*, under the command of the 73-year-old Sir John Ross, and by the ships of the American expedition under Capt. De Haven.

In the face of the horror of Franklin's fate, the Austin expedition built with their newspapers and theatrical productions a morale-boosting, illusion-confirming view of their habitation of the gelid frontier. Osborn and McDougall saw as the purpose of *Illustrated Arctic News* the need to show "that in the desolation of Land & Ice around us, the gentle lily Wisdom can still be culled—either in the contemplation of the ruins of the Old World, or in the strange, & ever changing phenomena of nature."[32] In the article "Notes from the Plank," Osborn demonstrates that the lily Wisdom of nature that the culler is meant to seek are the novel and picturesque aspects of the region:

> ...if nature here does not assume those rich & gorgeous forms under which the imagination becomes enthralled in more genial climes, yet the sweet and delicate tints thrown by her across the heavens, and filling up the background of some of her most striking tableaux leave a pensive and reflective effect upon the mind which cannot be well expressed or easily forgot.[33]

The parlance of the habit of viewing nature as pictures—"tints," "background," "tableaux"—governs what may be called an aesthetic strategy for survival in high latitudes. Over in the *Assistance*, the reinforcement of the illusion of the Picturesque took on a humorous but no less fanciful tone in the form of a newspaper advertisement for real estate in *Aurora Borealis:*

> To be sold or let, with immediate possession. Two new cottages, called Marble Villa and Cerulean Cottage, situated a short distance to the southward of 'Assistance,' in a very picturesque neighbourhood; they both face to the south, having extensive undulating grounds in front, over which fine healthy exercise may be taken; the climate is so well known, that it does not require the flowery language of a Robins to say anything in its praise.
> ...N.B.—There are good quarries of building material close to the cottages, and any quantity of water can be obtained by sinking wells of a few feet.
>
> WM. KNOCKMEDOWN,
> Auctioneer[34]

Landscape appreciation takes an obvious jibe from such a passage, but it is clear that what makes the joke possible is the widespread habit among the mariners of surveying the "fields" of ice from the elevated prospects of their ships' decks and of feeling inclined to transform desolate wastes and hummocks of ice into "undulating grounds" and cottage plots, induced in this by the spontaneous exertions of their aesthetic wills to survive. Numerous fanciful pictures are made in prose by "A.B.," whose journal extracts appeared in *Aurora Borealis* and were hailed by the editor as the most valuable sort of submission to the paper that the officers could make.

In the *Lady Franklin,* which was commanded by William Penny, Dr. P.C. Sutherland answers the advertisement, as it were, with the following single-paragraph description of the animated landscape he views in Assistance Bay from the deck of his ship on 23 September 1850:

> Assistance Bay was beginning to show signs of life and activity. On this point a party of strollers; on that level plain two boon companions with their guns; wending his way in a rugged ravine, charmed with its iron cascades, and wretchedly dreary, wild, and barren aspect, a solitary individual; and, chasing one another playfully along the beach, the dogs, were the objects that now began to meet and please the eye.[35]

A common narrative corollary to the picture frame, the paragraph form governs this single view. The here/there composition of a picturesque view in which vegetation, ruins, animals, and so on are set on an axis. The humanized, animated foreground contrasts ideally with the "wild, and barren aspect" of the ravine through which the solitary traveller wends his way in the middle ground. Sutherland's view attracts and merits attention less for the landscape than for the human activity going on in it.

Such is also the case with J. Coventry's picture "Assistance Bay..." (Fig. 4), which was selected as the frontispiece for the first volume of Sutherland's *Journal.* Its rendition of landscape, apart from the successful execution of the convention of hiding the sun on the horizon and behind a headland, a convention attributable to the most influential picturesque landscape painter, Claude (Gellée) Lorrain,[36] offers less interest than does the chronicle it provides of pedestrian excursions and games of field hockey taking place amid temperatures sufficiently cold to freeze mercury, and in a country whose windswept bareness is destitute even of a cover of snow in February. As well, the picture is interesting for its inadvertent suggestion that the Marble Villa and Cerulean Cottage of the advertisement in *Aurora Borealis* refer humorously to the two ice sheds in the foreground, built for the storage of explosives and flammable *matériel.* Coventry in art and Sutherland in prose, like the tars in action, throw the illusion of picturesque contentment over Assistance Bay, making a recognizable landscape of it.

FIG. 4. J. Coventry's "Assistance Bay 24th February 1851, The Coldest Day, Mercury Frozen." (Courtesy Metropolitan Toronto Library Board)

The Voyage of the Prince Albert in Search of Sir John Franklin (1851) offers many parallel responses to the arctic tundra, but one exceptionally fanciful response merits attention for its alliance of the North with landscapes visited on the Grand Tour by British travellers. William Parker Snow, who had been employed before the voyage of the *Prince Albert* in the summer of 1850 as the amanuensis to Thomas Macaulay, the historian whose first two volumes of the *History of England* appeared in 1849, quotes the third-to-last stanza of Byron's *Childe Harold* as the epigraph to his *Voyage*. Occasionally fancying himself a roaming child, charmed to a "pleasing fear" by the global oceans, in a work whose structure bears several signs of the sort of guidebook for the Grand Tour that Byron's poem in some ways is, Snow encounters at the top of Baffin Island the type of majestic vale that Childe Harold discovers after treks across "wild and rugged" mountain ranges:

> ...I could not help for the moment assimilating it, however great the difference might really be, to the far-famed Val d'Ossola first seen from the Simplon Pass in Italy. This arctic vale certainly gave as bright and pleasing relief at that moment, and among those wild and rugged scenes, as the other could in its own neighbourhood.[37]

Besides making his own aesthetic charting, Snow manages to align his summer "tour" to the Arctic (the *Prince Albert* did not stay the winter) with the most fashionable continental tours made by travellers who would not dare not to know their Byron.

As well as editing a newspaper, Osborn kept his own journal and edited for publication the diary of his friend Capt. Robert M'Clure.[38] M'Clure, who had sailed with George Back in HMS *Terror* in 1836–1837, and patrolled the Great Lakes on board HMS *Niagara* in 1838 and 1839 after the Upper Canada rebellion, commanded HMS *Investigator* to the Arctic by way of Bering Strait in 1850, having departed five months prior to the Austin expedition.[39] M'Clure was a strong-headed, exceedingly capable commander and was possessed of an apparently common Irishman's disregard for the aesthetics of landscape. (Neither of his countrymen who commanded expeditions to the Arctic—Richard Collinson and Francis L. McClintock—display any aesthetic interest in nature in their writings.[40]) The passages from M'Clure's own pen that are quoted at length by Osborn in *The Discovery of the North-West Passage* attest almost not at all to the character of the region through which he travelled from 1850 to 1854.[41] Likely, M'Clure recognized Osborn's own talent for composing "correct" landscape pictures and left it to his friend to embellish his own notes to suit public taste.

Because he published the journal in 1856, before discovery of the Franklin crew, Osborn still strikes the fanciful note in many of the descriptions of landscapes he himself had not seen. By way of picturing the icescapes over which a sledging party, led by M'Clure, passed on 22 October 1850, en route from the winter quarters of the *Investigator*, up Prince of Wales Strait to the top of Banks Island and Barrow Strait, Osborn employs a telling analogy: "After some difficulty in crossing ridges of broken ice—the *hedge-rows* of an arctic landscape,—they reached vast fields of smooth ice...."[42] This instance of fancifully identifying a feature of arctic landscape as English is not unique. At the top of Banks Island, the prospect extended out across the polar ice pack in Melville Bay and over to Melville Island, 75 miles distant. The view is sublime not just for its vastness but because it represents the first *published* sighting of a Northwest Passage: in the distance lay Winter Harbour, where Parry's first expedition spent the winter of 1819–1820.[43] Osborn enlarges the dimensions of the conventional picturesque representation but his description is not suitably sublime. He retains an England-based schema for the view: "great hills and dales of blue crystalline sea-ice rolled on before them."[44]

To obtain the nineteenth-century sublime response to this significant "Passage" view from Banks Island, one must turn to the work of Samuel Gurney Cresswell, the expedition's artist. His picture of this icescape is entitled "Melville Island from Banks [Is]Land" (Fig. 5). It appeared both as one of eight sketches published by Cresswell himself and in the M'Clure/Osborn collaboration.[45] The tiny pair of explorers are conventionally dwarfed by the wondrous vastness of arctic space. They gaze off into the interminable north from a cliff, which Osborn notes reaches 600 feet above the gelid sea. The succession of headlands on Melville Island rises like a series of spectres out of the refracted distance across M'Clure Strait. But the erubescent skies of a late October sunrise, which present the view's most sublime aspect, show Cresswell's adaptability to a vermilion lucidity of atmosphere not commonly found in English skies or in his other works. Such adaptation is fitting for an important painting of an imaginatively and topographically significant view, a view consecrates that aspect of the quest motif central to the geographical and aesthetic mapping of the North. Finally and ironically, one must note that the picture consecrates what would become a pedestrian but never a marine Northwest Passage. It marked perhaps the single most remote and wild excursion on any walking tour by a nineteenth-century British traveller.

Two members of M'Clure's expedition, its surgeon/naturalist and its chaplain, produced journals that were published. The minister was Johann Miertsching, a Moravian missionary in Labrador. In 1967, L.H. Neatby translated his journal, titling it *Frozen Ships*.[46] Not surprisingly, the missionary's chief concern lies with contacting the "Eskimaux" of the western Arctic, but his complete lack of interest in landscape shows, by contrast, how intensely aware of it the British officers for the most part were. Miertsching writes baldly of the various "frightful" situations of the *Investigator* in pack ice and of the "pleasant" arctic sunsets, his avocation for landscape touring virtually undeveloped in an otherwise fascinating journal.

Alexander Armstrong, on the other hand, follows the impressive aesthetic response to landscape by such navy surgeons before him as John Richardson and Peter Sutherland. Off the northern continental coast, west of Point barrow, on 6 August 1850, he demonstrates a keen perception of how his aesthetic habits tend to make over the natural phenomena before him, transforming and composing them into a recognizable picture:

FIG. 5. S.G. Cresswell's "Melville Island from Banks [Is]Land." (Courtesy Metropolitan Toronto Library Board)

The position from whence these fears [of becoming ice-bound] were entertained, could scarcely be supposed to have existence in the frigid regions of the north, from the picturesque beauty and loveliness of the scene which then met the eye; but when I say that ice and water alone contributed to form the landscape, it must be equally difficult to fancy that these elements could so closely imitate true lacustrine scenery. We lay with all our canvas set, hanging sluggishly from the yards on the glassy surface of a sheet of water some two or three miles in diameter, apparently ice-locked. The sun shone forth brilliantly, imparting to us all, the delightful warmth of his rays, and to the icy regions in the distance, that peculiar splendour produced by their reflective power in a highly refractive atmosphere. Masses of snow-white ice, in form resembling little islands were interspersed around, with intervening spaces of water. Numerous as they were, there was light sufficient to display the outline of each as they floated motionless on the surface of the sleeping sea, with the distant and uneven pack all around, forming a land-like but ice-locked boundary, resembling one of our own northern lakes in its wintry garb. There a vivid imagination might readily have taken a flight far from the Polar Sea, in contemplating the icy scene which surrounded us, the novelty of which was only surpassed by its beauty.[47]

Like Snow, who likens a Baffin Island valley to Val d'Ossola, or Back, who thinks of Alpine scenes when viewing the tundra,[48] or Chappell, for whom the powerful summer sun striking a calm arctic sea reminds him of a description of the Syrian desert,[49] or Franklin, Hood, and Richardson, who recall the picturesque aspects of the English Lake District when viewing the prospect from Fort Enterprise—indeed, like almost any explorer whose visual mode of perception involves the composition or, at least, the identification of landscapes—Armstrong perceives nature in terms of the natural world familiar to him and his readers. But his practice differs from some others in its degree of fancifulness since, as he notes, he finds himself making a terrestrial scene from an aquaeous one; that is to say, making a landscape from a seascape. The motionless ship in the foreground, the island-dotted (or lake-dotted) ocean in the middle ground, and the delimiting "distant and uneven pack" resembling hills in the background constitute a view sufficiently similar to its Lake District model as to enable Armstrong to chart it aesthetically.

Nevertheless, a picturesque illusion of a highly fanciful sort, however reassuring it may be momentarily, endures only as long as the "landscape" does; and with the ice continuously in motion, Armstrong soon finds himself greeting other prospects. The fear to which he alludes at the outset of his Lake District single-paragraph picture becomes a profoundly expressed emotion throughout the narrative account of the next three years. On the night of 8 October 1850, in Prince of Wales Strait, HMS *Investigator* was thrown up on the ice, amid

> a general movement in the pack; this commenced with a low rumbling noise, resembling the distant roar of the ship, when we were amazed at seeing immense masses of ice slowly and gradually raised to different degrees of elevation, others crumbling to pieces, or packed on each other, and the same force slowly but surely approaching ourselves. Our astonishment rapidly changed into intense anxiety for our own safety.[50]

Edmund Burke had argued in his *Philosophical Enquiry* that natural sublimity had to be kept at a distance for it still to enthrall the spectator: once it approached too near him, error erased any appreciation of it. Clearly a landscape enthusiast in the Burkean tradition, Armstrong falls silent, abdicating his self-proclaimed role as the expedition's aesthetic voice, once the harrowing litany of ice converges on the ship, thereby rapidly changing astonishment to intense anxiety.

Yet, just at this point of Armstrong's abdication, Cresswell comes into his own. Three of Cresswell's paintings depict the struggle waged between HMS *Investigator* and the pack ice. These paintings cover the period beginning with the night Armstrong's picturesque eye shrinks away, 8 October 1850, and extending one year, until 23 September 1851, during which time the ship coasted south out of Prince of Wales Strait and around Banks Island to Mercy Bay (Fig. 1)—its winter harbour and its grave.[51] Two of Cresswell's scenes set the ship in icescapes rather than seascapes: "H.M.S Investigator in the Pack..."(Fig. 6), and the famous "Critical Position of H.M.S. Investigator..."(Fig.7).[52] The ship is an aesthetic and navigational anomaly, involving its sailors in an aesthetic and navigational crisis. Indeed, the whole scene in each case is sublime in the sense that it lies beyond human navigational or imaginative control. This sense of the absurdly inconceivable actually being realized charges Cresswell's achievement with a distinctly profound gloom which is evoked by the curious glow of the cabin lantern shining against the moonlit onslaught of nature in the first work, and the tiny figures desperately scaling the mountainous iceberg in the second. The sense of impending doom which suffuses all the works and is effected principally by Cresswell's achievements with the technique of *chiaroscuro* mark a degree in the rendition of natural sublimity previously unattained in polar art and comparable to the sublime achievements of Cresswell's peer, Turner.

Armstrong's concerns as a doctor became paramount in his journal from the winter of 1851 onward. The *Investigator* remained beset in Mercy Bay through 1852 and M'Clure planned to send out the weaker half of his scurvy-ridden crew to seek the continental coast at the Mackenzie River in April 1853. This misguided and disastrous plan was averted only through the sudden arrival on 7 April, eight days prior to the scheduled departure of the infirm, of Bedford Pim, from HMS *Resolute*, which had wintered off Dealy Island (Fig. 1), 28 days' march away in the direction of Melville Island.

Over in Prince Regent Inlet, William Kennedy and the French volunteer, Joseph René Bellot, were icebound aboard the *Prince Albert*, the only ship to spend the winter of 1851–1852 in the eastern Arctic. The men survived an extremely rigorous winter and an unusually late spring. As if to give vent in February to his distaste for what appeared to be a continuous gale blowing from December until April, Kennedy fashions a singular outcry, echoing John McLean's lament[53] of a winter spent at Fort Chimo by quoting the same Miltonic passage:

The terrible enemies of travelling parties were the snowstorms and furious gales which prevailed with us during the greater part

FIG. 6. S.G. Cresswell's "H.M.S. *Investigator* in the Pack. October 8th 1850."
(Courtesy Metropolitan Toronto Library Board)

of the winter. A low temperature, even the lowest recorded in the
Arctic region, is elysium compared with a piercing nor'-easter
driving the sharp keen spiculae of snow-drift, like a shower of
red-hot sand in your face and through every pore of your body.
The comparison may seem Hibernian, but nevertheless gives a
very good idea of one's sensations under the pitiless discharge of a
hurricane of snow-drift in these regions, where as in Milton's
Pandemonium,

_____ "The parching air
Burns frore, and cold performs the effect of fire,"

I have a strong opinion that old Æolus, with his den of ruffianly
winds, that so shamefully belaboured the pious Æneas, must have
emigrated to North Somerset since the days of Virgil.[54]

A deeply religious man, Kennedy appears to doubt the existence of
Providence at the height of the tempest. Short of an outright expression of

FIG. 7. S.G. Cresswell's "Critical Position of H.M.S. *Investigator* on the North-Coast of Baring [Banks] Island, August 20th 1851." (Courtesy Metropolitan Toronto Library Board)

such doubt, he alludes to the region as a pre- or extra-Christian domain, where a "pitiless discharge" of climatic havoc is wreaked by a pagan god who seems bent on presenting a series of "terrible enemies" to "travelling parties." A native of Cumberland House and a resident of England, Kennedy alludes to Ireland ("Hibernian") in a way that recalls a view of it as a God-forsaken country in the minds of many Englishmen. The allusion also suggests, by way of the Miltonic quotation and the Virgilian comment, that the pious Kennedy regards himself sledging across the Arctic as the Englishman would touring Ireland—alternately as one of Milton's fallen angels in *Paradise Lost* passing across to the "frozen Continent" and as Virgil's epic hero questing through a hostile realm.[55]

The narrative of Joseph René Bellot lies, properly speaking, beyond the perimeter of this study, but it may be consulted briefly for the contrast it bears to the British response to nature. Initially, Bellot voices great pleasure in arctic landscapes. Like Goodsir, who did not penetrate Lancaster Sound, Bellot finds the ice in Baffin Bay enchanting: "There is more poetry in this than in the burning lava crust of a volcano. What pencil could reproduce the thousand beauties of the sun playing amid the ice? What pen could describe the thousand sensations experienced by the intellect and the heart?"[56] But the novelty of besetment soon wears thin, and two weeks later (9 August) Bellot's response to a rain-drenched landscape sounds more like Kennedy, Parry, and Ross:

> I cannot find hard words enough to say of these icebergs, for which I panted so long at the period of my feverish admiration for the sublime scenes of the north. The sense of its own impotence reacting on the human mind, makes it regard with rage mingled with terror and scorn...this ignoble triumph of number and of mere physical force....But Nature no longer feels her heart beat in the slumber of the north...Moral nature seems to have abdicated, and nothing remains but a chaos without a purpose, in which everything clashes confusedly and by chance.[57]

The Frenchman's landscape concerns strike a new chord, taking to a more profound level British complaints of, or efforts to mask, perceived monotony and uniformity in arctic nature. His inquiry, however casual, into the moral character of Nature was not indulged in by his British counterparts because of two aspects of the Picturesque aesthetic: its tendency to keep the landscape viewer's attention, as Christopher Hussey maintains,[58] on the surface features of nature, their textural values, tonal relations, and compositions; and the faith in a fundamental harmony between man and nature that still obtained in early nineteenth-century imperial Britain, and that helped to nurture the dream of Franklin's survival. For the most part, the response to nature by such pre-Huxleyan naturalists as John Richardson and David Douglas took the form of belief rather than inquiry.[59] Yet, British explorers who were exposed, not to moderate conditions of nature, but to chaotic and desolate extremities of climate and terrain do begin to voice doubt. Equipped only with the illusions of reality which were formed in response to moderate English nature, on the one hand, or the genial sublimity of the Alps which evoked a pleasing horror, on the other, and which produced descriptions of the Arctic that were more or less fanciful, the British explorer could not endure indefinite time searching for survivors in realms where nature relentlessly assaulted his prior conceptions of it. Sooner or later, he would come to doubt a faith he rarely had reason to question at home, a faith, to recall Wordsworth's enunciation that "Nature never did betray / The heart that loved her."[60] One finds this process of doubt engaged most openly in the work of John Ross but in other journalists and painters the doubt takes the form of silence and deliberate ignorance.[61] In either case, a fear is registered over the capability of the Picturesque and its attendant faith to represent reality, and a recognition is made of the possible existence of a natural force divested of moral purpose—a Demorgorgon, to cite Shelley's personification of raw potentiality[62] without a cultivated, beneficent character—which appears to be as capable of annihilating man as of protecting and nourishing his physical and aesthetic needs.

Searching for Franklin: The 1852–1857 Expeditions

The spring of 1852 saw the Admiralty launch another large-scale campaign. It was to be the last grand search for the crews of the *Erebus* and *Terror*, for after 1854 the Crimean War made its claims on Navy manpower and *matériel*: with the arctic voyages proving repeated failures, their continuation could not be countenanced against an arguably greater need. Capt. Edward Belcher was a Nova Scotian by birth.[63] He had sailed with Beechey aboard HMS *Blossom* in 1825–1828 as part of the third Parry and second Franklin expeditions, but with no more experience in ice-infested waters he was appointed to command the 1852–1854 voyages. He sailed in HMS *Assistance* with Comm. G.N. Richards. Accompanying them were Kellett in HMS *Resolute* and Comm. Francis L. McClintock and Capt. Sherard Osborn in the screw steamers *Intrepid* and *Pioneer*. Belcher and Osborn proceeded up Wellington Channel (Fig. 1:1) while Kellett and McClintock wintered at Dealy Island, whence the rescue expedition by Pim was initiated to save M'Clure and company from the same fate as Franklin. As well, HMS *North Star*, under Capt. Pullen, wintered at Beechey Island, ready as a supply ship to the other four if need arose; and need did arise.

FIG. 8. W.W. May's "Sledges in a Fair Fresh Wind, Going over Hummoky Ice."
(Courtesy Metropolitan Toronto Library Board)

Comm. Walter W. May, who had a serious falling out with Belcher during the voyage, produced *A Series of Fourteen Sketches* (1855). Two pictures record novel environmental events: the return of daylight, and sledging over a pool of water on a July ice floe. The second, "Sledge Party Returning Through Water during the Month of July,"[64] does not offer the intricate ice formations or variations of light captured so superbly by Cresswell in his picture of sledging across M'Clure Strait earlier in the same year (1853), but another of May's sketches does. "Sledges in a Fair Fresh Wind, Going over Hummoky Ice," (Fig. 8) is suffused with a sense of exposure to the sledgers' "terrible enemies."[65] The sky and billowing sails portend disaster as the weather appears on the verge of enveloping the icescape; it already has effaced any distinction between middle ground and background and threatens to throw a sublime obscurity over the sojourners. "The drift is so strong," writes May in his annotation to the picture, "that it makes some of the objects appear quite indistinct, and with the sky, drift and sledges all going together, a different picture is presented to any of the rest of the work."

Two more pictures serve to display May's range of execution and perception in these 14 works. These are "H.M.S. Assistance and Pioneer Fast to the Floe...,"[66] (Fig. 9) and "Division of Sledges Passing Cape Lady Franklin..."(Fig. 10).[67] May supplies a guidebook-like resumé for the first of these paintings:

> ...Cape Majendie is the northern boundary of Wellington Channel, fifty miles to the northward of which, in the Queen's Channel, H.M.S. Assistance and Pioneer wintered in 1852–3. The Sketch was made at midnight, the red cliff being covered by a table-cloth of white mist. There was about two miles of floe between us and the shore, which, together with Dundas Island on the left, completed the scene.

Perceived as a landscape picture ("scene"), the channel is portrayed like many of the seascapes of the Franco-Italian doyen of the picturesque style in landscape painting, Claude Lorrain. As in one of Lorrain's Mediterranean seascapes, the declining (here, the declined) sun is hidden behind the *coulisse* of Dundas Island on one side, while the headland on the other rises precipitately from the ocean floor. The intricately shaped ice in the right-hand, and the scene-enlivening ducks in the left-hand foreground echo the contrast perceptible in the geography in either side of the background. The stillness of the open water and the slumbering state of the ships with their sails reefed spread an impressive quietude over this picturesque midnight sunset view.

"Division of Sledges" (Fig. 10) illustrates several conventions. The variation in shade cast on the fore- and middle ground provides a depth into the picture, which in turn intensifies the height of what May in his notes calls "the tremendous barrier." The sublime force of nature is explicit, for the sea ice has been thrust against the cape itself. As well, May depicts the route of

FIG. 9. W.W. May's "H.M.S. *Assistance* and *Pioneer* Fast to the Floe, off Cape Majendie, Wellington Channel, 1853." (Courtesy Metropolitan Toronto Library Board)

FIG. 10. W.W. May's "Division of Sledges Passing Cape Lady Franklin; Extra-ordinary Masses of Ice Pressed Against the North Shore of Bathurst Land." (Courtesy Metropolitan Toronto Library Board)

the journey in a serpentine line, again probably in order to emphasize depth into the landscape since his concern in several of the sledging scenes is to define the space *through* which the sojourners journeyed. This concern arises out of the artist's fear that the sameness of the snow-covered landscape or icescape would strike the viewer of his work (as it strikes him) as a two-dimensional absurdity.

Identifying a middle ground proved a continual problem for sledgers: only what was right before them or far in the distance was visible; but because space could not readily be demarcated and approximated between the immediate foreground and distant background, many sledgers found themselves approaching for days a headland they believed no more than 20 miles distant. Of course, the fact that the characteristic English view rarely exceeds 10 miles—a recent edition of Turner's *Picturesque Views of England and Wales* includes only one landscape in 103 plates whose view appears longer than 10 miles—fosters perceptual habits that expect objects in the distance to lie only so far away.[68] The English reaction to repeated disillusionment in the middle-groundless and highly refracted environment was, as May's picture of the north shore of Bathurst Land illustrates, to superimpose on a given terrain or tract of ice the conventions of landscape viewing with which he was familiar. The serpentine line and varying bands of light and shade are what James Thomson saw from the hill overlooking Hagley Park when composing *The Seasons*, that poetic manifesto of picturesque landscape touring.[69] They are brought forcibly into play in the Arctic for the Englishman's aesthetic nourishment and spatial orientation and to permit him to make somewhere a place, to make it *mean* something that the English mind could endure. Such illusions rendered such "excursions" as McClintock's wondrous 105-day, 1200-mile trek across Melville Island, Fitzwilliam Strait, Eglinton and Prince Patrick Islands in the spring of 1853 aesthetically, psychologically bearable.

McClintock was based on the steamer *Intrepid*, wintering with Kellett's *Resolute* at Dealy Island in 1852–1853, and west of Byam Martin Island (Fig. 1) but still in Viscount Melville Sound in 1853–1854. The record of this half of the Belcher expedition was published in 1857 by George F. McDougall as *The Eventful Voyage of H.M. Discovery Ship "Resolute."*

Including some of his own sketches, McDougall's work expends much ink on the practical affairs of the expedition: the composition and achievements of the various sledging parties embarking from the *Resolute* and *Intrepid*, the effects of scurvy, the examination of Belcher's decision to abandon ship, and a detailed account of the recovery in 1855 of the *Resolute*. Perhaps because he also had accompanied Osborn in the *Resolute* in 1850–1851, McDougall finds polar landscapes no longer hold the allure of novelty for him that they did when he co-edited and illustrated the *Illustrated Arctic News*. His aesthetic response during the later expedition is comparatively slim, but perhaps this may be attributed to the drain on the physical network of the European constitution by the arduous sledging journeys across all the islands on the north shore of Viscount Melville Sound.

McDougall does, however, discuss the fate of Franklin in a manner that includes criticism of British perception of the arctic environment. While discussing the comparatively large numbers of animals on Melville Island, he argues that this profusion marks an exception to the findings on previous expeditions of a general paucity of wildlife in the polar archipelago:

> It must be apparent to the reader that I despair of Sir John Franklin and his brave companions still existing within these regions, the more so as the graves and other relics on Beechey Island prove that their first winter was spent in one of the most unproductive places within the arctic circle....
>
> Whilst fitting out, I overheard a very amusing discourse between an eccentric but talented Scotch gentleman (connected with one of the most important of our public institutions) and a young officer about to make his first trip to the Northern seas....
>
> "Now," said he [the Scot], "I see no reason for supposing, that Nature has entirely excluded the northern regions, from participating in the gifts so lavishly displayed, in the more favoured regions of the south. Not that I would have you expect an English landscape, with its meadow lands and picturesque groups of trees; but I venture to predict, that during the summer and autumnal months, you will find the shore of North Devon [Devon Island] abounding in rich vegetation, which forms the food on which the numerous animals in that locality exist. There, interspersed with gay mosses, you will find brilliant lichen, and luxuriant saxifrage, with the arctic poppy; the whole forming a delightful picture and instructive study to the inquiring mind."
>
> I leave the sojourners at Beechey Island, on board the "North Star," to confirm or refute the above statement. The numerous animals have dwindled down to an occasional solitary bear, whose flesh, even to hungry men, is anything but palatable; and the above description is far too glowing and imaginative, for the scanty portions of the floral world at Beechey, or in its neighbourhood; although it is true that gay mosses and brilliant lichens are to be found there, specimens of which, obtained by Dr. McCormick, may be seen in the Arctic collection at the British Museum.[70]

McDougall pinpoints the important aesthetic thesis on which, as Yi-Fu Tuan argues, the identity of man in relation to the external world is based.[71] Ordering sense impressions is a vital procedure in human conduct, but when the order being cast (in this case, by the Scot) over the outside world bears little relation to the phenomena actually there, it becomes questionable whether that order can stand for reality, and whether it can stand the burden of expectation which the illusions or schemata or taxonomies, that together one calls reality, must bear.

Just as the Picturesque permitted the eighteenth- and early nineteenth-century Briton to see the world with an English eye and to show off his landscape learning, it provided the nineteenth-century imperialist with a way to make other parts of the globe British and to show that he was abetting the effort to impart British/Christian values to foreigners and English scenes to foreign lands. Pope's and Thomson's intentions of making English views worthy of the Arts grew, with confidence, into the urge of the Victorian generations of imperialists to make other parts of the world identifiable by "correcting" them in terms of an English concept of nature. Arctic voyagers embarked, leaving behind what Charles Dickens called "an English hearth and Devon's waving trees,"[72] and, coming face to face with another form of nature, they attempted to "correct" it: first, by decoding the inscrutable sublimities of the terrain, or, citing Dickens, "the secrets of the vast Profound"; then, by "making a garden of the desert wide" in the name of British aesthetic principles, British science, and a British God. (The "Dr. McCormick" alluded to as the eccentric Scot by McDougall still spoke of an arctic landscape as "a fit subject for the pencil of a Claude" when he published his narrative in 1884.)[73] What the tenacious voyagers met was a resilient land which, like the sea, gave up its secrets very grudgingly. Through no fault of their own, the Britons deployed an ill-fitting aesthetic *matériel* that, because largely unadaptable, caused fanciful depictions and, in the end, several perceptual mistakes themselves productive of an unique aesthetic map of the North.

Finding picturesque and genially sublime views is, as has been seen throughout the examination of these pictorial and narrative responses to the Arctic, an aesthetic practice that conserves the traveller's idea of how space and time in foreign realms exist in relation to what he knows. But continuing to find picturesque views where they do not exist or where the relations between European man and nature which underlie the aesthetic principles do not obtain, opens a dangerous and not always bridgeable gulf between illusion and nature, those two components of geography as Watson defines it. And a perversion in response to nature, that is, increasingly fanciful responses, will, rather than sustain the viewer's sense of identity, imperil his chances for understanding what changes an altered state of nature demands of him. As George McDougall implies, fanciful pictures of the Arctic produce graves;[74] or, as John Ross noted, snow and ice in a Dutch landscape painting are not the same snow and ice which beset a scurvy-ridden crew of incarcerated sojourners at the greatest odds with the surrounding environment.[75]

The unquestioned belief in a harmony operating between man and nature promises a certain blindness to the threat posed by an environment unguided by the beneficent hand of the Deity. Neither the Sublime nor the Picturesque met the British explorer's imaginative needs in the North: only the apocalyptic efforts in the poetry of Franklin's peers—Byron, Shelley, and Keats—display an imaginative scope commensurate with that of the explorer, a few of Cresswell's paintings marking a possible exception. The void which these poets imaginatively confronted bears a certain affinity to the void which the arctic map of 1819 showed. Charting the map, filling the void beyond the mouths of the Mackenzie and Coppermine rivers and the east coast of Baffin Island, like the Romantic poets' struggles to map the imaginative provinces of the mind, would cost the dreamers nothing less than life. Shelley's poetic epitaph for Keats in *Adonais*—"Die,/If thou wouldst be with that which thou dost seek!"[76]—appears to be poignantly remembered in another line of heroically alliterative monosyllables, Tennyson's epitaph for the Franklin cenotaph—"They forged the last link with their lives." It was Franklin's crews who discovered the navigable Northwest Passage, but the discovery was like attainment of beauty in Keats's poetry: it came only with death. *Adonais* was Shelley's understanding of Keats's imaginative quest. Duncan Campbell Scott's comes in his poem entitled "Ode for the Keats Centenary."[77] Not surprisingly, perhaps, Scott gives Keats's soul the "fields of arctic moss" as a topographical haunt in which to seek "The wonder of the various world, the power/Of 'seeing great things in loneliness.' "

Between 1770 and 1860, explorers of northern British North America did not perceive the region's vastness in terms of its unique landscape properties; nor were the geomorphic names for and the sheer dimensions of these properties—eskers, tarns, permafrosted valleys, gravel beaches of immense sizes, badlands erosion, glacial flutings, tundra polygons, ice-covered pingos, and more fresh-water lakes than in the rest of the world—known to them. Rather, the Picturesque and the Sublime dictated how the terrain was perceived, and although along with astronomical computations, they told the Briton where he stood relative to the nature and geography of England, they pointed out what the nature of the North did *not* possess. Yet, just as the British explorers brought with them all their food and supplies, stubbornly yet understandably resisting adaptation to such proven survival techniques of the indigent peoples as a diet of pemmican and blubber (although the Ross expedition of 1829–1833 survived only because of forced adaptation to this diet), so they brought with them a perceptual baggage which they felt was equally elemental to their survival but which proved adaptable only with difficulty. Distance in a view could only be measured where a foreground was succeeded by a middle ground, and a middle ground by a background. Where this did not occur, the Britons quite naturally complained of monotonous, dreary extents, lacking variety and uncomposable by conventional techniques. Just as Franklin in 1825 insisted upon using specially designed boats, fabricated in London and tested on the Thames, to coast the north shore of the continent when Eskimos advised him that ice conditions necessitated sledge travel along the shore, so British explorers insisted with a wonderful tenacity upon making their landscape observations based upon made-in-England customs, made in England, where rock seldom meets sky without an intervening band of treetops, hedge rows, or, at the least, a plant- or soil-covering. Yet, this aesthetic tenacity not only sustained the early-century explorers in their searches for a passage, but it permitted the hundreds of mariners who searched for

Franklin to endure harsh, even imperilling conditions until the missing men and, with them, the key to a passage were found.

Undoubtedly, the tenacity with which the explorers attacked the North compensated in part for the unsuitability of their perceptual schemata; however, it left for subsequent generations a bewildering legacy of landscape perception which could only see the Arctic, almost without exception, as a vast uninhabitable, and annihilating realm.[78] The recent publication of poetry by F.R. Scott and by Al Purdy,[79] as well as the journals and sketches of A.Y. Jackson's first Arctic trip in 1927,[80] attest to the difficulties involved in altering perception to the extent demanded of artists of any age by the North. Still, such relatively modern developments as aerial photography and, as in Purdy's poetry, the appreciation of minute flora and fauna have suggested new ways of seeing the realm that Canadians are just now learning to appropriate into their imaginative nationhood. Only 20 years ago, I.N. Smith titled the book he edited *The Unbelievable Land*.[81]

Notes

1. C.P. Barbier, *William Gilpin: His Drawings, Teaching, and Theory of the Picturesque* (Oxford: Clarendon, 1963).

2. W. Wordsworth, *Guide to the Lakes*, ed. E.D. Sélincourt (Oxford: Oxford University Press, 1970).

3. J.W. Watson, "The Role of Illusion in North American Geography: A Note on the Geography of North American Settlement,"*Canadian Geographer* 13 (1969): 10.

4. E.H. Gombrich, *Art and Illusion: A Study in the Psychology of Pictorial Representation* (Princeton: Princeton University Press, 1960), 466.

5. E. Burke, *A Philosophical Enquiry into the Origin of Our Ideas of the Sublime and the Beautiful* (London: Routledge and Kegan Paul, 1958), 197.

6. S.H. Monk, *The Sublime: A Study of Critical Theories in XVIII-Century England* (Ann Arbor: University of Michigan Press, 1960), 250.

7. C. Hussey, *The Picturesque: Studies in a Point of View* (New York: Putnam, 1927), 307; J. Barrell,*The Idea of Landscape and the Sense of Place 1730–1840: An Approach to the Poetry of John Clare* (Cambridge: Cambridge University Press, 1972), 244.

8. D. Lowenthal and H.C. Prince, "The English Landscape," *Geographical Review* 55 (1964): 309–46; D. Lowenthal and H.C. Prince, "English Landscape Tastes," *Geographical Review* 55 (1965): 186–222.

9. Hussey, *The Picturesque*, 128.

10. C.C. Loomis, "The Arctic Sublime," in *Nature and the Victorian Imagination*, ed. V.C. Knoepflmacher and G.B. Tennyson (Berkeley: University of California Press, 1977), 95–112.

11. I.S. MacLaren, "Retaining Captaincy of the Soul: Responses to Nature in the First Franklin Expedition," *Essays on Canadian Writing* 28 (1984): 57–92.

12. R. Hood, *To the Arctic by Canoe 1819–1821: The Journal and Paintings of Robert Hood, Midshipman with Franklin*, ed. C. Stuart Houston (Montreal: McGill-Queen's University Press), 79.

13. J. McIlraith, *Life of Sir John Richardson, C.B., LL.D., F.R.S. Lond., Hon. F.R.S. Edin., Inspector of Naval Hospitals and Fleets; &c.&c.&c.* (London: Longmans, Green, and Co., 1868), 63.

14. J. Franklin, *Narrative of a Journey to the Shores of the Polar Sea in the Years 1819, 1820, 1821, and 1822* (Edmonton: Hurtig, 1969), 222.

15. McIlraith, *Life of Sir John Richardson*, 82–83.

16. W. Gibson, "Sir John Franklin's Last Voyage: A Brief History of the Franklin Expedition and an Outline of the Researches which Established the Facts of its Tragic Outcome," *The Beaver* 268 (June 1937): 44–75; L. H. Neatby, *In Quest of the North West Passage* (Toronto: Longmans Green, 1958); E.S. Dodge, *Northwest by Sea* (New York: Oxford University Press, 1961); P. Nanton, *Arctic Breakthrough: Franklin's Expeditions 1819–1847* (Toronto: Clarke Irwin, 1970); G. M. Thomson, *The North-West Passage* (London: Secher and Warburg, 1975); R. Owen, *The Fate of Franklin* (London: Hutchinson, 1978); H.N. Wallace, *The Navy, the Company, and Richard King: British Exploration in the Canadian Arctic 1829–1860* (Montreal: McGill-Queen's University Press, 1980).

17. I.S. MacLaren, "Arctic Exploration and Milton's ' Frozen Continent': A Note," *Notes and Queries*, n.s. 31 (1984): 325–26.

18. J. Richardson, *Arctic Searching Expedition: A Journal of a Boat Voyage through Rupert's Land and the Arctic Sea, in Search of the Discovery Ships under Command of Sir John Franklin*, 2 vols. (London: Longman, Brown, Green, and Longman's, 1851); W.H. Hooper, *Ten Months Among the Tents of the Tuski, with Incidents of an Arctic Boat Expedition in Search of Sir John Franklin, as far as the MacKenzie River, and Cape Bathurst* (London: J. Murray, 1853); B.C. Seeman, *Narrative of the Voyage of H.M.S. Herald during the Years 1845–1851 under the Command of Captain Henry Kellett, R.N., C.B.; Being a Circumnavigation of the Globe, and Three Cruizes to the Arctic Regions in Search of Sir John Franklin*, 2 vols. (London: Reeve, 1853).

19. W.H.J. Browne, *Ten Coloured Views Taken during the Arctic Expedition of Her Majesty's Ships "Enterprise" and "Investigator," under the Command of Captain Sir James C. Ross, R.N., K.T., F.R.S.* (London: Ackermann and Co., 1850).

20. W.E. Parry, *Journals of the First, Second, and Third Voyages for the Discovery of a North-west Passage from the Atlantic to the Pacific in 1819–1820–1821–1823–1824–1824–1825, in His Majesty's Ships Hecla, Griper, and Fury*, 5 vols. (London: J. Murray, 1828), V: frontispiece.

21. I.S. MacLaren, " '...where nothing moves and nothing changes': The Second Arctic Expedition of John Ross (1829–1833)," *Dalhousie Review* 62 (1982): 485–94.

22. R.A. Goodsir, *An Arctic Voyage to Baffin's Bay and Lancaster Sound, in Search of Friends with Sir John Franklin* (London: John van Voorst, 1850), 119.

23. Goodsir, *An Arctic Voyage*, 22–24.

24. McIlraith, *Life of Sir John Richardson*, 236–37.

25. Goodsir, *An Arctic Voyage*, 51–52.

26. J. Thomson, "The Seasons," in *The Complete Poetical Works of James Thomson*, ed. J.L. Robertson (London: Oxford University Press, 1980), ll.1001–3.

27. G. Back, *Narrative of the Arctic Land Expedition to the Mouth of the Great Fish River, and Along the Shores of the Arctic Ocean in the Years 1833, 1834, 1835*

(Edmonton: Hurtig, 1970), 415.

28. Goodsir, *An Arctic Voyage*, 79–80, 133.

29. Goodsir, *An Arctic Voyage*, 61–62.

30. S.T. Coleridge, *The Rime of the Ancient Mariner*, in *English Romantic Writers*, ed. D. Perkins (New York: Harcourt, Brace and World, 1967), 404–13, ll. 53–54.

31. W. Wordsworth, "Lines Composed a Few Miles above Tintern Abbey," in *English Romantic Writers*, ed. D. Perkins (New York: Harcourt, Brace and World, 1967), 209–11.

32. S. Osborn and G.F. McDougall, eds., *Facsimiles of the Illustrated Arctic News, Published on Board H.M.S. Resolute: Captn. Horatio T. Austin, C.B. in Search of the Expedition under Sir John Franklin* (London: Ackermann, 1852), 1.

33. Osborn and McDougall, eds., *Facsimiles of the Illustrated Arctic News*, 17.

34. *Arctic Miscellanies. A Souvenir of the Late Polar Search by the Officers and Seamen of the Expedition* (London: Colburn and Co., 1852), 36–37.

35. P.C. Sutherland, *Journal of a Voyage in Baffin's Bay and Barron Straits, in the Years 1850–1851 Performed by H.M. Ships "Lady Franklin" and "Sophia," under the Command of Mr. William Penny, in Search of the Missing Crews of H.M. Ships Erebus and Terror: with a Narrative of Sledge Excursions on the Ice of Wellington Channel, and Observations on the Natural History and Physical Features of the Countries and Frozen Seas Visited*, 2 vols. (London: Longman, Brown, Green, and Longman's, 1852), I: 380.

36. E.W. Manwaring, *Italian Landscape in Eighteenth Century England: A Study Chiefly of the Influence of Claude Lorrain and Salvator Rosa on English Taste, 1700–1800* (New York: Oxford University Press, 1925); M. Röthlisberger, *Claude Lorrain: The Paintings*, 2 vols. (New Haven: Yale University Press, 1961).

37. W.P. Snow, *Voyage of the Prince Albert in Search of Sir John Franklin: A Narrative of Every-Day Life in the Arctic Seas* (London: Longman, Brown, Green, and Longman's, 1851), 352.

38. S. Osborn, *Stray Leaves from an Arctic Journal on Eighteen Months in the Polar Regions in Search of Sir John Franklin's Expedition in 1850–1851* (London: Longman, Brown, Green, and Longman's, 1852).

39. G. Back, *Narrative of an Expedition in HMS Terror Undertaken with a View to Geographical Discovery on the Arctic Shores in the Years 1836–1837* (London: J. Murray, 1838).

40. R. Collinson, *Journal of H.M.S. Enterprise, On the Expedition in Search of Sir John Franklin's Ships by Behring Strait 1850–1855* (London: Sampson, Low, Marston, Searle, Rivington, 1889); F. McClintock, *The Voyage of the "Fox" in the Arctic Seas. A Narrative of the Discovery of the Fate of Sir John Franklin and His Companions* (Edmonton: Hurtig, 1972); F. McClintock, "Narrative of the Expedition in Search of Sir John Franklin and His Party," *Royal Geographical Society Journal* 31 (London, 1861):1–13.

41. R.J. Le M. M'Clure, *The Discovery of the North-West Passage by H.M.S. "Investigator," Capt. R. M'Clure 1850, 1851, 1852, 1853, 1854*, ed. Commander Sherard Osborn (Edmonton: Hurtig, 1969).

42. M'Clure, *The Discovery of the North-West Passage*, 134.

43. Parry, *Journals*.

44. M'Clure, *The Discovery of the North-West Passage*, 137.

45. S.G. Cresswell, *Dedicated by Special Permission, to Her Most Gracious Majesty the Queen, a Series of Eight Sketches in Colour (together with a Chart of the Route) by Lieut. S. Gurney Cresswell, of the Voyage of the H.M.S. Investigator (Captain M'Clure), during the Discovery of the North-West Passage* (London: Day and Son, 1854), no.6; M'Clure, *The Discovery of the North-West Passage*, opp. 256.

46. L.H. Neatby, trans., *Frozen Ships: The Arctic Diary of Johann Miertsching 1850–1854* (Toronto: MacMillan of Canada, 1967).

47. A. Armstrong, *A Personal Narrative of the Discovery of the North-West Passage; with Numerous Incidents of Travel and Adventure during Nearly Five Years' Continuous Service in the Arctic Regions while in Search of the Expedition under Sir John Franklin* (London: Hurst and Blackett, 1857), 89–90.

48. Back, *Narrative of the Arctic Land Expedition*, 170–78.

49. E. Chappell, *Narrative of a Voyage to Hudson's Bay in His Majesty's Ship "Rosamond" Containing Some Account of the North-eastern Coast of America and of the Tribes Inhabiting that Remote Region* (Toronto: Coles, 1970), 54.

50. Armstrong, *A Personal Narrative*, 248.

51. Creswell, *A Series of Eight Sketches in Colour*, nos. 3, 4, 5.

52. L.H. Neatby, "Samuel Gurney Cresswell (1827–1867)," *Arctic* 35, 4 (1982): 555.

53. J. McLean, *Notes of a Twenty-Five Years' Service in the Hudson's Bay Territory*, 2 vols., ed. W.S. Wallace (Toronto: The Champlain Society, 1932), 2:249.

54. W. Kennedy, *A Short Narrative of the Second Voyage of the Prince Albert, in Search of Sir John Franklin* (London: W.H. Dalton, 1853), 106.

55. J. Milton, *Paradise Lost* in *John Milton: Complete Poems and Major Prose*, ed. M.Y. Hughes (Indianapolis: Odyssey, 1957), bk. 2, 587–605.

56. J.R. Bellot, *Memoirs of Lieutenant Joseph René Bellot, Chavalier of the Legion of Honour, Member of the Geographical Societies of London and Paris, etc., with His Journal of a Voyage in the Polar Seas, in Search of Sir John Franklin*, 2 vols. (London: Hurst and Blackett, 1855), I:235–236.

57. J.R. Bellot, *Journal d'un Voyage aux Mers Polaires Executé à la Recherche de Sir John Franklin, en 1851 et 1852 par J.R. Bellot* (Paris: Perrotin, 1854), 91.

58. Hussey, *The Picturesque*, 248.

59. W. Morwood, *Traveler in a Vanished Landscape: The Life and Times of David Douglas* (New York: Clarkson N. Potter, 1973), 48.

60. Wordsworth, "Tintern Abbey."

61. J. Ross, *Narrative of a Second Voyage in Search of a North-West Passage, and a Residence in the Arctic Regions during the Years 1829, 1830, 1831, 1832, 1833* (London: A.W. Webster, 1835), 190–91.

62. P.B. Shelley, "Adonais" in *Shelley: Poetical Works*, ed. J. Hutchinson, rev. M. Matthews (London: Oxford University Press, 1970), 430–45.

63. R.A. Pierce, "Edward Belcher (1799–1877)," *Arctic* 35, 4 (1982):552; E. Belcher, *The Last of the Arctic Voyages; Being a Narrative of the Expedition in H.M.S. "Assistance," in Search of Sir John Franklin, during the Years 1852–1853–1854*, 2 vols. (London: Lovell Reeve, 1855).

64. W.W. May, *A Series of Fourteen Sketches Made during the Voyage up Wellington Channel in Search of Sir John Franklin, K.C.H., and the Missing Crews of H.M. Discovery-Ships "Erebus" and "Terror"; Together with a Short Account of Each Drawing* (London: Day and Son, 1855), no. 13.

65. May, *A Series of Fourteen Sketches*, no. 11.

66. May, *A Series of Fourteen Sketches*, no. 5.

67. May, *A Series of Fourteen Sketches*, no. 10.

68. E. Shanes, ed., *Turner's Picturesque Views of England and Wales 1825–1838* (London: Chatto and Windus, 1979).

69. Barrell, *The Idea of Landscape and the Sense of Place*, 21–22.

70. G.F. McDougall, *The Event Voyage of H.M. Discovery Ship "Resolute" to the Arctic Regions in Search of Sir John Franklin and the Missing Crews of H.M. Discovery Ships "Erebus" and "Terror" 1852, 1853, 1854, to which is Added an*

Account of Her Being Fallen in with by an American Whaler after Her Abandonment in Barron Straits, and of Her Presentation to Queen Victoria by the Government of the United States (London: Longman, Brown, Green, Longman's and Roberts, 1857), 280, 282–83.

71. Y.-F. Tuan, *Man and Nature*, Association of American Geographers Commission on College Geography, Resource Paper 10 (1971), 17.

72. R.L. Brannon, ed., *Under the Management of Charles Dickens, His Production of "The Frozen Deep"* (Ithaca: Cornell University Press, 1966).

73. R. McCormick, *Voyage of Discovery in the Arctic and Antarctic Seas and Round the World: Being Personal Narratives of Attempts to Reach the North and South Poles; and of an Open-Boat Expedition up the Wellington Channel in Search of Sir John Franklin and Her Majesty's Ships "Erebus" and "Terror," in Her Majesty's Boat "Forlorn Hope," under the Command of the Author*, 2 vols. (London: Sampson, Low, Marston, Searle, Rivington, 1884), 2:120.

74. McDougall, *The Event Voyage of H.M. Discovery Ship "Resolute,"* 278–79.

75. Ross, *Narrative of a Second Voyage*, 600–603, 698; McLaren, "The Second Arctic Expedition of John Ross."

76. Shelley, "Adonais," 430–55.

77. D.C. Scott, "Ode for the Keats Centenary" in *Selected Poetry of Duncan Campbell Scott*, ed. G. Clever (Ottawa: Tecumseh, 1974), 74–78.

78. McClintock, *Narrative of the Expedition in Search of Sir John Franklin*, 13.

79. F.R. Scott, *The Collected Poems of F.R. Scott* (Toronto: McClelland and Stewart, 1981), 223–39; A. Purdy, *North of Summer: Poems from Baffin Island* (Toronto: McClelland and Stewart, 1967), 29–30, 36.

80. A.Y. Jackson, *A.Y. Jackson: The Arctic 1927* (Moonbeam, Ontario: Penumbra Press, 1982).

81. I.N. Smith, ed., *The Unbelievable Land* (Ottawa: The Queen's Printer, 1964).

SECTION 2

INDIANS AND THE ADVANCE OF EUROPE

ON THE ABORIGINAL POPULATION OF THE KUTCHIN*

SHEPARD KRECH III

The aims of this paper are to analyze the postcontact population processes among the Northern Athapaskan Kutchin and to calculate the size of the aboriginal population. It is hoped that this effort will contribute to issues currently being debated by scholars interested both in native North American demography and in the implications of population estimates for theories of band organizations.

The renewed interest in prehistoric native North American demography during the last decade is due primarily to Henry Dobyns'[1] critical summary of aboriginal population and depopulation estimates, and his challenge of conventional estimates, and partially to the implications of upwardly-revised aboriginal estimates for historiography.[2] Dobyns' proposals of a New World depopulation ratio of 20:1 and a North American prewhite-contact population of roughly 10 million, approximately ten times the conventional estimates of James Mooney and A.L. Kroeber, are well known and have spawned a number of studies.[3]

The Athapaskan hunter-fishers of the Western Subarctic have not contributed substantially to these issues.[4] This is probably due mainly to the belief that the Subarctic environment is "as difficult and demanding to man as any in the world."[5] Small, low density populations are compatible with a delimiting environment[6] and Kroeber's Western Subarctic (Athapaskan) density of 0.87 persons per 100 square kilometers, the extreme low density for North America, is consistent with this assumption.[7]

A second reason for the neglect of Subarctic populations may be due to the fact that, compared with other native groups in North America, those in the Subarctic were contacted fairly recently by whites. The depopulation period was brief and many may feel that it has been adequately documented; hence, the conventional estimates may not need re-examination.

A third reason may be the belief that such population data that may exist in the accounts of the fur traders, missionaries, and explorers will not begin to

*Arctic Anthropology 15, 1 (1978): 89–104.

compare with the tribute lists, mission baptismal records, or accounts detailing epidemic mortality that have allowed population conversions and projections in other areas of North America.

In contrast, I would argue first, that the severity and harshness of the aboriginal environment remains to be demonstrated; second, that the admittedly brief depopulation period has not been adequately documented by those who have ignored primary archival sources; and third, with Dobyns, that "[o]ne either uses such data as may be available and learns something, however inadequate, or abjures such data and learns nothing."[8]

Following a brief consideration of the aboriginal distribution of the Kutchin, of their contact with whites, and of previous estimates of their population size, this paper will describe in detail postcontact processes and then will provide an estimate of the aboriginal Kutchin population .

Precontact Distribution and Euro-Canadian Contact of the Kutchin

The territory of the precontact Kutchin was north of the Athapaskan Hare, Tutchone, Han, east of the Tanana and Koyukon, and south of several Inuit groups (Fig. 1). This area encompassed roughly 317 000 square kilometers. The Kutchin were divided into nine bands, each of which hunted caribou and moose and fished for salmon (Pacific drainage) and whitefish in river drainage sections of the total territory. From east to west, the bands are named Mackenzie Flats, Peel River, Upper Porcupine River, Crow River, Black River, Chandalar River, Yukon Flats, Birch Creek, and Dihai Kutchin (Fig. 2). In this paper, the first three bands are collectively termed Eastern Kutchin, the rest Western Kutchin. Though the bands were distinguished by dialectical and cultural differences and never came together as a totality, all dialects were mutually intelligible and cultural differences were slight, increasing in complexity east to west. The bands were said to comprise "a unity on the basis of their own opinion, of language, of culture, and the use of Kutchin, 'one who dwells' as a terminological ending."[9]

In the late eighteenth and early nineteenth centuries, white traders approached the Kutchin from the south and west. North West and Hudson's Bay Company traders came down the Mackenzie River, beginning with Alexander Mackenzie's 1789 voyage. In 1804, the North West Company established Fort Good Hope, which from 1823 to 1827 was moved to the Hare-Kutchin boundary. Peel River Post was established in 1840, and this was the first post located in Kutchin territory; Fort Yukon was founded seven years later. Russian traders reached Nulato in Koyukon territory in 1836. Knowledge of the whites, and of white goods and diseases probably did not reach the Kutchin prior to 1750. Regular and direct trade with whites began between 1804 and 1850, depending on the particular Kutchin band.[10]

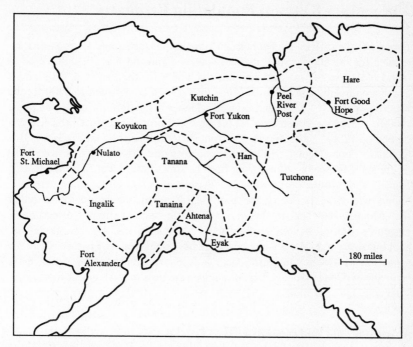

FIG. 1. Distribution of Northern Athapaskans and Some Trading Posts

SOURCE: Slobodin, *Band Organization*; Helm et al., ''Contact History of the
          Subarctic Athapaskans.'

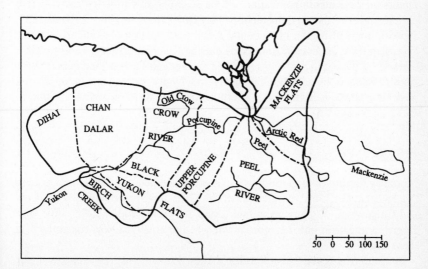

FIG. 2. Distribution of Aboriginal Kutchin Bands

Precontact Kutchin Population Estimates

James Mooney, A.L. Kroeber, and Cornelius Osgood have all provided estimates for the aboriginal Kutchin. Mooney estimated that "Kutchin" numbered 4600 prior to contact, but included in this several contiguous non-Kutchin Athapaskan bands;[11] the total should be adjusted to 2700 for the Kutchin proper.[12] Kroeber followed Mooney's published Kutchin estimate (4600).[13] Osgood stated that "at the time of European contact" the Kutchin numbered 1200.[14] This figure was from an 1858 census by the Hudson's Bay Company, but Osgood neither comments on the discrepancy between this figure and Mooney's estimate, nor does he stress here[15] that first face-to-face contact with whites occurred by 1789, seventy years prior to the census.[16] Others who have estimated the aboriginal Kutchin population follow either the Mooney-Kroeber totals or, sometimes with extreme reservations, Osgood's use of the 1858 census.[17] McKennan has argued, largely on ecological grounds, for a Chandalar Kutchin population that is essentially the same size as Mooney had estimated.[18] In the remainder of the paper, these estimates will be evaluated, first through an analysis of postcontact mortality.

Causes of Postcontact Mortality

Epidemic and endemic diseases, responses to disease, warfare, starvation, and female infanticide all contributed to postcontact fatalities. Epidemic diseases caused the greatest number of deaths. In this section, the influence of these factors on the Kutchin population will be documented chronologically, in five periods: prior to the establishment of Fort Good Hope in 1804; 1804 to 1839, a period marked by the indirect and direct participation of Kutchin in Euro-Canadian trade conducted from posts outside Kutchin territory; 1840 to 1865, marked by the extension of direct trade and regular face-to-face contact with Euro-Canadians by all Kutchin bands and by the establishment of trading posts in eastern, central, and western portions of Kutchin territory; 1866 to 1900; and post-1900.

Prior to 1804

Mortality during this period is unknown; whether any epidemic disease reached the Kutchin is problematical. In 1781, smallpox decimated the Cree and Chipewyan.[19] Chipewyan middlemen may have traded at that time with Dogrib and Slave, but it is not known whether smallpox was transmitted to these tribes.

In 1789, Mackenzie recorded that a Hare woman had "an Abscess in the Belly and is reduced to a mere Skeleton"[20] and he considered Slave to be "an ugly meagre ill made People particularly about the Legs which are very clumsy & full of Scabs....Many of them appear'd very sickly."[21] Though Mackenzie said that the scabs were a result of sitting too close to fires and this sickly appearance due to a "Dirty" life, endemic or epidemic diseases might have been responsible. Mackenzie Flats Kutchin appeared "healthy and full of Flesh and more cleanly" than other Indians.[22]

1804 to 1839

Kutchin population processes during the 1804 to 1820 period are unknown.[23] The 1810–1811 winter in the upper Mackenzie River region was very severe. Euro-Canadian fur traders and natives starved, the trade declined, and "many" natives died.[24] By this time, some Kutchin were deeply involved in the Fort Good Hope trade, but it is not known whether either starvation or disease affected their population during the 1810–1811 winter.[25]

In contrast, after 1820, the Kutchin and other bands trading at Fort Good Hope were ravaged by almost continual disease. The Bear Lake (or Hare) Indians were severely affected at least three times during the 1830s.[26] Mortality among Mountain Indians (or Hare) was high, especially in 1837–1838, when starvation and disease took a heavy toll.[27] In the 1820s, Hare were dying from a "dreadful sickness," a "contagious distemper" that killed adults and children.[28] This distemper, or delirium, may have been meningococcal meningitis or epidemic encephalitis; case fatality rates. vary widely (20–85 percent);[29] though "virgin soil epidemic" (i.e., relating to epidemics among populations not previously exposed to the disease in question) mortality probably would have been great.[30]

Kutchin were affected by this same disease in the mid-1820s, where one bout left at least "one dead and no less than 14 at deaths door" and in another instance, ten died "in the course of the winter and many more [were] in a sickly state." "Mortality so prevalent" caused a decline in trade.[31]

Due to the great amount of intertribal contact at Fort Good Hope, a contagious disease afflicting any single band would probably have readily spread to many others. When Fort Good Hope was located near the Kutchin-Hare boundary, many Kutchin came to trade. They came in contact with Hare and other Athapaskans and took away diseases with their trade goods. Mackenzie Flats, Peel River, Upper Porcupine River, and probably Crow River Kutchin all came directly to Fort Good Hope and traded through Kutchin middlemen. Kutchin participation was extensive and essential for the success of the Hudson's Bay Company trade, for by 1830, the trade depended on the Upper Porcupine River Kutchin.[32]

In the mid-1830s, Hare and Kutchin were again sick and dying from "the disease so prevalent among them";[33] symptoms are obscure and identification of the disease evasive, but the "cumulative value" of the testimony suggests substantial mortality.[34]

Prior to 1840, Western Kutchin may have been affected by diseases introduced from Athapaskan neighbours along the Yukon River. In the late 1830s, smallpox afflicted Alaskan native populations with very heavy mortality in some regions.[35] At Nulato, on the Middle Yukon River, the epidemic peaked in 1839. Koyukuk River Koyukon suffered in this epidemic, as they would in another epidemic in 1843.[36] Although it is not known whether Kutchin died in the 1839 smallpox epidemic, Russian goods were in Eastern Kutchin hands by 1825,[37] and these goods were highly valued by Western Kutchin in the 1840s.[38] Trade networks with the contiguous Koyukon or other western Athapaskans may have brought Western Kutchin Russian goods, but also smallpox, with consequent heavy mortality among Dihai, Chandalar River and Birch Creek Kutchin bands.

Responses to Disease

Kutchin responses to disease included phlebotomy, sweating and ingathering, and responses to death included self-mutilation and the destruction of property. The therapeutic values of some reactions to disease appear to have been limited.[39] In one case, bleeding may have been carried to excess.[40] Sweating is fatal therapy in diseases such as measles which are complicated by bronchopneumonia. Ingathering worked against the isolation of a disease:[41] in the twentieth century, measles spread rapidly from one case to a dispersed bush population in the lower Mackenzie and Peel River regions, in spite of quarantine efforts;[42] rapid dissemination has occurred in numerous other instances.[43]

Responses to death included food and property destruction and self-mutilation;[44] these would not have been adaptive in certain seasons and under specific conditions of food scarcity.

The Kutchin believed that illness was a result of sorcery, and that the appropriate response was vengeance. The result—a feud or war—may also have increased mortality.

1840 to 1865

In 1843, Peel River Kutchin suffered from a "very bad cough . . . from which children were cut off."[45] This may have been whooping cough.[46] Fatalities evidently occurred again in the mid-1840s, when the Hudson's Bay Company trader, A.H. Murray, reported, "The Russians were trying to incite the Indians here against us by telling them, that it was on account of our being in their country that so many of them had died in summer."[47] The next year, a "great number of [Han] women had died lately, and many were sick"; both Eastern and Western Kutchin traded with Han.[48]

The period from 1850–1853 was exceptionally severe. Many Eastern Kutchin were sick in the fall of 1851. Fatalities peaked in the 1852 spring, when it was remarked, "It is astonishing how rapidly the Indians are dying off";[49] "A great many Indians . . . died" during the next eighteen months.[50] Complicating disease in 1851–1852 was the failure of caribou to travel along their accustomed migratory route in Eastern Kutchin territory; severe hunger, and one death from starvation resulted.[51]

In the 1860s came scarlet fever. The Western Kutchin, Birch Creek, Yukon Flats, and perhaps other bands were devastated.[52] Dall said that all Birch Creek Kutchin died. Scarlet fever arrived in 1865 from the upper Mackenzie among Eastern Kutchin, and small bands of Mackenzie Flats Kutchin lost 10 to 33 percent of their population.[53]

Female Infanticide

In the 1858 Kutchin population there were 158 males and 100 females in the subadult population,[54] which may indicate that female infanticide was common.[55] Whether infanticide rates increased in the postcontact period from the precontact era, due to hypothetical increases in food shortages, or in male mortality in warfare is, however, problematical.

Feuding and Warfare

Intra-Kutchin and intertribal hostilities caused fatalities during the first half of the nineteenth century. Although some have suggested that "wars among [the Kutchin] and with the Esquimaux have sadly diminished them"[56] it is difficult to quantify mortality from warfare. Interband hostilities were generated by quarrels about women,[57] by desires for prestige and property and by revenge.[58] An important cause of hostility was sorcery; sickness and death were due to the malevolent actions of sorcerers, who might be members of other tribes or whites. Hudson's Bay Company traders John Bell and A.H. Murray were both accused of sorcery; John Bell of "throwing bad Medicine" by Mackenzie Flats Kutchin,[59] and Alexander Murray by Western Kutchin.[60]

Although the Kutchin and Eskimos fought often, and fatalities among Western Kutchin may have been extensive,[61] this does not appear to have been the case among Eastern Kutchin. In the lower Mackenzie drainage, Mackenzie Eskimos and Kutchin clashed almost every year, yet from 1825 to the middle 1850s, only approximately 30 Kutchin died.[62] Hostilities prevailed but fatalities were rare compared to those from disease.[63]

Hostilities may have increased in the postcontact period, as a consequence of disease and of the fur trade. Disease, due to sorcery, demanded revenge; and Kutchin committed to the trade both defended middleman positions, controlled access to posts, and competed with Eskimos for access to fur grounds. In 1856, the final fatalities occurred, probably because of the greater evaluation of trade-related factors.[64] For further discussion of various causes of warfare among the northwestern Athapaskans see McClellan.[65]

1866 to 1900

In the 1880s, diptheria arrived among several Western Kutchin bands.[66] In 1885, some types of disease killed Eastern Kutchin.[67]

The latter half of the 1890s decade was fairly severe: in 1897, scarlet fever killed at least one Eastern Kutchin; in 1898, scarlet fever appeared (but no fatalities resulted). There were a number of deaths in the Crow River and Upper Porcupine River Kutchin bands in 1899–1900.[68]

Starvation

In 1897, when "an epidemic of scarlet fever" struck the Kutchin, reports arrived of starvation east of the Mackenzie River and west of LaPierre House. In May, 1897, "15 deaths by starvation among Rat Indians near Old Crow" apparently occurred; twelve who died were children.[69]

In the nineteenth century, Euro-Canadian traders in the lower Mackenzie documented periods in which they suffered from severe hunger. Some winters they actually starved: in 1810 at the mouth of the Liard River,[70] in 1842 at Fort Good Hope.[71] At Peel River Post on numerous occasions, the Hudson's Bay Company traders either failed to exploit faunal resources or could not adjust to fluctuations in animal populations.[72]

However, with the exception of the 1897 incident, starvation does not appear to have increased significantly nineteenth century mortality among the Kutchin.[73] In 1841, when many at Fort Good Hope died[74] some Eastern Kutchin were hard pressed and ate beaver skins they had collected for the trade, but none died. In 1852, caribou failed to migrate along their accustomed route in Eastern Kutchin territory and one Kutchin died. This was "the only death I have heard of from starvation," commented a clerk who had recorded a number of cases of "starvation" over the preceding six years.[75] This was a severe winter in other sections of the Mackenzie.[76] In 1885, starvation again threatened the Kutchin, but none died—although many were ill from diseases.[77] Finally, in 1897 came disease and starvation.

When starvation threatened the Kutchin in 1852, 1885, and 1897 (and actually occurred in 1852 and 1897), disease also was prevalent. In 1852, the sole death from starvation occurred the same month that others died from "sickness";[78] scarlet fever and starvation concurred in 1897. The coincidence of disease and starvation affected Mackenzie Flats Kutchin and Mountain Indians in 1834 and 1838.[79]

While starvation may predispose susceptibility to disease,[80] disease may also preclude a successful subsistence quest.[81] Subsistence tasks that demand broad cooperation, such as those associated with caribou surrounds and fish weirs, may become impossible due to adult mortality in virgin soil epidemics. In 1865, some Batard-Loucheux (Hare) were unable to exploit the fall fishery, as a result of disease.[82]

Post-1900

In 1901, "A sort of cholera took many" Eastern Kutchin. The following year, measles coupled with pneumonia ravaged the Eastern Kutchin, with over 40 deaths in a population of approximately 300 at Fort McPherson, a death rate of 13 percent.[83]

With the exception of the 1902 measles epidemic, after the turn of the century, the greatest causes of mortality were endemic tuberculosis and influenza. At Eagle, a Han village, "tuberculosis far outweighs all other ailments . . . one notices everywhere evidence . . . in the form of humpbacks, hip disease, scrofula, and consumptive cough."[84]   At Fort Yukon in the period 1943–1949, there was an overall death rate of 33 per 1000, and 67 percent of the deaths were due to tuberculosis.[85]   The death rate from tuberculosis peaked between 1930 and 1950.

Influenza exacted a severe toll, at least among the Eastern Kutchin, twice during the twentieth century. In July, 1928, "influenza followed by lobar pneumonia" travelled with the steamer *Distributor* to each settlement on the Mackenzie and Peel Rivers, in a manner and with results similar to the 1895 scarlet fever epidemic: "At each settlement after the steamer departed, the people succumbed and the epidemic raged up and down the river, taking a final toll of more than three hundred Indians."[86]   At Fort McPherson, 31 in a population of approximately 300 died (10 percent mortality); the majority were either under age four or over age seventy. An epidemic of influenza struck again in 1948, when at Fort McPherson, 15 in a population of approximately 375 died.[87]

A striking demographic characteristic of the Kutchin population from 1950 to the present day is a decline in the death rate, especially in the infant mortality rate during the period 1950–1970 was 46 per 1000, a marked decline from an estimated rate of 93 per 1000 in the period 1920–1929. The death rate has shown a steady decline from 23 per 1000 in 1947 (in the flu year 1948, the death rate was 53 per 1000) to 14.6 per 1000 in 1952, and 3.3 per 1000 in 1970,[88] largely as a result of the extension and expansion of government health services. During this period, the birth rate has remained at a fairly constantly high of 43.8 (1952) and 42.4 (1970) per thousand. These two characteristics, a constant, high (or increasing) birthrate and a sharp decline in the death rate, are probably typical of the entire Kutchin area over the past 25 years and the Kutchin population has increased steadily during this time.[89] Offsetting this population growth has been emigration: at Fort McPherson, for instance, 23 percent of all people born during the twentieth century have emigrated.[90]

Population Changes, 1750–1973

In this section, the aims are to estimate postcontact population changes, the aboriginal population, and a depopulation ratio. Between 1847 and 1862, three estimates were made of the Kutchin population. By analyzing these data, it should be possible to calculate population changes in this period, and the results may then be applied speculatively to changes during other periods in postcontact era.

1847–1862

In 1847, A.H. Murray estimated the numbers of "men and boys able to hunt" (hunters) in several Western Kutchin bands.[91] In 1858, the Hudson's Bay Company took a census of the trading population at Fort Yukon, La Pierre House, Peel River Post, Fort Good Hope, and other posts in the Mackenzie River District.[92] In approximately 1862, the naturalist, Robert Kennicott, estimated the numbers of "hunters" in Kutchin bands.[93] These data, with only the number of adult males tabulated from the 1858 census, are presented by band (1847 and 1862) and by trading post (1858) in table 1.

TABLE 1   *Estimates of the Number of Adult Males or Hunters among the Kutchin, 1847–1862, by Murray, Ross, and Kennicott*[94]

	1847	1858	1862
Dihai Kutchin			4
Chandalar Kutchin	40		20
Birch Creek Kutchin			10
Yukon Flats Kutchin	90		50
Black River Kutchin			
Crow River Kutchin	80		25
Fort Yukon "Loucheux of Six Tribes"		256	
Upper Porcupine River Kutchin			15
Peel River Kutchin			30
Mackenzie Flats Kutchin			30
Peel River and La Pierre House		102	
Fort Good Hope "Loucheux and Batard Loucheux"		41	

Murray was concerned primarily with the Fort Yukon trade and he failed to provide population figures for Eastern Kutchin trading at Peel River Post. Among the Western Kutchin, he missed the Dihai band, perhaps because they did not trade in 1847 or because he merged them with the Chandalar Kutchin. The Birch Creek and Black River bands were undoubtedly included with the Yukon Flats Kutchin, which Murray "divided into three bands."[95]

In 1847, three hundred men from five Athapaskan bands (Yukon Flats Kutchin, including the Birch Creek and Black River bands, Chandalar Kutchin—possibly including the Dihai, Crow River Kutchin, Han, and "Tecounka"—a Koyukon band) traded at Fort Yukon. These 300 traders came from a total of 460 "hunters." Kutchin numbered slightly less than one-half of the total number of hunters. Han accounted for one-third of the population of traders and exactly one-half (230) of the "hunter" population.

In the 1858 census, it was estimated that the Kutchin numbered fewer than 1274: 337 Eastern Kutchin traded at Peel River Post, 842 Western Kutchin at Fort Yukon, and a population of 95 at Fort Good Hope (table 2).

The Peel River Post (and La Pierre House) population consisted mainly of Upper Porcupine River, Peel River, and Mackenzie Flats Kutchin. Apparently, some Mackenzie Flats Kutchin patronized Fort Good Hope in 1858, and in the census, they are counted with "Batard Loucheux" (Hare). Mackenzie Flats Kutchin probably numbered at the most one-third of all "Loucheux and Batard Loucheux" at Fort Good Hope.

TABLE 2   Census of the Kutchin, 1858[96]

		Married	Adult	Children	Total
Peel River and	M	81	21	83	185
La Pierre House	F	92	7	53	152
Fort Yukon: "Loucheux	M	135	121	218	474
of Six Tribes"	F	156	75	137	368
Fort Good Hope:	M	23	18	17	58
"Loucheux and	F	22	3	12	37
Batard Loucheux"					

The Fort Yukon count included "Loucheux of Six Tribes," said to be "all that resort to the Fort."[97] These certainly did not correspond to the six Western Kutchin Bands, but included contiguous Athapaskans, for the census abstracter regarded the Kutchin as "an exceedingly numerous and powerful people, if the various tribes inhabiting Russian America are to be taken into consideration. They occupy the northern waters of the MacKenzie from below Ft. Good Hope . . . as well as Peels River—They are found across the Rocky Mts. on the Rat River; on the Youcon . . . and on the lower Pelly—in fact they occupy the greater part of the interior of Russian America."[98] This territory encompassed non-Kutchin, most likely some Han, Northern Tutchone, and possibly Koyukon or Tanana.[99] I suggest that the "six tribes" trading in 1858 were: Yukon Flats (including Black River) Kutchin; Crow River Kutchin;[100] Chandalar (including Dihai) Kutchin;[101] Han; Northern Tutchone;[102] and either the Birch Creek (if separated from the Yukon Flats) Kutchin, or a Tanana or Koyukon band.[103]

If the numbers of actual Kutchin in the 1858 Fort Yukon population can be estimated, then it will be possible to measure the degree to which the population had changed from 1847. If Han were included among the 1858 "six tribes" (which is very probable), and if the proportion of Han/non-Han in the trading and total population attributable to Fort Yukon did not alter dramatically between 1847 and 1858,[104] then from 33 percent (traders) to 50 percent (total hunters) of the 1858 population was not Kutchin.[105] In numbers, from 422 to 703, or an arbitrary midpoint of 562, *were* Kutchin.

Two alternative estimates of population changes from 1847 to 1858 can now be made. The 1858 Fort Yukon Kutchin population estimate of 562 altered from an 1847 estimate of 210 Western Kutchin hunters (see table 1). If the ratio of married and adult males per overall population in the 1858 census population (1: 3.3) was roughly the same in 1847, and if the same age grades are included in 1847 hunters as are included in 1858 adult males, then the 1858 estimated population of 562 would represent a loss of 20 percent from the 1847 projected population of 693 (based on 210 "men and boys able to hunt"). In the total Fort Yukon tributary population, the 1858 "six tribes" population of trading adult males (256) would represent a loss of 204 men or 44 percent from the 1847 five band total "hunter" population of 460.[106]

Kennicott's data support a decline of at least 20 percent and tend to suggest that a population loss of 40 percent or more might not be excessive: from 1847–1862 (table 1), declines measured 40 percent among the Chandalar and Dihai Kutchin hunter population, 33 percent among the combined Yukon Flats-Black River-Birch Creek bands, and 69 percent among the Crow River Kutchin. The evidence of disease in this period is abundant. In addition, a number of factors might have affected the adult male per total population ratio. These include an under recording of infants and children in 1858, and under reporting of infant and child mortality, an epidemic similar to the 1843 whooping cough which severely afflicted children, or an extension to the Kutchin of the 1847 scourge that affected Han women and presumably the birth rate. Their effect would be to actually augment or appear to increase the proportional number of adult males during the 1847–1858 period, and thus, the 1847 population would be larger than a 1: 3.3 ratio implies.

At this point, population sizes at various points during the postcontact period may be estimated. First, population changes from 1862 back to a 1750 aboriginal baseline will be speculated, the dates (1862, 1858, 1847, 1840, 1804) corresponding either to post settlement or census dates. Following this, population changes from 1858 forward to 1970 will be detailed, and an attempt will be made to estimate a nadir population and depopulation ratio.

1862 and 1858 Population

Assuming that the 1858 census takers did include most Kutchin and that non-Kutchin were included in the Fort Yukon trading population in the proportion that has already been estimated, then in 1858 approximately 32 Kutchin traded at Fort Good Hope, 337 at Peel River Post, and 562 at Fort Yukon: a total of 931. In 1862, the population was surely lower, as suggested by Kennicott's data and by the ethnohistorical evidence. An estimate of 850–900 is probably not far out of place.

1847 Population

During the period 1847 to 1862, the Kutchin population declined an estimated 40 percent and in 1847, the population numbered 1552. This estimated decline is made on the basis of three sets of census data (1847 to 1862), of known mortality during twentieth century measles and influenza epidemics in Fort McPherson, NWT, and of the extensive ethnohistoric evidence for disease (especially in 1851 to 1852), all discussed in preceding sections of this paper. These data can be supplemented by mortality guides in epidemics in other regions of the Arctic and Subarctic. For example, in 1952, mortality in an Eastern Arctic measles epidemic was 5 percent;[107] and in the 1940s in British Columbia, successive epidemics of measles, diptheria, jaundice, whooping cough, German measles and meningococcal meningitis caused approximately 5 percent mortality, but in a second community, 25 percent died of pneumonia.[108] In these cases, therapeutic measures differed considerably from the nineteenth century reactions to disease and served to lower the mortality rates.

1840 Population

During the period 1840 to 1847, it is suggested that the Kutchin population declined 20 percent, and in 1840, the Kutchin numbered 1940 individuals. Diseases affected the Peel River Kutchin and perhaps other bands as well in 1843; the early 1840s were years of general hardship. A 20 percent decline is based on this ethnohistoric evidence, on the 1847 to 1862 depopulation estimate, and on known mortality from twentieth century flu and measles epidemics.

1804 Population

During the period 1804 to 1839, the Kutchin declined an estimated 40 to 60 percent, and in 1804, the Kutchin numbered from 3233 to 4850. I favour the higher estimate, 4850 (a 60 percent decline), mainly because Eastern Kutchin trading at Fort Good Hope appear to have been severely affected by constant disease. In addition, Western Kutchin may have been affected by virulent smallpox. Comparative mortality estimated in virgin soil epidemics does not make a 60 percent decline far-fetched.[109]

1750 Aboriginal Population

In 1750, prior to the period beginning in 1804 (when Fort Good Hope was established), there is a lack of population data for the Kutchin. However, first-hand contact with whites began in 1789, and there occurred at least one other

Euro-Canadian voyage to the Mackenzie Delta, through Eastern Kutchin territory, prior to 1804.[110] It may be unlikely, but not inconceivable, that one virgin soil epidemic reached the Kutchin prior to 1804, transmitted either directly by Euro-Canadians after 1789 or via contiguous Athapaskan groups either before or after that date. Mortality might have been approximately 10 percent of the population (a rate suggested by twentieth century comparative data detailed above), in which case, the aboriginal Kutchin numbered 5389, or roughly 5400.

Population Changes, 1862–1973

Census data for the Kutchin between 1862 and 1900 are uneven. After 1900, demographic data are more regular, but their interpretation quite complex. All data are presented in table 3 with a distinction made between source and adjusted population totals.[111]

Between 1862 and 1900, the Kutchin population may have declined below the 850–900 estimate of 1862. Petitot's 1865 total is non-specific and surely includes non-Kutchin trading at Fort Yukon. His estimate of 1400 contrasts sharply with Kennicott's adult role population, which if projected liberally on the basis of a ratio of one adult role to every five total population, would still be one-third lower than Petitot's figure. In 1880 (1880 to 1881), there were approximately 974 Kutchin, roughly the same as three decades before. This figure is probably low, as the 1890 (1890 to 1893) total is 40 percent greater.

In 1910 (1910 to 1911), there were an estimated 1547 Kutchin, a 13 percent rise from the 1890 estimate. The 1920 (1920 to 1922) total, however, represents a 25 percent loss in population. Some Kutchin south of the Peel River basin may not have been enumerated, and the loss not so great. The 1930 (1930 to 1940) totals are an 11 percent loss from 1930.

The 1960 (1960 to 1965) estimates are 38 percent greater than those two decades before, and the 1970 (1970 to 1973) totals represent a 35 percent rise over the 1960 estimates. Probable factors responsible for all these population changes have been discussed in the preceding sections of the paper.

Nadir Population and Depopulation Ratio

The Kutchin population fell to its nadir in the 1860s, when there was an estimated total of 850 to 900 Kutchin. This appears to indicate a loss of over 80 percent of the aboriginal population in approximately 100 years. In the 1860s, one Kutchin was alive where six had been originally.

The revised estimate of the aboriginal population of the Kutchin proposed in this paper is 5400. This compares with Mooney's published total of 4600, which was uncritically adopted by Kroeber, and Mooney's estimate of 2700 for Kutchin exclusive of contiguous Athapaskans, a total calculated from his manuscript notes. Thus, the revised estimate proposed here is exactly twice Mooney's, but only one-fifth higher than his published figure. The population density of the aboriginal Kutchin (5400 people in 317 000 square kilometers), is substantially higher than either Kroeber's or Steward's Athapaskan estimates.[112] This density still, however, is in the lowest section of the range of current hunter-gatherer densities.[113]

There were two principal reasons for the miscalculations of Mooney and others: their estimates were based on secondary sources; and they did not fully appreciate the effects of disease. Mooney relied heavily on Morice, Dall, and Richardson.[114] Morice had no first-hand knowledge of the Kutchin; Richardson, Dall, and Petitot were his sources.[115] Dall's visit to the territory of the Western Kutchin was fleeting. Richardson's data were mainly secondhand, provided by the Hudson's Bay Company traders, John Bell and Alexander Murray. The result of such a heavy reliance on secondary sources is an inevitable dilution of reliability. The solution is to rely on such primary sources as Hudson's Bay Company post journals, mission journals, and other materials.[116]

As for the second reason, the under rating of disease effects, little more need be said except that this is in part a consequence of neglecting the primary sources, which indicate clearly that the Kutchin suffered annually and severely the effects of disease. My conclusions here are the same as VanStone's for southwestern Alaskan Eskimos: "once European diseases had been introduced, they took a yearly toll that was not only great in terms of numbers of dead, but that greatly weakened the resistance of the survivors. In the many years of sickness, a few stand out as epidemic years, but the specter of ill health and death was continually present."[117]

Substantial depopulation appears to have occurred before Euro-Canadians actually settled in Kutchin territory. This conclusion suggests a modification of the hypotheses forwarded by some of the historical revisionists. Jacobs, for instance, proclaims that "we can scarcely portray the European invasion of the Western Hemisphere as the relatively quiet expansion of Europeans into sparsely populated lands"; and Jennings argues that "European explorers and invaders discovered an inhabited land."[118] These views are overstated. In the case of the Kutchin, the expansion ("invasion") was quiet not because the lands were sparsely populated aboriginally, but because major depopulation, due of course ultimately to diseases introduced by whites, occurred prior to substantial Euro-Canadian expansion.

Depopulation appears to have been extensive: it is estimated that, at the time of nadir, there was only one Kutchin for every six who had been alive prior to white contact. This depopulation ratio of 6:1 is significant, though it differs from Dobyns' hypothesized continent-wide ratio of 20:1.[119] Obviously, the latter does not apply to all areas.[120]

Finally, the major cause of depopulation was epidemic disease. Disease was a direct cause of death; it also led to further mortality from increased starvation and intergroup strife. It is difficult to assess the impact of starvation independent of disease in the postcontact period, for incidences of disease and starvation severity seemed to concur. Whether starvation was a significant cause of recurrent mortality among precontact Kutchin and other Northern Athapaskans, as some would argue, is problematical.[121] It is beyond the scope of this paper to examine this crucial issue, which is the subject of a separate analysis.[122]

TABLE 3   *Selective Kutchin Population Estimates, 1847–1973*

Date	Population	Source[123]	Adjusted Population	Comment
1847	210 hunters	Murray 1910		Western Kutchin adult males only.
1858	1179	Ross MS	931	All Kutchin; see text.
1862	184 hunters	Kennicott MS		Kutchin adult males only.
1865	1400	Petitot 1889		Trading population; non-Kutchin included.
1880	337	Petroff 1900		Alaska Kutchin.
1881	637	Russell 1898		Eastern and some Alaska Kutchin
1890	580	U.S. 1915		Alaska Kutchin
1893	787	Russell 1898		Canada Kutchin
1910	547	U.S. 1918		Alaska Kutchin.
1911	1180	Canada 1912	1000	Canada; includes some Alaska Kutchin.
1920	447	U.S. 1932	425	Alaska Kutchin, including some non-Kutchin.
1922	445	Moran 1923	745	Mackenzie and Peel River Kutchin.
1929	632	Canada 1929		Canada Kutchin.
1930	638	U.S. 1932	600	Alaska Kutchin, including non-Kutchin.
1934	546	Asia 1934	650	Canada Kutchin, less Old Crow.
1940	484	U.S. 1953	450	Alaska Kutchin; includes non-Kutchin.
1950	683	U.S. 1953	780	Alaska Kutchin; includes non-Kutchin, but less several villages
1960	306	U.S. 1973		Alaska Kutchin, less Fort Yukon.
1961	198	Balikci 1963		Old Crow Indian (140) and Métis (58).
1965	1114	Bissett 1967		Mackenzie & Peel River Indian and Métis.
1965	801	Bissett 1967		Mackenzie & Peel River Indians only.
1970	1205	Canada 1970	1086	Canada Band Lists.
1973	1549-1010	U.S. 1974	1451-969	Alaska enrolled-enumerated.

Notes

1. Henry Dobyns, "Estimating Aboriginal American Population: An Appraisal of Techniques with a New Hemisphere Estimate," *Current Anthropology* 7 (1966): 395–416 and "Reply" 7: 440–44.

2. Wilbur Jacobs, "The Tip of an Iceberg: Pre-Columbian Indian Demography and Some Implications for Revisionism," *William and Mary Quarterly* 31 (1974): 123–32; Francis Jennings, *The Invasion of America* (Chapel Hill, N.C.: The University of North Carolina Press, 1975).

3. James Mooney, *The Aboriginal Population of America North of Mexico*, Smithsonian Institution, Miscellaneous Collection 80, 7 (Washington, D.C., 1928); A.L. Kroeber, *Cultural and Natural Areas of Native North America*, University of California Publications in American Archaeology and Ethnology 38 (Berkeley: University of California Press, 1939); Douglas Ubelaker, "Prehistoric New World Population Size: Historical Review and Current Appraisal of North American Estimates," *American Journal of Physical Anthropology* 45, 3 (1976): 661–66.

4. Paul Thompson, "Estimating Aboriginal American Population, 2. A Technique Using Anthropological and Biological Data," *Current Anthropology* 7, 4 (1966): 417–24; Margaret Morris, "Great Bear Lake Indians: A Historical Demography and Human Ecology. Part 1," *Musk- ox* 11 (1972): 3–27 and Morris, "Great Bear Lake Indians,"*Musk-ox* 12 (1973): 58–80; Joan Townsend, "Tanaina Ethnohistory: An Example of a Method for the Study of Cultural Changes," in *Ethnohistory in Southwestern Alaska and the Southern Yukon*, ed. Margaret Lantis (Lexington, Ky: University Press of Kentucky, 1970), 71-102.

5. Walter Goldschmidt, Forward in *Athapaskan Adaptations* by James VanStone (Chicago: Aldine, 1974), vii.

6. William Laughlin, "Hunting: An Integrating Biobehavior System and Its Evolutional Implications," in *Man the Hunter*, ed. Richard Lee and Irven DeVore (Chicago: Aldine, 1968), 315; Nelson Graburn and B. Stephen Strong, *Circumpolar Peoples: An Anthropological Perspective* (Pacific Palisades, Ca: Goodyear, 1973), 4.

7. Kroeber, "Cultural and Natural Areas," 142.

8. Henry Dobyns, *Native American Historical Demography* (Bloomington: Indiana University Press, 1976), 7.

9. Cornelius Osgood, "Kutchin Tribal Distribution and Synonymy," *American Anthropologist* 36 (1934): 138. After Richard Slobodin, *Band Organization of the Peel River Kutchin*, National Museum of Canada Bulletin 179 (Ottawa, 1962): 66 in the use of "band" for each geographical unit, and after Robert McKennan, "Anent the Kutchin Tribes," *American Anthropologist* 32, 2 (1935): 369; Frederick Hadleigh-West, "On the Distribution and Territories of the Western Kutchin Tribes," University of Alaska Anthropological Papers 7, 2 (1959): 113–16, and Edwin Hall, "Speculations on the Late Prehistory of the Kutchin Athapaskans," *Ethnohistory* 16, 4 (1969): 317–33 in the inclusion of the Dihai Kutchin as a ninth precontact band.

10. June Helm et al., "The Contact History of the Subarctic Athapaskans: An Overview," in *Proceedings: Northern Athapaskan Conference, 1971* 1, ed. Annette McFadyen Clark, Museum of Man Mercury Series, Canadian Ethnology Service Paper 27 (Ottawa, 1975): 307–49.

11. Mooney, *The Aboriginal Population*, 26, 32.

12. Population, 1928, James Mooney Manuscript, Envelopes 5, Box 1 and 23, Box 2, Bureau of American Ethnology, Smithsonian Institution (hereafter Mooney MS). Included in Mooney's 4600 "Kutchin" are: "500(?)" Tanana, 200 Han, 100 Koyukon, and 1100 "Tutchone," Mooney MS. The derivation of these data is confused. For instance, it appears that Mooney depended on Morice for his Tutchone estimate. Morice's tenth Kutchin group is the "Tutsone-kut'qin," or Crow People, the *Gens des Foux* of the Canadians according to the English writers, and the Tathzey-kutchi of Richardson, who estimates them at 230 hunters, or about 1100 individuals divided into four bands; A.G. Morice, *The Great Dene Race*, Administration of Anthropos (Vienna: The Press of the Mechitharistes, n.d.), 27. Richardson did identify "Tathzey-Kutchin" as "people of the ramparts" or "Gens du Fou" and said they numbered 230 men in four bands; John Richardson, *Arctic Searching Expedition* (New York: Harper and Bros., 1854), 234. However,

Richardson depended for his data on A.H. Murray, who reported: "...the Fathzei-Koochin (People of the Ramparts) there are only about 20 men in this band. ...Between them and the natives of this place are the 'Han-Koochin' (People of the Water) known as the Gens du fous this is the largest band of any hereabout, there are in all 230 men. They are divided into four bands." Alexander Murray, *Journal of the Yukon, 1947–48*, Publication of the Canadian Archives 4 (Ottawa, 1910), 82. Whymper, who was at Fort Yukon in the mid 1860s, identified Han as "Gens des Foux" and Tuchone as "Gens de Bois," but Dall, there at the same time, did just the opposite: Han were the "Gens de Bois or Wood People," Tutchone "Crow People or Gens des Foux." Frederick Whymper, *Travel and Adventure in the Territory of Alaska* (New York: Harper and Bros., 1869), 177; William Dall, *Alaska and Its Resources* (Boston: Lee and Shepard, 1870), 271. Morice referred to Dall's distinctions; Morice, *The Great Dene Race*, 27.

Evidently, Murray's identifications were confused by Richardson; Dall (but not Whymper) followed Richardson's error; Morice followed Dall and Richardson and also projected a total population (1100) from 230 hunters. Mooney adopted these inaccuracies.

13. Kroeber, "Cultural and Natural Areas,"141. Kroeber's Canada and Alaska totals of 3000 and 1600 correspond to the groups labeled "Kutchin" by Mooney in his published figures, in *The Aboriginal Population*. Although Kroeber believed Mooney's totals in general to be "mostly too high," he did not alter the latter's Kutchin estimates; Kroeber, *Cultural and Natural Areas*, 132.

14. Cornelius Osgood, *Contributions to the Ethnography of the Kutchin*, Yale University Publications in Anthropology 14 (New Haven: Yale University Press, 1936), 15.

15. Osgood, *Contributions*.

16. Cornelius Osgood, *The Distributions of the Northern Athapaskan Indians*, Yale University Publications in Anthropology 7 (New Haven: Yale University Press, 1936), 14.

17. Diamond Jenness, *The Indians of Canada*, 3d ed., National Museum of Canada Bulletin 65, (Ottawa, 1955), 404; Slobodin, *Band Organization*, 7, note 2.

18. Robert McKennan, *The Chandalar Kutchin*, Arctic Institute of North America Technical Paper 17 (Montreal, 1965), 20.

19. Samuel Hearne, *A Journey from Prince of Wales Port in Hudson's Bay to the Northern Ocean ... in the Years 1769, 1770, 1771, and 1772*, ed. Richard Glover (Toronto, 1958), 115.

20. Alexander Mackenzie, *The Journals and Letters of Sir Alexander Mackenzie*, ed. W. Kaye Lamb (London: Cambridge University Press, 1970), 191.

21. Mackenzie, *Journals and Letters*, 183.

22. Mackenzie, *Journals and Letters*, 192.

23. A key primary source of demographic processes, the Fort Good Hope post journals did not begin until 1822. Fort Good Hope Journal, 1822–1841, Hudson's Bay Company Archives (hereafter HBCA), B.80/a/1–17, Public Archives of Canada (PAC), Ottawa.

24. W.F. Wentzel, Letters to the Hon. Roderick McKenzie, in *Le Bourgeois de la Compagnie du Nord-Ouest*, 1, 1st ser., ed. L.F. Masson (Quebec: A cote et cie, 1889–1890): 95, 106–7; George Keith, Letters to Mr. Roderick McKenzie, in *les Bourgeois de la Compagnie du Nord-Ouest*, 2, ed. L.F. Masson (Quebec: A cote et cie, 1889–1890): 79.

25. Wentzel, Letters to McKenzie, 110.

26. Fort Good Hope Journal, HBCA, B.80/a/11–15 passim.

27. Fort Good Hope Journal, HBCA, B.80/a/14.

28. Fort Good Hope Journal, HBCA, B.80/a/fol. 10d; Fort Good Hope Journal, HBCA B.80/a/5 fol. 5d.

29. Hugh Paul, *The Control of Diseases*, 2d ed. (Baltimore: The Williams and Wilkins Co., 1964), 353–97 passim.

30. Compare Henry Dobyns, ''An Outline of Andean Epidemic History to 1720,'' *Bulletin of the History of Medicine* 37, 6 (1963): 493-515.

31. Fort Good Hope Journal, HBCA, B.80/a/4/fol. 4,13; Fort Good Hope Journal, HBCA, B.80/a/5/fol. 2d; John Franklin, *Narrative of a Second Expedition to the Shores of the Polar Sea* (Philadelphia: Cary, Lea, and Carey, 1828), 41.

32. Fort Good Hope Journal, HBCA, B.80/a/5–15 passim.

33. Fort Good Hope Journal, HBCA, B.80/a/11/fol. 13.

34. Sherburne Cook, *The Conflict between the Californian Indian and White Civilization* (Berkeley: University of California Press, 1976), 26.

35. For example, James VanStone, *Eskimos of the Nushagak River* (Seattle: University of Washington Press, 1967), 99.

36. Henry Michael, *Lieutenant Zagoskin's Travels in Russian America, 1842–1844*, Arctic Institute of North American Anthropology of the North: Translations from Russian Sources 7 (Toronto: University of Toronto Press, 1967), 146.

37. Franklin, *Narrative of a Second Expedition*, 118-57.

38. Murray, *Journal of the Yukon*, 29.

39. Compare Alfred W. Crosley, ''Virgin Soil Epidemics as a Factor in the Aboriginal Depopulation in America,'' *William and Mary Quarterly* 33,2 (1976): 289–99.

40. Fort Good Hope Journal, HBCA, B.80/a/7/fol. 5.

41. Slobodin, *Band Organization*, 69–70.

42. Kenneth Ward, ''Arctic Interlude,'' *Canadian Medical Association Journal* 67 (1952): 292-98.

43. For example, John Marchand, ''Tribal Epidemics in the Yukon,'' *American Medical Association Journal* 123, 16 (1943): 1019–20; A.F. Peart and F.P. Nagler, ''Measles in the Canadian Arctic, 1952,'' *Canadian Journal of Public Health* 45,4 (1952): 146–56.

44. Fort Good Hope Journal, HBCA, B.80/a/5; Franklin, *Narrative of a Second Expedition*, 41, 54–55; William Hardisty, *The Loucheux Indians*, Annual Report of the Smithsonian Institution for 1866 (Washington, D.C., 1872), 317; compare Keith, Letters to McKenzie, 10.

45. Peel River Post Journal, 1840–1844, 1873–1879, 1881–1886, HBCA, B.157/a/3/fol. 12d.

46. Paul, *The Control of Diseases*, 104–10.

47. Murray, *Journal of the Yukon*, 69.

48. Murray, *Journal of the Yukon*, 69.

49. Augustus Peers, Journal of [Daily] Occurrences, 10 May 1852, Peel's River Papers MG19, D/12, PAC.

50. James Anderson, Correspondence and Reports, 24 November 1853, MG19, A/29, PAC.

51. Peers, Journal of [Daily] Occurrences, 5 April 1852, Peel's River Papers, MG19, D/12.

52. Mooney, *The Aboriginal Population*, 31; McKennan, *The Chandalar Kutchin*, 21, 24; Osgood, *Contributions*, 14f.; Cornelius Osgood, *The Han Indians: A Compilation of Ethnographic and Historical Data on the Alaska-Yukon Boundary Area*, Yale University Publications in Anthropology 74 (New Haven: Yale University Press, 1971), 134.

53.   Dall, *Alaska and Its Resources*, 100, 430–32; Emile Petitot, *Quinze ans sous le cercle polaire*, ed. E. Dentu (Paris, 1889), 166–94 passim.

54.   Letter from Mr. Ross to George Gibbs, with Detailed Information Relative to Chipewyan Tribes with Abstract of MacKenzie River Dist., 1 June 1858, Bernard Ross Manuscript 144a, Bureau of American Ethnology, National Anthropology Archives, Smithsonian Institution, Washington, D.C. (hereafter Ross MS).

55.   William West Kirkby, *A Journey to the Yukon, Russian America*, Annual Report of the Smithsonian Institution for 1866 (Washington, D.C., 1872), 418; Hardisty, *The Loucheux Indians*, 312; Catharine McClellan, "Feuding and Warfare among Northwestern Athapaskans," in *Proceedings: Northern Athapaskan Conference, 1971* 9, ed. Annette McFadyen Clark, Museum of Man Mercury Series, Canadian Ethnology Service Paper 27 (Ottawa, 1975): 241–42.

56.   Kirkby, *A Journey to the Yukon*, 417; compare Murray, *Journal of the Yukon*, 46, 88; Richardson, *Arctic Searching Expedition*, 229.

57.   Murray, *Journal of the Yukon*, 57.

58.   W.H. Hooper, *Ten Months among the Tents of the Tuski* (London: John Murray, 1853), 271f.; Murray, *Journal of the Yukon*, 57, 87; Fort Good Hope Journal, HBCA, B.80/a/4/fol. 14; Richard Slobodin, "Eastern Kutchin Warfare," *Anthropologica* 2,1 (1960): 2f.

59.   Fort Good Hope Journal, HBCA, B.80/a/5/fol. 20.

60.   Murray, *Journal of the Yukon*, 87.

61.   Hall, "Speculations."

62.   Fort Good Hope Journal HBCA, B.80/a/1–17; James Anderson, McKenzies River District Report, 1858, MG19, A/29, PAC; Hooper, *Ten Months among the Tuski*, 275; Richardson, *Arctic Searching Expedition*, 132f., 229.

63.   A few statements, such as the 1823 comment that Kutchin were "killed by the Esquimaux all winter," Fort Good Hope Journal, HBCA, B.80/a/1, are suggestive but difficult to quantify.

64.   Slobodin, "Eastern Kutchin Warfare"; Shepard Krech, "The Eastern Kutchin and the Fur Trade, 1800-1860," *Ethnohistory* (n.d.).

65.   See McClellan, "Feuding and Warfare."

66.   M.E. Westbrook, "A Venture into Ethnohistory: The Journals of Rev. V.C. Sim, Pioneer Missionary of the Yukon," *Polar Notes* 9 (1969): 41.

67.   Peel River Post Journal HBCA, B.157/a/5/fol. 55–59d.

68.   Saint Matthew's Mission Journal, 1895–1899, Fort McPherson, Northwest Territories.

69.   Saint Matthew's Mission Journal, 1897.

70.   Wentzel, Letters to McKenzie, 106f.

71.   Peel River Post Journal, HBCA, B.157/a/2/fol.6.

72.   Krech, "The Eastern Kutchin."

73.   This analysis is based on approximately 50 statements noting "starvation" in the Fort Good Hope Post Journals 1832–1829, HBCA, B.80/a/1–17, the Peel River Post Journals 1840–1844, 1873–1879, 1881–1886, HBCA, B.157/a/1–5, and the journals of Augustus Peers, 1847–1853. In the majority of notations, starvation is clearly equivalent to hunger, e.g., Eastern Kutchin arrived at Peel River Post "very ill from starvation," Peel River Post Journal, HBCA, B.157/a/1; in several instances, severity is problematical, e.g., we learn that the Fond du Lac and Rat Indians are "starving," Peers, Journal of [Daily] Occurrences, 2 July 1851; finally there are those (few) instances in which Indians are "in a wretched state of famish," Fort Good Hope Journal, HBCA, B.80/a/11-12d, and in which they actually do die.

74.   Peel River Post Journal, HBCA, B.157/a/2/fol. 3–31.

75. Peers, Journal of [Daily] Occurrences, 5 April 1852.
76. Anderson, Correspondence and Reports, 10 July 1852.
77. Peel River Post Journal, HBCA, B.157/a/5/fol. 39–57d.
78. Peers, Journal of [Daily] Occurrences, 5 April 1852.
79. Fort Good Hope Journal, HBCA, B.80/a/11/fol. 12; Fort Good Hope Journal, HBCA, B.80/a/14/fol. 16d.
80. Cook, *Conflict between Indian and White Civilization*, 290.
81. Carl Sauer, "Aboriginal Population of Northwestern Mexico," *Ibero-Americana* 10 (1935): 13; see Alfred Crosby, *The Columbian Exchange* (Westpoint, Conn.: Greenwood Press, 1972), 52–53.
82. Petitot, *Quinze ans sous le cercle polaire*, 163.
83. Saint Matthew's Mission Journal, 1901–1902.
84. Ferdinand Schmitter, *Upper Yukon Native Customs and Folklore*, Smithsonian Institution Miscellaneous Collection 56, 4 (Washington, D.C., 1910): 6. Tuberculosis may have been endemic in Alaska from the early eighteenth century on; J.D. Aronson, *The History of Disease among the Natives of Alaska,* Transactions and Studies of the College of Physicians of Philadelphia, 4th ser., 8 (1940): 31f. Petroff considered consumption and scrofulous diseases as the greatest contributors to mortality among native Alaskans; Ivan Petroff, "The Population and Resources of Alaska," in *Compilation of Narratives of Explorations in Alaska*, U.S. Congress, Senate Committee on Military Affairs (Washington, D.C., 1900), 104.
85. Demitri Shimkin, "The Economy of a Trapping Centre: The Case of Fort Yukon, Alaska," *Economic Development and Cultural Change* 3,3 (1955): 225. Compare Fellows, who estimates the death rate from tuberculosis on the Yukon River in the period 1926–1930 at 662/100 000; Ward's observations span a 20 year period, and stress the severity of tuberculosis among the Eastern Kutchin. F.S. Fellows, "Mortality in the Native Races of the Territory of Alaska, with Special Reference to Tuberculosis," *Public Health Reports* 49, 9 (1934): 293; Ward, "Arctic Interlude," 293–94.
86. Archibald Lang Fleming, *Archibald the Arctic* (New York: Appleton-Century Crofts, Inc., 1956), 285.
87. Shepard Krech, "Changing Trapping Patterns in Fort McPherson, Northwest Territories" (Ph.D. diss., Harvard University, 1974).
88. Krech, "Changing Trapping Patterns."
89. Asen Balikci, *Vunta Kutchin Social Change* prepared for the Northern Co-ordination and Research Centre, Department of Northern Affairs and National Resources (Ottawa, 1963), 70.
90. Krech, "Changing Trapping Patterns."
91. Murray, *Journal of the Yukon*, 81.
92. Ross to Gibbs, 1 June 1858, Ross MS, 144a; Anderson, "McKenzies River District Report."
93. Robert Kennicott, Tribes of the Kutchin Indians of Lower MacKenzie and Youkon Region (ca. 1865), MS, 203–b, Bureau of American Ethnology, National Anthropology Archives, Smithsonian Institution, Washington, D.C. (hereafter Kennicott MS).
94. Murray, *Journal of the Yukon*; Ross to Gibbs, 1 June 1858, Ross MS, 144a; Tribes of the Kutchin Indians, Kennicott MS, 203-b.
95. Murray, *Journal of the Yukon*, 82.
96. Ross to Gibbs, 1 June 1858, Ross MS, 144a; Tribes of the Kutchin Indians, Kennicott MS, 203-b.
97. Anderson, "McKenzies River District Report."

98. Ross to Gibbs, 1 June 1858, Ross MS, 144a.

99. Murray's gratuitous and confused extension of ''Kutchin'' to non-Kutchin bands continued through the 1860s:

Han	Tutchone	Tanana	Source
Han Kutchin		Tannin Kutchin	Murray, *Journal of the Yukon*, 82.
Hun-Koo-chin			Hardisty, ''The Lechoux Indians,'' 311.
Hong Kutchin			Strachan Jones, ''The Kutchin Tribes,'' *Annual Report of the Smithsonian Institution for 1866* (Washington, D.C., 1872), 321.
	Touchon-ta-Kutchin		Kirby, ''A Journey to the Yukon,'' 418.
Han Kutchin		Tanan Kutchin	Petitot, *Quinze ans sous le cercle polaire.*
Han Kutchin	Tutchon Kutchin	Tenan Kutchin	William Dall, ''On the Distribution of Native Tribes of Alaska and the Adjacent Territory,'' *Proceedings of the American Association for the Advancement of Science* 18 (1870): 270–71.
An Kutchin	Tatanchok Kutchins		Whymper, *Travel and Adventure*, 254.
An Kutchin	Tatanhak Kutchin		Charles Raymond, ''The Yukon River Region, Alaska,'' *Journal of the American Geographical Society* 3 (1873): 158–92.

Both Han and Northern Tutchone were said to have been ''accustomed to trade'' at Fort Yukon in the late 1860s; Raymond, ''The Yukon River Region''; compare Whymper, *Travel and Adventure*, 254f; Dall, *Alaska and Its Resources,* 109. Han had traded at Fort Yukon since its 1847 establishment; Tanana also were seen at Fort Yukon, for example Dall, *Alaska and Its Resources*, 109; Whymper, *Travel and Adventure,* 254.

100. Following Murray, *Journal of the Yukon*, Hardisty, *The Loucheux Indians;* Jones, ''The Kutchin Tribes''; *Dall, Alaska and Its Resources*; Whymper, *Travel and Adventure*; and Raymond, ''The Yukon River Region,'' all of whom place the Yukon Flats and Crow River Kutchin at Fort Yukon.

101. Following Murray, *Journal of the Yukon*; Jones, ''The Kutchin Tribes''; Hardisty, *The Loucheux Indians;* and Dall, *Alaska and Its Resources.*

102. After those in note 100 above, who place the Han at Fort Yukon; and after Raymond, ''The Yukon River Region''; and Whymper, *Travel and Adventure* who note the Tutchone.

103. Murray, *Journal of the Yukon*; and Whymper, *Travel and Adventure* probably would favour the Birch Creek Kutchin or a Tanana or Koyukon band; Hardisty, *The Loucheux Indians,* would favour the Black River Kutchin.

104. The assumption that demographic rates of these neighbouring populations were constant during this period ought to be accepted only with extreme caution. For example, the disease that affected Han women in 1847 may well have affected

the birth rate, but whether it spread to neighbouring Kutchin, with whom the Han were in frequent contact, is problematical.

105. I believe the 50 percent figure for non-Kutchin to be quite reasonable, for one band was included in the 1858 census which was not included in the 1847 trading population, and this probably was not a separately identified Kutchin band.

106. In the interest of exhaustion, the 1858 figures might have excluded non-Kutchin, in which case the adult male population of 256 might indicate an increase of 22 percent from the 1847 population of 210 Kutchin hunters. Although contemporary nineteenth century writers did append"–Kutchin" to non-Kutchin people; they also, however, distinguished from the true Kutchin the Gens de Bois (Tutchone), Gens des Foux (Han), and Gens des Buttes (Tanana); however confusing, this was the tendency to call the Chandalar Kutchin the Gens du Large (Chandalar being the corruption), the Yukon Flats Kutchin the Gens de Fort, the Crow River Kutchin the Gens de Rat, etc.

107. Peart and Nagler, "Measles in the Canadian Arctic."

108. Marchand, "Tribal Epidemics in the Yukon."

109. Dobyns, "An Outline of Andean Epidemic History"; Crosby, *The Columbian Exchange*; Crosby, "Virgin Soil Epidemics."

110. See: Notice of Attempts to Reach the Sea by Mackenzie's River Since the Expedition of Sir Alexander Mackenzie, *Memories of the Wernerian Natural History Society* 4 (Edinburgh, 1822): 19–23.

111. These demographic data are at times extremely confusing, and many of the figures must be adjusted. Some of the difficulties include: correction for non-Indians in United States Bureau of the Census (1910 to 1970) data and in some Canadian figures; correction for non-treaty and Métis natives in Canada and for natives enrolled, but not enumerated in Alaska in 1974; correction for nonresident members of band lists; exclusion of non-Kutchin-speaking Athapaskan (e.g., Koyukon in Beaver); early twentieth century under-enumeration of children; population changes due not to mortality, but to written-area shifts (e.g., to Inuvik from Arctic Red River and Aklavik, to Salmon Village from Chalkyitsik along the Black River).

112. Kroeber, *Cultural and Natural Areas*; Julian Steward, *Theory of Culture Change* (Urbana: University of Illinois Press, 1955), 146.

113. Richard Lee and Irven DeVore, "Problems in the Study of Hunters and Gatherers," in *Man the Hunter*, ed. Richard Lee and Irven DeVore (Chicago: Aldine, 1968), 11.

114. Morice, *The Great Dene Race*; Dall, *Alaska and Its Resources*; Dall, "On the Distribution of Native Tribes"; Richardson, *Arctic Searching Expedition*.

115. Richardson, *Arctic Searching Expedition*; Dall, *Alaska and Its Resources*; Dall, "On the Distribution of Native Tribes"; Petitot, *Quinze ans sous le cercle polaire*.

116. Fort Good Hope Journal, HBCA, B.80/a/1–17; Peel River Post Journal, HBCA, B.157/a/1–6; Peers, Journal of [Daily] Occurrences; for example Tribes of the Kutchin Indians, Kennicott MS, 203–b; Petitot, *Quinze ans sous le cercle polaire*.

117. James VanStone, *Eskimos of the Nushagak River* (Seattle: University of Washington Press, 1967), 100.

118. Jacobs, "The Trip of an Iceberg," 128; Jennings, *The Invasion of America*, 15.

119. Dobyns, "Estimating Aboriginal American Population."

120. Ubelaker, "Prehistoric New World Population Size."

121. June Helm, "Bilaterality in the Socio-Territorial Organization of the Arctic Drainage Dene," *Ethnology* 4, 4 (1965): 361–85; Robert McKennan, "Athapaskan

Groupings and Social Organization in Central Alaska," in *Contributions to Anthropology: Band Societies*, ed. David Damas, National Museums of Canada Bulletin 228, Anthropological Series 84 (Ottawa, 1969): 93–114.

122.   Shepard Krech, "Disease, Starvation, and Northern Athapaskan Social Organization," MS (n.d.).

123.   Murray, *Journal of the Yukon*; Ross to Gibbs, 1 June 1858, Ross MS, 144a; Tribes of the Kutchin Indians, Kennicott MS, 203–b; Petitot, *Quinze ans sous le cercle polaire*, 80–81; Petroff, "The Population and Resources of Alaska"; *Indian Population in the United States and Alaska, 1910*, U.S. Bureau of the Census (Washington, D.C.: Government Printing Office, 1915), 112; Fifth Census of Canada, 1911, vol. 1 (Ottawa, 1912): 170–71; Fifteenth Census of the United States: 1930, Outlying Territories and Possessions, U.S. Bureau of the Census (Washington: GPO, 1932), 9; Census of Indians in Canada, 1929, Department of Indian Affairs (Ottawa, 1929), 54, 70; Fifteenth Census of the United States, 9; *Census of the Population: 1950*. Volume II, *Characteristics of the Population, Parts 51–54, Territories and Possessions*, U.S. Bureau of the Census (Washington, D.C.: GPO, 1953) 51–56; *Census of the Population: 1970. Volume I, Characteristics of the Population, Part 3, Alaska*, U.S. Department of Commerce, Bureau of the Census (Washington, D.C. : GPO, 1973), 3–15; Don Bissett, *The Lower Mackenzie Region: An Area Economic Survey* prepared for the Industrial Division of the Department of Indian Affairs and Northern Development (Ottawa, 1967), 7; Bissett *The Lower Mackenzie Region*, 71; Balikci, *Vunta Kutchin Social Change*, 65; *Linguistic and Cultural Affiliations of Canadian Indian Bands*, Department of Indian Affairs and Northern Development, Indian Affairs Branch (Ottawa, 1970), 37; *Final Environmental Statement. Proposed Yukon Flats Native Wildlife Refuge*, Alaskan Planning Group, U.S. Department of the Interior (1974).

OF TWO MINDS: DENE RESPONSE TO THE MACKENZIE MISSIONS 1858–1902*

KERRY ABEL

Any attempt to understand the nature of the interaction between missionary and Indian in the Canadian North faces a double challenge. Neither the history of the aboriginal peoples nor the history of the missions has been well served. In the past, historians tended to focus on what had been done to Indian societies, rather than what those societies did themselves in response to the new pressures of European contact. Indians were presented as the passive recipients of Euro-Canadian economic, political and social demands. The Indian view is seldom heard because most natives understandably are reluctant to speak with outsiders on sacred matters. Modern social scientists also have tended to avoid the issues of mission history, perhaps because they find the curious rhetoric and difficult personalities of the missionaries to be outside the realm of quantification and rational analysis.

The most sensitive analysis to date is John Webster Grant's *Moon of Wintertime,*[1] which surveys the experiences of various Indian groups across Canada in their dealings with the missionaries. From the survey, Grant attempts to explain the result of this conflict: the acceptance of Christianity by natives throughout North America. Essentially, he relies on the "disaster and deprivation" thesis, arguing that once a society begins experiencing the hardships associated with its contact with white men, its traditional value system no longer seems adequate, and people turn to the alternative of Christianity.[2]

While much of Grant's analysis may not be applicable to the situation in the Mackenzie Valley, his approach is clearly more helpful than the popular and journalistic accounts which appeared during the 1960s and 1970s as part of the anti-colonialist movement. Missionaries became prime targets in this literature as imperialistic agents; thus catch-words like "cultural

*Kerry Abel, "Of Two Minds: Dene Response to the Mackenzie Missions 1858–1902" (University of Manitoba, 1987, unpublished paper).

genocide" and "Third World imperialism" have become meaningless. In the specific context of the Canadian North, missionaries were accused of forcing Indians into the permanent, "clergy-directed village" in order to "implement the agricultural life."[3] They erected industrial schools, like those on the plains, to acculturate Indian children by tearing them away from the influence of their families and by imposing savage punishments for crimes like speaking their native languages. "In their zeal to save and convert the 'savages to Christianity,' " two critics claimed, "... the missionaries tragically believed that it was necessary to try and wipe out all vestiges of cultural, religious, and economic values that the natives had practised...."[4] Contemporary church officials now accept culpability for the actions their forebears committed and respond with such gestures as the United Church of Canada's recent apology to native peoples. Non-church members equate the missionary's role in cultural dislocation with that of the Hudson's Bay Company: often the fur trader and the missionary are depicted as partners in crime. Even those who would agree with revisionist historians that the fur trade did not cause as great a disruption as once believed, still would argue that the case of the missionary was quite different. As one author confidently asserts,

> Things started to change permanently and fundamentally when the missionaries started to take over the souls of native people....
> There is no question that the practical result has been the destruction of one of the cornerstones of native culture.[5]

Besides the fact that such conclusions are based on sketchy research, there is a more disturbing element to such popular wisdom. Implicit in all of these commentaries is the assumption that native cultures were passive in the face of the onslaught, and as a result, European and North American missionaries were indeed able to impose their value systems on the Indians. Native culture is given no credit for strength, resiliency, or adequacy in the face of adversity and pressure. Essentially, these authors are committing the "crime" of ethnocentrism in assuming the superior strengths of their own culture—ironically the very crime of which they are accusing the nineteenth century missionaries. Obviously, a clearer understanding of both the native and missionary sides of the contact situation is required before any such conclusions can be drawn.[6]

The Dene (meaning "people") are Athapaskan, of the Western Subarctic. In the nineteenth century, they lived in bands composed of related people which ranged in size from a single nuclear family to large congregations of fifty or more. In the last century they could be subdivided into the Chipewyan, Slave, Dogrib, Yellowknife, Mountain, Hare and Loucheux (or Kutchin).[7] These people relied on hunting and fishing and were thus necessarily mobile, although each band had a recognized hunting "territory" throughout which it moved seasonally or as resource availability dictated. The fur trade had been incorporated into this economy by mid-century, such that part of each winter was devoted to trapping furs for the purpose of trade rather than of home use.

One or two visits would be made annually to a Hudson's Bay Company post, or goods would be traded with other Indians who in turn visited a post themselves.

Early European visitors often concluded that the Dene had no religion because they had no cathedrals, patterned rituals, or organized priesthood.[8] In fact, religion permeated every aspect of daily life for the Dene. They made no distinction between the "sacred" and the "profane" as did the Europeans. Rather than separating the natural and supernatural, the Dene saw themselves and their environment as an integral unit. A person's life was not a linear progression through a series of events culminating in a final passage to another world which was unknowable in natural or human terms. Instead, a lifetime was experienced simultaneously in both physical and spiritual worlds. Any event could be caused by the activities of spirits, and events were never randomly caused. For instance, a hunter was not "lucky" if he killed a caribou; the caribou had offered itself to the hunter. The universe was governed by moral rules, often unstated, but nevertheless unbreachable since severe consequences could result from infraction. There were community as well as personal taboos. If a law was not observed, a spirit might be offended and bring its power to bear against the lawbreaker. Animals would not give themselves to the hunter, or a person might become ill or insane.

People were by no means the passive victims of the spirits' whims, however. Besides avoiding breaches of the law, a person could also ally with useful or "good" spirits who would come to one's assistance in times of need, or advise one as to the correct behaviour in a given situation. It is not clear whether Dene children deliberately pursued the "dream quest" visionary experience which has been observed in other native societies, but there is no doubt that many people did adopt a personal spirit-mentor at some point in their lives. People with particularly powerful contacts in the spirit world might rise to prominence as shamans, and be asked to predict the future, cure the sick, or divine the whereabouts of game.

Dreaming was the vital key to travel between the spirit and everyday worlds. Through the dream, spirits would make themselves known to people and provide them with the means to power. During the dream, it was believed that the soul left the body and travelled to various places. A dreamer might be taught a special song by his spirit-mentor, or be given a song to be used for the benefit of the community.

Although the testimony of European observers provides even less sense of Dene cultural values than it does of Dene religion, clues to the former may be gleaned from the rich body of folk stories, some of which have survived and from others no longer told, but recorded in the past.[9] In Dene legends, the unity between human and animal kingdom is constantly demonstrated as people and animals interchange form. The tales also reflect the positive value placed on flexibility and adaptability. The traveller makes use of whatever one finds at hand to advance position. In an environment of climatic extremes and migrating food resources, flexibility would seem to be a necessary trait. This flexibility has been noted by many other observers of Dene culture. Always receptive to new ideas, there is evidence that people rapidly assimilated both tools and ideas of neighbouring cultures.[10]

The other crucial cultural value lay in Dene respect for the individual. Each person had access to spiritual power, so that while some might make better use of it than others, every person was still potentially powerful. Therefore, each Dene had to respect the wishes and beliefs of others. Social conformity existed only in the broadest sense of the term; the band accepted certain given rules, but each individual developed a personal relationship with the environment which was to be respected by others. Competition between individuals was often in evidence in hunting, personal relationships or recreation (such as the popular gambling-guessing game) as each person tested his individual strength. As a result of this individualism, personal taboos appear to have held precedence as a means of social regulation. Each person made his own choices about right and wrong, and those choices were respected by others.

It would be incorrect, however, to conclude that for the Dene, the individual's rights were paramount. The community was recognized as important for survival and for social reasons. Good hunters had a responsibility to assist those who were less capable. Reciprocity in interpersonal relationships, animal and human-spirit relationships were as important to the Dene as individual prowess. Thus, the Dene valued a balance between individual autonomy and personal responsibility. While the individual would ideally be self-sufficient and self-reliant, one would also respect the autonomy of others, and demonstrate that respect through generosity and hospitality. As result, a sense of social cohesion and an acceptance of tacit social rules could be maintained, even though formal social organization was limited.

Into their society came European missionaries, who arrived in the North during a period of relative stability and prosperity in the mid-nineteenth century. Both Roman Catholic and Church of England missionary societies had been interested in expanding their work into the far northwest following the establishment of bases at the Red River settlement, but shortages of money and personnel prevented such expansion in the early years. Methodist missionary James Evans visited Ile à la Crosse briefly in 1844. Abbé Thibeault followed the next year. The first permanent Roman Catholic mission in Athabasca was founded at Fort Chipewyan in 1849 by representatives of the Oblates of Mary Immaculate (OMI). The OMI was an ultramontanist order founded in France in 1826 to revitalize the faith in a country torn by the French Revolution and the Napoleonic challenges to the authority of the pope. The Church Missionary Society (CMS), an evangelical organization from England, was determined to counter the influence of "heathen" Roman Catholics in the North, and in 1858, decided to send its first representative to Fort Simpson. When the OMI discovered that an Anglican was preparing to establish a mission there, a delegation was hastily organized and representatives of the two mission societies arrived on the Mackenzie River in the same boat brigade. An open competition for souls soon became one of the chief features of the Christian mission effort in the Mackenzie Valley. Later, in 1902, the CMS began to withdraw funding; this and the impact of treaties 8 and 11 changed the character of missionary work.

Given the nature of the OMI and CMS, mission work in the Mackenzie Valley differed from the stereotypes. For instance, both organizations were more interested in preaching and spiritual salvation than they were in inducing material cultural change. Boarding schools were established by both Anglicans and Roman Catholics, but for many years most student were Métis offspring of fur traders; few "bush" Indians participated. Those children who did attend came only sporadically and seldom for more than one or two years. According to official policy, the CMS encouraged the teaching of Indian children in their native tongues, using books of scripture and prayers written in syllabics or Roman characters.[11]

Nonetheless, the missionaries as a group told the Dene that they were receiving religious truth, and that those who accepted that message would have to make changes in their lives. Missionaries were particularly opposed to polygamy, infanticide, and the ease with which the Dene terminated marriage arrangements. The Roman Catholics saw no conflict between Christianity and an economy based on hunting and trapping,[12] but some of the Anglicans were ambivalent on this issue. The CMS saw its role as evangelizer only, and initially discouraged its missionaries from involvement in industrial and agricultural projects. A number of its representatives, however, were uncertain about the validity of such a programme and felt it necessary to encourage Dene to adopt the material "fruits of the gospel" as well as its spiritual messages. Clearly, the missionaries presented the Indians with not only an alternative religious expression, but also with alternative economic and social structure arrangements.

How then did the Dene themselves respond to these strangers in their midst? If one were to take modern census figures at face value, one might conclude that nearly all northern Indian people are Christians of one denomination or another, mostly Roman Catholic in the south and Anglican in the north. Do these census figures indicate that the missionaries were successful in attaining their objectives? Were they able to achieve their other goals: change Dene moral concepts and abolish Dene spiritual values?

Certainly, the Dene received the missionaries with great hospitality. The first mission workers felt cheered by the receptiveness with which they were met. There is some evidence to suggest that in a few cases, the Indians themselves had invited representatives of the Christian church to visit them, probably having heard of the white man's religion through fur traders and their Métis contacts.[13] Both Anglican and Roman Catholic missionaries noted the "attention" and "evident interest" with which their preaching was received at first contact.[14] The novelty of missions even seemed to be drawing the Indians away from their normal pursuits, as Hudson's Bay Company traders occasionally lamented. Large numbers of adults came to the priests to be baptized. At both Fort Simpson (population approximately 745) and

Providence (population approximately 300), an average of thirty-three people were baptized annually during the first eight years of the work.[15]

It was not long before the numbers of baptisms began to decline and the missionaries to complain about what they interpreted as the Indians "laziness" and "indifference" in matters of religion. The Reverend W.D. Reeve reported a typical response at Ford Liard in 1872. "There are only a few Indians here," he wrote, "These I have attempted to teach but when, after making a few common place remarks, I pulled out my Indian book, they all got up and left the room."[16] Some clues to the reasons for this change of attitude have been preserved in the records. It seems that the Dene responded to the missionaries as they responded to their own shamans and prophets.[17] The missionaries, like the shamans, claimed to have a special ability to proclaim mysteries invisible to other people because they had special channels of communication with the unseen world, and had the power to improve the quality of life. So the Indians reacted in much the same way as they would if one of their own people had proclaimed such information: they listened, looked for practical proof, might have accepted the teaching for a time, and then they turned to other leaders if the one's powers seemed to fail. As one Mountain Indian explained to an Anglican minister about his encounters with a priest, "At first I thought the Holy Father was like God, then I believed him to be like Satan, but now I think he is a fool."[18]

Such a statement reveals that the Indians felt free to transfer allegiances to different churches or individual missionaries if one proved "stronger" than another. All missionaries despaired at this behaviour, which they interpreted as inconsistent and lacking conviction. The first real test of power for the missionaries followed a devastating scarlet fever epidemic which swept down the Mackenzie in 1864–1865. Unable to provide much in the way of medical assistance, the missionaries devoted considerable effort to comforting the sick and baptizing those who requested it, often in the hopes of inducing a recovery. Of course, many who had been baptized later died; the Roman Catholic ceremonies for the dying, last rites or baptism were unfortunately quite the opposite of what Indians expected for the occasion. Fathers Petitot and Grouard noted that the Fort Simpson Indians were not only losing interest in their teaching, but were even afraid of the priests. Grouard discovered that he was being held responsible for the death of a man whom he had baptized,[19] while W.D. Reeve lost one follower to the Oblates because "of some fancied slight during the time of the fever, and because his wife and two children died."[20] As a result, the number of baptisms for the years 1865 to 1871 at Providence and Simpson dropped dramatically; people turned to their own spiritual leaders for help in time of crisis.

Disease was not the only test of spiritual power. The crisis periods of game shortages as well challenged the priest and shaman. When an Oblate priest scolded an Indian for reverting to "magical" practices after having been baptized, the priest received the explanation that the Indian "could not see his relatives suffer from hunger and do nothing while he knew he could make the caribou come by his incantations."[21]

Nevertheless, the Dene were always careful to show consideration and respect for the missionaries, just as they would toward a shaman, because of the possibility that the individual might be able to cause harm. As David Kirkby of the CMS reported:

> In a few hearts amongst the Indians I believe there are some real feelings toward God, but for the most part they are very indifferent. They attend prayers, it is true, but I believe from either a 'superstitious' motive... or to please their ministers.[22]

Some Indians rejected the Christian message because it did not seem logical or consistent to them. One visitor to Fort Simpson recounted an incident in which an Indian asked the priest for a two dollar loan, and then at the next day's service deposited the sum on the offering plate with considerable display. After some time, the priest asked the Indian to repay the loan. The Indian responded that he had already repaid it, on the offering plate in church. When the priest protested that such money was not for him, but for God, the Indian replied that, "God did not need the money, that he was rich," and the priest himself had preached recently that where God lived, "all the streets were made of gold," so that the priest would be wiser to keep the money himself.[23]

In another instance, a man who had initially accepted the Christian message rejected it after a long period of illness. William Spendlove of the CMS reported that "he finds it difficult to understand how God should afflict him who tries to serve him while many are well in health whose lives are sinful."[24] To this man, the Dene explanation for the nature of illness seemed more convincing because it had practical proof. Others rejected the mission teaching because the white men themselves did not seem to be following it, nor could they seem to agree amongst themselves. Furthermore, the Indians resented what they considered the hypocrisy of the missionaries preaching morality while breaching laws which the Dene considered important. One visitor to Fort Simpson announced he was parting company with the Oblates because he was disgusted that they had "asked his children indecent questions respecting himself, his wife etc." during confession.[25]

The Indians soon appreciated the fact that the missionaries (and the Anglicans in particular) were very much one-sided in their demands, and exhibited none of the reciprocity which the Dene valued so highly in their interpersonal relationships. The missionaries were unwilling to be flexible and accept some of the Indians' rules, so they began to lose interest and often to demonstrate their resentment of the newcomers' rudeness in failing to observe this fundamental social law. Evidence of these tensions was manifest in many different ways. When Father Emile Grouard attempted to intervene in a dispute over a woman at Fort Liard in 1866, one of the community leaders visited him to say, "Why do you interfere in something which is none of your business? When you pray down there in your lodge, we leave you alone;

leave us alone as well, to manage our affairs as we see fit."[26] At another time, in response to W.W. Kirkby's appeal for converts other Indians are supposed to have replied:

> If you want us to adopt your prayers, here is the condition we make for it. You are a married man, you have sons and daughters; very well, consent to take our daughters as wives for your sons, and give your daughters as wives for ours. Maybe then we will have faith in your words.[27]

The Dene also soon learned that the mission teachings and the practical results of such teaching were incompatible. Inconsistencies were most clearly noted when it came to the mission schools. While supposedly being taught to respect their elders, (a value shared by the Europeans and Dene), the children who attended school returned to their families "unfit for camp life," finding "the demeanour of their parents...distasteful hence they disobey and dispise [sic] them."[28] The Indians disapproved of such behaviour, and for many years, few Indian children were sent to mission schools by parents who failed to see the promised advantages materialize.

There were also some practical reasons for the declining Dene interest in mission teaching. With time, both Anglican and Roman Catholic missionaries began to insist on certain preconditions for baptism, including the renouncement of polygamy by the prospective recipient. While showing understandable resistance to unnecessary cultural change, the Indians faced as well painful personal dilemmas. How could a man abandon his "extra" wife? Who would hunt for her? And how was a man to choose which wife to keep? As one Yukon Indian explained, "You know how people sometimes had two wives? Minister say, that's wrong. Choose one they say. Imagine that; live with two women all that time, have to choose one. That's hard, I think."[29] The priests and ministers seemed to have been quite insensitive to the problem.

The indifference of the Dene to the missions has been frequently attributed to the conflict between the Roman Catholics and Protestants.[30] This explanation can be rejected. Contests of influence and power were part of the shaman's life, and the Protestant or Catholic missionary's claim to possess the "Truth" about God was no different from any shaman's claim. Surveyor John Henry Lefroy was probably closer to an understanding of the situation when he commented on the conflicts between Anglican and Methodist missionaries at The Pas. "The Indians of course understand nothing of the question," he wrote, "And looked upon it precisely as they do on the disputes of their medicine men. He whose medicine is strongest gets the victory."[31]

Probably the most important reason for the decreasing interest which followed the initial curiosity among the Dene was the growing realization that at a fundamental level, there were important differences between teachings of the missionaries and Dene beliefs. The Anglicans in particular based their appeal on the belief that man was sinful by nature, and could be saved only by faith through the propitiation of Jesus Christ. The Dene, while they might believe that breaking moral laws could result in punishment, could never be convinced that they were fundamentally bad. W.D. Reeve noted their reluctance to learn a prayer for the forgiveness of sins. "One old woman said the Indians have no sins, they always walk 'straight', and therefore there was no need for that petition," he wrote. "From the few observations that I have made I think it is a difficult matter to convince these Indians that their hearts are naturally sinful."[32] Unable to get the Dene to accept this first step in the chain of Christian theological thinking, it is hardly surprising that these missionaries encountered resistance to other ideas.

Moreover, the Dene were not prepared to share the European view of the nature of the relationship between the clergy and their flocks. Both the Grey Nuns and the Anglicans recorded a number of instances in which Indians expected to receive payment for leaving their children at the mission school, or to be paid for agreeing to a clerical demand like giving up a second wife. Some Dene considered that a visit to a mission was a favour which they granted to the missionaries. They attempted to demonstrate to the Europeans that if the priests and ministers wanted to get their attention, they would have to indicate sincerity by forming social, political and economic alliances with the Indians. When these were not forthcoming, the Indians decided to use the missions to their own advantage. A visit to the church meant gifts of tea and tobacco. In times of hardship, small children could be conveniently left at the missions where they would be fed and housed for the winter. In exchange for the privilege of having the child, the missionaries were expected to provide good care and payment with food and clothing.

The problem was that the missionaries either failed to understand that the Dene saw social relationships in a different way, or else the missionaries refused to acknowledge these differences, and persisted in their demands that the Dene accommodate themselves to the Euro-Canadian interpretation of religious and social relationships. In fact, the missionaries attributed their problems with the Dene to nonexistent causes. The most common explanation advanced by both Anglicans and Roman Catholics was that the Indians were being misled by the underhand tactics of the opposing church. Both sides believed that the Indians were confused by the opposition and thus were unable to make the "rational" choice. A second common response was the conclusion that the Indians were intellectually or socially slow to realize the "proper" state of religious organization and behaviour. Those who proved more responsive to mission teaching were deemed more intelligent, while those who resisted were "stupid" or "lazy." The ethnocentrism of these nineteenth century Europeans was such that they assumed anyone who saw the world differently must be somehow "backward" or underdeveloped.

In spite of these disagreements and conflicts, and after a second phase of declining interest, the missionaries were accepted gradually as part of life in the North. Christian rituals and practices became widely known. More Dene began to identify themselves as Christians and by the 1890s, both mission societies began to see their role as being providers of pastoral care rather than proselytizers. As the Indians began to incorporate certain elements of mission teaching into their lives, relations with the churches became more congenial and regularized.

Yet the question remains whether the Dene became assimilated into Euro-Canadian culture, whether they had completely accepted the Christian value system. Certainly the missionaries themselves did not proclaim that they had "Christianized" the Dene. As Bishop Bompas explained to the CMS in 1891:

> You use a strange argument for handing over these Missions to Canadians, that many of the Indians have now been Christians for many years, as though the work was already done, when it is yet hardly begun. In Mackenzie River I fear there are very few real Christians though many professing ones. Our work has been so far a failure....[33]

Father A.G. Morice recognized the depth of integration of pre-mission ways of thinking in 1928, when he observed:

> The language of the best Christianized Dene has retained to this day unequivocal traces of these zootheistic ideas. If unsuccessful in the hunt after game, the modern Dene will not say: 'I had bad luck with this or that animal,' but: 'Bears or beavers,' as the case may be, 'did not want me.'[34]

As a non-church traveller put it, "I think that the missionaries over-estimate their success in making genuine converts."[35]

What in fact had happened was that the Indians had interpreted many elements of the Christian faith in their own way, and gradually incorporated those ideas which enriched their pre-existing spiritual beliefs and religious activities. Their fundamental world view remained unchanged; merely some details, and in other cases, only the vocabulary, were new.

A number of specific Christian rites found favour among the Indians. Baptism, which was seen by the Oblates as the mark of conversion and by the Anglicans as the beginning of a Christian life, was seen by the Dene in several rather different ways. Some saw it as a ceremony to protect from evil, much as was the purpose of certain shaman's ceremonies. As Monsignor Grandin reported after a visit to Fort Rae:

> A chief came urging me to baptize the shirt of one of his hunters who was dying too far off for me to be taken to him. Two mothers, whose children had died without being baptized, begged me to baptize their tiny bonnets. Devastated at not being successful on this point, they begged me to take these bonnets and keep them safe.[36]

To others, baptism represented respect shown to the missionary, and an alliance forged with a man of spiritual power. A northern chief wanted to give his son the name "Jesus Christ" at baptism, explaining, "I did that so that Jesus Christ will continue to remember him."[37]

Even more enthusiastically received by the Dene was the Roman Catholic confessional. Priests frequently noted the avid interest in expressions of penitence which, as Emile Petitot and others have observed, Dene shamans had made use of as part of their own ceremonies. Petitot recognized the similarity:

> This conformity between our blessed religion and several of their ancient practices will doubtless be for them a preservation against the poison of Protestantism, where they find neither confession nor fasting....[38]

Other Christian practices which the Dene enjoyed included the saying of prayers, and rosaries, playing music and viewing medals and pictures. As has been noted, music had always been an important part of Indian life, particularly in relation to the acquisition of spiritual power. The other items were provided by the Oblates during instruction or after baptism, much to the disgust of the Anglicans. As one minister noted, "there is a great hankering for the medals & crucifixes given by the priests. They are looked upon, for the most part, in the light of powerful charms which protect them from some evil thing."[39] The items provided by the priests became additions to the personal "medicine bundles" carried by many of the northern Indians.

Christian symbols might be incorporated into Dene life in other ways. When Hugh Brody visited the Beaver Indians of northeastern British Columbia in 1978, he was taken to the site of a "medicine cross" which had been erected at a place believed, according to a dream prophecy, to be rich in game. The cross would be hung with medicine bundles and decorated with sketches of animals in hopes that such would make themselves available for the hunt.[40]

The adoption of a new religious vocabulary and some new forms of religious practice has not changed all Dene activities associated with their view of the spirit world. When anthropologist June Helm visited "Lynx Point" in the 1950s, she discovered a number of pre-Christian ideas, such as the blood taboo against menstruating women; the belief that animal blood should be respected was universally held.[41] While many Indians attend church services, several observers have noted participation is very different from that in southern churches; one remarked, "...the service just carried on, the priest and teachers doing it their way, while the Indians did it theirs."[42] An anthropologist who visited the Chipewyan community of Snowdrift between 1968 and 1972 noted that the belief i꞉ko꞉ze (or spiritual power of individuals) was still prevalent among young and old alike.[43]

Certainly some changes promoted by missionaries occurred in Dene society. Notably, polygamy and infanticide were almost totally abandoned. Nevertheless, it cannot be proven that these changes were the result of mission society pressure. Long before the arrival of churchmen and women, the Hudson's Bay Company had expressed its dislike of infanticide, and its Indian trade partners sometimes commented that they would consider giving up the practice in order to cement a trade alliance.[44] Furthermore, the orphanages, hospitals, and schools which the missionaries brought to the North provided practical alternatives to abandoning the young, elderly or ill in times of crisis.

Following the visit of the Pope to Fort Simpson in 1987, all Canadians have become aware of the importance of the Roman Catholic church to the people of the Upper Mackenzie. Morris Zaslow attempted to explain the apparent preference for Roman Catholicism over Anglicanism:

> The more limited role in which the Roman Catholic clergy cast their native adherents, the stress of religious observances and ceremonies, the colour and pageantry of the ritual, were better suited to the particular situation than were the vaguer concepts of personal revelation and spiritual regeneration taught by the Protestant missionaries.[45]

Such a conclusion is not only an unfortunate generalization, but also little credits the northern Indian's ability to think in sophisticated and complex terms. Certainly, aspects of Roman Catholicism resemble those of Dene tradition: the confessional, the charismatic religious specialist, the concept of fasting and the many saints or spirits who could intervene in the course of events. On the other hand, the Anglicans professed some beliefs which were more like Dene traditions than analysts like Zaslow have recognized. The evangelical emphasis on the religious life was certainly in keeping with Dene ideals. Anglican ministers were also free to marry, and the Dene considered marriage a means of alliance and reciprocity; they valued highly a man who would thus form a tie with the community. Hence, it is not surprising that the Loucheux (Kutchin) still remember that missionary Robert McDonald married a local woman.[46] Perhaps this is one reason why the Kutchin are the only Mackenzie Dene people who generally identify themselves as Anglican. Furthermore, the Anglicans tended to be more closely involved with the Hudson's Bay Company at its Mackenzie District posts, in spite of the Company's policy of impartiality. Anglicans tended to situate their missions right at company sites, rather than at a distance, and senior Company officials were usually Protestants. Hence those Indians with economic motivations or a desire for political alliance might have been drawn more strongly to visit the Anglican mission.

Why then did most Dene choose to ally themselves with the Roman Catholic church? Once again, considering the Dene's view of the missions provides some answers. The Anglican missionaries supervised by Bishop Bompas made unyielding demands on the Indians and expected greater changes than did the Roman Catholics before administering baptism. These demands must have seemed quite unreasonable to the Indians given their interpretation of that ceremony. Second, the Anglican emphasis was on proselytizing, while the Roman Catholics assumed pastoral duties and maintained a large orphanage at Providence, which was highly valued by the Indians as an alternative to infanticide in times of difficulty. Hence, the Roman Catholic missions were offering more useful services to the Dene, while the Anglicans were never able to organize and successfully maintain equivalent projects. Thirdly, the Oblates tended to be more aware of native cultural values, and demonstrated a greater respect for them than did the Anglicans. Furthermore, the Oblates had a higher level of tolerance for manifestations of those native values in their Christian adherents. The Oblates saw little conflict between Christianity and the hunting economy, while the CMS missionaries counteracted their own society's instructions by planning farms and industrial schools. Finally, the evangelical Anglicans rejected the use of pictures, medals, and other religious objects in their public ceremonies and private devotions. The Roman Catholics, on the other hand, encouraged the use of such items as part of their traditional methods of reaching nonliterate audiences. The Anglican refusal to supply religious objects must have appeared very odd to the Indians, who associated such artifacts with personal power. Were the Anglican ministers thus refusing to share their powers or secrets with the Indians?

Therefore, while both mission societies' faiths shared different elements with the Dene concept of religion and power, both demonstrated important differences. The Anglican inflexibility may have been the deciding factor in its failure to attract adherents in the southern part of the diocese (although there are certainly many other reasons).[47] If the Dene had felt that the "old ways" were becoming ineffective, they might have seriously considered Anglicanism as a possible solution. It seems, however, that they were not questioning their traditional values at a fundamental level, and saw no reason to admit socio-economic changes suggested by the nineteenth-century Anglican missions. The Oblates' behaviour was more consistent with Dene expectations, their demands more consistent with Dene traditions. It is hardly surprising, then, that the Dene chose to exhibit more interest in the priests' discourses.

The Dene were not easily, automatically and happily "converted" to Christianity or to other values which the European missionaries attempted to teach. The Dene treated the missionaries as shamans: persons better able to contact the spirit world, hence of potential utility in the struggle to survive. Some people rejected the message entirely and openly; some listened cautiously and politely so as not to offend; still others adopted elements of Christian teaching which seemed appropriate in individual cases. There was no single response in this individualistic society. As a pragmatic people, they tested new ideas and accepted only those which proved useful. Even an individual missionary could be welcomed if he proved his power or rejected if his ways proved harmful.

Because of the tolerance in Dene society for individual expression, the same missionary might be admired by some and reviled by others simultaneously. There was no one simple response.

The Dene were clearly not passive recipients of missionaries' instructions. They made their own use of the mission presence. They learned to read and write, and these skills were utilised in attempting to secure trade and political advantages. They made use of the Oblate orphanage and school to support their children in times of food scarcity, rendering obsolete the desperate practice of infanticide. They looked to mission medical services as one alternative if others failed. They "begged" food and supplies from missionaries: a useful way to avoid Hudson's Bay Company prices and a means to circumvent their debts. They also made use of the missionaries in later dealings with the Canadian government. They showed approval for Roman Catholicism by accepting baptism and supporting the missions.

Ultimately, as has been suggested, the Christian missions did not make profound changes in the daily lives or cultural outlook of the Dene. Anthropologists have observed manifestations of pre-mission values and customs; Christian labels have been applied to non-Christian concepts; Christian rituals have been interwoven with traditional ceremonies. No agricultural communities have been established, and while there are increasing numbers of native Christian religious workers, the northern churches remain largely dependent on support from "outside" for funds and personnel.

Nevertheless, it is obvious that important cultural changes have occurred in the North since the period considered in this survey. Education and housing programs sponsored by the Canadian government have created permanent villages. Welfare and family allowance cheques play a significant part in supporting the family unit. An analysis of the period of government involvement in the North is obviously a necessity before any final conclusions can be drawn about the impact of Euro-Canadian society on the northern Indians. Clearly, however, it is just as simplistic and unfair to "blame" the missionaries for assisting in the alleged destruction of Dene culture as it is to assume that indigenous northern culture was too "weak" or "primitive" to face the onslaught of nineteenth century Europeans. The meeting of societies in the Canadian North was an interaction and exchange, not a unilateral imposition of ideas. Ultimately the northern Indians may not have been the *victors* in the cultural contact situation, but neither can they be viewed as passive *victims*.

Notes

1. John Webster Grant, *Moon of Wintertime* (Toronto: University of Toronto Press, 1984).
2. For other analyses of cultural contact which make use of this approach, see

Robert Conkling, "Legitimacy and Conversion in Social Change," *Ethnohistory* 21, 1 (Winter, 1974): 1–24 for the Algonkian; Richard Slobodin, *Métis of the Mackenzie District* (Ottawa, 1966), and Bruce Trigger, *Children of the Aataentsic* (Montreal, 1976) for the Huron. Calvin Martin's *Keepers of the Game* (Berkeley, 1978) uses this thesis to explain eastern game overkill.

3. E.P. Patterson, *The Canadian Indian: A History Since 1500* (Don Mills, 1972), 124.

4. Hugh and K. McCullum, *This Land Is Not for Sale* (Toronto, 1975), 174.

5. Colin Alexander, *Angry Society* (Saskatoon, 1976), 25.

6. For a more detailed study, see K. Abel, "The Drum and the Cross: An Ethnohistorical Study of Mission Work among the Dene, 1858–1902" (Ph.D. diss., Queen's University, 1984).

7. Contemporary Dene groups are Chipewyan, Slave, Dogrib, Sahtudene (or Bearlake) and Kutchin. The Dene Nation organization includes the Fort Smith and Hay River Cree for political purposes. *Denendeh* (Yellowknife, 1984).

8. Samuel Hearne, *A Journey from Prince of Wales's Fort in Hudson Bay to the Northern Ocean, 1769–72* (Toronto, 1958), 220.

9. Emile Petitot, *The Book of Dene* (Yellowknife, 1976); Edward Curtis, *The North American Indian* 18 (Norwood, Mass., 1928); Robert Bell, "Legends of the Slave Indians of the Mackenzie River," *Journal of American Folklore* 14 (1901); Paul Voudrach, *Good Hope Tales*, National Museums Bulletin 204 (Ottawa, 1968); J. Lofthouse, "Chipewyan Stories," *Transactions of the Royal Society of Canada* 10 (1913); R.G. Williamson, "Slave Indian Legends," *Anthropologica* 1, 2 (1955–1956); June Helm MacNeish, "Folktales of the Slave Indians," *Anthropologica* 1 (1955); plus others.

10. For instance, the Chipewyan adopted the larger canoe of the Cree for use in long journeys to the fur trade posts. See York Factory Journals, 1715–1717, Hudson's Bay Company Archives (hereafter HBCA), B.239/a/2–3.

11. For a full discussion of mission methods and ideas, see K. Abel, "The Drum and the Cross," and Martha McCarthy, "The Missions of the Oblates of Mary Immaculate to the Athapaskans 1846–1870: Theory, Structure and Method" (Ph.D. diss., University of Manitoba, 1981).

12. Robert Carney, "The Native-Wilderness Equation: Catholic and Other School Orientations in the Western Arctic," *Study Sessions* 48, Canadian Catholic Historical Association (1981), 61–78.

13. For example, see Bishop Provencher to George Simpson, 27 June 1849, HBCA, D.5/25, fol.313. Quoted in Gaston Carrière, "L'Honorable Compagnie de la Baie-d'Hudson et les missions dans l'ouest canadien," *Revue de l'Université d'Ottawa* 36 (1966), 254. See also Emile Petitot, *En route pour la mer glaciale* (Paris, 1888), 313.

14. W.D. Reeve, Annual Letter, Fort Simpson, 29 November 1869. Records of the Church Missionary Society on microfilm in Public Archives of Canada (hereafter PAC), reel A98; Emile Grouard to Sister Marie Colombe, Providence, 10 November 1864, Archives Deschâtelets, Ottawa (hereafter AD), HPF 4191. C75R–124.

15. Sylvio Lesage, "Sacred Heart Mission, 1858–1958," MS, AD, BPC 513.L62, 48. Population figures from James Anderson, "1858 Census of the Population of Mackenzies River District," MG19/A29, PAC; and Emile Petitot, "On the Athabasca District of the Canadian North-West Territory," *Proceedings* 5, 11, Royal Geographical Society (November 1883).

16. Reeve's Fort Simpson Journal, 19 September 1872, microfilm reel A100, PAC.

17. Charlotte Bompas, wife of Bishop Bompas, was one of the few Europeans to recognize this fact, which she explained to a friend in 1901. S.A. Archer, ed., *A Heroine of the North: Memoirs of Charlotte Selina Bompas* (London, 1929), 172.

18. William Spendlove, "A Wild Red Indian Tamed," MS, n.d., MR 250/1, Provincial Archives of Alberta (hereafter PAA).

19. Quoted in Sylvio Lesage, "Sacred Heart Mission," BPC 513.L62, 9.

20. W.D. Reeve, Fort Simpson Journal, 3 September 1869, microfilm reel A99, PAC.

21. Martha McCarthy, "The Missions of the Oblates," 305. Based on a letter from Father Séguin to Taché, 1 June 1887.

22. Kirkby to C.C. Fenn, Fort Simpson, 19 June 1890, microfilm reel A116, PAC.

23. Elihu Stewart, *Down the Mackenzie and Up the Yukon in 1906* (London, 1913), 240–1.

24. William Spendlove, Fort Simpson Journal, 8 May 1882, microfilm reel A110, PAC.

25. W.D. Reeve, Fort Simpson Journal, 20 January 1870, microfilm reel A99, PAC. Reeve later noted that these "vile questions" were "too disgusting to be written down."

26. E.J.B.M. Grouard, *Souvenirs de mes soixante ans d' apostolat dans l' Athabaska-Mackenzie* (Lyons, Winnipeg, 1923), 100.

27. Grouard, *Souvenirs*, 99. Translated by K. Abel.

28. William Spendlove to CMS, Fort Simpson, n.d. (received 3 March 1884), microfilm reel A111, PAC.

29. Quoted in Julie Cruickshank, *Athapaskan Women: Lives and Legends*, National Museums of Canada, Canadian Ethnology Service Paper 57 (Ottawa, 1979), 24.

30. For example, Edgar Laytha, *North Again for Gold* (New York, 1939), 43–44.

31. Lefroy to Anthony (?), Fort Chipewyan, 11 November 1843, in *In Search of the Magnetic North: A Soldier-Surveyor's Letters from the North-West, 1843–44*, ed. G.F. Stanley (Toronto, 1955), 74.

32. Fort Simpson Journal, 9 June 1878, microfilm reel A103, PAC.

33. Bompas to C.C. Fenn, Fort Norman, 2 May 1891, MR 170/2, PAA.

34. A.G. Morice, "Denes" in *Encyclopedia of Religion and Ethics* (New York, 1928), 638.

35. Michael Mason, *The Arctic Forests* (London, 1924), 61.

36. Journal of Monsignor Grandin, June 1862 to April 1963, in *Les Missions des Oblats* 5, 18 (June 1866), 220–21. Translated by K. Abel.

37. Journal of Monsignor Grandin, 221.

38. Petitot, "Etude sur la nation Montagnais," Fort Good Hope, 1 July 1865, in *Les Missions des Oblats* 6, 24 (December 1867), 508. Translated by K. Abel.

39. D.N. Kirkby to C.C. Fenn, Fort Simpson, 19 June 1890, microfilm reel A116, PAC.

40. Hugh Brody, *Maps and Dreams* (Penguin, 1983), 8.

41. June Helm, *The Lynx Point People*, National Museum of Canada Bulletin 176 (Ottawa, 1961), 117–20.

42. Brody, *Maps and Dreams*, 79.

43. David Smith, *ʔkoʼze: Magico-Religious Beliefs of the Contact-Traditional Chipewyan [sic] Trading at Fort Resolution, NWT,* Museum of Man, Mercury Series, Ethnology Paper 6 (Ottawa, 1973), 20.

44. For example, see John McLeod's negotiations to open trade with the

"Nahany" Indians, HBCA, B.200/a/4, fol.10d.

45. Zaslow, *The Opening of the Canadian North* (Toronto, 1971), 65.

46. Julie Cruickshank, *Athapaskan Women.*

47. The CMS mission was unable to generate sufficient funding, and could not form a coherent policy direction for the diocese. See K. Abel, "Bishop Bompas and the Canadian Church," in a collection of papers, ed. Barry Ferguson, the Anglican Church in Western Canada, forthcoming.

PERIODIC SHORTAGES, NATIVE WELFARE, AND THE HUDSON'S BAY COMPANY 1670–1930*

ARTHUR J. RAY

Today, various forms of government assistance provide the principal sources of income for many northern Canadian native settlements, thereby supporting a welfare society. It is widely believed that this modern welfare society emerged recently, as the fur trade declined and was no longer able to provide native people with the income they needed to obtain basic necessities. The historical chronologies that have been most widely used by ethnologists reflect this belief. The most recent example is the chronology employed as the framework in the Smithsonian Subarctic Handbook, which dates the end of the "stabilized fur and mission stage," the end of the era of fur-trade society in other words, at 1945. This was the time when the so-called "modern era" began, when, it is thought, "the Canadian government began to assume direct responsibility for native health, education, and welfare needs long neglected."[1] When reflecting upon this conceptualization of the economic history of native peoples, one must question whether it is a valid and useful way to view the cultural and economic transformations that have taken place in the North.[2] Does it, for example, give a proper appreciation of the continuities of northern Indian cultures and the roots of contemporary native economic problems? To answer this and related questions it is necessary to examine the problems of resource shortages in the North and the ways in which the native peoples and the incoming European traders dealt with them.

Today, opinions are divided whether hunting, fishing, and gathering societies generally faced a problem of chronic starvation—the more traditional viewpoint—or whether they were the original affluent societies, as Marshall Sahlins has suggested. Sahlins does not deny that occasional starvation plagued hunters and gatherers, but, as he points out, more advanced horticulturalists and farmers faced this problem as well. Of greater

*The Subarctic Fur Trade, ed. S. Krech III (Vancouver: University of British Columbia Press, 1984), 1–20.

importance, Sahlins posits that demand for basic commodities is curtailed in "primitive economies" and brought into line with available resources. He further argues that only a relatively small amount of time is devoted to basic subsistence pursuits.[3]

In Sahlin's terms it is clear that the parkland-grassland bison hunters, the barren ground caribou hunters, the Ojibwa fishing villagers, the Iroquoian horticulturalists, and the bison-moose hunters of the wooded Peace River country could probably be classified as "affluent." All had reasonably stable food resources that normally exceeded the requirements of the local populations. The situation of hunters of the full boreal forest at the time of contact is more uncertain. For this region, references abound concerning food shortages during the early years of contact. The problem with such accounts, however, is that native complaints of privation were part of their bargaining strategy, and therefore Indians not infrequently exaggerated their actual situation. This is not meant to suggest that Indians did not experience real hardships; rather, that it is risky to accept all such accounts at face value without carefully considering the contexts in which they were made.

More to the point, it is clear that native people had developed resource management and redistribution strategies in the precontact period which served to minimize the risk of severe privation as a consequence of localized short-term scarcities of basic staples. Traditionally, most native groups had the capability of exploiting a wide range of resources even in areas where hunting activities were highly focused on single species such as the grassland bison, moose, or barren ground caribou. If these primary game were not readily available, secondary ones such as red deer (wapiti), woodland caribou, and beaver were pursued.[4] Furthermore, in many areas, such as the flanks of the shield uplands, the parklands, and the northern transitional forests, the seasonal hunting cycle took groups on lengthy migratory routes that exposed them to a wide variety of ecological niches, any one of which could be resorted to in times of need. Furthermore, these cycles of movement lessened the risk of overhunting in any single locality. The need for spatial flexibility in precontact big-game economies was recognized in the territorial control system that emerged. As E.S. Rogers has shown, in the boreal forest, native groups tended to hunt in the same areas every year—their hunting range. However, if game was scarce in that range, they could temporarily hunt on the lands of their neighbours to obtain basic necessities.[5] On the other hand, hunting or trapping for essentially commercial purposes was not permitted under the hunting range system.

While potential scarcity was minimized by exploiting diverse ranges (parkland-grassland, parkland-boreal forest, shield upland-Hudson Bay lowland, and northern transitional forest-tundra) and by having the capability to hunt a number of different species of game, the possibility of serious shortages stemming from unusual weather conditions, forest fires, and faunal epidemics still existed. To deal with these occasional hard times, native economies were structured to reinforce co-operation and sharing. Under such a system, general reciprocity was the dominant mode of internal exchange. Individuals were expected to share whatever surpluses they had with their families, close relatives, and members of their band. Indeed, as European traders learned, aid was often extended to strangers. According to the rules of general reciprocity, one did not expect an immediate return for aid rendered nor was any economic value placed on the obligation. The reciprocal obligation that accrued was generalized. The giver simply expected help in return when he was in need. In this way, general reciprocity served to knit groups together by a series of mutual obligations to render aid. This increased the survival chances of all members of the group. Sharing basic necessities of life with neighbouring groups was accomplished through the hunting-range system described above. To reinforce the co-operative orientation of their cultures, most groups, except perhaps those in the grassland area, negatively sanctioned the hoarding of wealth by individuals.[6] This does not mean that Indians were not interested in gaining access to wealth. Rather, individuals derived prestige from wealth by giving it away. For instance, generosity was a virtue that was expected of all chiefs or "captains," as the Europeans called them. It appears that most Indian trading captains distributed their wealth to their followers, thereby enhancing their social position.[7]

The fur trade negatively affected Indian economies in two fundamental ways. It served to increase the risk of serious shortages for native groups. At the same time, it increasingly undermined their ability to deal with this problem. For example, the fur trade tended to favour economic specialization among all native groups who took part in it. One of the earliest forms of specialization involved commercial trapping. Native people had always taken furs for their own use in making clothing. Probably the best known example was the use of beaver pelts to make beaver robes and coats. Indians began to hunt more selectively when they trapped for commercial purposes, often choosing furs that fetched the best prices. Initially, beaver and marten loomed large in the trade.

Very quickly, another specialty emerged: engaging in the trade as middlemen. Indians who became middlemen devoted little or no time to commercial trapping activities. Instead, they obtained furs from other Indian groups in exchange for trade goods they had acquired from Europeans. Middlemen often travelled great distances to carry on this exchange. It meant that less time could be spent than traditionally had been the case in food-gathering activities in the summer. To compensate, food supplies had to be secured from Europeans, from other Indian groups, or by increasing the role of women and children in food-gathering activities.

Still other groups specialized by becoming commercial hunters who supplied trading posts with provisions or "country produce," as it was called. Probably the most notable early examples of these types of groups were the homeguard Indians of the Hudson Bay lowlands—Cree at Moose Factory, Fort Albany, Fort Severn, York Factory, and Fort Churchill in the early years and Chipewyan at the latter post by the late eighteenth century; Ojibwa in the region between Lake Superior and Lake of the Woods, who supplied wild rice and, later, corn; and plain-dwelling Assiniboine, Blackfoot, and Cree, who supplied pemmican in the Parkland area.[8] Indeed, by the early nineteenth century, the number of Indians who specialized as commercial hunters was probably very large, given the proliferation of trading posts that took place during the period of intensive competition and considering that each post received a sizeable portion of its food from local natives.

The commercialization of native economies and the concomitant specialization of resource orientation began to favour a shift in traditional attitudes toward sharing among unrelated groups. Though it appears that bands continued to be willing to share basic survival resources with their neighbours, to define survival needs clearly became increasingly difficult. For instance, in the precommercial era it was easy to determine how much hunting of any given species was necessary for a group to meet its immediate requirements for food, clothing, and shelter. But with the advent of the fur trade and the growing dependence on imported technologies, it was no longer a simple task to define need. Rather than directly applying an aboriginal technology to the local environment to obtain food, clothing, and shelter, the Indians, through the process of technological replacement, were increasingly caught in the trap of having to buy the tools that they needed to hunt, fish, and trap, to say nothing of utensils, blankets, and cloth. Native groups thus faced a problem which had an impact on resource use that was both circular and cumulative. Items of European origin that originally were basically novel or luxury articles—firearms, hatchets, knives, and kettles, to name a few—became essentials. Partly for this reason, despite a traditional conservational attitude—in the sense that animals were hunted only to the degree that they were needed for food or clothing—once they began to trade, Indians overexploited many of their environments in response to the demands of an open-ended market.

The implications of this development for interband relations, resource use, and group survival can perhaps best be illustrated by examining the situation of the Blackfoot and their neighbours. In the 1750s, Anthony Henday accompanied a group of the Assiniboine and Cree who travelled from York Factory to the lands of the Blackfoot. Henday learned from his companions that the Blackfoot would allow them to hunt bison freely. The situation with regard to beaver was more complex, however. Henday tried to persuade the Assiniboine and Cree accompanying him to trap beaver. They refused. Not only was trapping unnecessary, since trading in the spring would give them more furs than they could carry in their canoes, but they indicated that the Blackfoot would kill them if they trapped beaver in Blackfoot territory.[9] Curiously, perhaps, subsequent entries in Henday's journal indicate that his Indian companions were trapping beaver. The women, however, were using the pelts to make winter clothing.[10] In short, the Blackfoot prohibition related only to commercial trapping. The prohibition caused no hardship for the Assiniboine and Cree at this time because the Blackfoot provided more furs to trade than the former middlemen needed to satisfy their trade good requirements and allowed them to collect the furs they needed to survive the winter.

A century later the situation had changed drastically. Many former luxuries had become necessities. Growing trapping pressures led to the serious depletion of many fur-bearing animals in the area. Fortunately, while animal populations were under growing stress, the trade offered Indians of the parkland-grassland area an alternative economic opportunity. Bison could be commercially hunted to meet the burgeoning provision requirements of the fur trade. This was a significant development for the Blackfoot and their confederates as well as for their former trading partners, the Assiniboine and Cree. The expansion of the fur-trade operations of the Hudson's Bay and the North West Companies had displaced the Assiniboine and Cree from their middleman positions and provided the Blackfoot with direct access to European trading posts. For this reason, the Assiniboine and Cree who lived in the parkland became suppliers of provisions. By selling pemmican and grease to the traders, they could still obtain the European articles that they formerly obtained through their prairie trading networks.[11]

The commercialization of the buffalo hunt had several unfortunate results. Hunting pressures began to deplete this once abundant food resource. By the 1850s, bison ranges were beginning to contract. Increasingly, Assiniboine and Cree groups were forced to encroach on Blackfoot lands in pursuit of the dwindling herds. As the bison diminished in numbers, they became more valuable. Also, bison were absolutely essential for the highly specialized economies that had developed among the plains Assiniboine, Blackfoot, and Cree. Not surprisingly, the Blackfoot were no longer willing to share this resource with their neighbours.[12] They now competed with the Assiniboine and Cree for control over a valuable, commercial subsistence resource that was in rapid decline. Consequently, persistent hostility developed between the Assiniboine-Plains Cree and the Blackfoot.[13]

The growing unwillingness of the Blackfoot to share their territory occurred in many other areas of Rupert's Land as an outgrowth of resource depletion. For instance, by 1821 beaver and other valuable fur-bearing animals were becoming scarce throughout the woodlands between James Bay and the Churchill River. Hudson's Bay Company traders and Indians alike began to see the need for conservation. However, the traditional tenure system was not well suited to a situation in which scarcity had become a chronic and widespread problem instead of an occasional and localized one. When certain Indian bands attempted to husband the fur resources in their hunting and trapping ranges by curtailing trapping activities, their neighbours frequently moved in and collected the furs.[14] While this might have been appropriate according to old customs, it meant that conservation schemes were virtually impossible to implement when the need for them arose. Local Indian bands apparently grew resentful of the incursions of their neighbours for trapping, but the band organization of the Subarctic offered no effective means of rationalizing access to or use of resources that were being depleted at an accelerating rate. The situation was particularly complicated with respect to beaver. This animal had always been a secondary source of food after moose and woodland caribou. With the destruction of these two big-game animal populations because of overhunting, beaver took on added significance in the provision quest of groups living in the boreal forest. Thus, beaver was not purely the commercial resource that some other fur bearers, such as marten, mink, and otter, were.[15]

Under the direction of Sir George Simpson, the Hudson's Bay Company attempted to use its considerable economic power to introduce a conservation programme. In areas where it held a monopoly, it began to exert pressures on local bands to restrict their trapping activities to assigned territories. The company's efforts were effective only in those areas where caribou populations had already declined sharply, forcing the Indians to shift to food sources that were less mobile, usually fish and hare.[16] In other places, particularly in districts where competition persisted, such as along the American border, encroachment of bands on each other's territories continued to be a vexing problem and the subject of considerable commentary in Hudson's Bay Company correspondence.[17]

Thus, as resources became valuable commercially and in turn more scarce as a result of heavy hunting and trapping, more rigid and spatially restrictive land-tenure systems began to emerge. The hunting range was supplanted by the system of band territories in many areas by the middle of the nineteenth century. During the late nineteenth century and the early part of this century, the trap line replaced this system in most of the woodland areas. In this way the mobility of the native peoples was increasingly curtailed.

Resource depletions depressed native economies in another important way. By the early nineteenth century, reduction of game had forced many woodland groups living south and east of the Churchill River to rely more intensively on less valuable fur-bearing animals, such as muskrat, and on alternative sources of food, such as hare and fish. This trend increased the hardships that several groups experienced because many of these less valuable species, fish excepted, exhibited more erratic fluctuations in their population cycles. For example, beaver and marten populations vary less from high point to low point, enjoy greater population wave lengths, and endure less erratic cycles than do muskrat and hare. Because of resource depletion, Indians were forced to spend more time hunting and trapping species of lesser value and more uncertain yield. In the 1820s Governor Simpson remarked, not surprisingly, that the Ojibwa living in the muskrat country of the lower Saskatchewan River area had a feast-and-famine economy, owing to oscillations in the population of this aquatic animal.[18]

Similarly, in areas where hare had become the dominant food source in the late nineteenth and early twentieth centuries, native economies were on a very precarious footing. This was especially true of the Hudson Bay-James Bay lowlands. When hare populations dropped sharply, Indians were forced to divert their attentions from trapping to the food quest.[19] Consequently, fur returns from posts like Moose Factory and Fort Albany exhibit great fluctuations. These variations are often more a consequence of the changing availability of hare than a reflection of the population cycles of the principal fur bearers (various fox) in the area.[20] Only those Indians who had access to a good fishery, usually sturgeon or whitefish, escaped the hardships that resulted from overdependence on hare.

The plight of Indians who took up residence in the Hudson Bay-James Bay lowland area was not brought about solely by overhunting. It was also in part the consequence of a major alteration that they made in their precontact ecological cycle. As noted earlier, prior to European penetration into their region, Indians apparently did not inhabit the lowlands throughout the year. There simply was not enough game. Therefore, they only visited the region during the summer to hunt geese and to fish, retreating to the Shield uplands in winter. Nevertheless, the arrival of the Hudson's Bay Company and the establishment of trading posts on the shores of the Hudson and James Bays meant that a need developed for post hunters. These hunters were particularly important for the spring and autumn goose hunts, and geese became one of the principal ingredients in the men's diet at the posts.[21] But to obtain a maximum return on the fall hunt, Indians often had to remain in the lowlands near the posts long after they normally would have returned inland to hunt and trap. In this way, specialization as post hunters favoured the permanent occupation of the Hudson Bay-James Bay lowlands and curtailed the spatial mobility of the Cree and Chipewyan who were involved. In essence, they discontinued the aboriginal practice of moving through their hunting range to seasonal surpluses, and instead developed a symbiotic relationship with the Hudson's Bay Company post where regional surpluses were stockpiled. When the Indians faced privation, usually in the winter, they turned to the company for relief, which was always provided.

Even when Indian groups did not attach themselves to trading posts as provision suppliers, involvement in the fur trade often curtailed the exploitation of a diverse environment in favour of a new scheme that was more narrowly focused and riskier in terms of the food quest. For example, as noted above, the Chipewyan originally occupied the food-rich northern transitional forest-tundra zone, where they subsisted principally on moose and barren ground caribou.[22] This was not prime fur country, however. As the Chipewyan were drawn into the fur trade in the eighteenth century, bands responded in three ways. Some drew near to Fort Churchill and became post hunters, with results that have already been described. Others became middlemen. Still others began to trap. Both of the latter two groups were drawn southwestward into the boreal forest where furs were more plentiful. These forests were located northeast of Great Slave, Athabasca, and Reindeer Lakes. While this ecozone was a better trapping environment, however, it was not as well stocked with game as their aboriginal homeland had been.[23] The increased population pressure on local resources that would have been the consequence of this historic migration must have further undermined the ability of these micro-environments to support a sound big-game economy.

When these developments are considered together, it is clear that one of the most far-reaching aspects of European expansion into the North involved overturning basic aboriginal ecological strategies. While precontact Indian bands often followed extensive migration circuits to take advantage of seasonal food surpluses, Europeans were unable to adopt this approach. Trade required the maintenance of large, spatially fixed settlements, together with rigid time schedules for cargo shipments along set routeways. This meant that the European companies had to devise sophisticated logistical systems that could move food from surplus areas to their posts for storage and redistribution. Needless to say, this was a revolutionary ecological strategy for northern Canada.

Generally, the significance of this revolution has been overlooked. Surely it was as important as the technological innovations that were introduced to the native economies, but most attention has been addressed to this latter issue. By being able to move large stocks of food from surplus areas (the grassland, the Peace River country, the fisheries on the edge of the Shield, and wild rice areas) and by importing it from eastern North America and Europe, the traders not only managed to maintain their posts, but also were increasingly able to sustain native populations in many areas that were either initially marginal in terms of provisions or became so because of overhunting. Indeed, as the late nineteenth century progressed, country provisions became more unreliable in most areas of historic Rupert's Land, and foodstuffs imported from eastern Canada and Europe or purchased from the developing prairie farming community of Red River had to be counted on more and more. Throughout the old areas of Rupert's Land native peoples grew to depend on the trading posts for food. This dependence emerged partly out of necessity and partly out of the deliberate policy of the Hudson's Bay Company. As noted, when country food stocks declined, native people had to spend more time searching for food; therefore, they had less time to devote to trapping activities. To combat this trend, in many areas the Hudson's Bay Company imported flour and sold it well below cost to the Indians.[24] It was hoped that this subsidy would encourage trapping. The policy was generally effective, although it served to further reduce native self-sufficiency in subsistence and to orient their diet towards a much higher starch intake than had been the case traditionally.

As native vulnerability to shortages of basic staples increased, the European traders were better able to manipulate them to serve their own interests. After 1821, one of the principal concerns of the Hudson's Bay Company involved maintaining a sufficiently large and low-cost labour force in the regions south and east of the Churchill River to assure that a profitable fur trade would continue. This meant that large scale emigration of native people from seriously depleted areas, such as Nelson and Hay River territories, to non-fur-producing regions, such as the Red River Colony, was strongly discouraged.[25] Furthermore, company hiring policies largely excluded Indians from occupations that involved work during the winter trapping season.[26] Instead, Indians were generally employed during the summer when they were hired to man boat brigades and carry on unskilled maintenance work around posts or to serve as hunters and fishermen. Significantly, there never was enough of these low-paying seasonal jobs to hire all who might have wished to be employed. Therefore, the practice developed of awarding summer jobs only to the most reliable hunters and trappers, mainly those who had paid their debts. Housing was also often provided for them at the post.[27] In this way, the employment practices of the Hudson's Bay Company were specifically designed to encourage Indians to remain in the traditional hunting and trapping sector of the economy well beyond the time that many were finding it difficult to do so.

Additional support for, and control of, native people was achieved by the extension of credit as well as by the distribution of gratuities. The former was made available to able-bodied adult males; the latter to widows, orphans, the aged, and the infirm. The use of credit in the fur trade can be traced back to the earliest days of the Hudson's Bay Company's operations. By advancing to Indians outfits of goods, the company, and other traders as well, hoped to secure the future returns of hunts; credit, as well as gratuities, served to tide Indians over during times of poor hunting and trapping. Thus, from the beginning, debt and gratuities became essential to the fur trade. When European competition for Indians' furs was modest and the fur market steady or rising, the system was not too costly, and it gave Europeans greater control over the Indians.[28]

The debt-gratuity system became increasingly troublesome for the fur traders as time passed. When Indians specialized economically, and as resource depletion became an ever more serious problem, Indians grew more vulnerable to shortages of food and low fur returns. Hard times occurred with increasing frequency, and in some areas, such as the Hudson Bay-James Bay lowlands, inadequate supplies of food had become a chronic problem by the turn of this century.[29] While traditional sharing practices continued to operate within Indian bands, deprivation could only be alleviated by increasingly resorting to the Hudson's Bay Company posts for gratuities and credit. At the same time, the ability, and perhaps willingness, of Indians to repay their debts seems to have diminished.

Reflecting these changing conditions, by the late nineteenth century the Hudson's Bay Company adopted a policy of discounting the face value of all Indian debts by 25 percent at the time they were issued. Thus, for every 100 Made Beaver (MB) of credit issued to an Indian only 75 MB was entered into the account books. Furthermore, any credit outstanding after one year was written off as a bad debt.[30]

The company could well afford to write off debts in this fashion. The standards of trade that it used to value goods and furs allowed for a very considerable gross profit margin.[31] Indeed, it could be argued that the standards not only served to underwrite the credit/gratuity system, but that they increasingly made it necessary. For instance, the resource base continued to decline to the point that in some areas native purchasing power was no longer adequate to serve basic Indian consumer requirements. The Hudson's Bay Company could have relieved the plight of the Indians by lowering the prices it charged for staple items or by advancing the prices it paid for furs. James Ray, the district manager for James Bay, considered this option as a solution to the problems that native people at Great Whale River faced in the early 1920s. He rejected this course of action as others had done before him. In explaining his decision, he wrote:

> Beyond the slight reductions mentioned (for ammunition which has been selling at 200 percent of cost land price) I am not in favour of reducing our selling prices for it would be difficult to raise them again when better times shall come to the natives. So it seems the only solution, if it can be called a solution, to the problem is for us to go on advancing to these peoples as if for debt, though they have little hope of ever paying it . . . . If we continue as I proposed, the debt system as a means of keeping the natives alive during the lean years, the Company may in some small measure—be reimbursed by the amounts the natives may be persuaded to pay when the fat years shall come again and in the main, I imagine it will be more easily handled than any system of gratuity we may devise.[32]

Thus, Ray preferred the large scale use of credit instead of resorting to a system of more flexible prices or to straightforward welfare.

Indians living in the southern James Bay area and the Montreal Department had been aware for some time that the Hudson's Bay Company's practice of issuing credit in the form of relatively high priced merchandise was aggravating their economic hardships. Therefore, when the Canadian Pacific Railroad was built, opening the southern portions of Rupert's Land to renewed competition in the late nineteenth century, Indians began to pressure the Hudson's Bay Company traders to give them credit in the form of cash advances, that is, consumer loans. The Indians intended to take this money to the "line" where they could buy their outfits at reduced prices. Indeed, some were said to be prepared to go as far as Montreal and Trois Rivières to get cheaper goods.[33] Not surprisingly, the company traders did not willingly comply with this request. Non-payment of credit in goods represented a potential loss of something less than 50 percent of face value of the loan. Furthermore, as Inspecting Officer P. McKenzie noted in 1890, "There is no profit to be made in cash advances to Indians in large amounts even supposing they . . . pay up their accounts in full every year."[34]

Of fundamental importance, the extensive use of credit under near monopoly conditions favoured the persistence of a credit/barter economy, using the Made Beaver standards. It was not simply the result of Indian conservatism or an inability on their part to operate in a monetized economy. It served the company's interest to conduct the trade in this fashion until the late nineteenth century. Holding a near monopoly, the Hudson's Bay Company was able to maintain high prices, low seasonal wages, and put the Indians under an obligation to it through the extension of credit.

By the final quarter of the nineteenth century the old order was, however, coming under increasing stress. The construction of the Canadian Pacific Railroad along the southern periphery of Rupert's Land not only increased competition, but it also brought a new kind of competitor. Rather than bartering furs for goods as in the past, increasingly, company opponents paid cash for the Indian's returns.[35] The Indians were able to take the money and search out the best prices for the commodities they needed. Traditionally, the prices of trade goods had been relatively constant and most bargaining was focused on the values assigned to furs and country provisions. Direct competition in trade good prices began in most areas of southern and southwestern Rupert's Land in the 1870s with the signing of treaties. Treaty payments injected cash into the local economies and encouraged small travelling peddlers to compete with the Hudson's Bay Company for the treaty money. The building of the Canadian Pacific Railroad thus served to accelerate a new trend by offering small fur buyers and merchants relatively cheap access to the North. The Indians benefited by being able to seek out the best prices for furs and goods rather than having to continue to deal with a single company which largely monopolized fur purchases and goods sales in most areas of the North.

Reflecting this new development, by 1899 the Hudson's Bay Company employed cash and barter standards in all districts except Mackenzie River, and Fur Trade Commissioner C.C. Chipman recommended that steps be taken immediately to introduce it to that district.[36] As map 1 shows, by 1922–1923 a significant portion (6–35 percent) of the merchandise transactions of the fur-trade division of the Hudson's Bay Company consisted of cash sales. In the Lake Huron, Lake Superior, and Athabasca areas, competition was strong and major inroads were being made into the old credit/barter system of trade.

As competition escalated, the issuing of credit became risky once again as it had been in the days of sharp rivalry between the Hudson's Bay and North West Companies in the period from 1790 to 1821. A significant number of Indians simply preferred to deal with whomever offered the best prices for furs in the spring, regardless of whether or not they owed debts to someone else. Consequently, to offset the growing number of bad debts, in the 1890s the Hudson's Bay Company began a concerted effort to curtail the use of credit in the hope of eventually operating the business on a basis of ready barter or cash. This objective was given the highest priority in so called "frontier districts," or areas open to intensive competition. Such districts included all areas lying within fifty miles of a railway line. Indeed, Indians adjacent to the line were regarded as unreliable because they roamed up and down it looking for the best prices.[37]

Other pressures were also mounting that encouraged the Hudson's Bay Company to curtail the credit/barter trade and to seek relief from the escalating expenses it was incurring by giving gratuities to sick and destitute Indians. When fur returns were at a sufficiently high volume, the rate of advance built into the standard trade provided the company with a gross profit margin that

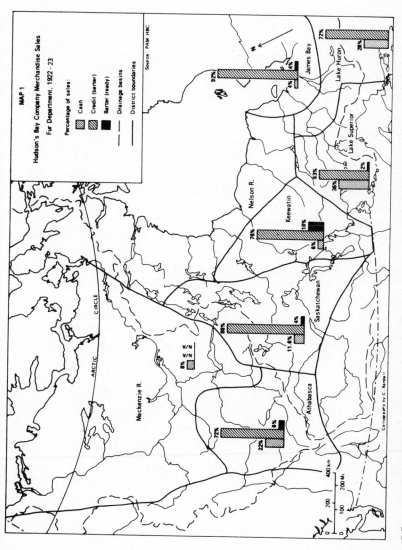

MAP 1. Hudson's Bay Company Merchandise Sales, Fur Department, 1922–1923

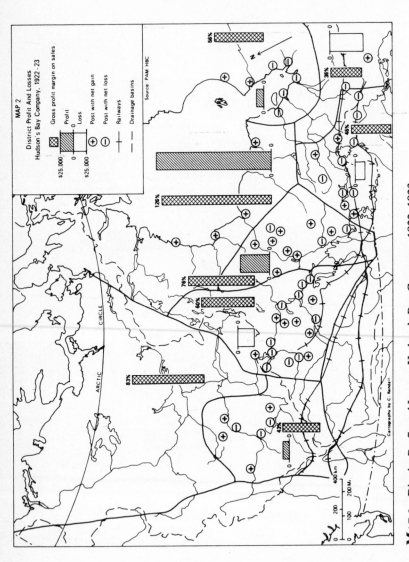

MAP 2. District Profit and Losses, Hudson's Bay Company, 1922–1923

was sufficient to cover overhead costs and assure it an ample net return. By the late nineteenth century, however, the turnover at many posts had declined to the point where this was no longer the case. As map 2 shows, by the early 1920s, the Hudson's Bay Company registered net losses in three of its more southerly trading districts. Furthermore, the net gains made in the Moose River and Athabasca districts were relatively small and were based on the operations of a few posts that did not experience strong competition.

In the late 1870s and early 1880s, York Factory, one of the company's oldest posts, had so taxed its local environment during its heyday that the trading returns of the local Indians were no longer sufficient to cover the post's operating expenses. W.J. Fortescue, who was in charge of the post at that time, thought the Indians there should be encouraged to enter into treaty negotiations with the government. Fortescue believed this arrangement desirable because the Indians' welfare would then become a government responsibility.[38] In addition, the annuity payments would constitute a new source of revenue for the company.[39] Thus, by the late nineteenth century, some interest in having the government assume the growing burden of Indian welfare needs was beginning to develop within the company.

While Fortescue was somewhat ahead of his time in making this suggestion, by the early part of this century the government was beginning to underwrite these expenses even outside treaty areas. For example, in the James Bay district, where Company gratuity expenses were particularly large compared to other regions, the Hudson's Bay Company frequently submitted bills for this cost to the government. The government usually paid them.[40] In this way, the process of transferring responsibility for a welfare system that was an integral part of the fur trade from the Company to the government began in the late nineteenth century. It happened slowly because the government was not eager to assume this burden. And, for humanitarian as well as practical business reasons, the Hudson's Bay Company could not simply abolish the practice of providing gratuities to needy Indians before alternative arrangements had been made. The Company's predicament in this regard was illustrated by the problems that it faced in the Richmond Gulf area in 1924. In that year the Hudson's Bay Company provided over $31 000 in assistance in the form of gratuities, unpaid advances, and sick and destitute accounts. In discussing what should be done about the problem, District Manager Jim Ray noted:

> It is true that the natives are our assets, that we must keep them alive for future profits even though we carry them at a loss till such time shall come. On occasion we have taken large profits out of the post as the following figures will show; Outfit 249 (1919) profit $51,724, Outfit 250 profit $250,497. (Year of high realizations) Outfit 251 profits $1,017. (Year when slump in prices occurred) Outfit 252 profit $46,141. Outfit 253 profit $99,430. But the question arises, is it consistent with good business to go on assisting these people to the sum of $25,000 a year till such times

> as good tax years return to us? There are limits to what the
> Company may consider generous and judicious treatment.[41]

Clearly the company faced a dilemma. Resources were seriously depleted in
the Richmond Gulf area and the natives were reduced to a heavy dependence
on two species: hare to serve as food; fox as fur. When either failed, the Indians were destitute. When hare and fox were plentiful, the Indians lived well
and the Company reaped handsome profits. Similar circumstances prevailed
elsewhere.

From the Company's economic position, the ideal solution would have the
government assume the financial burden of carrying the Indians through lean
years. Then, despite deteriorating conditions, the Company would be free to
continue to prosecute the fur trade on a highly profitable basis. This eventually transpired, and by the 1940s the government was heavily involved in a
wide variety of welfare programmes for native peoples. From the point of
view of the traders, one of the negative aspects of this development—a
problem apparently not forseen by Fortescue—was the loss of their control
over the local Indian populations. Unlike the Company's scheme, government
assistance did not carry any obligations to hunt and trap.

From this discussion it is clear that the modern welfare society of the North
is not a post-World War II phenomenon. It is deeply rooted in the fur trade.
The welfare system was a necessary by-product of several processes:
economic specialization by native peoples, a concomitant decreasing spatial
mobility, European control of food surpluses and the depletion of resources.
Reinforcing these were the labour policies, wage schedules, and standards of
trade that assured the Hudson's Bay Company large gross profit margins in
good years under near monopoly conditions, but that also allowed native
peoples only a marginal return. Some scheme for the additional redistribution
of excess profits to the Indians in the form of gratuities and "debt" to supplement their meagre returns from hunting and trapping was absolutely essential.
Otherwise, the company could not have stemmed a migration of Indians from
the boreal woodlands, and the loss of this labour force would have seriously
undermined the prosecution of the trade in many districts south and east of the
Churchill River.

Finally, it is clear that we must reconsider the stereotype of the Indian as essentially conservative economically. By holding a virtual monopoly on most
aspects of the northern economy until the last quarter of the nineteenth century, the Hudson's Bay Company was the key determinant for development
and change. In many areas of the North, it was in the Company's interest and
ability to perpetuate the use of a credit/barter or truck system until the late
nineteenth century. The arrangement discouraged, and often prevented, Indians from leaving this part of the primary resource sector of the economy,
even in regions where resources were so depleted that only marginal
livelihoods could be sustained. The system failed to encourage the spread of
the cash economy through cash buying of furs, partly to insure a higher gross

profit margin and partly to minimize losses from bad debts. In summary, the Hudson's Bay Company was partly responsible for limiting the ability of the Indians to adjust to the new economic circumstances at the beginning of this century. Debt-ridden, repeatedly blocked from alternative opportunities for over a century, and accustomed to various forms of relief over two centuries, Indians became so evidently demoralized in this century, but the groundwork for this was laid in the more distant past.

welfare state of fur trade
Limited choice of natives to do anything else.
we made them insufficient in ways. we bracht
them to way they are.

Notes

1. June Helm, Edward Rogers, and James Smith, "Intercultural Relations and Cultural Change in the Shield and Mackenzie Borderlands," in *Handbook of North American Indians, Vol. 6, Subarctic*, ed. June Helm (Washington, D.C.: Smithsonian Institution, 1981), 145–57.

2. Charles Bishop and Arthur Ray, "Ethnohistoric Research in the Central Subarctic: Some Conceptual and Methodological Problems," *Western Canadian Journal of Anthropology* 4 (1970): 116–44; Shepard Krech III, "The Influence of Disease and the Fur Trade on Arctic Drainage Lowlands Dene 1800–1850," *Journal of Anthropological Research* 39 (1983): 123–46.

3. Marshall Sahlins, *Stone Age Economics* (Chicago: Aldine, 1972), 1–100 passim. Some ethnologists question whether even big-game hunters like the Caribou-Eater Chipewyan could be said to have had an aboriginal affluent society; James Smith, "Economic Uncertainty in an 'Original Affluent Society': Caribou and Caribou-Eater Chipewyan Adaptive Strategies," *Arctic Anthropology* 15, 1 (1978): 66–68.

4. Arthur Ray, *Indians in the Fur Trade* (Toronto: University of Toronto Press, 1974), 27–50.

5. Edward Rogers, *The Hunting Group–Hunting Territory Complex among the Mistassini*, National Museum of Canada Bulletin 195 (Ottawa, 1963).

6. After the horse was adopted into the northern plains culture in the early eighteenth century (in Canada), it became a symbol of wealth and Indians did try to accumulate as many as possible. However, it is uncertain whether or not this was simply a postcontact development or was built on earlier traditions.

7. Arthur Ray and Donald Freeman, *Give Us Good Measure* (Toronto: University of Toronto Press, 1978), 63–69.

8. Ray, *Indians in the Fur Trade*, 51–57. Ray and Freeman, *Give Us Good Measure*, 39–51; Wayne Moodie, "Agriculture and the Fur Trade," in *Old Trails and New Directions*, ed. C. Judd and A.J. Ray (Toronto: University of Toronto Press, 1980), 272–90.

9. L.J. Burpee, ed., "Journal of Journey Performed by Anthony Henday: to Explore the Country Inland and to Endeavour to Increase the Hudson's Bay Company's Trade, A.D. 1754–1755," *Transactions* 3d ser., vol. 1, sec. 2 (Royal Society of Canada, 1907): 91–122.

10. Burpee, ed., "Journal of Journey Performed by Anthony Henday," 91–122.

11. Ray, *Indians in the Fur Trade*, 131–35.

12. Ray, *Indians in the Fur Trade*, 223–26.

13. This situation had apparently developed sometime after 1774, judging from the account of M. Cocking, who visited the Blackfoot territory in 1772–1773. Trade between Assiniboine-Cree was still going on. However, shortly thereafter, the inland expansion by the Nor'Westers and the Hudson's Bay Company upset this arrangement.

14. Arthur Ray, "Some Conservation Schemes of the Hudson's Bay Company, 1821–50: An Examination of the Problems of Resource Management in the Fur Trade," *Journal of Historical Geography* 1, 1 (1975): 61; Charles Bishop, "The Emergence of Hunting Territories among the Northern Ojibwa," *Ethnology* 9 (1970): 10–14.

15. Ray, "Some Conservation Schemes," 65.

16. Ray, "Some Conservation Schemes," 61; Bishop, "The Emergence of Hunting Territories," 10–14.

17. Many comments of this nature can be found in Governor Simpson's correspondence in the Hudson's Bay Company Archives (hereafter HBCA); Fur Trade Commissioners Correspondence, HBCA, A.12/FT, Public Archives of Canada (hereafter PAC), Dr. Irene M. Spy, personal communication with author, 3 March 1981.

18. For discussion of population cycles see C.G. Hewitt, *The Conservation of Wild Life in Canada* (New York: Charles Scribner and Sons, 1921); Simpson's observation is cited in Ray, *Indians in the Fur Trade*, 121.

19. According to the various documents dealing with the James Bay district between 1880 and 1920, one of the most common causes of poor fur returns was the failure of hare. See, for example, letters from Moose Factory to the Hudson's Bay Company Secretary, 1871–1889, HBCA, A.11/47, Public Archives of Manitoba. In particular, the letter of 15 September 1890 noted the very poor return and claimed:

> The causes of ... falling off is attributed to scarcity of rabbit, the
> principal food of the Indians thus preventing them from hunting being
> occupied all of their time in procuring food. This is most apparent in
> Rupert River where the decline in these skins is no less than 900 per
> cent. As you are probably aware this scarcity arises from disease, and is
> periodical running in a cycle of ten to eleven years, with three years of
> maximum and three years of minimum.

20. This was also true inland on the Shield uplands of northern Ontario; B.P. Winterholder, "Canadian Fur Bearer Cycles and Cree-Ojibwa Hunting and Trapping Practices," *American Naturalist* 115, 6 (1980): 873–74.

21. Reflecting the importance of these hunts, the correspondence between the posts on the Bay almost always commented on the success or failure of the local hunts. The record pertaining to York Factory indicates that geese were one of the cheapest provisions that could be obtained before 1880. Fortesque to Armit, York Factory, 1 December 1880, Moose Factory Correspondence Outward 1871–1880, HBCA, A/119a, fol.149.

22. Beryl Gillespie, "Territorial Expansion of the Chipewyan in the Eighteenth Century," in *Proceedings: North Athapaskan Conference 1971* 2, ed. A.M. Clark, National Museum of Man Mercury Series, Canadian Ethnology Service Paper 27 (Ottawa, 1975), 350–88.

23. C. Yerbury, personal communication with author.

24. For example, the Inspection Report for Cumberland District in 1886, recommended using cheap flour in the northern portion of the district to discourage Chipewyans from hunting deer; Inspection Report for Cumberland District 1886, HBCA, P.25/1/1. Similar recommendations were made for other parts of the district.

25. Ray, *Indians in the Fur Trade*, 218.

26. Carol Judd, "Native Labour and Social Stratification in the Hudson's Bay Company's Northern Department, 1770–1870," *Canadian Review of Sociology and Anthropology* 17 (1980): 307.

27. William Anderson, Fort Albany, May 1980, personal communication with author. Mr. Anderson served as a company clerk in James Bay.

28. In the early years credit even may have been used to increase Indian fur outputs beyond the level that could have been achieved otherwise. In offering an historical overview of the fur trade, the Fur Trade Department Annual Report for 1929 included the following observation: "It was found then [after natives adopted European goods] that only sufficient game would be killed to meet the natives' own requirements, and so a plan was adopted to overcome that. Advances were given through the chief. These Chiefs and clans were a proud lot .... The clan with the largest advance was the most influential, and in order to remain influential all debt had to be paid," Fur Trade Department Annual Report 1929, HBCA, A.74/43. Regarding the declining ability of the environment in some areas to cover these costs, see Fortesque, HBCA, A.11/119a.

29. Beaver were said to be in steady decline as of the early 1890s. Other furs showed the normal cyclical variations. The problem was that the principal food was rabbit, which was said to run in ten to twelve year cycles with three years maxima and three years minima. The low points in the cycle frequently caused starvation (see note 19 above). Many other examples of the adverse effects of food shortages on trapping activities in this area between 1880 and 1930 could be cited. For example, Inspection Reports, 1888–1890, HBCA, 5.54/4–10; Annual Reports, 1890–1894, HBCA, A.74/1–3; Fur Trade Reports 1912–1924, HBCA, DFTR/1–19.

30. Rules and Regulations, London, 1887, rules 72–76, HBCA, D.26/3. These rules specified further that "doubtful" debts, those beyond current outfit but less than a year old, were to be entered in the accounts at 50 per cent of original value.

31. On several occasions traders pointed out that the indebtedness of the Indians shown in their accounts did not represent the money actually owed the company, given that the debt was in terms of goods advanced and valued as per the standard of trade. The debts thus represented a loss of potential profit. As the inspection report for Bersimi in 1890 indicated, "the profit on goods (supposing the hunter or hunters had been paying up pretty regularly for a few years previous) ought to be sufficient to prevent actual loss to the Company," Inspection Report for Cumberland District, 1886, HBCA, D25/4.

32. Throughout the Company's records, suggestions to lower prices are always turned down with the same explanation—that is, Indians would not allow them to be raised again; Fur Trade Annual Report, 1912–1924, HBCA, DFTR/19.

33. Indians dealt with CPR employees. Also, the railroad had a store car. In the Bersimis and Saguenay Districts cash advances had to be given to combat competition despite Company opposition; Inspection Report for Cumberland District 1890, HBCA, D.25/4.

34. Of course, the profit margin would be reduced, given that it became a fur-cash transaction rather than fur and goods in which the company extracted profit both ways; Inspection Report for Bersimis 1890, HBCA, D25/4.

35. By 1898 cash tariffs and barter standards (MB) were in use in the southern portion of the Montreal, Southern, and Northern Departments. Hudson's Bay Company Commissioner C.C. Chipman indicated that the Company would have to introduce it to the Mackenzie Department before opponents did, as had been the case elsewhere; Fur Trade Commissioners Correspondence, HBCA, A.12/FT 229/3.

36. Evidence of this can be obtained from a variety of sources. In 1880, W.J. Fortescue indicated that the MB tariff for goods was inelastic but that of furs was

not; Moose Factory Correspondence Outward 1871–1880, HBCA, A.11/119a.

37.   From the earliest years of the Company's history there were efforts to curtail credit when competition was strong. The efforts usually were unsuccessful, and this was true in the 1880s also; Inspection Report for Cumberland District 1890, HBCA, D.25/4.

38.   Arthur Ray, "York Factory: The Crisis of Transition, 1870–1880," *The Beaver* (Autumn 1982), 26–31.

39.   A concerted effort was made in treaty areas to obtain as much of this money as was possible. Also credit was extended against Treaty payments; Moose Factory Correspondence Outward 1871–1880, HBCA, A.11/119a.

40.   See Fur Trade Commissioners Correspondence, HBCA, A.12/FT 243/1 dealing with Destitute Indians and Treaties.

41.   Fur Trade Annual Reports, HBCA, DFTR/19.

SECTION 3

THE GOLD MINING FRONTIER

FLUX AND AUTHORITY IN A SUBARCTIC SOCIETY: THE YUKON MINERS IN THE NINETEENTH CENTURY*

THOMAS STONE

Throughout the last quarter of the nineteenth century, steadily increasing numbers of gold-seeking adventurers moved into the region of the upper Yukon drainage. Between the arrival of the first prospectors in 1873 and the arrival of Charles Constantine of the North West Mounted Police in 1894, no formal positions of authority or formal organizational structures emerged among the miners. Nonetheless, the inhabitants of the district did not function as isolated individuals. Partnerships were essential, n ot only to the prospecting and mining enterprise but also to one's chances of survival. The men often formed traveling or working parties of substantial size, and upon occasion collective action was organized on a scale of an entire community. For twenty years, the miners in the district demonstrated their ability to organize frequently and well in pursuit of collective interests while their society retained its strong egalitarian character.

In the absence of formal authority, the miners' capacity for concerted group activity was sustained by a form of conflict management not unlike that observed among hunter-gatherers[1] and intimately linked to patterns of recurrent population movement with attendant fluctuation in the size and composition of local groups. In this article, the patterns of mobility and fluctuating group composition which characterized the miners' society are described, and the interplay between these patterns, the management of conflict, and the nature and functions of leadership and authority are analyzed. In the case of these early Yukon adventurers, mobility and group "flux"[2] provided an alternative to the elaboration of relationships of formal authority as a means of resolving a fundamental problem in the organization of any human

*Ethnohistory 30, 4 (1983): 203–16. The staff of the Yukon Territorial Archives, the Public Archives of Canada, and the Crumb Library, Potsdam, New York, all contributed in important ways to the study from which this article derives. I would also like to record special thanks to Elinore Vorse, Kathy LaClair, and Nancy Perkins.

society, i.e., how to sustain a capacity for concerted social action in the face of variable and conflicting individual purposes and judgments.[3]

A Society in Flux

The first serious prospectors entered the upper Yukon region in 1873, by way of the Mackenzie Valley and the Hudson's Bay Company portage to the Peace River.[4] Three of them—Leroy McQuesten, Al Mayo and Arthur Harper—were to become prominent figures in the early history of the district, as they established and maintained the principal trading posts along the upper Yukon. After 1878, when George Holt and his party pioneered the route over the mountain passes from the Alaska Panhandle for prospectors, the number of miners in the district began to increase steadily. Many of the new arrivals would work only through the summer then leave permanently or winter outside the district, sometimes traveling back over the mountains, or commonly, continuing downriver to St. Michael, Alaska. Smaller numbers stayed through the winter, but with each passing season, the size of the wintering population, like the size of the summer immigration, tended to grow. Nonetheless, the population of miners in the region during this early period remained small by comparison with the years of the Klondike rush; Goodrich, for example, estimates that fifty miners were wintering in the district in 1882, the number increasing in succeeding years to 200 in 1886, 300 in 1890, and 1000 in 1894.[5]

Prior to 1885, the prospecting and mining activities in the region remained scattered and desultory, until strikes on the Stewart River and then in the Fortymile River district tended to concentrate activity. A trading post was established in 1886 at the mouth of the Stewart, but by summer 1887, although the post was retained, much of the clientele had abandoned the Stewart for Fortymile. Another post was constructed here to accommodate the new center of mining activity, and around this post a town quickly developed. In 1894, the development of the Birch Creek district in Alaska led to the creation of another new town, Circle City, which quickly rivaled Fortymile in both its size and in the variety of its accoutrements. But the population of the district was growing sufficiently so that the growth of Circle City by no means led to the disappearance of Fortymile. Both continued as lively centers of activity until the discovery on Rabbit (later named Bonanza) Creek in August 1896 which initiated the rush to the Klondike.

Throughout the period from the 1870s to 1894, the Yukon district remained without any official agents of Canadian government control. In the interest of not driving a population of largely American miners across the 141st parallel to Alaska (and thus impairing the development of the region) Ottawa adopted a deliberate policy of laissez-faire. By 1894, however, concern for Canadian sovereignty in the area began to be felt in Ottawa, and at that point the North West Mounted Police were sent to establish government control in the district.

Through most of the twenty year period preceding the arrival of the NWMP, the miners remained highly mobile, following a recurrent seasonal pattern of concentration and dispersal, accompanied by a continual reshuffling of group affiliations. The seasonal and transient nature of the mining and prospecting activities during this period and the resulting patterns of population movement are revealed both in the accounts of a variety of the early observers and chroniclers of the mining history of the Yukon,[6] and in the personal accounts of several early prospectors, chronicling their own travels and experiences in the district in the years before the Klondike rush.[7] The patterns of mobility which characterized the miners' society during this period were significantly influenced by the nature of the prospecting and mining enterprise on the one hand, and by the requirements for survival in the Yukon environment on the other. But recurrent movement, concentration and dispersal also provided readily seized opportunities for the deliberate shifting of social alignments.

Something of the flavour of the miners' mobility and its impact on social relationships over time can be gathered from a summary of Chris Sonnikson's activities in the Yukon in the years 1886 and 1887.[8] Sonnikson crossed the mountains with his partners Charley Braises and Old Solomon in late March 1886. By late May or early June, they had moved on through the lakes to the upper Yukon where they had built a boat to take them on down the river to the Stewart. As they began the trip, however, they changed plans and decided to stop to prospect and work the bars on the upper Yukon. Having made this decision, they joined forces with another party of five who had independently decided on the same course of action. Both parties had in turn been swayed from their original plan to go to the Stewart by observing that Frank Densmore, a veteran prospector in the district, had stopped with his party to prospect the upper river.

The eight man group thus formed detailed some members to prospect while others worked the most promising bars; watches were also detailed to keep an eye on the Densmore party's activities. By 18 June, the water had risen so high that the bars where members of the group had been finding good pay could no longer be worked. Sonnikson and Braises decided at that point to prospect the Salmon River, where the water had already fallen. Sonnikson's other partner, Old Solomon, did not want to go and drew out to remain with the others on the upper Yukon, waiting for the river to fall there. After prospecting up the Salmon, Sonnikson and Braises also separated temporarily; Sonnikson joined with a man from another party they had encountered and the two of them went on to prospect the Hootilinqua, while Braises returned to the Yukon, where Sonnikson later met and rejoined him. Sonnikon and Braises then headed back to the bar they had abandoned when the water rose on the Yukon, but when they reached their former site, they discovered that the rest of the group they had been working with had restaked the bar for themselves as soon as the water had fallen and it had become workable.

Sonnikson and Braises moved on to find another bar, but their partnership did not endure long. Braises decided to go out to Juneau for the winter, so he sold his share in the new bar to Sonnikson and joined the Densmore party, traveling out with them in the later part of September.

Sonnikson then began building a boat to take him down to the post on the Stewart to winter, but he was shortly joined on his bar by two others to whom he sold ground for a few dollars. One of these men planned to winter at the Stewart; the other, a man by the name of Doty, planned to go out later on the ice to winter at Juneau. Doty helped Sonnikson with his boat, and in the course of their conversation convinced him to go out to Juneau. They quit working in November and began waiting for the river to freeze. The freeze was late in coming, so with the river still open in early December they began moving out. Sonnikson, however, found Doty's rate of travel impossibly slow and estimated they would never make it out with their available food, so he decided to return to the bar and live throughout the winter on flour which had been cached there. Doty was afraid to make the attempt to get out alone, so he returned with Sonnikson. They were back at the bar, with winter now fully set in, by 23 December. They found at least five others wintering in the same vicinity. The winter was a hard one; supplies ran short, game at times proved terribly scarce, and several men showed signs of scurvy.

In May 1887, the ice broke and the summer influx of men from Juneau began to arrive, bringing supplies. Sonnikson had begun working his bar in April, but following the breakup he sold it and started downriver with the incoming crowd from Juneau, now all bound for the Fortymile River. He formed a partnership with one of his wintering companions who also wanted to prospect the Fortymile district, a man named Davis, and by the end of May they had reached the site of the new community of Fortymile and were moving up the river. Encounters with other prospecting parties were frequent, word of prospects was freely passed around and some small stampedes occurred, but by July Sonnikson and Davis had not settled on any one spot to work. They were running short of supplies, so they returned to Fortymile to meet the steamer *New Racket* which was due in with supplies for the post.

After the steamer arrived two weeks later, Sonnikson again changed partners. He had hatched a plan to avoid those areas where gold had already been found and concentrate instead on prospecting a virgin territory; by now he had concluded that there was gold on all the rivers and the best way to make a fortune was to find it and clean it up before anyone else heard about it. Davis was apparently less than enthusiastic about this idea, but Sonnikson managed to convince a man by the name of Berndt to go along with him; they formed a partnership and headed on down the Yukon below Fortymile, prospecting the tributaries along the way. The prospecting appears to have brought only indifferent success, and after they had reached the Seventymile River, they met and briefly teamed up with Frank Densmore and J. Bender. After the four of them had worked an apparently good prospect which had quickly played out, Densmore and Bender decided to continue on down the river where they intended to winter.

Sonnikson and Berndt, however, decided to return to Fortymile, secure a full year's outfit, and come prospecting downriver once again, stopping to winter wherever they happened to be when freezeup caught them. They began moving downriver again about the first of September and reached the deserted site of Fort Yukon after about a week. Continuing to prospect on down the Yukon, with trips up various tributaries, the pair finally stopped to winter near the mouth of Beaver River at the end of September. Through the winter some company was provided by a neighbouring camp of Indians, but hunting was poor and at times the Indians as well as Sonnikson and Berndt experienced acute shortages of meat.

In June, with the river open again, Sonnikson and Berndt remained to prospect in the Beaver River vicinity. They encountered traveling parties on the river and also the steamboat coming upriver with supplies; from these contacts they learned that 140 men had wintered at Fortymile, where thirty-seven had suffered from acute scurvy or other sickness and three had died.

Two of the steamboat passengers decided to get off to prospect and joined Sonnikson and Berndt in a trip up the Beaver beginning June 10. By the 4th of July they were back at the mouth of the river and encountered the vanguard of a small rush to the Beaver from Fortymile. The steamboat captain had triggered the rush with his report that one of the passengers had left the boat so excitedly after talking to Berndt and Sonnikson that he had forgotten his purse.

The prospecting in the area had, in fact, proved disappointing, and Sonnikson at this point became disgusted with hearing Berndt complain that it "was all work for nothing." He went with Berndt to put him aboard the steamer when it returned on its way out, and here they parted company. Sonnikson then joined forces with two men who had arrived at the head of the rush to the Beaver from Fortymile, and the three continued to prospect together on down the Yukon.

Sonnikson's account, like those of the other prospectors whose travels during this period are recorded,[9] reveals clearly the varying and transient nature of local groups. From the standpoint of the individual prospector, his accessible "personal community"[10]—the circle of others whom he could rely on at any point for support—was constantly in flux. Both its size, and the particular personnel it embraced were highly unstable and the social exchanges and forms of mutual support which transpired within it were a matter of ad hoc temporizing agreements to collaborate.

The fluidity of local group composition which is revealed in these accounts was linked to a seasonal pattern of summer population dispersal in small, unstable and highly mobile groups and winter concentration in larger, sedentary and more stable aggregates, typically centered at the trading posts. This seasonal pattern, in turn, was rooted in the exigencies of productive work and survival as dictated by the miner's technology and the Yukon environment.

The summer season was the time when all of the prospecting and, before 1888, virtually all of the significant mining was done. This was the time when men could—and did—move easily through the territory, following their own hunches, following or avoiding other miners, combining their fortunes in partnerships with one or a few others, and upon occasion joining then separating from other groups in the course of their travels. How long a man stayed in any one place depended on what he found, and if he discovered ground that proved to pay well; it depended on how long the paydirt lasted. In any case, there were few men who could not be tempted by rumors of richer ground somewhere else to abandon their current diggings in the hope of finding more lucrative ones.

Between the time of break-up and freeze-up on the rivers, two favoured routes provided access into and out of the mining district. One was by way of the Yukon from its mouth; steamboats could move unimpeded from the Alaskan port of St. Michael all the way to the supply centres in the mining districts. Passengers, as well as supplies, came in during the summer by this route—if not by steamboat, then by raft or homemade boat. Men taking this route drifted downstream to St. Michael (and passage south) or to other favoured wintering spots in Alaskan territory along the way.

The second route was over the mountain passes from the Alaska Panhandle. Chilkat Indians who at one time had jealously guarded access to the interior by this route had become willing packers by the late 1880s. Once over the mountains, newcomers (the majority of them entered the territory by this route) typically encamped to cut and saw lumber at the lakes providing access to the upper Yukon, building boats or rafts which took them to their destination in the mining district. This same route, followed by poling or tracking upriver, could be taken out of the territory by the end of the summer season.

Within the district, men moved throughout the summer by rafting and boating up and down the Yukon itself, and along its tributaries and the branches of its tributaries. Along the smaller creeks, the prospectors proceeded to the headwaters and back on foot, occasionally moving across the divides separating the headwaters of streams in order to prospect up one and down another.

During this summer season, access to supplies was not likely to be a serious worry. Once the rivers were clear, men were soon appearing from outside packing new outfits, sufficient to sustain themselves and also providing a temporary source of supply for those already in the country who might have run short by the end of the winter. And once the steamers arrived, usually in July, the posts (at least for the time being) were well stocked. With the relatively easy travel which this time of year afforded, getting to a post with supplies, or even outside, was always a ready possibility.

With the freeze-up on the rivers and the arrival of winter, travel was a different matter. On the Yukon itself, wide enough for the wind to keep the ice blown clear of deep snow, sledding could proceed without inordinate difficulty, but remained hard work. Moving a full outfit (900 pounds) by sled would typically require "triple-tripping," i.e. taking three sled loads over any given distance; five times the distance finally covered was actually traveled in this process. This was no mean effort, even on clear ice, inasmuch as the sleds were manhauled in these early years when dogs and dog traction were a rare commodity in the mining district. A favourable wind, permitting the use of a sail, might upon occasion be employed to advantage to reduce the effort involved in this kind of travel. On other creeks and rivers, with narrower valleys, conditions for sledding in the winter were likely to be much worse. Here, drifts as deep as five to ten feet could be anticipated as a regular obstacle to travel.[11]

Movement during the winter, even under the best of traveling conditions, was also a risky business. Lack of shelter, fatigue, and constant exposure on the trail to deep and penetrating cold could combine to make an extended trip, remote from help and additional supplies, a foolhardy venture. For this reason, men in the interior rarely attempted to travel out of the district after freeze-up.[12]

The assurance of sufficient supplies of imported foodstuffs was affected by seasonal conditions and access to these supplies was a matter which weighed heavily on miners' decisions about their movements. Few if any of the miners were willing voluntarily to take their chances at living wholly off the country.[13] Their reluctance to do so was probably well advised; certainly, most of these men (many of them new to the territory) did not have the skills to match the Indians in their ability to live off the land. Even the Indians could become hard pressed for food during the winter and when they were sometimes observed in what looked like serious straits the lesson was not lost on the miners.[14]

In part, however, the miners' dependence on outside supplies was a matter of taste. Ogilvie, for example, reports that Arthur Harper, one of the first to begin prospecting and trading in the district, told him prospecting could be cut short when "shortness of supplies prevented them thinking of aught else than getting to some place where they could renew their stores" even though "meat they could get in abundance, but a straight meat diet is very trying except for a short period."[15] Notwithstanding Harper's feelings about the abundance of meat, a major consideration for others was the uncertainty of game, an uncertainty which could become all too apparent during the winter when supplies of imported food might run low.[16]

Against lean periods in the availability of local game, the Indians managed to survive by resorting to caches of fish, located at strategic points along the river to provide for such emergencies.[17] The miners, of course, did not devote their summer hours to accumulating supplies of fish. They sought their security instead in the size of their "outfits" of imported foodstuffs or in easy access to locations where such supplies would be readily available.

Winter weather, with its attendant difficulties and risks, induced large numbers of men to spend this season outside the mining district. Some, of course, departed more or less permanently for the "outside"; others found what they regarded as sufficiently congenial wintering sites at towns in the Alaska Panhandle, or at the site of posts on down the Yukon in Alaska.[18] For those who did remain in the mining district, company and the enhanced security of a larger pool of available supplies led them to cluster in the vicinity of the trading posts.[19] The posts were not, however, the exclusive choice as wintering sites; upon occasion groups might form elsewhere on the river or partners might winter alone.[20] But even when partners wintered apart from any larger concentrations of men, they were often within reach of one of the winter trading settlements, where they made periodic visits for supplies or company. And certainly the arrangement which attracted the large majority of miners who had wintered in the mining districts in the period before 1894 was to settle in with a large group at the site of a supply post.

During the years from the opening of the district to 1894, the techniques employed by the miners in their mining operations did not remain static, and the change which occurred here began to affect the mobility of at least some of the population. Prior to the winter of 1887–1888, the mining being done in the district was limited to working the bars and banks of streams, mostly as what was termed "skim diggings." This involved working on the two to four feet of surface gravel on river bars and along the banks of creeks; below this depth water was encountered which "prevented profitable work."[21] The discovery of "coarse" gold in the Fortymile region, however, stimulated interest in the kind of bedrock mining common to the more southerly placer fields. The Yukon miners assumed that there, as elsewhere, the best pay could be found at the lowest depths, in the gravels lying immediately above bed-rock. But the presence of permafrost posed the problem of how to dig through twenty to forty feet of frozen ground to reach and follow a pay streak.[22]

William Ogilvie, the Dominion Land Surveyor wintering in the vicinity of Fortymile in the 1887–1888 season, suggested a technique he had earlier seen used in the streets of Ottawa to reach defective gas and water pipes during the winter months: building fires on top of the frozen ground, then removing the thawed layer of dirt, rebuilding the fire to thaw the next layer, then removing it, and so on.[23] This technique of burning down was little more than an extension of one already used by miners in the district who were accustomed to burning on bar gravels to loosen frozen dirt uncovered at times of exceptionally low water during the winter season.

The new technique was adopted, and permitted winter mining.[24] A hole would be burned to bed-rock, and then, using the same method, the pay streak could be followed under the frozen ground. The gravels extracted in this way were simply piled as they were taken out during the winter season, then, with the spring thaw, the "clean-up" would follow as the thawed gravels were sluiced to extract the gold.

This new technique, applied to the richer "coarse" gold gravels of creeks in the Fortymile district, made for more profitable and also more sedentary mining operations. Now it was possible to find profit in staying in one place for an extended period of time and it was possible as well to be fully engaged in mining activity throughout the year. In time, this new style of mining promoted a comparatively sedentary existence for at least some miners who had located sufficiently lucrative gravels for themselves. By 1895, for example, Ogilvie could report that the new technique "keeps scores of (miners) on their claims all winter."[25] Similarly, in 1896, Josiah Spurr observed many small camps, far removed from the post town at the mouth of the Fortymile, where small groups of miners were settled in, working claims steadily year round and only occasionally traveling out for supplies or a break in their work routine.[26]

But the seasonal pattern associated with "skim diggings" was by no means entirely nor quickly eliminated after the discoveries at Fortymile and the development of the new mining techniques. For the majority of men working in the district, prospecting continued to absorb as much if not more of their time than mining, and continued to demand high mobility. And factors other than winter working conditions were involved, too, in sustaining the usual winter exodus. Before 1890, regardless of what might appear to be the advantages of working a claim year round, supplies sufficient to sustain only about one-third of the summer population through the ensuing winter were all that could be transported into the post at Fortymile.[27] Even after 1890, when larger steamboats removed this limit to the number of miners who could winter in the district, the familiar peripatetic pattern continued for most men. These were men either without established claims on profitable ground, or those who were motivated to avoid settling on any one spot in the continuing hope of uncovering ground that was richer. Writing as late as 1897 in a report on his Yukon fieldwork during the summer of 1896, H.B. Goodrich could still assert:

> Of those who stay from one year to the next it is nearly impossible to make an estimate, on account of their wandering habits, which lead them sometimes hundreds of miles from the mining camps....It is impossible, therefore, to make anything more than a rough estimate of the miners who are comparatively fixed, and it should be borne in mind that even in a few days the distribution may be entirely changed.[28]

There can be little doubt, then, that throughout the period from the opening of the district to 1894, the lack of stable local group composition, set within a pattern of seasonal mobility and population concentration and dispersion, remained a hallmark of the miners' society.

Organization, Flux and Authority

In hunter-gatherer societies, patterns of population movement and changing group composition have significant functions which go beyond necessary adjustments to seasonally varying ecological conditions. Fluctuating group size and composition has been viewed as "the very mechanism that gives these societies their cohesion";[29] it provides for the management of conflict in a way which sustains coordinated, cooperative group activity in the absence of formal authority. Turnbull[30] first called attention to this function among the Mbuti and Ik, but the role of seasonal concentration, dispersal, and shifts in the membership of local groups as a form of conflict management is now widely acknowledged as a typical feature of nomadic hunting societies.[31]

Among hunter-gatherers, this function is evident in both the occasions of group fission and fusion and in the particular readjustments of personnel that result: as Turnbull puts it, "the process of fission and fusion follows lines of dissent rather than those of descent."[32] When conflict emerges, fluctuating group composition permits contending parties to separate and enables regrouping to occur which will preserve cooperative relationships and the potential for smoothly running collective activity among the members of the reconstituted group. When the opportunity to employ fluctuating group composition in this manner is reduced, then alternative forms of conflict management must appear, if group activity is to be maintained. This is likely to take the form of the emergence of more formalized and coercive authorities to whom disputes can be appealed and who come increasingly to exercise rights of command over group members.[33]

Among the Yukon miners, the evident patterns of movement and transient association worked in a similar fashion. Sonnikson's account,[34] summarized earlier, reveals how groups traveling and working together could vary substantially in size, from a single pair of partners to a larger traveling or working party, or a much larger group sharing winter quarters at a particular location. Such associations might last anywhere from a matter of hours to months. At the root of these constantly shifting affiliations there was the inviolable autonomy which every miner retained with regard to his own movements and prospecting activities. The details of the creation and termination of each partnership recounted by Sonnikson make this apparent. Whenever individuals disagreed on plans, there was no argument, they simply parted company and, by the same token, where men found agreement, they allied with one another as partners for however long their own preferences coincided.[35]

Larger groups, whether they were traveling, working, or wintering together, were also created and endured only so long as the separate plans of those involved coincided and made the association expedient.[36] Partners, of course, recognized an obligation to share work, the products of their labour and (ideally) to be continually responsive to one another's needs for safety and well-being. But the more ad hoc forms of collaboration among men who did not count themselves as partners were equally varied, ranging all the way from the provision of food when supplies were short, to assistance in travel or working a bar, to mutual entertainment. None of these collaborative and supportive arrangements, however, were guaranteed; no one apparently felt that they had any clear right to demand or expect such cooperation. When it came, it had to be by mutual agreement at the time. In fact, expectations could run quite counter to the likelihood of such support. Sonnikson's account[37] alludes more than once to suspicions that the movements of another party were a "blind" (unfounded suspicions, it turned out, in the incidents he recounts) designed to throw others off the track of a particularly promising discovery.

But the important fact remains that at any point where parties (whether partners or not) failed to agree on a course of action, no issue was really joined; the simple expedient was for those in disagreement to part company and regroup with those who shared compatible purposes and views. As a result, even in the absence of formalized relations of command and obedience which could require that group members suspend compliance with their own purposes and judgments, dissent could hardly overwhelm and negate the capacity for group action. Where significant divisions of opinion occurred, groups simply divided, to be re-formed along lines of essential consensus.

No one in the Yukon miners' society exercised any formal authority to coordinate and control group activities. Nevertheless, leaders who often exercised substantial amounts of informal influence did emerge to play a vital role in the society's organization. These informal leaders—exercising only consensual authority over their followers—were able to organize collective activity on a major scale. The role of such men as a source of informal authority and as a focus for community organization in the miners' society is illustrated by the events surrounding the rush to Fortymile from the Stewart River in March 1887.

Coarse gold was discovered in the Fortymile district in the summer of 1886. The men responsible for the discovery had been prospecting on the Stewart earlier in the summer, and in keeping with "the code of the country" they returned to Stewart post in October 1886 to report their discovery there.[38] A modest stampede to the Fortymile followed but did not leave the Stewart completely abandoned.[39] Miners from upriver continued to arrive at the Stewart post and as many as seventy to eighty remained there through the winter.[40]

According to George Snow's account of the events of the following spring, in March 1887, a letter arrived at the Stewart which provided the catalyst for the wholesale abandonment of the Stewart in favour of the Fortymile.[41] The letter was from Leroy McQuesten, the most respected of the early traders in the area, to Al Mayo, one of McQuesten's longtime associates in the trading business who was managing the Stewart post at the time. It informed Mayo of the quality of the Fortymile discovery, pointed out there was plenty of ground for everyone, and instructed Mayo to tell the "boys" on the Stewart to get down to Fortymile before the "Cheechakos" (new prospectors in the district, whose numbers were increasing every summer) began to arrive. McQuesten also advised that if anyone did not want to make the trip to Fortymile, they should be encouraged to explore the Stewart to its head, where McQuesten believed there was a strong possibility of finding coarse gold. The letter went on to instruct Mayo to announce that McQuesten and Mayo would see to it that travelers up the Stewart were properly outfitted, and if they came back with nothing they would be provided with a full outfit for the next year. If only two men made the trip, McQuesten said, he would also try to have a piece of ground "laid over" for them at Fortymile, in the event they struck nothing on the Stewart.

The courier bringing the letter had reached the Stewart in the midst of a celebration following a hockey game, and Mayo immediately read it to the assembled community. He then went on to suggest that probably not everybody was going to stampede to the Fortymile, since a number of men had good ground on the Stewart. Accordingly, and seemingly without any question that McQuesten's suggestion would be followed, he proposed that the men going back up the Stewart to their present diggings ought to help the volunteers going to the headwaters to move their outfit as far as the river falls, some 160 miles upstream. Mayo then invited the gathering to break up, think over the situation, pack for travel the following day, and reassemble in the evening at his establishment where he intended to give everyone a final "blow-out."

Traveling up the narrow, snow clogged valley of the Stewart without dogs and packing a complete outfit would be no easy task, but the next evening, when the miners gathered at Mayo's cabin, one pair of partners volunteered to prospect the headwaters as McQuesten had suggested. Others not joining the Fortymile rush agreed to assist them in getting their outfit up as far as the falls. One of the miners going to Fortymile protested to the gathering that the men joining the rush should contribute something to the outfit of the volunteers rather than let Mayo provide it all. Mayo responded that they would need all their grub at Fortymile and could do their bit by assuring that the recorder there would lay over ground for the pair exploring the Stewart.

The following morning, the men left for Fortymile and completed the trip in four days; travel was much easier on the Yukon than on the Stewart, with much of the broad expanse of the former cleared of snow by the wind. At Fortymile, where over 100 men were now gathered, a meeting was held on 28 March at McQuesten's cabin where Fred Harte, another of the early traders and prospectors in the district, was elected recorder for the new district and the size of claims was set.

As the organization of the rush to Fortymile shows, informal "suggestions" proposed by a man like McQuesten or Mayo were not likely to be ignored. In any collective deliberation, their words, proposals, and judgments could be expected to carry more weight than those of most other men. The response of the Stewart camp to McQuesten's letter concerning the Fortymile discovery involved the forging of public policy and a decision as to collective and coordinated courses of action to be taken by the group. In all of this, the key role of informal leaders, serving to crystallize and coordinate a community response, is evident.

The men who functioned as leaders of this sort had come into the Yukon early and had combined their own prospecting activities with the work of establishing and managing the trading posts. In their role as traders, they were of course the source which prospectors in the district often depended upon for supplies which were essential for their subsistence and their prospecting activities. The traders readily extended credit and they could be counted on to "grubstake,"a miner with no capital of his own in his prospecting ventures. From time to time, like no one else, they were in a position to sponsor personally the development of a new area by offering to outfit men who would be willing to prospect it.

But men like McQuesten and Mayo not only occupied a key position with respect to the dispensation of material goods; they were also the preeminent purveyors of essential knowledge to the miners in the district. The peripatetic miners, who were often working in some isolation and many of whom were comparatively recent arrivals in the district, accorded special respect to the knowledgeability of these men, and stood ready to follow their suggestions. The traders were known to have been among the first whites to enter the district, had themselves traveled (and prospected) widely through the area, had accumulated the longest terms of residence there, and perhaps most importantly, they served—given the miner's patterns of movement—as a focus for the reception and dissemination of information concerning the activities and discoveries of the myriad small prospecting parties working in the district. The mobility and transiency of the rest of the population thus served to foster the power of a few men as the consensual leaders of the mining community, but the prominence in forging public policy which they achieved was not dysfunctional. The informal allocation of influence in this nineteenth century Yukon setting worked toward the maintenance of a functional congruence between decision making power and information control.[42]

The only formal office of government which existed in the district was the position of recorder; one man was typically appointed to this position on each creek or gulch by popular vote. The recorder held no executive powers, but was responsible for recording the names of claimants and the location of their claims, and also for recording claim sales.[43] Beyond the office of the recorder, the only sort of institutionalized authority to be found in the mining district was that exercised by the "miners' meeting," a gathering of all men who chose to attend when someone called an assembly to discuss a particular issue or dispute or to formulate any rules which were going to be recognized in a particular camp.[44] A chairman was elected each time a meeting was called, opposing sides were allowed to present their case, and ultimately the issue was decided by a simple majority vote of those present. The jurisdiction of the meetings was potentially wide ranging: they could be called to consider any matter which any member of the community deemed appropriate. Adjudication of what could be considered civil as well as criminal cases, setting of mining regulations, or any other rules which might be established for a particular area, all fell within their purview. The decisions of the meetings carried the sanction of community opinion, and a committee was appointed to see that these decisions were executed if this was deemed necessary.

Through the institution of the miners' meeting, the miners in any particular locale of course retained their own autonomy, setting their own standards for their collective life and making their own judgments. Since the decisions of the meetings were not necessarily binding outside the particular locale and group where they were promulgated, those who could not agree or accept them had the option of removing themselves from the local group. To be effective, the decisions of the meetings had either to reflect or generate a significant degree of local consensus, and mobility still remained the ultimate solution to the serious failure of consensus or persisting threats of serious conflict.

In cases where the miners' meeting acted to deal with a miner whose behaviour had come to be viewed as criminal, for example, it relied primarily on banishment as a form of punishment. But banishment in one place did not necessarily seal a man's fate elsewhere. In the winter season of 1886–1887, Frank Leslie and another man known as Missouri Frank were both banished from the vicinity of the Stewart River, Missouri Frank for the theft of some butter from the Stewart post after he had already received his winter's allotment, and Frank Leslie for attempting to murder his four partners.[45] In the spring of 1887, Missouri Frank showed up at the camp where Chris Sonnikson and a number of other miners had wintered on the upper Yukon. He was so worn out that he fainted when he reached the camp but he made no attempt to cover up what had happened to him, relating the whole story of his theft and banishment. Impressed by his honesty and his difficult condition, the men at the camp gave him flour and let him stay for a time. He joined with Sonnikson, helping him to work a bar he had staked. In relating his story of the incidents of the preceding winter on the Stewart, Frank also informed Sonnikson and the others about the banishment of Frank Leslie.[46]

About the 1st of April, some two weeks later, a man from the Stewart arrived bringing word that the Indians had gone on the warpath and were coming only a few days behind him; he claimed to have been sent upriver to warn the incoming men of the danger. Pale, haggard, and emaciated, he looked as though he had just managed to escape the kind of debacle at the Stewart which he described. The man was Frank Leslie. Sonnikson and some others, taking note of some inconsistencies in Leslie's story, were inclined to accept Missouri Frank's version of Leslie's identity and events on the Stewart. Others, however, were more ready to believe Leslie's account; the result was an Indian scare which prompted some men to flee in haste.[47] Over a month later, Leslie was still working his way out and spreading his Indian story as he encountered parties on the way in. On May 24, William Ogilvie, making his first trip into the district as Dominion Land Surveyor, encountered Leslie at Haines Mission.[48] Leslie was telling the same story and needless to say caused Ogilvie "much apprehensive anxiety for many miles of my journey downriver."[49] Peter Roblin also met him on June 10 and was told about the Indian killings downriver and that Leslie was running for his life. The story, according to Roblin, caused his party considerable anxiety, and was cause for fearfully dodging Indian camps, and fleeing on at the sight of Indians until the party reached the Stewart and the truth became known.[50]

Although the miners' meeting did involve some of the trappings of a formalized mechanism of local government, it bestowed only transient and limited formal authority on any individual or select sub-group. One could easily speculate that informal leaders like McQuesten or Mayo could carry an assembly with their views, but if they did, their influence was felt through a process which appeared scrupulously to avoid concentrating authority in any formal sense in any offices or persons. Although it might be really their voice, it appeared to be the authoritative voice of the formally constituted community in council which stood behind any decisions taken through the meetings.

In all phases of life in the early Yukon, then, organized, collective social activity was much in evidence. For all its lack of formal organization and authority, Yukon society was far from totally individualistic and anarchical: organized group life was essential to all phases of existence here. Concerted action was sustained through patterns of mobility and flexible group composition which obviated the problem of dissent and fostered the power of the traders as informal community leaders.

But the circumstances of life and labour which sustained the flexibility of association among the early miners did not persist indefinitely. As noted earlier, the phase of the Yukon gold industry which has been described here, characterized by its emphasis on prospecting, "skim diggings," and only a very transitory committment of effort to any particular location, ultimately gave rise to increased sedentarization of the working miners with the development of bed-rock mining in the richer gravels. By the later 1890s, established claimholders and other propertied members of the community came to be differentiated from a growing population of men without claims of their own, men who drifted through the territory prospecting and frequenting the growing post towns or hiring on as labour for settled claim owners.

Under these circumstances, there was no system of regular population movement capable of managing conflict so as to sustain normative consensus. This situation contributed to the abandonment of the miners' meeting and the acceptance of the Mounted Police as the primary source of public authority in the territory after 1894. In the increasingly differentiated Yukon community, divided by conflicting interest and values which could no longer be adjusted by mobility,[51] consistency and clarity in the affirmation and sanctioning of community norms came to be served by the concentration of public sanctioning power in the hands of a specialized body identified with one particular set of values and interests.[52] Following the Klondike rush, the Yukon gold industry was further transformed with the development of hydraulic and dredging operations which required massive capital investment and the consolidation of holdings; at this point mining operations in the district assumed the character of highly formalized large scale, bureaucratic enterprises.[53] By this time, forms of social organization, law, and authority in the Yukon were virtually indistinguishable from those prevailing "outside" in the rest of Canada and the United States.

The Yukon case would certainly make it appear that hunter-gatherer societies are not alone in linking social "flux," i.e., "constant changeover of personnel between local groups"[54] with an egalitarian system of largely consensual, informal authority. As in these societies, flux in the miners' society reduced the need for formal, coercive authority with the right to prescribe behaviour and adjudicate conflict. And, much as Lee[55] observed in the case of the !Kung Bushmen, once increasing sedentarization appeared among the miners, more structured forms of formal authority began to find acceptance and the prevailing mode of conflict management significantly changed.

A diversity of motives and understandings and the need for "organization of diversity" has come to be recognized as characteristic of all societies.[56] Stanley Milgram, in his landmark study of obedience to authority,[57] shares with others the opinion that the limitation of individual discretion, particularly through the elaboration of relationships of formal authority, is essential to overcome the problems posed by such variability of individual purposes and judgments in the interests of concerted action.[58] When relationships of authority are activated, with their attendant rights of command and duties of obedience, subordinates are constrained to suppress their autonomous judgments and interests to act instead simply as "agents" of the authority in question.[59] Unity of purpose and action is thereby achieved within the group.

But the Yukon miners, like the small-scale societies of hunter-gatherers so familiar to ethnology, serve as a reminder that the elaboration of formal authority is not the only solution. In relatively mobile, undifferentiated, small scale societies—even where the institutions of private property and a market economy prevail—alternative means of coping with variability are available and social "flux" may figure prominently here.

Notes

1.   Colin Turnbull, "The Importance of Flux in Two Hunting Societies," in *Man the Hunter*, ed. R.B. Lee and Irven DeVore (Chicago: Aldine, 1968), 132–37; Joel Savishinsky, "Mobility as an Aspect of Stress in an Arctic Community," *American Anthropologist* 73 (1971), 604–18; Richard Lee, "The Intensification of Social Life Among the !Kung Bushmen," in *Population Growth: Anthropological Implications*, ed. Brian Spooner (Cambridge: MIT Press, 1972), 343–48; Richard Lee, *The !Kung San: Men, Women, and Work in a Foraging Society* (Cambridge: Cambridge University Press, 1979), 33–400.

2.   Turnbull, "The Importance of Flux," 132.

3.   Stanley Milgram, *Obedience to Authority* (New York: Harper and Row, 1974), 123–34; Robert Edgerton, *Deviance: A Cross Cultural Perspective* (Menlo Park, CA: Cummings Publishing Co., 1976), 102–10.

4.   Allen Wright, *Prelude to Bonanza: The Discovery and Exploration of the Yukon* (Sidney, BC: Gray's Publishing Ltd., 1976), 123–27.

5.   Harold Goodrich, "History and Conditions of the Yukon Gold District to 1897," in *Geology of the Yukon Gold District Alaska*, ed. Josiah Edward Spur (Washington: Government Printing Office, 1897), 132.

6. George Dawson, *Report on an Exploration in the Yukon District, NWT and Adjacent Portions of British Columbia*, Annual Report, Geological Survey of Canada, n.s. 3, pt.1 (Montreal, 1889), 180B–183B; R.G. McConnell, *Report on an Exploration in the Yukon and McKenzie Basins, NWT*, Annual Report, Geological and Natural History Survey of Canada, n.s. 4 (Montreal, 1891), 139D–140D; Charles Constantine, Report of Inspector Constantine, October 1894, in *Report of the Commissioner of the North-West Mounted Police Force, 1894* (Ottawa: The Queen's Printer, 1895); Goodrich, "History and Conditions of the Yukon Gold District," 108–19, 129; M.H.E. Hayne, *The Pioneers of the Klondike* (London: Sampson, Low, Marston, 1897), 89.

7. George Snow, comp. and ed., Snow Papers of the Yukon, 1896–1925, Baker Library, Dartmouth College, Hanover, New Haven, (microfilm). These are unpublished accounts of Chris Sonnikson, Peter Roblin, G.W. Carmack, Peter Nelson, John Burke, and John McCloud. The accounts are contained in the Snow Papers of the Yukon assembled by George Snow as a result of a resolution by the Yukon Order of Pioneers in 1896 which authorized him to prepare a history of the Yukon Valley and pledged the support of all members of the organization in carrying out the subject. Snow never completed his history, but the reminiscences, correspondence and manuscript material he had compiled before his death in 1925 were kept by his daughter, Mrs. Crystal Snow Jenne, and microfilmed at Baker Library, Dartmouth College, in 1964. Leroy McQuesten, *Recollections of Leroy N. McQuesten: Life in the Yukon, 1871–1885* (Dawson, 1952); Henry Davis, "Recollections," in *Sourdough Sagas*, ed. Hebert Heller (New York: World Publishing, 1967), 28–84; Frank Buteau, "My Experiences in the World," in *Sourdough Sagas*, ed. Herbert Heller (New York: World Publishing, 1967).

8. Sonnikson MS, Snow Papers of the Yukon.

9. Snow Papers of the Yukon; McQuesten, *Recollections*; Davis, "Recollections"; Buteau, "My Experiences in the World."

10. Jules Henry, "The Personal Community and Its Invariant Properties," *American Anthropologist* 60 (1958): 827–31.

11. Snow MS, Snow Papers of the Yukon.

12. Carmack MS, Snow Papers of the Yukon; Goodrich, "History and Conditions of the Yukon Gold District," 115–16.

13. Peter Nelson MS, and Carmack MS, Snow Papers of the Yukon; Constantine, Report of Inspector Constantine, 10 October 1894, 75.

14. Sonnikson MS, Snow Papers of the Yukon.

15. William Ogilvie, *Early Days on the Yukon* (New York: John Lane, 1913), 99–100.

16. Sonnikson MS, Snow Papers of the Yukon; William Ogilvie, Report of William Ogilvie, D.L.S., Annual Report of the Department of Interior for 1899, Part 8 (Ottawa: The Queen's Printer, 1889), 1–114.

17. Sonnikson MS, Snow Papers of the Yukon; Cornelius Osgood, *The Han Indians*, Yale University Publications in Anthropology, no.74 (New Haven: Yale University Press, 1971), 102, 106.

18. Carmack MS, Sonnikson MS, Snow Papers of the Yukon; Goodrich, "History and Conditions of the Yukon Gold District," 128; Wright, *Prelude to Bonanza*, 137–39.

19. Ogilvie, Report of William Ogilvie, 16; Constantine, Report of Inspector Constantine, 77, 81; Carmack MS, Snow Papers of the Yukon; McQuesten, *Recollections*, 2–3, 5, 7.

20. Sonnikson MS, Snow Papers of the Yukon; McQuesten, *Recollections*, 13.

21. Ogilvie, *Early Days on the Yukon*, 138.

22. Ogilvie, *Early Days on the Yukon*, 139–40.

23. Ogilvie, *Early Days on the Yukon*, 140. In his version of the introduction of this technique, Adney credits Fred Hutchinson with the first application of the innovation which led to its adoption by others; Tappan Adney, *The Klondike Stampede* (New York: Harper and Brothers, 1900), 241–42.

24. Adney, *The Klondike Stampede*, 241–43.

25. William Ogilvie, Extracts of Reports of William Ogilvie, D.L.S., Annual Report of the Department of the Interior for the Year 1896, pt. 2, no. 9 (Ottawa: The Queen's Printer, 1896), 40.

26. Josiah Spurr, *Through the Yukon Gold Diggings* (Boston: Eastern Publishing, 1900), 110–206.

27. Ogilvie, *Early Days on the Yukon*, 112.

28. Goodrich, "History and Conditions of the Yukon Gold District," 129.

29. Turnbull, "The Importance of Flux," 132.

30. Colin Turnbull, *Wayward Servants: The Two Worlds of the African Pygmies* (Garden City: Natural History Press, 1965); Turnbull, "The Importance of Flux."

31. Richard Lee and Irven DeVore, "Problems in the Study of Hunters and Gatherers," in *Man the Hunter*, ed. R. Lee and I. DeVore (Chicago: Aldine, 1968), 9; Savishinksky, "Mobility as an Aspect of Stress."

32. Turnbull, "The Importance of Flux," 137.

33. Lee, *The !Kung San*, 366–69.

34. Snow Papers of the Yukon.

35. Carmack MS, Nelson MS, Sonnikson, MS, Snow Papers of the Yukon; McQuesten, *Recollections*, 11–13; Davis, "Recollections," 44–67 passim; Buteau, "My Experiences in the World," 102.

36. Sonnikson MS, Snow Papers of the Yukon, McQuesten, *Recollections*; Davis, "Recollections;" Buteau, "My Experiences of the World."

37. Snow Papers of the Yukon.

38. Ogilvie, *Early Days on the Yukon*, 111.

39. Adney, *The Klondike Stampede*, 238; Wright, *Prelude to Bonanza*, 162.

40. Adney, *The Klondike Stampede*, 237.

41. Snow MS, Snow Papers of the Yukon.

42. John Roberts, "The Self Management of Cultures," in *Explorations in Cultural Anthropology*, ed. Ward Goodenough (n.p., 1964), 433–54.

43. Goodrich, "History and Conditions of the Yukon Gold District," 128.

44. The nature and functions of the miners' meetings are described in more detail in Thomas Stone, "The Mounties as Vigilantes: Perceptions of Community and the Transformation of Law in the Yukon, 1885–1897," *Law and Society Review* 14 (1979), 83–114.

45. Ogilvie, *Early Days on the Yukon*, 42–50, 267–70.

46. Sonnikson MS, Snow Papers of the Yukon.

47. Sonnikson MS, Snow Papers of the Yukon.

48. Ogilvie, *Early Days on the Yukon*, 37–39.

49. Ogilvie, *Early Days on the Yukon*, 50.

50. Roblin MS, Snow Papers of the Yukon.

51. Charles Brown, Report to Charles Constantine, 9 February 1985, MS Records of the Royal Canadian Mounted Police, RG18, 1344, file 190–1895, Public Archives of Canada (PAC), Ottawa; Hayne, *The Pioneers of the Klondike*, 122–24; Charles Constantine to Officer Commanding the NWMP, Regina, 13 July 1896, Constantine Papers, MG30/E55, 4, PAC.

52. Stone, "The Mounties as Vigilantes."

53. Lewis Green, *The Gold Hustlers* (Anchorage: Alaska Northwest Publishing

Co., 1977); David Morrison, *The Politics of the Yukon Territory, 1898–1909* (Toronto: University of Toronto Press, 1968).

54. Turnbull, "The Importance of Flux," 132.

55. Lee, "The Intensification of Social Life"; Lee, *The !Kung San*, 368–69.

56. Anthony Wallace, *Culture and Personality* (New York: Random House, 1970), 22–36; Edgerton, *Deviance*, 68–69; Edward Boldt, "On Aligning Actions in Simple Societies," *Canadian Review of Sociology and Anthropology* 16 (1979): 249–59.

57. Milgram, *Obedience to Authority*.

58. Milgram, *Obedience to Authority*, 123–34; Wlodzimierz Wesolowski, "Some Notes on the Functional Theory of Stratification," in *Class, Status and Power*, ed. R. Bendix and S.M. Lipset (New York: The Free Press, 1966), 68–69; Richard Hall, J. Eugene Haas, and Norman Johnson, "Organization, Size, Complexity, and Formalization," *American Sociological Review* 32 (1967): 911.

59. Milgram, *Obedience to Authority*, 123–34.

THE YUKON: NORTHERN DEVELOPMENT IN A CANADIAN-AMERICAN CONTEXT*

MORRIS ZASLOW

To most Canadians, mention of the Yukon Territory brings to mind the exciting story of the mad dash from the four corners of the earth to the small circle of ridges and ravines through which flowed creeks lined with gravel flecked with gold—the movement known for all time as the Klondike gold rush. An economic historian, H.A. Innis, observed that, "It is doubtful if, in rapidity, size and intensity, the Klondike gold rush has ever been equalled in the whole range of economic expansion,"[1] and a sociologist, S.D. Clark, has remarked that, "Within this four-year period [1898–1902] the development of the Yukon passed through the full cycle of social disorganization and reorganization; for study of these social processes, few social laboratories could be more revealing."[2] A student of gold rushes, W.P. Morell,[3] perceived in the gold mining camps of British Columbia and the Yukon an interesting contrast, in their methods of operation and their "styles" of activity, with other mining camps being developed in California and Alaska. He attributed this contrast to the differing political systems of British America and the United States, as did H.F. Angus, F.W. Howay, and W.N. Sage, the authors of that excellent study, *British Columbia and the United States.*

These judgments—selected from among many others—demonstrate a few of the differing vantage points from which the Klondike gold rush may be viewed and studied. The gold rush was a complex bundle of interrelated phenomena extending across the broad range of human behaviour. Because of its complexity, as well as because of the abruptness, scale, and dramatic intensity of its manifestations, the gold rush can be made to yield insights into problems that are characteristic of all the northern districts of Canada, and which, by marking them off from other, more settled portions of the country, give grounds for considering "the North" as a distinctive region of Canada.

* *Regionalism in the Canadian Community 1867–1967*, ed. Mason Wade (Toronto: University of Toronto Press, 1969), 180–97.

At the same time, because northern Canada is comprised of many districts that differ from one another in their geographical, historic, and sociological aspects, "the North" cannot be considered a true region if uniformity and homogeneity are regarded as essential qualities in the definition of a region. Thus at one and the same time, "the North" is—and is not—a true region of Canada. As for the phenomena exemplified by the Klondike gold rush, some are common to all parts of northern Canada, whereas others are peculiar to itself alone.

The Yukon Territory, one of Canada's most fascinating districts, still carries the marks of that cataclysmic event. Important as was the rise and fall of gold mining, it is not the sole, or even most important factor in the evolution of the Yukon Territory. This is to be found, more broadly, in the interaction between the settlers and the physical environment, as revealed in the social, cultural, administrative, and economic developments of the period.

The examination of the evolution of the Yukon Territory discloses the importance of one aspect of this interaction—that of the district government with the people and their environment. In the Yukon Territory we see the interaction between official Canadian policies and Canadian institutions and a community largely comprised of Americans and expressing the American frontier ideology. The outcomes—the imposition of a Canadian system of external controls upon the developing community, and the integration of the Yukon into the Canadian polity, economy, and society—are fascinating, little-understood sides of the region's history.

An important comparative aspect is seen in the history of the wider Yukon region of Canada and Alaska during this period. Canada and the United States followed widely contrasted approaches towards the settlement and development of their frontier territories that were reflected in the histories of their colonial dependencies along the Yukon River during this period. Those histories are a unique opportunity to view the two opposed experiments in frontier administration under almost ideal conditions. Most of the elements in both situations were the same—the time, the physical environment, the type of settler, and the settler's goals. The major variable, the contrasting effects of the colonial programmes of the controlling powers during the period of the Klondike gold rush, can readily be gauged. By examining this wider situation one may come to a better understanding of the salient features of Canada's programme of frontier control and development. From that, one may better approach the regional trait that is shared by all of Canada's northern territories—their colonial dependence upon Ottawa or the provincial capitals.

The Yukon region had been divided at the 141st meridian by the Anglo-Russian Treaty of 1825, but until 1895 almost identical conditions prevailed in the Alaskan and British-American sectors. Both were dominated by the river, the sole means of travel and communications; both were frequented by the same nomadic hunting and trapping Indians of the Loucheux, Tukudh, or Kutchin tribes, to which were added a few white settlers engaged in the fur trade or mission work. British interests controlled the region until 1869.

Entering the district from the east by way of the Mackenzie and Porcupine Rivers, the Hudson's Bay Company in 1847 established Fort Yukon at the junction of the Porcupine and Yukon Rivers. This post was almost a hundred miles inside Russian territory, although Company employees professed to believe they were still within the British boundary. Other trading posts had been established for a time along the upper Yukon River, really within British territory, but these were soon given up because of the hostility of the Indians and the difficulty of supplying them by way of the Liard River. Besides, the Company reached an agreement with the Russians that enabled it to dominate the trade of the upper Yukon from the coast. In the wake of the English traders, and each supporting the other, came Church of England missionaries who also made Fort Yukon their major westernmost base of operations.

The situation changed very quickly after the United States purchased Alaska in 1867. An official American party under Captain C.W. Raymond came up the river in 1869 and took possession of Fort Yukon, handing over the fur trade to Hutchinson, Kohl and Company, a San Francisco firm. The Hudson's Bay Company commenced a slow withdrawal up the Porcupine River, establishing three Ramparts Houses in succession, each a little further towards or inside British territory. However, after 1891 the trade of the Ramparts House-Lapierre House area also was attacked from the north by American whaling vessels based on Herschel Island. In 1893, during an economy drive to reduce expenses, the Hudson's Bay Company abandoned the entire operation west of the Mackenzie delta region. The Anglican missions also withdrew, retiring from Fort Yukon in 1879 and leaving the western territory to the rivalries of American Episcopalians, Presbyterians, and Roman Catholics.

After the British interests had been driven from Alaska they proved unable to halt the Americans from advancing into British territory. The fur trade in Alaska came under the control of the Alaska Commercial Company which imported goods cheaply from the Pacific coast of the United States by way of Bering Sea and the Yukon River. In Canadian territory a number of small traders established themselves along the upper Yukon and operated as clients of the Alaska Commercial Company. Other Americans began entering the territory after 1880, mainly from the south, over the mountain passes, as part of the wave of American gold seekers that had been swept into western America by the California gold rush. Drawn by rumours of gold, they moved from one likely location to another, sometimes in British territory, other times farther west in Alaska, the boundary being completely ignored. In the early 1890s another large American trading organization, the North American Transportation and Trading Company, entered the country. It was based at Dyea, at the head of Lynn Canal, the gateway to the interior, and operated its own vessels and outposts along the Canadian Yukon waterway. To all intents and purposes, the Canadian Yukon was a part of the American frontier, inhabited by American (or Americanized) miners and its trade monopolized by American mercantile interests. The sole British voice in the district was the Anglican missionary operation, headed by Bishop W.C. Bompas of Selkirk, who began organizing the diocese after 1891 from a base in the American mining camp of Fortymile, just inside the Canadian boundary.

The 141st meridian boundary held no administrative significance either; no effective system of government existed on either side of it. The interior of Alaska was in a state of anarchy, for nothing had been done to put the Organic Act of 1884 into effect in the interior. As for the Canadian portion of the Yukon, the first evidence of a government presence was the joint survey by G.M. Dawson and R.G. McConnell of the Geological Survey and William Ogilvie of the Department of the Interior in 1887–1888. Ogilvie's advice to the Dominion government was to leave well enough alone for the present but to keep a watchful eye on the district with a view to future action. He argued that the imposition of Canadian laws and taxes would put the district at a disadvantage as compared with Alaska and would militate against the development of its mineral resources. Besides, he added, the miners were Americans and used to American rules, which were more suited to local conditions than were those of Canada.

The American system—or lack of system—that prevailed in both sections of the Yukon seemed designed for just such a situation as existed there in the 1870s and 1880s. The district judge held courts only at Sitka and Wrangell; the commissioners were located at these and at two other coastal settlements, Juneau and Unalaska. There was no law (or taxes) in the Yukon country, and the principal legal provision drafted with the region expressly in mind, the prohibition of the importation of liquor, was a dead letter. Such neglect was quite logical in terms of American political philosophy enshrined in the Constitution of the United States. Governments were the agents rather than the masters of the people. The principle that governments should be instituted by the people on the spot in keeping with their own needs had been further enshrined in the mid-century ideal of "squatter sovereignty." The United States government saw no need for the precipitate or premature imposition from outside of government institutions or controls upon a new territory in the absence of some major reason necessitating its intervention.

To meet this absence of external authority at this stage of Alaskan development the frontiersmen, particularly the veteran free miners, had been evolving their own system of rules and regulations in the hundreds of mining camps that flourished briefly in the half century after the California gold rush. In each camp the miners elected their recorder, fixed the recording fee, decided on the mining regulations that would be applied, and passed bylaws on other matters. Their regulations, derived from their past experience, were determined by majority vote. Though they were supposed to fall inside the broad limits of the appropriate federal legislation, sometimes, as with liquor prohibition, they completely ignored the federal enactments. Miners' meetings also heard suits between miners and decided on punishments for criminal acts. Penalties were usually fines or expulsion from the camp or district, but could extend as far as hanging. This system operated reasonably well without outside interference in the early days in Alaska, and by extension, in Canada. The miners settled their own problems and disputes and kept internal order. They paid no taxes, but neither did they ask for any services from government.

The system also had its disadvantages, particularly as the size and complexity of the camps increased. Occasionally persons simply defied the rulings of the miners' meetings and the miners could not always compel compliance. Since they tended to decide cases on the basis of their knowledge of the individuals concerned, rather than on the issues, the results sometimes favoured the popular person's suit; or a chivalric sense could overcome the members' sense of justice; or judgments were pronounced purely on frivolous grounds (particularly when the saloons became the major meeting places). As Joseph Ladue, a pioneer trader, commented:

> The Miners on the Yukon are shrewd, experienced men, and sometimes they are tricky. I do not like the kind of government they set up for themselves, except in the very first stages. It is all by miners' meetings. They begin by being fair, but after a while cliques are formed, which run things to suit the men who are in them, or, what is just as bad, they turn the sessions into fun. Nobody can get justice from a miners' meeting when women are on one side.[4]

Nor were miners' meetings infallible. Lacking legal experts they could not determine questions of law, or, sometimes, questions of fact. Ogilvie cited examples of miners' meetings committing serious mistakes in assigning claims, being deceived by false testimony, being swayed by secretly interested parties planted in the midst of the meeting to affect the result, or deliberately ignoring known rules of law to prevent the perpetration of a suspected fraud.

In 1893 the time seemed right for the Canadian government to enter the Yukon to uphold Canadian authority, though as yet there were almost no Canadians or Canadian interests in the Yukon. From Ogilvie, back surveying the boundary along the Alaska Panhandle, from Bishop Bompas at Fortymile, from C.H. Hamilton, the manger of the North American Transportation and Trading Company, came requests for the Canadian government to take control. In 1894 it sent out a North West Mounted Police inspector and a staff-sergeant to look into the situation. Inspector Constantine came to Fortymile, collected some customs duties and mining fees, left the staff-sergeant to carry on, and returned to Ottawa to report that a large police force was needed to enforce the whole body of Canadian laws and regulations in the Canadian Yukon. In 1895 he returned with half the force he had asked for, a squad of twenty men. He built a police post in the tradition of the prairie forts with buildings arranged in a square, and began to enforce Canadian laws to the best of his ability, while back in Ottawa the government proclaimed the existence of a District of Yukon.

Thus two diametrically opposed principles for the government of a pioneer environment confronted one another. The American philosophy, exemplified by the mining camps, was libertarian and laissez-faire, based on the principle of squatter sovereignty; the Canadian approach was authoritarian or colonial. It began with the premise that the authority of the Crown and of the law predated the establishment of the frontier settlement, that the institutions of the frontier, as for any other section of Canada, were imposed by the fiat of the governing authority and remained applicable to the frontier until some provision was made for it to receive some portion of the authority of the central government and began to legislate for itself. In the meantime it was the duty of the frontier to accept the regulations of the superior authority and the agents sent by the authority to administer the affairs of the region. Constantine and his men as agents of the federal authority in the Yukon District were not simply police officers; they were agents of every branch of the Dominion government that had any interest in the Yukon region.

The affirmation of the authority of the Canadian government in the years 1895–1897 quickly made the system based on the miners' meetings useless, if only because it enabled those aggrieved by miners' decisions to disregard them with impunity and appeal for a new hearing according to Canadian law. Besides, Constantine was determined to make the miners accept his authority and he missed no opportunity to do so. "The men who live this sort of life are old miners from the Cassiar & Cariboo Districts of BC Men from Idaho, Montana, Nebraska, Nevada, New Mexico & Washington states—who have been used to no control except that of their own sweet will & who preserve order in their camps by stern law, if not justice in all cases."[5] He proceeded to send detachments of his men to collect customs duties, issue mining licences, register mining claims, and enforce other rules, at the same time asking Ottawa to institute regulations that would lessen the discrepancies between the two systems or improve upon the rules the miners imported from outside, as for example, by enacting a system of proper liquor licences to stop the manufacture of "home brew."

There were one or two incidents where the miners seemed inclined to question this assertion of Canadian authority, especially at Glacier and Miller Creeks, close enough to the border that they could argue against accepting Canadian jurisdiction until the boundary had been definitely located. Constantine accepted no excuses; he reported in August 1896, after one or two incidents, that "The action taken has shown the American miner who does not care for constituted authority, that they [sic] can't run the creeks on our side and has had a very quieting effect on gentlemen of that stamp."[6] Ogilvie was inclined to stress that the helpfulness of the Canadian authorities induced the American miners to accept the new system for the sake of convenience, rather than because of the compulsion implied in the reports of the policeman Constantine. As Ogilvie told a private correspondent on 22 May 1897, at the close of the NWMP's second winter in the Yukon and the end of the first winter's diggings on the Klondike creeks:

Owing to the diversity of character, nationality, traditions, and number of the locators on these creeks, the inevitable soon became apparent, confusion, and confliction, of which you have no doubt heard a great deal; but, I think, I know there is now and will be a healthier, and higher standard set up in the country. There is now a desire for the knowledge of mining laws, which twelve months ago was conspicuously absent, that augers well for the future peace and harmony of the camp; even hardened old timers have admitted to myself that "Miners Meetings" as a means of adjudication are generally unsatisfactory and often unjust.

The cry everywhere is "let us have law administered by disinterested men who are above influence and reproach" as a proof of this sentiment I have only to say no miners' meetings have been held in the District for over six months, though there were occasions when the temptation was sorely trying. Many old miners have stated to me "I'll never attend another miners meeting while I live." We have Magistrates and police men in the country who if they cannot stamp out vice and injustice, will at least preserve order, and prevent robbery and have a terror to evil doers, and I think I can assert confidently for the Canadian Government that their condition will be maintained as long as the need for it is apparent.[7]

Just as in British Columbia forty years earlier, the American miners found the practical convenience of accepting the authority of the state greater than the incentives to follow their older tradition of local autonomy. The question of whether the miners would continue to make their own rules or be governed by laws made in Ottawa and administered by its agents in the field was decided in favour of Canada before the influx of gold seekers began in earnest. With these came a renewed, more serious challenge to Canadian authority than that posed by the earlier free miners.

The rush that followed the news of the great gold discovery in the Klondike came in three waves. The first, in the autumn and winter of 1896–1897, caused the abandonment of the camps at Fortymile, Circle City, and other nearby centres, bringing to the Klondike men who were already prospecting or mining in or near the Yukon basin. The news reached the outside world in the spring and early summer of 1897, in time for experienced travellers in the Canadian northwest or along the Pacific coast to reach the Klondike that autumn or early winter of 1897, if they hurried. Most would-be Klondikers spent that autumn and winter preparing for their journey, planning to reach the Yukon in the spring of 1898 when navigation reopened along the waterway. During the winter of 1897–1898 they travelled by sea to ports on the Lynn Canal or Wrangell to begin the spring rush over the trails and passes to the headwaters of the Yukon. Boom towns sprang up at Dyea and Skagway as the many thousands began hauling their supplies back and forth over the passes to the tent and boat-building city along the margin of Lake Bennett. This largest group of gold seekers was overwhelmingly American, reflecting the effectiveness of American publicity, the good communications with the Yukon by way of the ports on the Alaska Panhandle or Bering Sea, and the intense appeal that the opportunities in the Klondike held for footloose west coast Americans ready to take big chances to achieve great rewards.

These newcomers were not miners accustomed to the traditions of self-regulation, but they presented a challenge of another sort. They were adventurous, chauvinistic Americans in a highly jingoistic age. They were rebels, breaking loose from the shackles of convention and conformity in quest of a new life of adventure and fortune. Some in fact, were fugitives—from unsuccessful business activities, unhappy domestic situations, or the law. They played for high stakes, and did not appreciate being cramped, confined, regulated, or ruled by Canadian functionaries who could not be reasoned with since they had no authority beyond referring petitions and requests to Ottawa. Besides, their administration was extremely incompetent in the early stages, characterized by mixups and worse in the Dominion Lands Office where there was a certain amount of corruption in the allotment of claims. The Americans felt they had settled the country and organized its social fabric. They considered that the mining camps, the mining techniques, the businesses, and the city of Dawson all were American creations. They felt that the Canadian presence in the Yukon was only a geographical or diplomatic accident, that the country was the creation of American skills, labour, and capital and belonged to the people who could make the best use of it in the interests of civilization.

This not unfamiliar argument in our own time was even more strongly felt in the social Darwinian, white man's burden climate of the turn of the century. Such a feeling had inspired the British in their relations with the Boer republics of South Africa from the Jameson Raid to the Boer War. Some Americans in the Klondike (and more outside) felt they were Uitlanders too, as regards their position in the Yukon and the political disabilities under which they suffered—and some of them drew the same conclusions as the British were doing in South Africa.

Was there any chance of a takeover of the Klondike by the United States? The international situation did not rule this out completely, for Anglo-American relations were in a precarious state through much of the period. Even the building of Fort Constantine in 1895 had not gone unnoticed. The *San Francisco Examiner* and other west coast newspapers printed alarmist reports that Canada was building stone forts along the Yukon and sending in troops to occupy the ground in force and to undermine American claims to the disputed territory[8] (which some Americans assumed to be the entire Yukon country, just as most Canadians today seem firmly convinced that the boundary award deprived Canada of the whole of the Alaska Panhandle and gave it to the United States). This misunderstanding had barely been allayed when the touchy Venezuela-Guiana boundary dispute erupted, and the State Department intervened belligerently with the Olney Declaration. The *Examiner* carried a succession of articles on the military position of Canada[9]—whence might come British assaults upon the United States, and where the United States might best direct its counterblows. On the international front there was the excitement aroused by the Spanish-American War, an easy victory that increased American impatience with a situation like that of the Klondike, and the British involvement in the Boer War. Troubles over the location of the boundary in the vicinity of the Lynn Canal, and disputes over transit and transhipment rights in northwestern America were irritants closer to home that might have touched off a Canadian-American war. To these should be added the possibilities of on-the-spot insurrections that could bring American intervention in force in the Yukon. There are hints of conspiracies organized in Skagway in the NWMP comptroller's references to "the occurrences of last winter when the futile attempt was made to organize a conspiracy to obtain possession of our Territory."[10] The counter-measures of the Canadian government indicate how seriously it took the danger. However, no attack or insurrection occurred. The British and Canadian governments took care to avoid letting their relations with the United States get out of hand. As for the chances of an uprising, Tappan Adney, perhaps the ablest of all the contemporary observers of the social scene, commented apropos of the attitude of the American settlers that, "If there were not serious disorders it was due less to the quality of government than to the orderly character of the population, and to the fact that men were there enduring the privations of an Arctic climate to make their fortunes and get away, not to help set in order the political households of their Canadian friends."[11]

Instead, the American threat to the Klondike remained at the economic-social-cultural level, represented by the domination of the Yukon by American settlers and businessmen from within and American transportation and trading interests from outside. It was indicated in the predominance of American social modes and customs, including wide-open gambling, sale of liquor, and prostitution, that were characteristic of the American west but were completely alien to the Victorian respectability that prevailed almost universally in contemporary Canada.

On the other hand, the new wave of Americans was met with a stronger affirmation of Canadian authority than that proclaimed by Constantine on 22 July 1895. Americans arriving in the Yukon over the passes during the winter of 1897–1898 were met by strong NWMP forces at the summits and subjected to stringent inspection. The police insisted that all persons entering the Yukon had to carry sufficient food (a year's supply, at a rate of three pounds per person per day) to remove any danger of starvation in that barren country. They used the occasion to examine the credentials of each intending immigrant, and turned back undesirables. They gave the immediate impression that the Yukon was under control, in complete contrast with conditions currently prevailing in the Alaska Panhandle. The police action obviously accorded with the best interests of the territory and of the newcomers and was accepted by most, though a few voices were raised against interference with the personal liberty of Americans to go where they chose. Others contended that the process was designed to blackmail Americans into paying tribute in the guise of customs duties, to compel them to purchase inferior Canadian goods, and to establish a Canadian claim to advanced positions in the territory under dispute, within ten marine leagues of the coast. The regulation respecting the food supply was disallowed by the Dominion government, but it had done its work. The police had passed 30 000 000 pounds of food in the winter of 1897–1898, "sufficient to feed an army corps for a year,"[12] and notwithstanding the enormous increase in the population, there was no food shortage in the Yukon during 1898–1899.

The police also took other unaccustomed measures of control. The Canadian, rather than the American, practice respecting firearms was enforced in the Yukon, representing another marked difference from Alaska or even from the contemporary western states. Under the domineering Superintendent S.B. Steele the police also assumed control of the movement of the Klondikers down the Yukon River. After some loss of life on scows attempting to run the White Horse Rapids, Steele improvised and put in force a set of compulsory rules:

> There are many of your countrymen who have said that the Mounted Police make the laws as they go along, and I am going to do so now for your own good, therefore the directions that I give shall be carried out strictly, and they are these...No women or children will be taken in the boats....No boat will be permitted to go through the canyon until the corporal is satisfied that it has sufficient free board to enable it to ride the waves in safety. No boat will be allowed to pass with human beings in it unless it is steered by competent men, and of that the corporal will be judge. There will be a number of pilots selected, whose names will be on the roll in the Mounted Police barracks here, and when a crew needs a man to steer them through the canyon to the foot of the rapids, pilots will be taken in turn from that list....The rate now charged, 5 dollars, for each boat, seems to be reasonable.[13]

The manner in which these rules were elaborated without discussion, without reference to any outside authority, and without any appeal being allowed against the rulings, shows that Steele's action was the almost perfect affirmation of the authoritarian tradition in territorial administration in Canada.

The police performed a multitude of other services, including carrying the mail (an important activity when much gold had to be carried out of the Yukon) when the delivery by private contractors broke down. They patrolled the waterways, the gold-mining operations on the creeks, the city of Dawson and other communities, enforcing federal and territorial laws, and acting as agents for government departments that did not have their own officials in the territory. As Morrell observed, "The firm yet tactful and informal authority of the police won the admiring respect of American observers, who doubtless noted the absence of the political undercurrents apt to interfere with the course of justice in the Western States."[14] They were also vital to the security of the Yukon. They kept the criminal element under constant surveillance and ordered potential troublemakers out of the country. Their detectives infiltrated miners' and citizens' organizations to ensure that these were not used for purposes of subversion. Their numbers were raised to 250-300 between 1898 and 1904, powerful enough to cope with small insurrections, and the government in 1898 sent in a 200 man militia contingent, the Yukon Field Force.

The civil administration also was greatly enlarged to parallel the increase in settlement. As chief executive officer and commissioner the government sent Major J.M. Walsh to the Yukon in the autumn of 1897, and appointed a council of leading government officials to assist him in legislating for the Yukon District. He was given wide powers to alter mining and other regulations and to remove any federal government official, judges excepted, at his own discretion. These powers were withdrawn from his successors, and for the decade after his departure the Minister of the Interior kept close rein on activities in the Yukon. A judicial district was established and a judge was sent out to try cases in the area. A Dominion Lands Office was set up to regulate the all-important registration of mining claims, under the supervision of a gold commissioner. After a dispute with the Northwest Territories legislature, which asserted its right to legislate for the Yukon District, Parliament in June 1898 passed an act establishing the Yukon as a separate Territory (for a time it appeared as though it would be named "Klondike" instead of "Yukon"). In this way the Dominion retained control in its own hands rather than sharing it with the autonomous government springing up in Regina. This step made possible the future advance of the Yukon towards separate self-governing status, but for the present it placed the Territory under the control of a regime less well attuned to pioneer conditions and aspirations than was that in Regina.

Between 1897 and 1900 the size and scope of the bureaucracy grew rapidly. The mining administration was represented by mining recorders at the major gold-bearing creeks. The legal system was reinforced with a variety of court officers, while two more judges were appointed to make a bench of three judges able to act as a supreme court as well as to process the multitude of lawsuits arising from mining disputes. A wide variety of inspectors, recorders, administrators representing most branches of government appeared in the Territory, including after 1902 agents of the territorial government in such fields as public works and education. Everything was quickly brought under regulations and controls in the Yukon, and the spirit of salutary neglect so typical of Alaska or the earlier Yukon was nowhere in evidence.

In its decisions respecting the political organization of the Yukon the Dominion government was careful to avoid inflaming American opinion or aggravating the delicate situation in the territory. It delayed granting self-government due to fears that Americans might gain control of these institutions if they were allowed to participate; alternatively it feared that giving Canadians a monopoly of these institutions while the population was predominantly American would be regarded as discrimination and might awaken resentments akin to those aroused in the Transvaal. So the government retained control over the Yukon and refused to share it with the inhabitants for some years; and only gradually did it introduce measures of political reform while the complexion of the population changed in Canada's favour. Thus it introduced open council legislative sessions, granted two elected members to council (1901), then five elected against five appointed (1905), then all ten elected in 1908. The Territory received representation in the House of Commons by its own MP in 1902 while Dawson was granted an elected municipal government in 1901. In every case the electorates were limited to British subjects, but these were rapidly becoming the majority in the declining population of the Yukon.

All these steps were in marked contrast to the development of government control and authority in Alaska. Under the Organic Act of 1884, which specifically forbade the calling of a legislature or the granting of representation in Congress, Alaska was organized as a District, with an appointed governor but with administrative control exercised by the Secretary of the Interior. But no attempt was made to administer to the interior of Alaska, and even the coastal settlements were most ineffectually administered, as was evidenced by developments at Wrangell and particularly at Skagway during the height of the gold rush in 1897–1898. Alaskan authorities were quite powerless to curb the operations of a criminal gang in Skagway that preyed on Yukon-bound travellers, notwithstanding the presence there of a deputy marshal and during part of the worst period, of a detachment of United States Marines. In the end, after a year of uncontrolled depravities, the citizens who wanted reform were compelled to organize themselves to take the law into their own hands. They were met head-on by the ringleader of the criminal element, "Soapy" Smith, who was shot and killed in a street gun duel in the best wild-west tradition. Following this drastic action the gang, to avoid being lynched by the aroused citizens, was rounded up by the suddenly-visible agents of the law, and hustled aboard ship to face trial outside for their crimes.

The Klondike gold rush, the example of the Yukon Territory, and the advent of would-be miners to Birch Creek, Nome, and other sections of Alaska, at last brought action by the American government to institute an effective system of government for the interior where "non-interference with liberty by the central government has been but another name for neglect."[15] Under a law of 6 June 1900, prohibition was repealed, saloons and other businesses were licensed (constituting the first local taxation in the District) and a new criminal code especially designed for Alaskan conditions was enacted to replace that of Oregon which had been followed previously. A new civil code provided that two of the three judicial divisions be in the north, at St. Michael and Eagle City. Provision was made for the establishment of municipalities with limited powers of taxation, while appointed commissioners were put in charge of the principal communities. However, it was not until 1908 that a gesture towards Congressional representation was allowed, when the people of Alaska gained the right to send a non-voting delegate to the House of Representatives, and only in 1912 was Alaska at last constituted a Territory, with a wholly elected Senate and House of Representatives able to legislate for and administer to its local concerns.

In all these measures Alaska lagged behind the Yukon, which had received full representation in Parliament in 1902, an entirely elected territorial council in 1908, and possessed a much larger administrative and judicial establishment. Moreover, the sad tale of misgovernment at Nome indicated that the system of government provided from Washington was not an entirely satisfactory solution to the problem of colonial government. The trouble there arose from the appointment, through the influence of a North Dakota political boss, of a corrupt federal judge and court officials who concocted a scheme to enrich themselves by getting control of the mining claims. The case of Nome indicated the inability of the federal government to avoid making unsatisfactory partisan appointments or to exercise adequate supervision over its local agents. The Canadian government, though it could certainly not be accused of neglecting partisan appointments for the Yukon, nevertheless retained extremely close supervision over the Territory, which prevented large-scale corruption at the local level. In fact, in 1899 it went so far as to prohibit government officials from involving themselves in mining properties. There was more danger of corruption originating in or engineered from Ottawa, but there the glare of publicity on Yukon affairs (greater than upon Alaskan affairs in Washington), the system of governmental responsibility, and the vigilance of the parliamentary opposition, all combined to make an operation like that at Nome virtually impossible in the Canadian Yukon. Above all, the Canadian system of administration benefited from the all-powerful NWMP and the large, impressive judicial system. Curiously, when it became fully developed after 1900, the Canadian system furnished the Yukon at one and the same time with a more powerful, authoritarian bureaucracy and more fully representative institutions than Alaska enjoyed.

The contest between Canada and the United States for the control of the Canadian Yukon turned strongly in Canada's favour particularly after 1900, largely because of the efforts of the police and other agencies of the government in the Yukon itself. At the same time, from outside the Yukon, other Canadianizing agencies were also attacking the American outpost in the Yukon Territory. The monopoly enjoyed by American trading concerns and port cities was challenged by vigorously advertising the advantages of securing outfits and supplies in Canada rather than in the United States, and by strict enforcement of Canadian customs regulations to make these words come true. A serious effort was made to build, or have built, an all-Canadian access route to the Yukon to reduce the dependence upon American transportation. Branches of Canadian banks in the Yukon handled the financing of mining operations and helped stabilize the economy, hitherto operating with gold dust as the sole medium of exchange.

To fight the monopoly enjoyed by Seattle and San Francisco in the marketing of the gold dust—which in turn gave those cities powerful commercial holds on the Yukon—a government assay office was set up in Vancouver to enable miners to convert their earnings into goods and credit in Canada rather than in the United States. Canadian manufacturing concerns were cajoled and given tangible incentives to compete for the supply trade, while companies were encouraged to set up branches and agencies in the Territory. Despite the tendency of American-controlled companies and American nationals to look to the United States for supplies, by 1902 Canadian firms were reported to be doing about 60 percent of the Yukon trade.

The reconquest of the Yukon by Canadian business was actually helped by the economic decline and stabilization of its economy on a low level. As the returns from the Yukon diminished and the chances for large financial coups disappeared, businesses in San Francisco, Seattle, and Portland found the market in the Yukon for which they competed too small and awkward. They abandoned the field to Canadian firms that enjoyed the advantages of government protection and patronage and were content with more modest gains. The opening of the White Pass and Yukon railway was a particular boon to Canadian business chances in the Yukon because it had the effect of segregating the trade of the Territory from that of the major part of Alaska. The railway also afforded a convenient, direct trade route between Vancouver and the Yukon that was quickly seized by the CPR and other shipping interests and rapidly displaced the more roundabout route via the Bering Sea and the Yukon River. Henceforth Vancouver became the principal trading and communications centre for the Yukon.

While encouraging Canadian participation to the full with a view to hastening the integration of the Yukon into Canadian life, the government did little to discourage the participation by Americans in its economic life. No attempt was made to prohibit American citizens (apart from those banned by the police) from settling anywhere or holding mining claims, as was the case with Canadians and other foreigners in Alaska. No effort was made to prevent an American-controlled company, the White Pass and Yukon Railway (financed largely in Britain), from building the only railway link into the area from the port of Skagway, or to keep American capital from playing an important role in integrating gold mining operations in the highly successful Yukon Gold Company, organized by the Englishman A.N.C. Treadgold but financed by the Guggenheim mining interests of California.

The Canadianization of Yukon society also went forward rapidly after 1900. Canadian churches and fraternal organizations put forward determined efforts to convert the Yukon into a portion of Canadian society as they conceived it. The presence of Canadian officials and institutions, and the adoption by the federal government of policies reflecting the attitudes of southern Canada, were other potent forces in the remaking of Yukon society. Church groups in particular complained endlessly against the "un-Canadian" demeanour of Dawson—the gambling halls, saloons, and houses of ill-fame operating openly and non-stop along the principal streets of Dawson. Left to themselves, the police and local government were content with regulating these activities so as to ensure that the games were honest, the customers were not victimized, and no crimes were committed. They argued that such activities were bound to take place in the present state of the society, and so long as they were conducted openly they could at least be policed and controlled. But the pressures of Canadian settlers wanting to bring their families to the Yukon, and the outcry from groups and societies in southern Canada that could bring considerable pressure to bear upon the Dominion government, would not let the matter rest. The houses of ill-fame were banished to a back-street, then expelled from Dawson across the Klondike River, and the gambling houses and dance halls were closed. Above all, strict observance of the sabbath—the hallmark of the Canadian way of life at the time which differentiated it most sharply from that of the United States—was instituted and enforced. By 1900 Dawson was a suitable place for orderly family living, and by 1902 it was reported to be as Canadian as Toronto.

A measure of Canada's success in winning control of the Yukon was the change in its population structure, as revealed in the censuses. At the height of the gold rush, Americans probably numbered three-quarters or more of the estimated 40 000 persons who reached the Yukon before 1900. Yet by the census of 1901, when the total population was given as 27 219, the American group had declined to 8700 persons, 32 percent of the total, most of their number having already departed for home or for the new gold rush at Nome. The exodus continued and few replacements arrived, so that by the 1911 census there remained only 1891 Americans in the Territory, 22 percent of the whole. At the same time the Canadian population, which was said to have constituted no more than 10 percent of the advancing human wave, began to grow in relative importance if not in absolute numbers. Canadians tended to remain longer in the Yukon than the Americans, and to be replaced by other Canadians when they departed, the large government establishment furnishing a source of employment and a stable economic base. By 1911 there were 3850 Canadians in the Territory, double the number of American nationals, and 45 percent of the total population of 8512, making, with the 1346 British, a Territory 61 percent of whose population were British subjects.

Ironically, the triumph of Canadian interests in the Yukon was a pyrrhic victory, for the population continued to plummet even further, to the 4000 level in the censuses of 1921 and 1931. Consequently, the political fortunes of the Yukon took a turn for the worse and its political lead over Alaska was eliminated. What had been regarded as a future province with all the powers of self-government associated with that status, had become by 1911 a Territory that scarcely seemed to warrant its present levels of administrative services and self-governing status. Indeed, it was a question whether or not the Yukon should be relegated to the common level of colonial administration that Canada provided for its undeveloped northern territories. From 1904 onwards the bureaucracy was considerably reduced, the judicial system was curtailed, and a plan was instituted to replace the elected council with a small appointed council. This fate was averted, but the council was reduced from ten to three members in 1919. At the same time, with the curtailment of a diversified civil service, many of its duties fell once more upon the shoulders of the smaller but still sizeable police establishment. The Indian Affairs administration—the very exemplar of the concept of Canadian trusteeship over her dependent territories and peoples—which had been almost entirely absent until this time, began to emerge in full force in 1914 as a means of regulating and controlling a native population that now accounted for half the Territory's inhabitants. By the 1920s the Yukon, reduced to a shadow of its former self, was hardly distinguishable from the settlements of the Mackenzie valley sector of the Northwest Territories. Only the river steamers, railway, roads, the churned-up beds of the former Klondike creeks, and the decayed government buildings, amusement halls, business places, and dwellings of Dawson were left as a reminder of the glorious years when the Yukon stood on the threshold of becoming Canada's first northern province and was an object of feverish contention between Canadian and American cities, national governments, societies, and cultures.

Notes

1. H.A. Innis "Settlement and the Mining Frontier," in A.R.M. Lower and H.A. Innis, *Settlement and the Forest and Mining Frontiers* (Toronto, 1936), 183.
2. S.D. Clark, *The Social Development of Canada* (Toronto, 1942), 326.
3. W.P. Morrell, *The Gold Rushes* (London, 1940).
4. F.W. Howay, W.N. Sage, and H.F. Angus, *British Columbia and the United States* (New Haven and Toronto, 1942), 350.
5. Charles Constantine to L. Herschmer, 15 August 1896, "Superintendent's Letter Book, 1895–1898," Constantine Papers, MG30 E2, 4, Public Archives of Canada (hereafter PAC), Ottawa.
6. Constantine to Herschmer, Constantine Papers, MG30 E2, 4.
7. William Ogilvie to J.M. Wilson, Fortymile, 22 May 1897, TS copy, Ogilvie Papers, MG30 C2, PAC.
8. *San Francisco Examiner*, 4, 5, 7, 9 November 1895.
9. *San Francisco Examiner*, 16 December 1895, et seq.
10. F. White to F.C. Wade, 11 October 1902, "Alaska Boundary, 1902–1942," F.C. Wade Papers, RG18, 4, entries 15 October 1902 and 25 January 1902, PAC.
11. T. Adney, *The Klondike Stampede*, cited in Clark, *The Social Development of Canada*, 353.
12. S.B. Steele, *Forty Years in Canada* (Toronto, 1915), 312.
13. Steele, *Forty Years in Canada*, 311–12.
14. Morrel, *The Gold Rushes*, 389.
15. Adney, *The Klondike Stampede*, cited in Clark, *The Social Development of Canada*, 353.

SECTION 4

AFTER THE GOLD RUSH

"BETWIXT AND BETWEEN": THE ANGLICAN CHURCH AND THE CHILDREN OF THE CARCROSS (CHOOUTLA) RESIDENTIAL SCHOOL, 1911–1954*

KENNETH COATES

From 1891, when William Carpenter Bompas of the Church Missionary Society first opened his Forty-Mile mission to child boarders, the residential school was an important component in the Anglican clergy's program for the moral and cultural improvement of the Indians of the Yukon district.[1] Though the Church of England missionaries continued their itinerant efforts among the nomadic bands and offered regular missions and day schools at central meeting places, most believed their greatest hope for the native children of the North lay in residential schools. Through repeated appeals to the Canadian government, the church secured the funds necessary to erect a sizeable facility at Carcross in the southern Yukon. Money and commitment, however, were not enough, for the boarding school concept proved at best a mixed blessing. An examination of clerical and government intentions and a consideration of the school children's experiences during their stay and after their departure illustrates the weaknesses of the residential format in the Yukon.

The suggestion that the missionaries' efforts were of dubious or negative benefit to the Yukon Indians, in this case the residential school children, is not made in order to belittle the clergy's efforts or, even less, to challenge their sincerity. Instead, like much of the recent literature on native-missionary activities, this article is designed to move beyond hagiographic descriptions of

*B.C. *Studies* 64 (Winter 1984–1985): 27–47.

the work of these wilderness saints which have so dominated the historiography in past generations. Writing on missionary activities, long the preserve of the religious community,[2] has attracted an increasing number of secular scholars. The simultaneous expansion of work on native–white relations, both polemical and analytical, has resulted in a decidedly less favourable, though unquestionably more comprehensive, treatment of missionary activities.

Contemporary historians have shifted the focus from the missionaries to the impact of proselytizing on native populations. The missionaries clearly wished to recast Indians values and customs. Their efforts to undermine native spirituality, supplant indigenous leadership and denigrate long-standing customs represented a major challenge to native societies. Whereas earlier work lauded the efforts of the back-country clerics, most recent studies are concerned more with the meeting of cultural systems and the identifiable ramifications of the introduction to Euro-Canadian religious leadership.[3] In the often used parlance of Ralph Linton, the clergy were agents of directed culture change, representatives of an expansive, ethnocentric Euro-Canadian culture determined to leave their imprint on the less advanced, "heathen" societies of the undeveloped world.[4]

Through the boarding school program, the missionaries and the government hoped to transform the children into "better" Canadians, offering the intellectual and technical skills deemed necessary for fuller participation in the larger Euro-Canadian society and the Christian values required to separate the students from their "heathen" past. In so doing, of course, the residential schools called into question existing native habits and values, setting the children against the standards of their parents and home communities. Though recent studies in Canada and the United States suggest that the program failed to achieve the desired results, most agree that the institution represented a systematic attempt to supplant native cultural forms.[5] The experience of the Carcross Residential School illustrates both the founders' enthusiastic if unrealistic expectations and the rather serious cultural and social impact on many of the children passing through its portals.

Bompas' first institution at Forty-Mile on the Yukon River could hardly be called a true boarding school. His students were primarily orphaned or abandoned native children, although several mixed-blood students came to live at the mission as well.[6] To Bompas, education, and particularly in a residential school, was essential even in the 1890s. Though he repeatedly argued that "schooling is the most hopeful branch of mission work," the London office of the Church Missionary Society refused his requests for extra money. Bompas' difficulties with the funding agency originated in his insistence that priority be given to educating mixed-blood children, an acknowledged departure from CMS practice. Bompas declared that "such half-breed children are liable to become if untrained and left wild, the bitterest enemies and most formidable obstacles to our mission, whereas if trained in the mission schools they may become our foremost and most useful friends."[7] Clearly, Bompas feared that such children, if not provided a viable option, would remain with their native mothers. To the missionary, the loss of their "whiteness" would significantly harm the mixed bloods' adaptation to an evolving Yukon society. His requests brushed aside, Bompas proceeded without assistance. In 1894 his small boarding school contained four mixed-blood girls and two Indian girls.[8]

When Bompas transferred his diocesan headquarters to Carcross in 1900, he initially left his small, unofficial school behind. He would not, however, permit the project to die. Convinced of the need for a permanent boarding facility, he appealed directly to the Department of Indian Affairs:

> I am wishing now to apply to the Government to open a new Indian Boarding School for orphaned and other destitute Indian children either at Whitehorse or here at Caribou Crossing (Carcross) and to maintain it themselves. I think this the only way to make the remnant of the Indian race in the next generation useful members of society.[9]

His request rejected, Bompas nonetheless transferred the Forty-Mile students to Carcross, opening in larger quarters and expanding his foster home to accommodate approximately two dozen children. When Bompas died in 1906, resident Anglican clergyman John Hawksley assumed responsibility for the school. The new bishop, Isaac O. Stringer, continued his predecessor's campaign for permanent government assistance.[10]

The Anglican Church's appeal for a boarding school came at a most inappropriate juncture. From 1871, when the federal government signed its first treaty with the Indians of western Canada, education and negotiated settlements went hand in hand. Modelling its western policy on eastern programs, the government organized boarding schools on reserves and, in 1883, opened an industrial school at Battleford. "It is self-evident," the government confidently declared, "that the prime purpose of Indian education is to assist in solving what may be called the Indian problem, to elevate the Indian from his condition of savagery, to make him a self-supporting member of state and eventually a citizen in good standing."[11] Though the goals remained intact, by the early twentieth century many educators and bureaucrats had come to acknowledge the apparent failure of the boarding-industrial school format.

Typically wary of increased expenditures, the government especially feared further involvement in an allegedly flawed and costly experiment. Frank Pedley, a senior official in the Department of Indian Affairs, argued for a more flexible program. "It would seem to be good policy at this junction," he wrote, "to attempt to devise a better system of Indian education, applying to each locality methods which would best achieve the desired result."[12] Pedley was alluding to the failure of the boarding school format to prepare the students adequately for their "after life." Advanced technical training or literary skills served little purpose for native children destined for life on a reserve or a trapline. The Anglican Church agreed with the government's assessment of the institutional deficiencies. A Special Committee of the Missionary Society of the Church of England in Canada (MSCC) recommended that teaching be limited to basic literacy and computational skills, plus "additional work as will fit the child to take his place as a workman in the locality in which he is to live."[13]

Frank Oliver, the Minister of the Interior, offered more explicit criticism. The residential school was flawed not only from an educational perspective; in addition, the cultural restructuring attending the rending apart of families had to be taken into account. Defending the less expensive day school program, Oliver argued:

> My belief is that the attempt to elevate the Indian by separating the child from his parents and educating him as a white man has turned out to be a deplorable failure....The mutual love between parent and child is the strongest influence for the betterment of the world, and when that influence is absolutely cut apart or is deliberately intended to be cut apart as in the education of Indian children in industrial schools the means taken defeats itself.[14]

Despite the fact that both the federal government and the MSCC viewed the boarding schools with increasing disfavour, Bishop Stringer proceeded with his appeal. The main reason for this apparent obstinance was that the Roman Catholic Church continued its efforts to secure government funding for a similar school in Atlin, British Columbia. In the continuing "rush for souls" in the North, the Anglicans could not afford to allow the Catholics to gain the upper hand in this key area. Under Stringer's direction, the 1907 Synod of the Diocese of the Yukon endorsed the need for a new residential school,[15] as did T.G. Bragg, superintendent of schools for the Yukon Territory.[16] Resistance at the national level, however, persisted.[17]

In part to quiet the persistent appeals from Bishop Stringer, McLean in 1908 directed British Columbia Indian school inspectors A.W. Vowell and A.E. Green to assess the need for a facility in the Yukon. As McLean noted in passing on his instructions:

> It would seem necessary before establishing a system of education which would entail considerable expense to ascertain how the Indians of the Yukon maintain themselves and what kind of education could be imparted to them in a Boarding School which would improve their condition and render them better able to fight the battles of life in their peculiar environment.[18]

During the summer of 1908, Vowell and Green travelled through the southern Yukon, discussing the matter with resident clergy, visiting accessible native villages and commissioning reports on distant Indian bands.[19] Their final report staunchly supported the Anglican position. Their submission to the Department of Indian Affairs cautiously noted:

We would, in all due deference to the opinion of the Department, state that, in our opinion, the Boarding Schools are, under the conditions prevailing, the most suitable for the education of the Indians. At these institutions can be taught everything that at the present time is needful for the advancement of the Indian so as to enable him to continue to be self-supporting and to meet on equal terms, from an educational point of view, those persons with whom he may be thrown in contact in his efforts to obtain a living for himself and his family.[20]

Their enthusiasm was muted by a pessimistic assessment of the prospects for further development in the territory. Noting that hunting and trapping would likely remain as the mainstays of the native economy, the school inspectors recommended that educational programs be restricted to basic literacy, computational skills, health care and carpentry. Vowell and Green tempered their recommendations by echoing their superiors' concerns that "to go beyond that would be rather to unfit them for their condition in life."

Although personally unconvinced, Minister Oliver reluctantly complied with his agents' recommendations.[21] As the Anglican church requested, a suitable facility was constructed near Carcross, the site of Bishop Bompas' small school. Built in 1911, the school initially housed thirty students. The new structure, complete with dormitory and educational facilities, was enlarged several times and remained in operation until destroyed by fire in 1954 when, after protracted debate about the possibility of relocating the institution, the government decided to erect a structure big enough for 150 students on the old site.[22] Beginning in 1911, then, the Anglican Church had the facility it had long demanded and had guarantees of sufficient funds to operate the school. It did not, moreover, have much difficulty developing a school curriculum, for the missionaries had a clear and comparatively consistent view of their educational goals.

The Anglican missionaries greeted their new responsibility with enthusiasm. To them, the school held out the best prospect for "elevating" the Yukon Indians. Their idealism was tempered, however, by the pessimism of the federal government and their own assessments of the prospects for northern development. Accepting the cautionary note offered by inspectors Vowell and Green, the missionaries limited their educational goals. Recognizing that most would return to their families and a hunting lifestyle, the teachers adopted special northern priorities. Instead of "white" Indians, versed in the techniques and routines of the industrial plant, the school sought to make "better" Indians, schooled in the necessities of health, hygiene, motivation, Christian social mores and the Protestant work ethic, yet armed with the requisite skills of the northern harvester.[23]

The scholastic program, featuring an amalgam of education and practical training, changed little from 1911 to 1954.[24] Different principals, of course, had their own particular emphasis. With the exception of H.G.M. Grant in the late 1930s, however, most stayed away from specific industrial training. Instruction in reading, writing and arithmetic typically occupied the morning, with the remainder of the day allocated to work around the school and occupational lessons. Boys chopped wood, fished, and worked in the carpentry shop and garden. Girls assisted in the kitchen and with household chores throughout the facility. Teachers expanded their lessons beyond basic instruction, offering the girls training in moccasin making and beadwork, pursuits which would "be useful and profitable to them in after life." There were deviations from the pattern, including the installation of a student-run printing press, which was used to print the church quarterly *Northern Lights* for several years, and an expanded industrial workshop.

From 1911, school officials repeatedly reiterated their concern that the instruction "be useful in the kind of life the children will likely lead."[25] Despite the fact that the school included such programs as agriculture, blacksmithing, carpentry and mechanical skills for the boys and industrial cooking for the girls, administrators repeatedly stated that it was their intention to prepare their charges for re-entry to the native village. In 1939, for example, school principal Rev. H.C.M. Grant noted: "I am convinced that the best way to fit the Indian children for the life they will have to live when they leave school is to have their life in school as similar as possible to the life they will have to live at home." How then did he justify his personal emphasis on an expanded industrial education program and strict social control? Grant simply assumed that "hunting and trapping, the natural life of the Indian," would soon be "a thing of the past." The Indians would then "have to turn to some other means of livelihood."[26] Grant's incorrect assessment of the future of the North was to cause hardship for many of his students. The missionaries sought, however, to provide necessary skills (albeit as defined for the natives by a clergy who, had regional realities supported a more industrial or agricultural economy, would have preferred an end to the harvesting lifestyle) for a successful return to the Yukon native society.

Whereas work-related instruction did not explicitly seek to disrupt existing skills, the school's social program proved more difficult to accommodate within standard native child-rearing practices. The key was a repeated insistence upon a strict, often authoritarian code of discipline. Administrators severely restricted socialization in the schools. Under most principals, boys and girls came in contact only in formal and strictly supervised settings. As principal from 1918 to 1920, Dr. Grasset-Smith allowed virtually no interaction between the sexes, a level of control even other missionaries found objectionable.[27] Most agreed, however, that extended contact between the students and the Carcross community, a predominantly native settlement, had to be curtailed.[28] To enforce these and other regulations, educators established firm disciplinary procedures. Breaches of school regulations, especially theft, malicious damage or unauthorized socialization, were dealt with firmly. Facing a rash of thefts in 1940, H.C.M. Grant cut all the hair off any child caught breaking school ethics. As he succinctly noted, "It checked stealing at once."[29] Programming varied as principals and staff passed swiftly through the school. Throughout, however, a rigid work schedule, limited socialization, firm discipline and forced adherence to the teachers' guidance characterized school life.[30]

The combination of an apparently flexible instructional program and rigid behavioural control was fraught with contradictions. Concern for the students' "after life," so evident in occupational programs, was not a major part of the residential school social environment. Interpersonal skills were, at best, not taught. At worst, they were actively repressed. The firm discipline and work schedules, both designed to instil appropriate Euro-Canadian work values, lacked relevance to the native way of life. Most importantly, the concerted effort to improve native hygiene and to inculcate different work habits of necessity called into disrepute the mannerisms and standards of the children's parents. The children were taught new practices of personal and home care—practices notably different from those of the native village. This, of course, was perfectly consistent with the school's general purpose: to prepare students so that they could return and reform their own villages. Ironically, though supposedly educationally prepared to re-enter native society, the students were taught through the residential school to abhor that environment, to look with disrespect if not disgust upon their families' customs. Before the Carcross School was constructed, Frank Oliver had noted:

> To teach an Indian child that his parents are degraded beyond measure and that whatever they did or thought was wrong could only result in the child becoming...admittedly and unquestionably very much less desirable a member of society than their parents who never saw the schools.[31]

The Anglican clergy in the Yukon now faced the consequences of failing to heed his prescient advice.

Once released from school, the graduates were to be harbingers of a new social order, missionaries assisting with the further "modernization" of native society. The experiment was, however, far less successful with the natives of the Yukon than the founders had hoped. From the beginning, the Anglican clergy encountered difficulty securing recruits, battled with the school's decidely negative image among the Yukon's Indian population and, the ultimate irony, had to ease the difficult, often painful transition of the graduates back into native society.

The first problem facing the church was locating suitable students. In attempting to fill out enrolment, the clergy sought to satisfy two different, often conflicting goals. Administrators wished to maintain Bompas' original purpose of providing a home for the destitute and orphaned. More importantly, they also hoped to use the school as a training centre for a new generation of native leaders. Removed from the baneful influence of an allegedly "backward" home environment and cloistered from the insidious depredations of avaricious whites, boarders would be educationally and morally prepared to return to their villages as disciples of the Church's social and moral message. The school would help more than just the students, for they in turn would serve as instruments of "civilization" for the dispersed native population. The missionaries, therefore, attempted to identify the poor and deprived, but sought in particular to recruit "the best both in health and intellect, so that the graduates of the School may form in their several camps a foundation on which the missionaries can build, in their endeavors for the physical and spiritual benefit of the natives."[32]

Finding students for the school proved more difficult than initially anticipated. Ongoing efforts to "procure" children were directed specifically at the offspring of well-placed Indians. Bishop Stringer was understandably distressed that "some of our best and most influential Indians object to sending their children away to school."[33] Stringer carefully cultivated his territory-wide contacts, often offering special arrangements to attract prized students. Administrators allowed the mixed-blood daughter of trader Poole Field to enrol in 1918 because, as Stringer wrote, her father had "an immense influence over the Liard and Pelly Indians, and can do a great deal in getting children for our school."[34] Despite these extensive efforts, the clergy often found parents unwilling to part with their children.

Evidence from registration records before 1945 suggest that the goal of drawing students equally from around the territory was far from realized. The southern districts accounted for more than 70 percent of the registrants. It is significant that children from these areas typically returned to their families each summer, maintaining at least some semblance of contact while enrolled in school. (Occasionally parents resisted when the students were scheduled to return in the fall. School administrators, supported by the government, refused to condone such absences for fear of setting a damaging precedent. The students were forced to return. See table 1.)

TABLE 1   *Origins of New Registrants, Carcross Residential School, 1930–1950*

	South[a]	Central[b]	North[c]
1930–1944	81	17	12
1945–1950	41	16	35

[a] Includes Carcross, Tahltan, Tagish, Atlin, Whitehorse, Kluane, Champagne, Teslin.
[b] Big Salmon, Carmacks, Pelly, Selkirk.
[c] Peel River, Mayo, Mooshide, Old Crow.

SOURCE: Registration documents, Carcross School, RG10, vol. 6481, file 940-10, pt. 4 to pt. 6. The collection of registration forms does not appear to be complete.

The missionaries' efforts succeeded to a limited degree, for they managed to keep enrolment close to capacity. A number of parents accepted the clergy's argument that their children's future lay with literacy, advanced training and religious guidance. Many native catechists, already strongly influenced by the church's teachings, sent their children to the school.[35] The attempt to attract what the missionaries viewed as the "better class" of Indians, however, fell far short of its goal.

A more detailed examination of registration records reveals the church's difficulties in attracting suitable candidates. Ideally, educators wanted children as young as legally possible and sought to draw them equally from around the territory. Such a policy, they hoped, would have the greatest possible impact by dispersing trained graduates throughout the district. The church had as much difficulty securing young children as they did in maintaining a regional balance. Although students as young as six (and occasionally younger in the case of orphans)[36] came to the school, the average age of entry ranged from nine to eleven years. Despite their comparatively advanced age, most came to Carcross with little educational background, except for temporary sessions at Anglican day schools (table 2).

The Carcross School did considerably better as a home for destitute and orphaned children. Between 1930 and 1950, a minimum of 30 percent of all new students came from identifiable situations of family distress (table 3). Missionaries, government agents and police officers readily noted children in need of special care and ensured that they were sent to the school.[37] The facility continued to meet Bompas' original purpose, providing a home for children who otherwise might have suffered. It was noticeably less successful in attracting those selected children whom the clergy hoped would serve as the future leaders of the Yukon Indians.[38]

TABLE 2 *Characteristics of Students, Carcross School Enrolments, 1930–1950*

	Recorded Registrations	Average Age[a]	None[b]	Previous Schooling		
				Less Than One Year	More Than One Year	Previous Residential
1930–1934	40	9.1	25	7	5	3
1935–1939	30	9.2	14	11	5	0
1940–1944	51	10.8	29	10	4	8
1945–1950	99	9.3	67	0	28	4

[a] At admission.
[b] Either identified as no previous schooling or simply no entry in the relevant blank on the registration form.

SOURCE: See table 1.

The natives' reluctance to send their children stemmed, in part, from the school's very poor public image. Epidemics, including an outbreak of influenza in 1920 which claimed four lives, frequently hit the school. The death of children at the institution was not uncommon, although they typically succumbed to tuberculosis or other diseases contracted before their arrival. The school soon earned a reputation as a dangerous place for children, an image that gained currency with each death or serious illness.[39] The already tarnished image was further worsened by a seemingly endless series of rumours concerning the school. Repeated tales of poor food, harsh discipline and cramped quarters found a ready audience among natives who already looked upon the school with suspicion. Though many of the rumours had some basis (if only tenuous) in fact, others, like the 1938 allegation that students were being fed "floor sweepings" and "dog rice" represented more slanderous assaults on an already vulnerable institution.[40] The clergy had great difficulty overcoming parental reticence constantly reinforced through rumours and news of more student deaths.

TABLE 3 *Status of Parents, New Registrants, Carcross-Residential School, 1930–1950*

	Both Alive	Both Alive Destitute[a]	Mother Dead	Father Dead	Both Dead	Total	%Family Distress
1930–1944	70	4	8	18	7	107	34.6
1945–1950	69	2	8	18	2	99	30.3

[a] Destitution as can be ascertained from supporting documents. The number is likely understated considerably.

SOURCE: See table 1.

Recruitment efforts continued in an ongoing attempt to overcome parental hesitation. The notable increase in attendance after 1940 illustrates changing economic conditions, extended government and missionary recruitment efforts, and, after 1945, the introduction of compulsory education measures by the federal government. (See table 4.) It was also only after the imposition of government enforced education that the geographic distribution of students shifted. Between 1945 and 1950, fewer than half (45 percent) came from the south. The Old Crow district, which had provided no children for the school in the preceding fifteen years (at least according to extant records), sent twenty-two, or almost one-quarter of all new registrants. Government legislative intervention, and not relentless church appeals, provided the impetus for wider enrolment. It was only after 1945 that the school consistently attracted the number and range of students administrators had long anticipated. (See table 1.)

Recruiting students proved only the beginning of the school's difficulties. The clergy's greatest—and certainly most unexpected—problem came with the return of students to their villages. Children left the school at different ages and for a variety of reasons. Many stayed until graduation, leaving at age sixteen. Others departed much earlier. Several students were deemed

TABLE 4 *Carcross School Enrolment, 1910–1950 (Yearly Averages)*

	Boys	Girls	Total
1910–1914	15	14	29
1915–1919	17	16	33
1920–1924	17	19	36
1925–1929	18	20	38
1930–1934	17	18	35
1935–1939	22	24	46
1940–1944	32	31	63
1945–1950	28	28	56

SOURCE: *Annual Reports*. Department of Indian Affairs.

incapable of learning, often because they entered the school at an advanced age or maintained regular contact with their families. Such students were returned to their parents. Similarly, students who could not be contained by the institution's strict disciplinary standards were hurriedly shipped out for fear they would set a bad example for other potential malcontents. A sizeable number of parents attempted to pull their children out of school, either because they had heard and believed several of the rumours circulating about the institution or because the children were needed at home. The school's administrators and the government typically rejected the first reason, believing that they were acting in the child's best interest by keeping him or her in school. Those requests involving demonstrable need were more often accepted, particularly if the children were needed to assist an invalid or ailing parent.[41] Students leaving before graduation were in the minority, however, as most returned home only after completing their schooling.

Removed from nomadism at a young age, the students faced a difficult, often traumatic transition when they attempted to return to their native villages. Initially, the clergy enthusiastically welcomed the students' departure. To them, it represented the end of their work, each child a new mission worker assisting in the general improvement of the Yukon Indians. Expectations shortly turned to despair, as missionaries came to realize the serious consequences of the students' return to village life. An Old Crow commentator wrote pleadingly to Bishop Stringer in 1926:

> If Caroline Moses' girl comes back, she is going into the filthiest hovel in the country....A dirt floor, two tiny windows which cannot be seen for the flies, stinking meat and fish hung all over the cabin, the stench unspeakable, six people already living there, and now a seventh, and under the willows on the dirt floor, all the filth of a long winter throwing off a deadly effluvia, in a stifling heat....Bishop, I plead with you not for humanity's sake, but for the sake of the Dear Lord who redeemed us, not to send a decent

girl back to untold misery and evil, where she cannot help but curse the very day she was born.[42]

Allowing for morally inspired excess, the writer makes an important point. Village life for many children was far removed both geographically and culturally from the Carcross dormitory. Even at this early date, there was general concern as to whether the students were adequately prepared for the transition.

It is easy to identify those who made a "successful" adaptation, particularly in the early years when comments on graduates filled the church's reports. These young adults, products of Bompas' closely-knit boarding home rather than the more impersonal Chooutla institution, often secured adequate placements upon graduation. Frequently orphans, the students struck out on their own, the girls seeking positions as domestic helpers, the boys attempting to find manual work. The girls enjoyed greater success as the church secured jobs for them from Dawson City to Victoria, British Columbia. Facing a more competitive, and often exclusionist job market, the boys encountered difficulty finding anything other than short-term positions.[43] In later years, the clergy offered frequent reminders of the exploits of the more notable graduates.[44] James Wood, Jacob Njootli and Maggie Daniels, for example, served the church as day school teachers or native catechists, conforming closely to the church's expectations for the graduates. Johnny Johns demonstrated the utility of a residential school education in another way. He established himself as a businessman of note in the Carcross area and later became widely regarded as the best (and only native) big game guide in the territory.[45] Several others utilized their school skills to make a more complete entry into white society. Two boys, trained on the school's printing press, found employment with a Whitehorse printing firm. Others settled near Whitehorse or Dawson city, sought employment and in several instances even applied for enfranchisement.[46] Others attempted to build on their school experience in less noticeable but perhaps more important ways. The church took particular pride in the efforts of one female graduate who, upon returning to Selkirk in 1939, effected a radical change in her family's habits and manners.[47] Such successes were few, however, and noted by the church all the more for their uniqueness.

Most of the children found themselves upon returning to their homes, torn between school values and the realities of camp life. Some of those who visited their families each summer readily discarded years of education and re-adopted village mannerisms and customs. For those who had assimilated substantial portions of their teachers' message, however, a more painful transition ensued. As a summer missionary at Carmacks noted in 1934 "They are potential outcasts of their own people and are not quite up to the standards of the white intellect. In other words, they are 'betwixt and between'—a condition of pitiful helplessness."[48] Schooling had taught them to disdain their parents' customs, but their race and lack of formal education precluded a more permanent integration into an exclusionist white society.

The lack of systematic records on the graduates' experiences, compounded by the wide and rapid dispersal of students upon leaving the schools, makes it impossible to follow these children through later life with much precision. Scanty evidence of enfranchisement application suggests, as would be expected, that many of those applying for full rights as Canadian citizens had come through the residential school program.

The bulk of the evidence, however, suggests that the students faced a rough transition. As one commentator noted in 1926:

> It is utterly wrong to send these nice well-trained girls, who have been used to decent living, back to homes such as they have to go to, where they know nothing of their native life, are a burden on their people who are already half-starved, as soon as the first welcome wears off, are regarded as a useless encumberance [sic].[49]

Sarah-Jane Essau, a native woman from Moosehide, echoed these sentiments when she wrote to Bishop Stringer, "When they are too long at school they won't have anything to do with us; they want to be with white people; they grow away from us."[50]

These attitudes were widely shared. An Old Crow woman noted in 1937:

> When they [ex-pupils] return their lot is not an easy one, for they have to go back to primitive conditions, and the majority of them can never hope to change their people. They told me it would be impossible to do anything with the old people. Consequently they slip back into careless ways and many go astray....I am sure those who spent many years of their lives trying to teach these children a higher standard of living both physically and morally would be horrified about their morals.[51]

The Indians of that community made the same point eight years later, although their emphasis was notably different. In a petition to the federal government asking for a residential school in their area, they noted that the graduates were poorly prepared for the harvesting way of life, had trouble adjusting to the harsh northern climate, and tended to "look down upon their parents and our (and their) natural way of life." The negative experience with Carcross graduates had been such that no children had been sent to the school for more than ten years.[52]

A major difficulty facing the former students lay, ironically, with their occupational training. Though the clergy repeatedly restated their desire to prepare students for their "afterlife," experience illustrates that the clergy's mix of practical and technical skills was inadequate for most students. Male graduates occasionally found temporary work as railway hands, labourers, guides, meat wholesalers or, more often, school assistants. The regional economy, however, emphasized skilled labour on a seasonal basis, and provided few regular openings for the partially trained students. The experience of Harry Davis is not untypical. After graduating in 1939, he remained in Carcross for a year attempting to secure suitable employment. Unsuccessful in his efforts, he applied to the school for funds to travel to Dawson City, where it was rumoured he could find work.[53] If Davis' career paralleled that of other graduates, he would have been unsuccessful in this effort as well.

The missionaries tried very hard to secure positions for their graduates, particularly the more promising ones. Their efforts were often unsuccessful and, with regret, they noted that the students returned to their home villages. By itself, this was often interpreted as a sign of weakness. When a promising young scholar, James Tizya, sought permission to return to Old Crow in 1933, former Anglican missionary and territorial Indian Agent John Hawksley commented: "I am inclined to think his decision is to some extent influenced by a desire for freedom and the somewhat lazy life of the Old Crow Indian."[54] These children did not return easily to the harvesting way, for their education had not offered sufficient skills. At the same time, however, the students lacked the inclination to turn wholeheartedly to a Euro-Canadian lifestyle. Those who attempted such an integration typically found their way blocked by exclusionist attitudes, their educational attainments of little practical use. The clergy, while focusing their attentions on the students, had done little to smooth a path for the natives in a still strongly segregationist white society. These graduates of the Carcross Residential School were clearly caught in the middle, unsure of their place, uneasy in both worlds and unclear as to what the future held.

Because so much of their mission rested on the students, the Anglican clergy maintained a close watch on their progress, revelling in their accomplishments, despairing in their troubles. To protect their investment, missionaries endeavoured to keep the young people from the twin evils of village life and white-dominated urban centres. The church ended up protecting the students from the very environment they were supposed to reform. Several of the better students (defined by academic competence) were kept at the school after graduation as over-age students, teaching assistants and labourers. The teachers hoped that the extra years' grace would prepare them more adequately for the unenviable challenge ahead. Most clergy viewed the intermarriage of graduates as the best means of protecting those versed in the new morality and customs, and they encouraged suitable marriages, occasionally over the graduates' protests.[55] Their efforts to save this one group only served to highlight their distinctiveness and compounded the difficulties of returning to the village. While few supported one theology student's recommendation that a separate village be established for the young graduates,[56] most missionaries privately acknowledged that the residential school children could not be left entirely to their own devices.

The post-graduation experience of the Carcross Residential School graduates was difficult for the missionaries to accept. Cautioned by the federal government to make their instructional program relevant to the student's "afterlife," the clergy had modified their curriculum. The intention was to impart rudimentary literary and computational skills plus extended training in directly relevant occupational activities. Though the technical training proved of limited utility, the students equipped for neither the hunting nor the mining camp, the real difficulty lay in the school's social program. Through their system of rigid discipline, social control, Christian teaching and moral guidance, the clergy sought to substantially revise native attitudes. These teachings, however, set the students on a collision course with the values and customs of their Indian villages. Accommodating these vastly different attitudes made the transition from residential school to hunting camp an onerous one.

It is understandable that the clergy refused to modify their social goals. The central theme of the institution was a desire to provide the native students with a new outlook on life, health and work, all in a Christian framework. Those values could not be compromised. To do so would have meant denying the fundamental purpose of the Carcross School and the missionaries' aspirations for the Yukon Indians. The problems encountered by the graduates upon reentry therefore originated with the basic structure of the institution and the underlying aims of the Anglican church's mission to the northern natives. Conflict between long-separated children and parents, between school ideas and those of the native village, was as inevitable as it proved painful. Designed to provide a generation of leaders for the Yukon Indians, the facility instead produced children caught "betwixt and between" the contradictory values of their parents and their teachers.

The construction of a new 150 student facility in 1953–1954 radically altered the nature of the Carcross Residential School. Reflecting a post-World War II surge in social welfare programming, the federal government's policy toward the northern native changed dramatically in favour of increased intervention. Far removed in time and outlook from Frank Oliver's warnings, government officials clamoured for a major extension of residential education and in particular for the implementation of a more formal and intensive scholastic and training program. The Anglican clergy and teachers were quickly pushed to the sidelines. In the years that followed, as Richard King demonstrated in his study of the school in the 1960s,[57] the new civilian teachers went noticeably beyond the limited program developed by their Anglican predecessors. It was imperative to the government that native children be brought to a level of scholastic attainment, equaling that provided by territorial public schools. To fail to do so, many believed, would doom the Indian children to a life outside the mainstream of a rapidly modernizing northern economy. As had been the case in the Anglican period, however, little thought was given to the impact of the social, cultural and educational programs on the children or to the difficulties they would encounter upon graduation. In moving the institution much closer to the norms of the public schools, and therefore making it even less relevant to the natives' cultural and economic background, school administrators and Department of Indian Affairs officials unwittingly accelerated the problems facing the students upon returning to their homes.

Acting with great sincerity and a firm conviction that their program was best for the native children, the Anglican clergy readily (though never adequately) modified their educational offering to make the school relevant to life in the native village. Their best efforts could not, however, overcome the underlying fact that their institution demanded through its social and moral structure a rejection of parental and community values. The Carcross Residential School failed to provide the native students with an obvious route into either native or white society.

Notes

1. For a summary of Anglican activities in the North, see T.C.B. Boon, *The Anglican Church From the Bay to the Rockies* (Toronto: Ryerson Press, 1962).

2. See the discussions on missionaries by Morris Zaslow in *A Reader's Guide to Canadian History 2: Confederation to the Present*, ed. J.L. Granatstein and Paul Stevens (Toronto: University of Toronto Press, 1982), 306–7.

3. Jean Usher, *William Duncan of Metlakatla* (Ottawa: National Museum of Man, 1974) and Robin Fisher, *Contact and Conflict* (Vancouver: University of British Columbia Press, 1977), chapter 6, offer useful assessments of missionary activity in British Columbia.

4. Ralph Linton, *Acculturation in Seven Indian Tribes* (New York: Appleton-Century Co., 1940). This approach is applied directly in Fisher, *Contact and Conflict*.

5. J. Gresko, "White 'Rites' and Indian 'Rites': Indian Education and Native Responses in the West, 1870–1920," in *Shaping the Schools of the Canadian West*, ed. D. Jones, N. Sheehan, and R. Stamp (Calgary: Detselig, 1979), 84–106; D.W. Adams, "Schooling the Hopi: Federal Indian Policy Writ Small, 1887–1917," in *American Vistas: 1877 to the Present*, ed. L. Dinnerstein and K. Jackson (New York: Oxford University Press, 1983), 3–20.

6. T.C.B. Boon, *The Anglican Church*. Additional information can be found in H.A. Cody, *An Apostle of the North* (New York: E.P. Dalton, 1908); A.S. Archer, *A Heroine of the North* (London: Macmillan, 1929).

7. Bompas to Church Missionary Society (hereafter CMS), 3 January 1894, CMS.

8. Cody, *Apostle of the North*, 253–72; Boon, *The Anglican Church*, 222–23; "Incidents in the Life of R.J. Bowen," Bowen Papers, 100, Public Archives of Canada (hereafter PAC), Ottawa.

9. Bompas to Hon. J.H. Ross, 7 March 1903, Department of Indian Affairs (hereafter DIA), 3962, file 147, 654–1, pt.2, PAC.

10. Cody, *Apostle of the North*, 310–36; M. Gibbs, "History of Chooutla School," Anglican Church Records (hereafter ACR) 82/77, Yukon Territorial Archives (hereafter YTA); David Greig, "The Anglican Mission Schools and the Beginning of Carcross Residential School from 1890 to 1907," in J.D. Wilson, "Schooling on

a Distant Frontier,'' MS, ACR 82/526, YTA.

11.   F. Pedley, Deputy Superintendent General of Indian Affairs to Reverend L. Norman Tucker, 21 March 1906, Missionary Society of the Church of England in Canada (hereafter MSCC), ser. 2–14, 75–103, Anglican Church General Synod Archives (hereafter GSA).

12.   Pedley to Tucker, 21 March 1906, MSCC.

13.   Memorandum on Indian Missions and Indian Schools, submitted on behalf of the Special Indian Committee of the MSCC, 14 March 1906, GSA. The concurrence of Anglicans, Presbyterians and Methodists with Pedley's comments is found in S.H. Blake, Memorandum of a Conference, 24–27 March 1908, MSCC, 75–103, GSA.

14.   Frank Oliver to A.C.C., 28 January 1908, MSCC, ser.2–14, 75–103.

15.   Journal of the Synod of the Diocese of the Yukon, Whitehorse, 1907, Vancouver School of Theology, GSA.

16.   T.G. Bragg to Hon. Alexander Henderson, 14 December 1907, YRG1, ser.4, 13, file 308, YTA.

17.   J.D. McLean to A.W. Vowell, 4 April 1908, DIA, 3962, file 147, 654–1. The comments came directly from a subordinate's letter; Accountant to Deputy Superintendent General, 20 February 1908, DIA, 3962, file 147, 654–1.

18.   Accountant to Deputy Superintendent General, 20 February 1908, DIA, 3962, file 147, 654–1.

19.   The supporting reports can be found in Anglican Church, n.s., 1983, YTA.

20.   Report of Messrs. Vowell and Green, 14 August 1908, Anglican Church, n.s., 1983, file 2.

21.   Notes of Interview with F. Oliver, 26 February 1909, Anglican Church, n.s., 1983, file 2.

22.   Gibbs, ''History of Chooutla School''; Church of England in Canada, *Chooutla Indian School* (Missionary Society, Indian Residential School Commission, n.d.); A. King, *The School at Mopass* (Toronto: Holt, Rinehart and Winston, 1967), 36–38. On the debate to relocate the school see C. Clark, ''An Educational Survey with Reference to the Relocation of Carcross Indian Residential School,'' 8 September 1950, DIA, 8762, file 906/25–1–001.

23.   On the general Anglican mission to Canadian Indians see Jean Usher, ''Apostles and Aborigines: The Social Theory of the Church Missionary Society,'' *Historie Sociale/Social History* 7 (April 1971): 28–52. For reports of the program in action at Carcross, see Report of E.D. Evans, 29 April 1921, and Report of W.T. Townsend, 31 March 1914, ACR, Carcross School file 2; Report of Chas. Johnson, 31 March 1918, ACR, C.F. Johnson file 2; also useful are the regular summaries in *Northern Lights*, the journal of the Yukon diocese.

24.   The summary is based on: ''Report of the Supt. of Indian Education,'' *Annual Report 1909–1910*, DIA, 351; Ross to Congdon, 16 April 1904, Ross to DIA, 2 April 1906, T.G. Bragg to McLean, 1 May 1907, and Bragg to Secretary of DIA, 21 April 1910, DIA, 3962, file 1457, 654–1, pt.2; Stockton to Deputy Supt. General, 29 November 1912, Stringer to Secretary of DIA, 31 March 1913 (a reply to Stockton's criticism), and Hawksley to J.D. McLean, 7 January 1915, DIA, 6479, file 940–1, pt. 1; Hawksley to A.F. McKenzie, 25 March 1931, and H.C.M. Grant to Supt. Indian Affairs, 5 February 1940, DIA, 6479, file 940–1, pt. 2; E.D. Evans to J.D. McLean, 29 April 1912, ACR Carcross School file 1; Report of Venerable Archdeacon T.H. Canham, 31 March 1913, *Annual Report 1912/13*, DIA; Collins to Blake, 27 April 1904, 13 March 1909, and 11 February 1909, MSCC, ser.2–14, 75–103. *Northern Lights* is the best source, covering the entire period in question.

25.   *Northern Lights* 15, 1 (February 1927): 1.

26. *Northern Lights* 28, 2 (May 1939): 5.

27. C.E. Whittaker to Dr. Smith, 2 July 1919, ACR Carcross file.

28. There are numerous examples of school restrictions on socialization with members of the Carcross community. With few exceptions, principals refused to allow the children to visit the town without direct adult supervision; Hawksley to MacKenzie, 25 March 1931, DIA, 6479, file 940–1, pt. 1.

29. Grant to Supt. Indian Affairs, 5 February 1940, DIA, 6479, file 940–1, pt. 2.

30. The limits on socialization characterized industrial schools generally. See J.D. Wilson, "A Note on Shingwark Industrial Home for Indians [Sault Ste. Marie]," *Journal of the Canadian Church Historical Society* 16, 4 (December 1974): 66–71.

31. Oliver to A.C.C., 28 January 1908, MSCC, ser.2–14, 75–105.

32. *Northern Lights* 15, 1 (February 1927): 1.

33. Stringer to Dr. Westgate, 19 April 1923, ACR, Westgate file.

34. Stringer to Johnson, 24 August 1918, ACR 79/52. He made similar arrangement for the entry of mixed-blood Jeff van Dorder from Ross River at the same time.

35. Regarding the children of A. Njootli, one of several catechists to send his children to the school, see Stringer to Njootli, 26 January 1947, ACR, Amos Njootli file.

36. B. Neary to R. Meek, 19 August 1949, DIA, 6481, file 940–19, pt. 6.

37. See various sets of correspondence in DIA, 6481, file 940–10. Re: the Chitzi children of Old Crow, sent to the school following their parents' separation, see Gibbon to Secretary, J.A.B., 23 May 1945 and 16 July 1946, DIA, 6481, 940–10.

38. Hawksley to McLean, 16 April 1923, DIA, 6479, file 940–1, pt. 1; Hawksley to McLean, 15 October 1929, RG91, 9, file 1491, pt.4, PAC; Meek to Welfare and Training, 17 January 1947, DIA, 6481, file 940–10, pt. 5. On one occasion, agents were instructed to attempt to recruit students from close to Carcross to reduce expenditures; Phelan to Commissioner, RCMP, 9 September 1940, DIA, 6481, file 940–10, pt. 4.

39. Gibbs, "History of the Chooutla School," 11; Stockton to Deputy Supt. General, 29 November 1912, DIA, 6479, file 940–1, pt. 1; King, *The School at Mopass*.

40. Grant to Capt. Binning, 12 May 1938, DIA, 6481, file 940–10, pt. 4; Roth to Gibben, 30 September 1942, DIA, 6479, file 940–1, pt. 2. For Bishop Stringer's response to a series of allegations (see Stockton's letter above) that reached federal officials, see Stringer to Secretary of DIA, 31 March 1913, DIA, 6479, file 940–1, pt. 2.

41. For specific cases see Sarah-Jane Essau to Bishop, 31 August 1919, ACR, Moosehide file, YTA; Grant to Dewdney, 17 November 1941, Phelan to Grant, 8 August 1938, Grant to Phelan, 24 August 1938, Binning to Secretary DIA, 11 April 1938, Grant to O.C., RCMP, 2 March 1934, Meek to I.A.B., 18 August 1947, T.B. Caulkin to Principal, 16 March 1935, and Binning to Secretary DIA, 15 December 1937, DIA, 6481, file 940–10, pt. 4; Meek to J.A.B., 29 August 1947, and 4 April 1949, DIA, 6481, file 940–10, pt. 6. Many more students were removed from school for disciplinary or academic reasons than were returned at their parents' requests.

42. Wood to Stringer, 14 April 1926, ACR, McCullum file, YTA.

43. Report of Rev. W.T. Townsend, 31 March 1914, ACR, Carcross School file; Report of E.D. Evans, 31 March 1912, ACR, Carcross School file; *Annual Report 1909–1910*, DIA, 314; *Annual Report 1912/13*, DIA, 618. Finding jobs for graduates became progressively more difficult due to territorial economic problems and entrenched segregationist attitudes.

44. Gibbs, "History of Chooutla School," 13–14. *Northern Lights* provided regular updates on the progress of noted graduates.

45. Johns' career is discussed at length in Robert McCandless, "Yukon Wildlife: A Social History," MS, 79/13, YTA.

46. Hawksley to Mackenzie, 7 March 1930, RG91, 1490, pt. 5, PAC. Enfranchisement files are, of course, closed. The government, however, clearly favoured Carcross graduates when reviewing such applications.

47. Robinson to Dickson, 7 March 1939, ACR, Selkirk Children Reports, YTA.

48. Report of Missionary Work carried on from 23 May to 31 August 1934 in and about Carmacks, ACR, Carmacks-Little Salmon file. Similar components, supporting what follows, can be found in Whittaker to Dr. Smith, 2 July 1919, Anglican Church Carcross file; Stringer to Johnson, 31 October 1917, ACR, C.F. Johnson file; T.G. Bragg to Secretary DIA, 23 June 1910, DIA, 3962, file 147, 654–1, pt. 2; Hawksley to Principal of Chooutla School, 27 May 1933, DIA, 6479, file 940–1, pt. 6; McCabe to Coldrick, 11 December 1933, ACR, Old Crow file; E.D. Wood to Stringer, 14 April 1926, ACR McCullum file.

49. E.D. Wood to Stringer, 14 April 1926, ACR, McCullum file.

50. Sarah-Jane Essau to Bishop, 31 August 1919, ACR, Moosehide file.

51. McCabe to Coldrick, 11 December 1937, ACR, Old Crow file.

52. Peter Moses et al. to Indian Agent, 28 August 1945, DIA, 6478, file 932–1, pt. 1.

53. Grant to Hoey, 20 July 1940, DIA, 6481, file 940–10, pt. 1.

54. Hawksley to Principal of Chooutla Indian School, 27 May 1933, RG91, 11, file 2335, pt. 6, PAC.

55. Stringer to Whittaker, 20 February 1915, ACR, Whittaker Papers; Stringer to Townsend, 28 January 1916, ACR, Townsend file; Stringer to Miss Bennett, 13 July 1918, ACR, Bennett file. Bishop Stringer was a particular advocate of this approach. Subsequent bishops followed the same line but with less zeal.

56. Report of Missionary Work, 23 May to 31 August 1934, ACR, Carcross-Little Salmon file.

57. King, *The School at Mopass*. For a more favourable view, prepared by a principal of the school, see M. Gibbs, "The History of Chooutla School."

EAGLE OVER THE ARCTIC: AMERICANS IN THE CANADIAN NORTH, 1867–1985*

WILLIAM R. MORRISON

Critics of the American imperialist impulse of the nineteenth and early twentieth centuries have pictured the United States as a country expanding greedily in every direction, engulfing a large part of Mexico, and more distant territories from Puerto Rico to Hawaii. Even Canada, America's most inoffensive neighbour, felt the breath of the imperialist whirlwind after Confederation, particularly in the North during the Alaska boundary dispute of 1903.

Canadian nationalists of an earlier generation were prone to see this dispute as the act of a bully: Canada, valiantly clinging to its northern heritage, was unfairly robbed of a portion of it by the threats and obstinacy of a powerful neighbour. In fact, Canada's case was weak.[1] Moreover, the Canadian attachment to the country's North was a fickle one. Canadians were alarmed and affronted when the United States seemed to threaten the North, but when the danger passed, they ignored the region. Since Confederation it has been Canadian indifference, not American aggression, which has weakened Canada's presence in the North, and on occasion even called into question her claims to sovereignty there.

When in 1870 and 1880 Canada acquired title to what is now the Yukon and Northwest Territories, the size of the Dominion was increased by 1.5 million square miles. Canada had gained what has proved to be a national treasure. But since its acquisition the Canadian government has treated the North as a national attic—an unimportant superstructure to the country, to be ignored and relegated beyond the periphery of national development. Canada was roused from its indifference only when the government perceived that Americans were finding opportunities in the North which had seemed invisible to Canadians. When Canada's static conception of the region was challenged by the more dynamic American view, the Canadian government was moved to assert its rights there.

* *Canadian Review of American Studies* (Spring 1987), 61–75.

At the centre of Canadian-American relations in the North since 1867 has been the question of sovereignty. From the purchase of Alaska in the year of Canadian Confederation to the present, the questions of sovereignty over Canada's North and developmental activity in it have focussed almost exclusively on the United States. To those unfamiliar with the chequered history of northern sovereignty in Canada, it may come as a surprise that it should be a "question" at all, rather than an issue long since settled to the satisfaction of Canada and other countries. But sovereignty is indeed an unsettled question in Canada, as the 1985 voyage of the American ship *Polar Sea* through the Northwest Passage has shown.

Though the concept of sovereignty in international law is one with many complicated ramifications, it may be usefully simplified for the purposes of understanding the history of Canadian-American relations in the North. The kind of sovereignty which Canada has traditionally exercised in the North may be called "symbolic" sovereignty[2]—that which is concerned with actions which are universally recognized in international law, particularly the formal occupation and legal administration of territory. Such actions as raising a flag and taking possession of territory in the name of a monarch or a government are symbols of sovereignty, as is operating a post office, collecting customs duties, and conducting a census.

Because it was based on symbols rather than development, the Canadian concept of sovereignty was essentially a passive one, more image than reality. It arose out of a desire to have formal possession of the North, combined with a lack of ideas as to what to do with it, or a general indifference to it—what J.L. Granatstein has called "a fit of absence of mind."[3] The traditional attitude of Canadians towards their North may be described as "mappism"— pride in the extent of the country as it appears on the map combined with ignorance of what the North is actually like, and a disinclination to do more than daydream about it or idealize it. Moreover, what actions Canadians have taken in their North have as a rule not been spontaneous, but have been forced upon them from outside.

The attitude of Americans towards their North, and indeed towards the rest of the world, may be seen in developmental rather than symbolic terms. This is a vision of the North which does not depend on symbols and dreams, but instead on practical exploitation and development, either, as originally, for commercial purposes, or, as in the last fifty years, increasingly for military purposes. Because the American North is small compared to the Canadian, because Canadians have shied away from active participation in their own North, and because the Canadian North has been seen as vital to the defence of the continent, Americans have tended over the past hundred years to fill a vacuum there. Though the main thrust of nineteenth century Manifest Destiny was to the south and west, it did lead some Americans northward as well.[4] This process, which became evident almost from the moment the United States acquired territory in the north, is particularly evident today in the search for new petroleum resources in the Arctic region. Thus the history of the

Canadian North is in part a history of the relations of two differing national concepts of the North, in which the active, developmental concept, as represented by the Americans, interacts with the more passive, or symbolic concept of sovereignty represented by Canada. Moreover, for over a century now it has often been intrusions by Americans which have stimulated Canadians to take action in their North. The phlegmatic Canadian beaver was only with difficulty persuaded to challenge the eagle.

An early illustration of the American attitude towards the North occurred in 1869, two years after the purchase of Alaska from the Russians. In the new territory, near the junction of the Porcupine and Yukon rivers, the Hudson's Bay Company had in 1846 built Fort Yukon.[5] The post was situated well over a hundred miles inside Russian territory, but the location was so favourable from the point of view of transportation to British North America, and the trade so profitable, that the British took the risk that the Russians would take no action to oust them. For twenty years the Hudson's Bay Company poached on Russian territory, with the Russians too weak, or too indifferent, to take action. But when the United States purchased Alaska in 1867, the Hudson's Bay Company found the new owners "much more energetic and much less lackadaisical than their Slavic predecessors."[6] Within a year a Hudson's Bay Company ship had been denied passage up the Stikine River, the navigation rights of the 1825 Anglo-Russian treaty having lapsed with the cession.[7] In 1869 Captain Charles W. Raymond, a U.S. army engineer, was sent to accompany an American commercial expedition up the Yukon river, with instructions to order the British Company out of American territory. Raymond determined by astronomical observation that the post was indeed well within American territory, and ordered the Company's men to leave, which they did in the spring of the next year.[8]

Although the traditional historical interpretation is that the United States had little interest in Alaska in the nineteenth century, and that the abrupt ejection of the Hudson's Bay Company from Fort Yukon was mostly a case of twisting the lion's tail, the United States government's interest in its North was obsessive compared to that of the Canadian government's in what would become the Canadian North. In 1870, the year the servants of the Hudson's Bay Company finally left Fort Yukon, the organization transferred all of what is now the Yukon and the continental part of the Northwest Territories to the government of Canada.[9] It now fell to Ottawa to explore, defend, and develop northern Canada. Yet the official attitude towards the North was, for thirty years, an almost totally passive one. The Canadian government was heavily involved in the settlement of the prairies and in building the Canadian Pacific Railway. There was still plenty of "frontier" in southern Canada in the 1880s and 1890s, though perhaps significantly, the frontier in the forty-eight American states was to close in 1890. Although there were some gestures made by way of symbolic sovereignty in the eastern Arctic—periodic voyages were made to that region beginning in 1897[10]—there was no permanent representative of the Canadian government resident in the Yukon before 1894, and none in the eastern or western Arctic until 1903. In fact, the Canadian government was so uninterested in the Arctic that there was opposition in the Canadian Parliament to the transfer of the Arctic islands from Britain in 1880 on the grounds that the territory would be valueless and expensive to administer.[11] Canada's reaction to the gift was to ignore it for nearly forty years; as one commentator put it:

> Canada was content to permit the residual Northwest Territories to remain a deserted and forgotten national attic. The government might be striving to extend that attic to the north pole, but it had no intention of furnishing it with meaningful government if the expense could be avoided.[12]

The early commercial history of Canada's western Arctic shows the difference between the clarity of the American commercial purpose and the passivity and dithering of the Canadians. The commercial value of this region lay in the whales that could be caught there, and also in the opportunities for trading with the Inuit inhabitants. When in 1888 rumours began to circulate among the Pacific whaling fleet that whales were plentiful in the Beaufort Sea, an employee of the American-owned Pacific Steam Whaling Company was sent to the Mackenzie Delta region to investigate. He reported to his employers that the rumours were true, and in the next year, 1889, seven whaling ships headed for the new field. With them came a U.S. Navy vessel, the U.S.S. *Thetis*, assigned by the American government to assist the whaling fleet, and commanded by Lieutenant-Commander C.H. Stockton, who made a survey of the region around Herschel Island[13] and named the most prominent geographical features of the region. It was thus an American vessel which explored this corner of Canada; no Canadian government ship was to call there for another forty years.[14]

The next fifteen years saw a whaling boom in Canada's western Arctic, as American whaling ships came north for trips that lasted two or three years. The profits were considerable at first: in 1891 the *Grampus* out of San Francisco returned home with nearly a quarter million dollars of cargo. It was estimated that by the end of this period, when synthetic materials destroyed the market, whales worth about $13.5 million had been caught in the waters of the western Canadian Arctic, as well as furs worth about $1.5 million.[15] Not a penny of duty was paid to the Canadian government on any of this.

In contrast to the American attitude towards encroachment on its sovereignty in Alaska—an immediate order to the Hudson's Bay Company to desist and depart—the Canadian government, though well aware of the situation in its western Arctic, did nothing about it for nearly fourteen years. What moved Canada to take steps to assert its sovereignty in the western Arctic was the possibility of public embarrassment arising from complaints that the government's lack of assertiveness was leading to the abuse of its citizens. In 1893 a young Anglican missionary, Isaac Stringer, arrived on Herschel Island.

Although Stringer was welcomed by the whaling captains as an asset to the island's social life, he sent reports to his superior, Bishop W.C. Bompas of the Diocese of Mackenzie, outlining the debauchery which was occurring there. Whaling captains made a practice of taking Inuit women as concubines for the long winter months. The crews also supplied the Inuit with liquor, and taught them to make home-brew. In the eyes of the clerics the result was unspeakable debauchery; complaints were forwarded to Ottawa by the bishop and after 1895 by the Mounted Police in the Yukon:

> The carryings-on of the officers and crews of the whalers there was such that no one would believe...large quantities of whiskey are taken up in the ships...as long as the liquor lasts, the natives neither fish nor hunt, and die of starvation in consequence....The captains and mates of these vessels purchase for their own use girls from nine years and upwards....[16]

Even after several years of such reports, Canadian officials were reluctant to assert their authority in the region. Early in 1901 Frederick White, Comptroller of the Mounted Police, advised Clifford Sifton, Minister of the Interior—the man responsible for the Territories—that "it is certainly desireable [sic] that Canada should assert her authority in the Arctic Ocean, but it is questionable whether the results would justify the expenditure, at present."[17]

What makes such passivity so remarkable is that at the same time a similar situation was developing in the eastern Arctic. American whaling ships sailing out of New England ports had been operating in Hudson Bay since the early 1860s. They had a wintering station at Cape Fullerton on the northwestern coast of the bay. This area, like the western Arctic coast, had become part of Canada by the purchase of Rupert's Land in 1870, but as was the case to the west, the Canadian government largely ignored the whaling and trading activities of the Americans. The difference between the two whaling centres, as far as Canadian sovereignty was concerned, was that Canada then laid no claim to sovereignty over the waters of the Beaufort Sea, but did claim Hudson Bay as part of the territorial waters of Canada.[18]

As in the west, what brought the question to the attention of the authorities was not the loss of revenue due to trade goods and whales on which duty was not paid, but the harm done to the culture of the Inuit in the region.[19] Yet not even reports of cultural dislocation and general debauchery were enough to move the government to action. What finally tipped the scales was a combination of events affecting Canadian sovereignty in the North which took place around the turn of the century. The first and most famous of these was the Yukon, or Klondike gold rush of 1897–1899. Here again was an example of Americans asserting, for a time, a *de facto* sovereignty over a part of Canada.

Most of the early development of the Yukon gold fields was carried out by Americans, many of them veterans of the California and British Columbia gold rushes.[20] Miners began to prospect in the Yukon in the mid 1880s, and within ten years there were more than five hundred miners operating in the region as well as two U.S.-owned trading companies, which controlled its commercial life.[21] Though a few Canadian officials had travelled in the country for the Geological Survey of Canada,[22] the area, and particularly its social organization, was virtually *terra incognita* in Ottawa.

Though Washington never made any formal or informal claim to the Yukon, Canada's sovereignty over the region was clouded, not only by the absence of any official presence in the area, but also because the miners, for lack of any official structure, had created their own. Because there were no Canadian officials in the Yukon, and thus no mining laws and regulations, the miners ran the camps by means of the "miners' meeting"—a sort of direct democracy based on the mining laws of the western United States. Under this code any miner with a grievance could call a meeting of his fellows who would hear the case, discuss it, and render a decision which was binding on the community. William Ogilvie, an early observer, reported that "each locality makes its own by-laws, elects its recorder, fixes the amount of the recording fee, and decides the size of the claim."[23]

The miners' meeting, an institution to gladden the heart of Frederick Jackson Turner, was also an example of the American approach to sovereignty in the North. The miners were engaged in developmental rather than symbolic sovereignty. They made no claim that the Yukon was part of America; rather, they developed it in their own interests. In the absence of Canadian authority, the miners administered the Yukon as they saw fit. Title to the Yukon may have been Canadian, but it was the Americans who were benefiting from its wealth.

It was this fact, along with the complaints from the local missionary bishop that the miners were debauching the Indians, that finally spurred the Canadian government to action. The possibility of revenue from customs duties on trade goods and perhaps on gold also was an inducement to action, as the government was less reluctant to assert itself in the North if there was some possibility of profit. Thus in the summer of 1894 two members of the North West Mounted Police went to the Yukon on a reconnaissance mission. The leader of the expedition, Inspector Charles Constantine, collected $3200 that summer in customs duties from the miners, who grumbled somewhat, but paid. This was an important demonstration of symbolic sovereignty, for the collection of such fees was an important proof of sovereignty under international law.

In the summer of the next year, 1895, the government sent a detachment of twenty Mounted Police to the Yukon, and it was in that year that an event occurred which symbolized the new, more assertive Canadian approach to the Territory. A miners' meeting seized a claim for default of wages, in contravention of Canadian law. Inspector Constantine sent an armed detachment of ten men to the claim with a note to the miners warning them to give the claim back to its legal owner. This they did, and the only organized challenge to Canadian authority in the Yukon vanished.[24]

The history of the Yukon gold rush is well known. Gold was discovered in large quantities in 1896, and in the next two years tens of thousands of people came to the Territory. The police controlled it with a firm hand, closing the saloons on the Sabbath, confiscating hand guns, and ordering bad characters out of the country, particularly the kind of American which one police officer described as "the scum of the coastal cities." The "shoot-em-up" image which the rest of the world had of the city of Dawson and the gold-rush society in general was a fantasy; it was probably the most orderly gold rush in history—the government, once roused to action, on this occasion spared neither effort nor expense in asserting Canadian authority and control in the region. Perhaps to its surprise, it was brilliantly successful in doing so.[25]

There is also significance to the fact that in this period Canadian-American frictions were simultaneously evident in four distinct areas of the North: in the western Arctic, in the Yukon, in Hudson Bay, and in the disputed Alaska panhandle region where American activities caused unease in Ottawa. The resolution of the Alaska boundary dispute in 1903 caused a considerable public outcry in Canada,[26] not because of the value of the lost territory, but because of the perceived public humiliation,[27] and it was largely for this reason that the Canadian government resolved not to let sovereignty over the western or eastern Arctic again fall into question. The result of this determination was the dispatching in 1903 of Mounted Police detachments to Herschel Island in the western Arctic and to Cape Fullerton on the northwest coast of Hudson Bay at the mouth of Chesterfield Inlet. In both places the police raised the flag and enforced formal obedience to Canadian law. The effect on the actual operations of the American whalers was minimal—in any case, the whaling industry was in rapid decline.

Twenty years later, in the next spasm of activity in the field of sovereignty undertaken by the government, it was again fear of American "spread-eagleism" in the North that spurred the Canadian government to action.[28] The American explorer Donald B. MacMillan, who had discovered and explored much of western Ellesmere Island during the First World War, was preparing an expedition for 1925 which would carry out aerial explorations of the polar region from bases on Ellesmere and Axel Heiberg Islands. When the Canadian government heard of his plans, it informed him through the British ambassador in Washington that Canadian licences were required if he wished to take specimens of Arctic fauna, but MacMillan ignored letters to this effect.[29]

The attitude of the Canadian civil service was, as usual, dilatory. The bureaucrat most directly responsible for the administration of the North had earlier asked in a letter whether the Arctic archipelago was worth bothering about. "Do we want them, or do we not?" he asked. "Apparently if we want them we have to do something to establish our title."[30] His answer was that Canadian public opinion would not permit the North to become American by default; thus some show of sovereignty had to be made:

One has but to recall the outburst of public indignation and protest in Canada at the decision of the Alaskan arbitration [of 1903] to realize what public opinion would be if any neglect on the Government's part resulted in the loss of an area thousands of times larger and more important than was involved in the Alaskan case.[31]

Of course, since the government of the United States had shown no interest in the formal acquisition of northern territory, it had never moved to consolidate any claims it might have had in the North arising from the explorations of its nationals. Nevertheless, the Canadian government eventually moved in the mid 1920s to establish Mounted Police posts at strategic points in the eastern Arctic. The most northerly one, on the east coast of Ellesmere Island at Bache Peninsula, was just north of the 79th parallel. Despite the fact that there were no human beings living within hundreds of miles of the place, except some Greenland Inuit at Etah, the police ran a post office at Bache Peninsula, since operation of a post office was internationally accepted as a symbol of sovereignty. Mail delivery was once a year, except in years when the ice was bad in August—then it was every other year.[32]

The modern period of Canadian-American relations in the North began after the outbreak of the Second World War in 1939, and particularly after the Permanent Joint Board on Defence was set up by the Ogdensburg Agreement of 1940. Here at last was something in the Canadian North that the American government truly wanted—a defence perimeter. And what it wanted, it got: the Alaska Highway, the Northwest Staging Route, and the CANOL project.

The general history of these mammoth defence projects has been well documented.[33] The airfields and particularly the highway were build in record time with traditional American "can do" enthusiasm. But there were ominous implications for Canadian sovereignty in the tens of thousands of American service personnel working in the northwest without even the most rudimentary supervision by Canadian officials. The story that American army headquarters in Edmonton used to answer the telephone with the greeting "U.S. Army of Occupation" may be apocryphal, but was widely believed. It seems certain that the U.S. officials in the North had a casual attitude towards Canadian sovereignty.

And yet the Canadian government, far from being roused from its traditional apathy to the North by the fact that the incursions on its sovereignty taking place this time were real ones, was even more complacent than it had been when the threats were largely figments of the government's imagination. As Richard Diubaldo has pointed out, "the Canadian government had had little say in the planning and execution of these wide-ranging projects and appeared oblivious to the long-range problems such activities could create....Canada seemed satisfied as long as proper channels were followed and ruffled feathers avoided."[34] It was not that the American government had conscious designs on Canadian sovereignty; rather, they had a clear idea of what they wanted and needed in the Canadian North, and saw no reason why what was in their interests should not be in the interests of the Canadians as well. To the Americans it was largely a question of developmental sovereignty; they were indifferent to its symbols.

In retrospect it seems almost beyond belief, even given the indifference of the Canadian government towards the North, that more than thirty thousand American servicemen should have been permitted to operate in the Canadian northwest in 1942 virtually unsupervised, with Ottawa not knowing, and apparently not much caring, what they were doing. Besides the usual indifference, there was the added excuse of the pressures of war, such as the loss of a Canadian army brigade at Hong Kong in December 1941 and the Dieppe disaster in August 1942. Then too, Prime Minister Mackenzie King tended to acquiesce freely in the continentalist defence plans put forward by his friend Franklin Roosevelt. Certainly it is remarkable that the alarm was sounded not by a Canadian, though there was a small group of informed Canadians who were concerned about the situation, but by a British diplomat.

Malcolm MacDonald, the British High Commissioner to Canada, who had gone on two tours of inspection of the defence projects, reported to the Canadian government in 1943 that "these vast undertakings were being planned and carried out with a view to the post-war situation."[35]

In a note to his superiors in Britain, he outlined the dangers of the American actions to Canada:

> ...It is surely unfortunate that the Canadian authorities have little real say as to, for example, the exact placing of these airfields, and the exact route of these roads on Canadian soil. The Americans decide these according to what they consider American interests. Responsible American officers will tell you frankly in confidence that ...they are designing those works also to be of particular value for (a) commercial aviation and transport after the war and (b) waging war against the Russians in the next world crisis.[36]

Here was a perfect example of American developmental sovereignty, but in this case Canada did not have even the satisfaction of symbolic control, since it was the Stars and Stripes that flew over the northwest defence projects.

After these warnings, Ottawa finally set about to negotiate a removal of the American "occupation" of its northwest, a process which was accomplished, successfully from the Canadian perspective, after two years of bargaining. Much of the responsibility for this success lay with the "northern nationalists,"[37] a small but dedicated group of bureaucrats in a number of government departments who, alarmed by the "almost cavalier attitude of the Canadian government towards the region they considered a key to Canada's destiny,"[38] resolved that Canada must take action in developing its North, lest the Americans' taste for its mineral and strategic value grow even stronger.[39] As Escott Reid of the Department of External Affairs, a member of this group, put it, a northern focus could prove therapeutic to Canadians:

After the emotional debauch of the war there is going to be a bad hangover in all the former belligerent countries. In order that people's lives will not feel too empty, some peacetime equivalents to the exciting national objectives to the war must be found. The opening of a new frontier in the Canadian north can, I think, become a national objective of some importance to the Canadian People. Even if, from the point of view of securing the highest possible national income, the Canadian North is not worth a large expenditure of national energy and capital, a very large expenditure might nevertheless be justified in an effort to realize an inspiring and somewhat romantic national objective.[40]

It is notable that even a northern nationalist like Escott Reid doubted the practical value of the North, seeing it primarily as an outlet for post-war nationalistic energies—not as a place where things might be accomplished, but as an object for aspirations and fantasies.

The post-war period saw a basic shift in the relations of Canada and the United States in the North. For the first time the American government had a clear military goal in the North, while the official Canadian approach remained vague—Prime Minister John Diefenbaker's ill-defined "northern vision" of 1957 was a classic example of symbol without substance. Since the Americans felt strongly about the question of defence, and since in any case they were in the process of becoming the champions of democracy in the cold war against communism, their encroachment into the Canadian North after 1945 seemed well-nigh irresistible. Particularly controversial in Canada was the Distant Early Warning, or DEW line, a chain of radar stations strung along the Arctic coast, allowed under an agreement of 1955, constructed and operated by the American armed forces. What made Canadians uneasy about the DEW line was what James Eayrs called "a general sense of misgiving,"[41] made up of a feeling that de facto control of the Canadian North was passing into American hands, and perhaps some sense of shame that it should be so.

The passage of time and the advent of the Intercontinental Ballistic Missile have rendered the DEW line somewhat obsolete and thus less controversial in Canada.[42] Such is not the case, however, with the North American Air Defence agreement of 1957, which acknowledged that "the air defence of Canada and the U.S. might be considered as a single problem."[43] NORAD is not entirely a "northern" phenomenon, and the opposition to it in Canada has less to do with concerns over northern sovereignty and more to do with the general question of Canada's role as "peacemaker or powder-monkey," to quote the title of James M. Minifie's book. Nonetheless it has great implications for the Canadian North as the frontier and perhaps the future battleground of the superpowers, and it remains an affront to some nationalistic Canadians who resent the "U.S. strategic perception of Canada as a useful polar barrier against trajectories of weapons targeted on the United States which cross Canadian territory."[44]

Two incidents which have taken place in the past twenty years show the persistence in Canada of popular interest in the symbols—as opposed to the realities—of sovereignty. Whereas debate over NORAD and NATO has been confined to political scientists and other academics, what captured public interest in the question of northern sovereignty were Arctic voyages made by U.S. vessels—the *Manhattan* in 1969 and 1970, and the *Polar Sea* in 1985— both of which caused great public controversy. The *Manhattan* voyages, coming two years after the great outburst of nationalistic feeling during the centennial celebrations of 1967, seemed to strike a particularly raw nerve. The *Manhattan* was an oil tanker specially adapted for icebreaking, and its voyages were tests of the feasibility of Arctic routes to bring oil to the south from the Beaufort Sea. Canadian newspapers carried news of the voyages on the front page, and the National Film Board made a film about them.[45] What caused official unease about the *Manhattan*'s voyages was that they emphasized the official American refusal to accept Canada's claim that all the waters of the Arctic archipelago were Canadian. The popular outcry was more the result of a perception that Canada's newly minted sense of national pride was being wantonly flouted.

The *Manhattan* incident continued the passive-reactive tradition of official Canadian response to perceived threats by Americans against its sovereignty in the North. The government did little about the voyage until news reports threatened to embarrass it. Then it was spurred to introduce legislation to emphasize its sovereignty over the Arctic waters, most notably in the control of pollution. But the basic question remains unsolved, since the American government has yet to agree to Canada's definition of the limits of its control over these waters. This is why the voyage of the *Polar Sea* in 1985, which echoed those of the *Manhattan*, again aroused public controversy.[46]

The furor over the *Manhattan*, compared to the relative lack of public interest in Canada's continuing membership in NORAD and NATO, may be taken as indicative of Canadians' approach to their North. Membership in these two organizations has effectively continentalized the defence of the North, and thus a good deal of the control over it. Yet perhaps because these are complex issues which do not fit well into the thirty second analysis of a television newscast and are not easily symbolized (and perhaps because to a degree many Canadians have accepted the realities of continental defence), there is little public discussion of them. On the other hand, there is lively public interest in the symbols of sovereignty—the flying of flags, the official letters of permission—and when these are slighted, there is inevitably an outcry. Perhaps this is because for the Canadian government and some of its citizens the North itself has always been a symbol or an abstraction rather than a reality— the "True North, strong and free" of the Canadian national anthem.[47] For the United States the North has been a practical proposition—something not to be symbolized, but to be employed in the national interest when needed.[48]

This neglect of the North also illustrates some truths about Canada and Canadian-American relations. One is that there is a wide gap between the image and the reality of Canadian development: the image persists that Canada is a northern country, but in reality this is true only in a geographical and in some sense a mythological way. Canada's North has served as an attic in more ways than one. Like an attic, it holds things of value, and successive generations of Canadians have rummaged about in it. Also like an attic, it holds memories and images—of explorers, miners, and Mounted Policemen. But it is not where Canadians want to live, except for the native people, the adventurous, or the merely eccentric. It is not where the thrust of economic development lies, except for the extraction of resources. Perhaps because the material wealth of Canadians permits many to live or travel where they wish rather than where they must, there are tens of thousands who have visited Disney World for every one who has visited Baffin Island. The anomaly of a northern country in which the overwhelming majority of the population lives within a hundred miles or so of the southern border is a commonplace of the human geography of the country.

There are truths here too for the student of Canadian-American relations. It has often been remarked how easily the brittle feelings of Canadians are bruised by the Americans, and this has been as true in the North as elsewhere. Yet on balance it is difficult to fault the Americans, unless one assumes *a priori* that everything the United States does in its foreign relations is malevolent. Over the past hundred years the Americans have acted in their own interests in the Canadian North. Since much of the time they were operating in a power vacuum, it is little wonder they behaved on occasion as if the territory was theirs to exploit. If there was no Canadian military presence to speak of in the northwest in 1941, why should not the American military feel almost like discoverers of new land? Certainly it is true that when at last pressed by a reluctant Canadian government, the Americans willingly observed the proper diplomatic niceties. The exception is the current matter of the Arctic waters, and here the Americans do in fact have at least an arguable case.

The conclusion to be drawn from these events is that the Canadian North is not a good forum for those wishing to indulge in anti-American rhetoric. The United States has never wished to assert formal sovereignty over Canada's North; rather, from time to time it has had specific interests there, and has done what seemed necessary to further them. The United States has not been bellicose in the Canadian North, or, with the exception of Teddy Roosevelt, even very aggressive; rather, it has seen its opportunities and it has taken them. When at the time of the Alaskan controversy of 1903 John Hay, United States Secretary of State, called Canada's attitude to the North that of a "spoiled child,"[49] he was not far wrong. In this respect, Canadians have been prone to long periods of indifference, punctuated by sudden tantrums and periodic sulks, and have tended to blame Americans for their own shortcomings. They would do better to complain less and think more about whether they want their North to continue as merely a source of symbolic nationalism, or whether, after more than a century it is to become truly a part of Canada.

Notes

1. See Norman Penlington, *The Alaska Boundary Dispute: A Critical Reappraisal* (Toronto, 1972) for a dispassionate account of the episode.
2. Symbolic sovereignty is discussed in W.R. Morrison, *Showing the Flag: The Mounted Police and Canadian Sovereignty in the North, 1984–1925* (Vancouver, 1985), and in W.R. Morrison, "Canadian Sovereignty and the Inuit of the Central and Eastern Arctic" (Paper presented to the Fourth Annual Inuit Studies Conference, Montreal, November 1984).
3. J.L. Granatstein, "A Fit of Absence of Mind: Canada's National Interest in the North to 1968," in *The Arctic in Question,* ed. E.J. Dosman (Toronto, 1976).
4. William Seward, acquisitor of Alaska, also cast covetous eyes on Greenland.
5. The name was spelled "Youcon" in the nineteenth century; it was Americans who changed the spelling. For a history of this incident, see B.D. Lain, "The Fort Yukon Affair, 1869,"*Alaska Journal* 7,1 (1977); K.S. Coates, *The Northern Yukon: A History*, Canadian Historic Sites Manuscript Report Series (Ottawa, 1979); K.S. Coates, "Furs Along the Yukon: Hudson's Bay Company-Native Trade in the Yukon River Basin, 1830–1893,"(M.A. diss., University of Manitoba, 1980).
6. Lain, "The Fort Yukon Affair," 13.
7. Under the Treaty of Washington (1871) British subjects were granted the right of free navigation on the Yukon, Porcupine, and Stikine rivers, all three of which rose in Canada and flowed to the sea through Alaska. The purpose of this provision was to guarantee British and Canadian traders—particularly the Hudson's Bay Company—access from the Pacific to the interior of the northwest. It was largely negated when the Americans began to require that a paid U.S. official accompany each party travelling upriver through American territory. This was probably illegal, and was a tremendous nuisance during the Klondike gold rush, but little protest was made. See D.J. Hall, *Clifford Sifton, I: The Young Napoleon* (Vancouver, 1981), 168–79.
8. They established a new post at Rampart House, up the Porcupine River. In 1889, J.H. Turner, an American surveying the international boundary where it crossed that river, found that Rampart House was thirty miles inside Alaska. The lone agent of the Hudson's Bay Company had the fort dismantled and towed upstream across the border, where it operated until 1893. See Lain, "The Fort Yukon Affair," and Coates, "Furs Along the Yukon."
9. The Arctic islands were transferred to Canada in 1880.
10. See Daniel Francis, "Staking Canada's Claim to the Arctic Islands," *Canadian Geographical Journal* 95 (August-September 1977).
11. Thomas M. Tynan, "Canadian-American Relations in the Arctic: The Effect of Environmental Influences upon Territorial Claims," *Review of Politics* 41 (July 1979).
12. J.A. Bovey, "The Attitudes and Policies of the Federal Government towards Canada's Northern Territories, 1870–1930" (M.A. diss., University of British Columbia, 1967), iv. This was true of the Arctic islands, but not of the entire North—the exception was the government's action in the Yukon during the Klondike gold rush, discussed below.
13. Herschel Island lies in the Beaufort Sea just off the north coast of the Yukon Territory, about thirty miles east of the Canadian-American boundary. It has the only good harbour in the region.
14. The RCMP schooner *St. Roch* was the first to do so, in 1928.
15. "Report of Inspector A.M. Jarvis," *Sessional Papers, 1908* (Ottawa: The

King's Printer, 1909), 140.

16. Inspector C. Constantine to Commissioner L.W. Herchmer, 4 September 1895, Comptroller's Correspondence, RCMP Papers, RG18, A-1, vol. 135, Public Archives of Canada (hereafter PAC) Ottawa.

17. White to Sifton, 23 January 1901, Comptroller's Correspondence, RCMP Papers, RG18, A-1, vol. 314.

18. The Beaufort Sea was part of the open ocean, but Hudson Bay was largely closed in by land, and was thus held to be territorial waters. See Gordon Smith, "The Historical and Legal Background of Canada's Arctic Claims," (Ph.D. diss., Columbia University, 1952), especially Chapter 17, "Jurisdiction over Polar Waters."

19. Diamond Jenness, *Eskimo Administration: II. Canada* (Montreal, 1964), 11–12, describes the process.

20. The Yukon, or Klondike gold rush is still a part of American folklore, and many Americans think that the Yukon is in the United States. If this seems hard to believe, consider "Great America," a "family entertainment centre" 45 miles south of San Francisco, which in 1986 included "five historic American areas: Hometown Square, Yankee Harbour, Great Midwest Livestock Exhibition and Country Fair, Orleans Place, and Yukon Territory."

21. The Alaska Commercial Company and the North American Trading and Transportation Company.

22. For the early history of the Yukon, see Allen A. Wright, *Prelude to Bonanza* (Whitehorse, 1980).

23. William Ogilvie, *Early Days on the Yukon* (London, 1913), 245. For a modern analysis, see Thomas Stone, "Flux and Authority in a Subarctic Society: The Yukon Miners in the Nineteenth Century," *Ethnohistory* 30 (1983), and Thomas Stone, "The Mounties as Vigilantes: Reflections on Community and the Transformation of Law in the Yukon, 1885–1897," *Law and Society Review* 4,1 (1974).

24. The incident is recounted in detail in Inspector Constantine's report to Comptroller White, 13 July 1896, Comptroller's Correspondence 123v, RCMP Papers, RG 18, A-1.

25. For a fuller discussion of the establishment of government control in the Yukon, see W.R. Morrison, *Showing the Flag*, Chapters 3, 4, and 5.

26. On this see John A. Munro, "English-Canadianism and the Demand for Canadian Autonomy: Ontario's Response to the Alaska Boundary Decision, 1903," *Ontario History* 57 (December 1965).

27. President Theodore Roosevelt had hinted that he would use force if a settlement were not reached in favour of the United States, and it was widely believed in Canada that the British negotiator in the dispute had sided with the Americans and sold out Canada's case to curry favour with them. See Penlington, *The Alaska Boundary Dispute*, Chapters 5 and 6. He remarks on page 119 that the episode "puts the United States in a bad light and Canada in a worse light."

28. The initial alarm in the post-1918 period was over the activities of Greenland Inuit, loosely under the control of Denmark, hunting on Ellesmere Island.

29. The main documents are printed in Lovell C. Clark, ed., *Documents on Canadian External Relations, III* (Ottawa, 1970), 575–80.

30. J.B. Harkin, minutes of a special meeting of the Advisory Technical Board, 1 October 1920, J.B. Harkin Papers, MG 30, C-63, vol. 1, PAC. Harkin was the Commissioner of Dominion Parks.

31. Harkin to W.W. Cory, Deputy Minister of the Interior, 26 May 1921, Harkin Papers, MG 30, C-63, vol. 1.

32. It must be emphasized that at no period in the history of American

involvement in the Canadian North did the United States government make any formal claim to sovereignty there, nor does it seem that it ever contemplated making such a claim. A recent study concludes that Washington was more interested in the sovereignty question as it applied to the Antarctic rather than the Arctic. The few pronouncements on the subject that came from the State Department confirmed Canada's sovereignty; a letter of 1935 stated that there was "no reason for intimating...that there may be islands to the north of Canada the Canadian sovereignty of which is not universally acknowledged." In 1944 Cordell Hull, the Secretary of State, voiced the same opinion. S.W. Boggs, Office of the Historical Advisor, Department of State to Mr. Hill, 11 September 1935, State Department File 800,014 Arctic/40, U.S. National Archives, Washington, D.C. quoted in Tynan, "Canadian-American Relations."

33. For recent scholarship on the Alaska Highway see Kenneth S. Coates, ed., *The Alaska Highway: Papers of the 40th Anniversary Symposium* (Vancouver, 1985).

34. R.J. Diubaldo, "The Alaska Highway in Canada-United States Relations," in *The Alaska Highway*, ed. K.S. Coates.

35. Quoted in Diubaldo, "The Alaska Highway." See also Curtis B. Nordman, "The Army of Occupation: Malcolm MacDonald and U.S. Military Involvement in the Canadian Northwest," in *The Alaska Highway*, ed. K.S. Coates, 83–94.

36. Nordman, "The Army of Occupation," 88.

37. Shelagh Grant, "The Northern Nationalists: Crusaders and Supporters of a New North, 1940–1950" (Paper presented to the Canadian Historical Association annual meeting, Ottawa, 1982).

38. Nordman, "The Army of Occupation," 85.

39. Diubaldo, "The Alaska Highway," 106.

40. Quoted in Diubaldo, "The Alaska Highway."

41. James Eayrs, *Canada in World Affairs: October 1955 to June 1957* (Toronto, 1959), quoted in Tynan, "Canadian-American Relations."

42. But in 1984 the American government approached Canada with a suggestion that the DEW line be given a $6 billion renovation, three-quarters of the funding to come from the United States. John Honderich, "North of the Border," *New Statesman* 109 (24 May 1985).

43. Quoted in Roger Swanson, "NORAD: Origins and Operations of Canada's Ambivalent Symbol," *International Perspectives* 1 (November-December 1972).

44. Lincoln P. Bloomfield, "The Arctic: Last Unmanaged Frontier," *Foreign Affairs* 60 (Fall 1981).

45. T.M. Tynan, "The Role of the Arctic in Canadian-American Relations" (Ph.D. diss., The Catholic University of America, Washington D.C., 1976) is an invaluable source on the *Manhattan*. Also significant are the articles in Dosman, ed., *The Arctic in Question*, particularly Granatstein, "A Fit of Absence of Mind" and Dosman, "The Northern Sovereignty Crisis 1968–1970." Among the many journal articles arising out of the interest in this episode were M.A. Galway, "Arctic Sovereignty," *Canadian Forum* 49 (November 1969); D.M. McRae, "Arctic Waters and Canadian Sovereignty," *International Journal* 38 (Summer 1983); P. St. Pierre, "Arctic: Problems of Sovereignty and Development," *Canadian Business* 43 (January 1970); D.E. Milsten, "Arctic Passage—Legal Heavy Weather," *Orbis* 15, 4 (1972); A.H.G. Storrs, and T.C. Pullen, "*S.S. Manhattan* in Arctic Waters," *Canadian Geographical Journal* 80, 5 (1970).

46. Peter Burnet, executive director of the Canadian Arctic Resources Committee, said "Canada must strive to put itself in a position to prepare for an international challenge for the waters. Any nation with moxie defends its boundaries, and we shouldn't be seen retreating from the Arctic." Bruce Wallace, "An American

Challenge in the Arctic,'' *Maclean's* 98 (22 July 1985).

47. In the official version of the anthem the words "True North" are capitalized—an apostrophe to an ideal.

48. The American approach to their own North in Alaska is also practical rather than idealized, as Kenneth S. Coates points out in "Controlling the Periphery: The Territorial Administration of the Yukon and Alaska, 1867–1959" (Paper delivered to the Pacific Coast Branch of the American Historical Association, August 1986).

49. Quoted in Penlington, *The Alaska Boundary Dispute*, 47.

TRANSIENCY IN THE FAR NORTHWEST AFTER THE GOLD RUSH: THE CASE OF THE *PRINCESS SOPHIA**

K.S. COATES AND W.R. MORRISON

Some of the most powerful nineteenth century images come from the far northwest;[1] notable among these is the long line of would-be prospectors inching up the steep incline of the Chilkoot Pass. The lures of the North—gold, adventure, and exotic locales—worked powerfully on the minds of North Americans, drawing tens of thousands to the Yukon and Alaska in 1897 and 1898. There exists a rich legacy from this northward migration—the poetry of Robert Service, the stories of Jack London, Charlie Chaplin's "Gold Rush"— all describe the region's appeal, and its impact on those who came, in Johnny Horton's phrase, "North to Alaska."

Northern writers have long noted, generally impressionistically, the importance of transiency and migration in the history of North America's far northwest. Sad dockside farewells of prospectors seeking better fields to the north or west, of disgruntled miners, bitter from isolation or cold, these are familiar elements in northern literature. Historians and historical geographers have done little more than echo these observations using selected quotations in place of systematic demographic analysis of a phenomenon that, because it is central to northern society, deserves closer study.

There is a fundamental element missing from popular culture's one-dimensional portrayal of northern migration. People came north to Alaska, or more likely to the Yukon first, but very little of their movements within the region has been described. Virtually no effort has been made to discover where these northern adventurers went after they left the goldfields, whether to the next boom town, a new mining frontier, or to a job and domestic tranquility in the south. Moreover, the narrow, nationalistic attitudes of Canadian and American

---

*Coates and Morrison, "Transiency in the Far Northwest after the Gold Rush: The Case of the *Princess Sophia*," (University of Victoria, 1988, unpublished paper).

scholars has led to a separate historiography and popular culture for each of the two areas. This regional chauvinism has resulted, unfortunately, in a neglect of the inter-relatedness of territory and state located in the Yukon River basin, and of the routine movement of people across the 141st meridian.[2]

Historical Demography and the Frontier

The issues of population movement on the mining frontier have not attracted much scholarly attention. In contrast, historical demographers have provided numerous analyses of transiency and mobility in North American urban settings. These studies have drawn on manuscript census data, city directories and other systematic statistical sources that, through computer linkages, permit detailed examination of individual movements and community mobility patterns. The techniques of these studies have generated much debate, and have caused constant revision of the methods of community-level demographic analysis. The result, though not perfect, is a much more sophisticated analysis of urban population shifts than was ever possible through recourse to purely literary sources.[3] The very nature of frontier societies, and those of the North in particular, makes use of new techniques for historical demography problematic. The lack of usable documentation, the constant flux of a population with unbalanced sex ratios, the transiency of workers, and the lack of government authorities to record population movements mean that standard approaches are inadequate.[4] Yet transiency as a social phenomenon in the North merits greater attention from scholars.[5]

Fortunately, the records exist for such a study. In addition to standard documents such as tax records, city directories, and land registers, there are other, unique documents collected for antiquarian and genealogical purposes; these permit a more elaborate examination. The card index in the "Trail of '98" museum in Skagway, for example, indicates the place of origin, date of arrival, and date of departure for thousands of gold prospectors. Mounted Police registers of incoming (and in some case outgoing) people provide dates of arrival and places of origin.

Even more important is a unique document, a list compiled by Benjamin Craig, postmaster at Dawson City in the first quarter of this century. For reasons which are unclear, Craig kept notes of all "old-time" Klondikers who left Dawson City during his tenure. These surprising lists, which are made up of nearly 15 000 cases, indicate date of departure and destination, and give a much more comprehensive portrait of migration in and out of the far northwest.[6]

Few such records, however, reveal much about the nature of seasonal mobility. Only special demographic events like the sinking of the *Princess Sophia* illuminate this vital theme. This disaster offers a unique perspective on the extent and character of seasonal movements in and out of the Yukon river valley.

Northern population movements were basically of two types, the second more difficult to analyze. The first kind is immigration and emigration; tied closely to the boom and bust cycles of the northern economy, these can generally be traced through aggregate census data. The second kind is seasonal mobility, which defies easy quantification and analysis, but is of equal if not greater importance to an understanding of northern society.

Several early commentators noted the annual fall departure of many individuals, a cross-section of northern society, and their return in the spring. But the timing of these movements was such that these people largely escaped the attention of the standard indicators of movement. Census takers and compilers of city directories either recorded their data in the summer or relied on land registry data, and thus missed such important, though temporary, relocations. It was possible for a person's name to show up consistently in the Dawson City directories and in the census data compiled over a ten year period; thus one appeared to be a "permanent" member of the community, even though actually living in the community for no more than five or six months in any year. The newspapers' social pages recorded the seasonal movements of leading members of the community, but those of the less socially prominent generally passed without notice, and assessing the characteristics of those migrations is thus even more difficult.

Post-Gold Rush Patterns of Northern Mobility

This mobility had widely ranging social and economic effects on the northwest in the years following the Klondike gold rush. In the twenty years after 1897, thousands of people migrated into the region, and moved about within the Yukon River valley. The discovery of gold at Atlin and Nome in 1898–1899 drew people away from the Yukon gold fields, but kept them within the region. Some abandoned the North altogether, disenchanted with unfulfilled visions of Eldorado; but others remained, many establishing a rhythmic movement north or south with the seasons.

The reduced population[7] formed the basis of a unique northern trans-border society. Transportation along the White Pass and Yukon Route, and steamboats moving passengers and supplies along the Yukon River linked people from Skagway to Iditarod through a long, sparsely populated region. By 1910, Dawson, once the jewel of the North, had become a company and government town, dominated by the concession holders who had taken over the gold fields.[8] Whitehorse, the head of navigation on the Yukon River operated according to the seasonal traffic on the White Pass and Yukon Route. Nome and Tanana, much smaller now that their rushes were over, had also changed according to the dictates of corporate mining.

There were other communities in the network, smaller and newer, more reflective of the frontier ethos that continued to dominate the region's public image. Life in mining towns like Mayo, Iditarod, and Ruby, and in trading communities like Fort Selkirk, Circle, and Eagle was controlled by the onset of winter, the return of spring, and by the patterns of river transportation.

These seasonal rhythms were the mainspring of northern patterns of mobility. Each spring, as the river cleared and the sternwheelers slipped out of dry dock and into service, workers, businessmen, tourists, and adventurers arrived from the south to follow the route of 1898 into the Yukon River valley. The influx continued throughout the summer. Then, starting in the late summer and continuing until the end of October, the flow reversed. Many of those who had arrived in late May once more boarded the steamers and headed to Whitehorse, Skagway, and points to the south. In the years after the gold rush seasonal migrants were often joined by those leaving the North forever.

By 1910, and particularly during World War I, this autumn migration increasingly sapped the region's social and economic vitality. During the war, Yukoners (and by 1917 Alaskans) sought to demonstrate their enthusiasm for the cause by volunteering in large numbers for overseas service, and by contributing large sums to charities. Ironically, the war effort proved how vulnerable the North really was, for the departure of hundreds of men for military service and war work cut badly into the already declining population.

Laura Berton, one of the North's best chroniclers, returned to Dawson City in the early 1920s, and offered a poignant description of the sad but inexorable decline of northern society:

> At first glance Dawson looked exactly as it had on the day I first saw it from the decks of the riverboat—the same grey-roofed buildings, the same helter-skelter of cabins. But on second glance there was no doubt at all that we were living in a decaying town. The population had now sunk to eight hundred, though there were buildings enough for ten times that number. Dozens more houses were standing empty, dozens more lots were vacant, dozens more buildings were slowly falling to pieces....Dawson had shrunk in towards the core.[9]

As this process continued, the season's last boat came to symbolize the regional decline:

> The last boat's departure was a considerable rite in Dawson City, for it effectively marked the beginning of winter. It was invariably a sad and sentimental occasion. The dock was jammed with people, for the entire town turned out for the ceremony of leavetaking. The last boat was always packed with the wealthy going out for the winter, the fortunate going out for ever, and the sick going out to die. The atmosphere was electric with brave

untruths. Every last soul on the boat pretended to be returning the following spring, but in point of fact few ever did so. The last boat had a curious and depressing quality about it. For some reason those people who were quitting the country for good always waited for the last boat, and the last moment, before they did so. Thus it became more than just another boat leaving town; it became a symbol of the town's decay.[10]

The principal question arising from these population movements is, how can they properly be assessed? A first step is to study a case, and an opportunity to do this is provided by a prosopographical analysis of the victims of one of Canada's most tragic, yet least known disasters, the sinking of the *Princess Sophia*. This Canadian Pacific steamship, in October 1918, two weeks before the armistice that ended the Great War, sank off the coast of the Alaska panhandle killing all on board—278 passengers and 75 crew.

At first glance, the deaths of these people offer scant opportunity for this kind of research. In fact, however, the timing of the disaster, which reveals northern transportation patterns, also shows that the movements of the *Princess Sophia* passengers are surprisingly representative of broad patterns of northern transiency.

The importance of the *Princess Sophia* to the study of migration is that it carried the last men and women to leave Dawson and the Yukon River valley at the end of the 1918 navigation season. Early in October 1918, the last riverboats of the year left the ports of west-central Alaska, working their way slowly upstream toward Dawson, taking on passengers anxious to get out before freeze-up. By October 12 the steamers from Alaska had reached Dawson City, where several dozen more passengers joined the southward migration. On October 16, two sternwheelers, the *Yukon* and the *Casca* left for Whitehorse, where the ships were pulled on shore for the winter.

By the time the travellers boarded the train at Whitehorse, the migration had become the largest in the history of the North. Recruits from Alaska, eager to get at the Hun before the war ended, swelled the number. Others joined the exodus at Carcross, where the lake steamers serving Tagish and Atlin lakes met the narrow-gauge line heading for Skagway.

News of the unusually large number of passengers had reached the Canadian Pacific Company headquarters in Victoria, and as the *Princess Sophia* made its way up the coast of British Columbia, the crew worked to add additional berths, allowing the ship to crowd in as many extra fare-paying travellers as regulations permitted. There was chaos in Skagway, for the local hotels had been unable to contain all the would-be passengers, and some had to camp out in abandoned houses or in tents.

For old-timers, particularly those leaving the North for the last time, as many were that October, the excitement of the scene was tempered by the melancholy of bidding farewell to friends and familiar settings. Although their own economy was dependent on the declining fortunes of the Yukon valley, the residents of Skagway, as they had for many years, hosted a send-off party for the migrants. After several days, on October 23, everyone was relieved when the *Princess Sophia* docked in Skagway harbour.

At 2:00 a.m. on October 24, a few hours after leaving Skagway, while steaming full-speed through a heavy snowstorm and badly off-course, the ship ran on to Vanderbilt Reef. Caught fast, it was buffeted by strong winds and high seas. For almost two days, rescue ships hovered around the stranded vessel, but the continuing storm and the precarious situation of the *Princess Sophia* made removing the passengers too risky, and the rescuers waited for calmer seas. When the storm blew up again, the waiting ships ran for shelter, and at about 7:00 p.m. on the evening of October 25, a strong northerly wind dragged the *Princess Sophia* across the reef, ripped open her hull, and sent the ship to the bottom.

Many passengers were caught unawares, and died in their cabins. Those who had thought to put on life jackets and stay on deck fared no better, however, for the wounded ship leaked bunker oil, and people who jumped into the water suffocated in thick sludge. Only a dog survived the greatest maritime disaster in the history of the northwest Pacific coast.

This catastrophe, which sent shock waves through the region, claimed about 353 victims.[11] Messages of concern and condolence poured into Juneau, site of a temporary morgue. Representatives of the governments of Alaska and the Yukon arrived to help identify the bodies. Former northerners, now scattered across the continent, met in small groups to remember friends who had perished. Newspapers from Victoria to Fairbanks published lists of the dead, and obituaries of the more prominent among them.

Allegations were made that the ship's commander, Captain Leonard Locke, had been negligent in piloting his vessel through the dangerous waters of the Lynn Canal at full speed in a snowstorm.[12] It was also alleged, falsely, that Locke had refused to let the passengers leave the ship, a charge which resulted in the establishment of a Royal Commission to investigate the affair. The victims' families also launched a civil action against the Canadian Pacific Railway Company, owner of the steamship line. This case went to court in 1919, but was not finally decided until 1932, when a court of appeal ruled in favour of the company.

The lengthy legal proceedings which followed the disaster, combined with press accounts, provide an unusually detailed body of prosopographical data on the people aboard the *Princess Sophia*. Obituaries in northern and hometown papers contain much valuable information on their lives and careers. Court documents, including statements relating the personal histories of each victim, and responses of relatives to direct and cross questioning by counsel, provide a wealth of information on age, occupation, personal history, and migration patterns.[13] The data is incomplete, especially for those of modest means or lower class origins. Still, it permits an examination of the mobility habits of a cross-section of northern society.

The passengers of the *Princess Sophia* were a varied lot. Of the 278 passengers, 92 were employees of the White Pass and Yukon Route, representing the better part of five riverboat crews going south for the winter. The other passengers, numbering 186 (of whom the occupations of 163 are known), included 55 miners, 14 labourers, 16 managers or businessmen, 1 doctor, 1 fur trader, 13 housewives, 20 children, 5 soldiers, 3 nurses, and people with various other occupations. It is clear that the migration was not limited to the professional or business classes; if the *Princess Sophia* is representative, then a true cross-section of northern society was on the move that fall.

The ship's passengers came from throughout the North, from small mining camps and from Dawson, from fur trading districts and from government centres. This multiplicity of origin seems logical, given the nature of the transportation system; people embarked from river towns as far apart as Iditarod and Atlin, and funnelled through the port of Skagway, hence the destinations of the passengers reveals some interesting patterns.

The destination of 79 passengers is definitely known, and of another 22 also, although less confidently. Individual passengers planned to travel to New York (3), Ontario (2), Wisconsin, England, Texas, Panama, Florida, and a variety of other places. Most, however, were heading for the Pacific northwest, the region that provided much of the impetus for the gold rush, and which still retained its interest in the northern economy. Counting both known and likely destinations, 27 were bound for British Columbia, 18 for California, 11 for Oregon, and 17 for Washington. It is important to note that there is no direct relationship between the territory in which the journey began—that is, Alaska or the Yukon—and that of destination—either British Columbia or the west coast of the United States. Because people lived in the Yukon did not mean they were more likely to be heading for British Columbia, nor were people from Alaska more likely to be heading for the United States.

The data for the White Pass and Yukon Route employees shows a slightly modified pattern. The destination of 39 of the 92 individuals is known (22 with certainty, 17 very likely). The White Pass and Yukon Route seems to have drawn a majority of its workers from British Columbia; 31 of the 39 were heading for that province, while only 2 were destined for California and 6 for Washington.

There is further evidence of the nature of seasonal and permanent mobility. A majority (47) of the 64 passengers for whom data on this point is available had been in the North for 10 years or more. Or, to be more precise, these people had first gone north as early as 1908, and had returned with some regularity thereafter. Only one of the 64 had been in the North for less than a year, although no doubt this was also true of some for whom no information was available. Thirteen had been in the North for 5 to 10 years, and three from 1 to 4 years. These were not, therefore, casual transients; rather, many had deep, if not unbroken, roots in the North.[14]

Perhaps most importantly, the data indicates that the majority of those travelling on the *Princess Sophia* intended to return north. Among the regular passengers (information is available for 78 of 192), 49 planned to return the passengers (information is available for 78 of 192), 49 planned to return the following spring.[15] Only 29 indicated their intention to relocate, or leave the North permanently. As might be expected, the White Pass and Yukon Route employees followed a standard pattern of working in the North during the summer months and returning south to find work as winter approached. Of the 22 employees who died on the ship for whom data is available, 19 were leaving the North only temporarily, and were planning to return in the spring. It is worth noting that there was a correlation between rank in the riverboat service and commitment to the North. Masters, engineers and other skilled employees were more likely than unskilled workers to return annually to the North.

The migration behaviour of the *Princess Sophia* passengers provides a perspective on the nature of northern transiency. The migrants represented a cross-section of northern society, drawn throughout the Yukon River valley. Some, affected by the decay of the regional economy in the decades after the gold rush, were leaving for good. Others, particularly miners, businessmen and riverboat workers, were following an annual migratory pattern, moving north in the spring and returning to families, investments, and different occupations in the fall. The travellers' intended destinations also indicate the continuing connection between the Yukon River valley and the Pacific northwest, a relationship established during the Klondike rush and still strong twenty years later. Most strikingly, the mobility patterns suggest that, in 1918 as before, Americans were more actively involved in the North, even in the Canadian portion of it, than were Canadians.[16]

The patterns established by the examination of the passengers of the *Princess Sophia* are supported by additional demographic data. An investigation of the city directories for Dawson City and Whitehorse indicates a rapid turnover of population and a steady decline in the number of people with long-term commitments to the region (see table 1).

TABLE 1 *Percentage of 1907–1908 Populations of Dawson City, Whitehorse, and Forty-Mile Still in Residence Four, Eight, and Sixteen Years later*

City	1907–1908	1911–1912	1915–1916	1923–1924
Dawson*	100	41.4	19.3	7.1
Whitehorse**	100	46.0	28.5	8.8
Forty-Mile***	100	56.0	24.0	n/a

*   1163 residents
**   274 residents
*** 25 residents

SOURCE: Yukon business directories for the years indicated

A study of two decades of movement out of Dawson City further corroborates these patterns. There was a steady bleeding of the population as boom gave way to partial bust, and as the frenzy of the rush surrendered to the stability of the company and government town. The timings of these permanent relocations and seasonal migrations deviated somewhat from the description offered by Laura Berton. Overall, for the more than 14 000 cases of departure recorded between 1900 and 1920, 75 percent occurred between the beginning of June and the end of October. Early in this twenty year period, September was the most likely month of departure, as almost a quarter of the migrants left then; more than 10 percent left in each of June, July and August. In later years, better steamship service, a longer season for dredging and hydraulic machine use, and greater confidence in the ability to predict the weather pushed back the effective work period by a month; thus people wishing to stay as long as possible, yet wanting to get out before freeze-up, were able to postpone their departures. In 1900, 5.1 percent of people leaving Dawson City did so in October, but in the years between 1910 and 1918, 20 to 25 percent of the departures occurred in that month (see tables 2 and 3).

TABLE 2 *Total of Recorded Departures from the Yukon, by Month, 1900 to 1920*

Month	Number	Percent
January	426	3.1
February	300	2.2
March	269	1.9
April	221	1.6
May	737	5.3
June	1770	12.7
July	1979	14.2
August	2095	15.0
September	2963	21.2
October	2068	14.8
November	569	4.1
December	551	4.0

SOURCE: "Lists of Old-Timers, Dawson City," Benjamin Craig Collection, Yukon Territorial Archives.

It is especially interesting to note the massive movement of people from Dawson City to the United States during the period, since this progress confirms the migratory paths noted for the passengers on the *Princess Sophia*. Between 1900 and 1919, 75 percent of those leaving Dawson were heading for the United States. Not all were leaving the North, however, as about 44 percent were going to Alaska (it is not known how long they stayed there). Leaving aside those who were going to Alaska or to other places in the Yukon, a somewhat different balance emerges. Of those leaving the North, 32 percent were heading to southern Canada, and 64 percent to the different states. Again, continuous contact with the Pacific coast is evident: 60 percent of the south-bound migrants were heading for British Columbia or Washington, and another 12 percent for California.

TABLE 3 *Departures from Dawson for Selected Months and Years, Expressed as a Percentage of the Total Number of Departures for Each Year.*

	July	August	September	October	November
1900	15.7	13.0	10.0	5.1	0.4
1905	11.5	10.0	28.0	12.7	3.9
1910	11.2	14.4	18.3	22.8	7.1
1918	6.6	14.5	19.7	25.9	10.1

SOURCE: See table 2.

Although further analysis remains to be done, this research substantiates the claims made concerning the passengers of the *Princess Sophia*. Their month of travel and destinations conform to patterns well established in the North. At the same time, the details of occupations, places of residence, and lengths of stay in the North which are available through court and other records created as a result of the disaster add to an understanding of the significance of these migration patterns, seasonal and permanent, which were characteristic of post-gold rush society.

Significance of Transiency in the Far Northwest

The nature and extent of seasonal transiency, in combination with the gradual decline in regional population, have important implications for the history of the far northwest. Examination of the behaviour of the passengers of the *Princess Sophia* suggest a number of probable regional effects of these movements.

It seems clear that the regular departure of key businessman drained much capital and entrepreneurial energy from the region. The practice of making money in the North by mining, retail sales, or hotels, and of then investing the profits in the south, seriously affected the long-term stability of the regional economy. The business elite, those needed in order to expand and diversify the economic base, by leaving the region every fall ensured that this diversification would not occur. Many of these people evidently regarded the North as a place to exploit rather than as a home, and such an attitude undermined the efforts of those trying to create a viable regional economy; probably they did much more harm to the North's economy than did the myopic and south-centered federal policies that were usually blamed for the North's weak, resource-based economy.

There are numerous examples from the passenger list of the *Princess Sophia* of those participant in two economies. Murray and Lulu Mae Eads were two of Dawson's most prominent citizens. They owned three of the town's hotels (she had been a famous dance-hall girl), but he also owned shares in the State Bank of Seattle and in other southern businesses. William Scouse struck it rich during the rush, and had managed to hold on to his money. He owned several northern mining properties, but went south to spend each winter with his wife, who lived permanently in Seattle. Captain James Alexander and his wife began the Engineer mine near Atlin, and built a valuable property. In 1918 they received an offer from a southern mining consortium, and were going to Toronto to negotiate, hoping to leave the North forever. William O'Brien, a Dawson City councillor, was travelling south with his family to scout out new business opportunities in Detroit.

Lest too harsh an attack be levelled at the business elite, it should be noted that the *Princess Sophia*'s passenger list makes it clear that seasonal travellers were of no one class. Ships' captains and deckhands, mine owners and laundresses alike followed the rhythm of northern seasons. Much of this movement depended on northern economic cycles. The economy, influenced by dredge mining and river transport operations was buoyant primarily during the summer months. There were widespread layoffs each fall, forcing many workers to leave for the 'outside'. The absence of a year-round transportation system limited the availability of supplies and added to an already high cost of living. It is not surprising therefore that hundreds of workers returned summer after summer, and departed each fall for the lower costs and more plentiful jobs of the south.

However inevitable this mobility was, it obviously tended to produce more transiency. The departure of workers and of a major part of the business elite drained much consumer demand from the local economy. These people left for sound economic reasons, but in leaving they further limited the prospects for regional stability. Businessmen who remained curtailed operations or even shut down for the winter, further reducing the workforce.

The implications go further. Just as people who left took their wages and profits south, so incoming people brought many of their supplies and business goods with them to the North each spring. Given the high cost of buying goods in the North, and the lack of a full range of suppliers, this was probably cost-effective, but it further undercut the viability of the northern retail trade. The southern grubstake, a commonplace of northern life, took its toll on the region.

On a different level, lack of commitment to the North also hampered the development of forms of protest. The migration of workers, for instance, was probably a major reason why trade unionism failed to take root in the North. Those who disliked the conditions of employment simply left and did not return. The transiency of the business class, and of the region's political representatives hampered political organization and prevented the development of a unified regional political voice. There were outbursts of regional anger, but these were usually directed at the federal government for its efforts to control or regulate the local economy. Neither the Yukon nor the interior of Alaska produced the sustained, regionally-based political protest that so characterized the transition of other North American frontiers to stable and permanent societies.

The migrants from the North travelling to the Pacific northwest maintained the connections between the two regions. Vancouver and Seattle had, from the days of the gold rush, battled for control of the economy of the far northwest. Seattle won the first round, and, as later mobility patterns demonstrate, maintained its hold on the region. Americans had dominated the first rush, and enjoyed most of the economic benefits of the Klondike discoveries; as the ties still in place suggest, Americans continued to dominate the region.

This seasonal mobility also set the pattern for the northern labour market. Labourers and skilled tradesmen moved easily in and out of the northern economy. The fact that a sizable number continued to come north each spring indicates that northern work was reasonably remunerative. Equally significant is the fact that northern work seems to have fitted easily into work patterns in the Pacific northwest, permitting workers to move with comparative freedom between regions. From scattered evidence, largely anecdotal, it seems that many northern employers sought workers in the south, and did little hiring in the North. While this practice initially may have resulted from the absence of surplus labour in the region, it further reduced the opportunities for those seeking to remain permanently in the North. Because employers had quick and easy access to the Pacific northwest labour pool, there was no need to develop a local labour force, much less to recruit unskilled native workers. Having transportation and telegraph systems meant that skilled workers could be readily recruited in the south, and a large annual migration north of would-be prospectors provided the necessary supplements to the unskilled labour pool. In this way, therefore, seasonal mobility of the workforce both resulted from and created an incomplete labour pool, and determined much of the social foundation of northern communities.

These observations on the importance of seasonal mobility only re-enforce the significance of this theme in understanding the evolution of northern society, and point to the need for further research in this field. It is important, when studying mobility, to find out how long people stayed in the North, where they went when they left it (especially how their destination relates to their southern origins). A sense of mobility caused by occupation and age would help illustrate the issue.

There is, ironically, an additional aspect of the *Princess Sophia* disaster that confirms the pervasiveness of transiency in the far northwest. The tragedy, which so devastated the region in 1918, has all but disappeared from regional folk memory. There are no memorials to the victims, and few songs or stories to record one of the most catastrophic events in the history of the North. The explanation for this is simple. Mobility in the Yukon was such that most of those in the North in 1918, except native people unaffected by the disaster departed within a few years, continuing the pattern established before the gold rush. Within a decade of the sinking there were few in the North with personal memories of those who had died, few to record the event and to pass the memory on to another generation. This surely is the ultimate irony in the story of the *Princess Sophia*, and one which provides another telling insight into the nature of northern society.[17]

Notes

1.   Defined for the purposes of this paper as the Yukon Territory and the interior of Alaska.

2.   The one attempt to link the history of the Yukon and Alaskan gold rushes is Melody Webb's *The Last Frontier*.

3.   For a useful review of the issues of urban mobility studies see Donald Parkerson, "How Mobile Were Nineteenth Century Americans," *Historical Methods* 15, 3 (Summer 1982): 99–109.

4.   See Ralph Mann, "The Decade After the Gold Rush: Social Structure in Grass Valley and Nevada City, California, 1850–1860," *Pacific Historical Review* 41 (1972): 484–504; William G. Robbins, "Opportunity and Persistence in the Pacific Northwest: A Quantitative Study of Early Roseburg, Oregon," *Pacific Historical Review* 39 (1970): 279–96.

5.   There has been some work undertaken on immigration to Alaska. See Frank Norris, "North to Alaska: An Overview of Immigrants to Alaska, 1867–1945," *Alaska Historical Commission Studies in History*, no. 121 (June 1984); for an attempt to model the migration process, see David Reaume, " Migration to Alaska: a Closer Look," (incomplete working paper), Alaska State Library.

6.   There are admittedly some problems with this data. Craig, though he used the phrase, did not indicate what he meant by "old-timers," or if the people on his lists were leaving the North temporarily or forever. Nonetheless, the very large number of cases should correct for these and other problems. Some of the passengers on the *Princess Sophia* were old-timers, others were not.

7.   The population of the Yukon, at its height in 1898–1899, was probably well over 30 000, though no accurate census was taken until 1901, when it was 27 219, of whom 3300 were native. At its lowest, in the 1921 census, it was just over 4100, of whom 1400 were native. Between 1898 and 1921 the non-native population thus dropped by more than 90 percent, from more than 30 000 to 2700, of whom by no means all were year-round residents.

8.   Hal Guest, "A History of Dawson City, Yukon Territory, 1898 to 1920" (Ph.D. diss., University of Manitoba, 1982).

9.   Laura Berton, *I Married the Klondike* (Toronto: McClelland and Stewart, 1967), 143.

10.   Berton, *I Married the Klondike*, 96–97.

11.   It is impossible to be precise about the number who died, since there may have been stowaways; many bodies were not recovered, passenger lists were not

complete, and the names of several crew members and passengers were inaccurately recorded.

12.   See Berton, *I Married the Klondike*, 146.

13.   "Princess Sophia," Admiralty Court Records, R21, A4553, National Records Centre, Seattle.

14.   The information on the White Pass and Yukon Route employees, though incomplete (information on this aspect is available for only 11 of 92), indicates similar patterns. Seven of the 11 had been in the North for more than ten years; three more had between five and ten years' experience on the Yukon River.

15.   This figure must be addressed with caution. As Laura Berton pointed out, the emotions associated with leaving the North in the fall were such that many, anxious to hide their true intentions, said they were planning to return when, in fact, this was not true. Because of this difficulty, care has been taken where possible to corroborate their statements with additional evidence.

16.   For a discussion of the role of Americans in the Canadian North, see W.R. Morrison, "Eagle Over the Arctic: Americans in the Canadian North, 1867–1985," *Canadian Journal of American Studies* (Spring 1987).

17.   Material on the *Princess Sophia*, her passengers and crew, from Coates and Morrison, *The Sinking of the Princess Sophia* (forthcoming).

SECTION 5

THE INUIT

CHIPEWYAN AND INUIT IN THE CENTRAL CANADIAN SUBARCTIC, 1613–1977*

JAMES G.E. SMITH and ERNEST S. BURCH, JR.

Relations between Chipewyan and Inuit along the forest-tundra ecotone west of Hudson Bay have been described as characterized by continuous and extreme hostility by practically every author who has written on either group, e.g., Birket-Smith, Chappel, Ellis, Gabus, Knight, Rasmussen and Williams.[1] Despite the overwhelming predominance of this general view, relatively few instances of actual bloodshed between the two groups can be reliably confirmed over the three and a half centuries of history covered by this paper. On the contrary, documented instances of peaceful contacts outnumber confirmed cases of violence by a wide margin, but they are invariably explained away— without supported evidence—as being entirely the result of peacemaking efforts by the Hudson's Bay Company.[2] Accepting that general view as correct, Glover[3] has argued more specifically that an initial state of hostility was followed by steadily improving relations between Chipewyan and Inuit. More recently, however, Janes[4] reviewed the published literature and concluded that Chipewyan-Inuit relations have been a complex mixture of animosity and coexistence since the very beginning of the historic period.

Arctic Anthropology 16, 2 (1979): 76–101. For assistance in the preparation of this paper, we thank A.S. Budzinski, Janet Cosby and F. Kaiser. We also wish to acknowledge our debt to Thomas C. Corell, Beryl Gillespie and Dale Russell for many stimulating and informative conversations on topics dealt with here. Both authors have conducted research in the Hudson's Bay Company Archives. We are grateful to the Company for the privilege of working there, and to Shirlee Ann Smith, Archivist, and to Garron Wells, Assistant Archivist, for their valuable assistance. Quotations from the Archives are published by permission of the Hudson's Bay Company. Field research was carried out by Smith in 1967–1968, 1969–1970, 1973 and 1976, supported by the National Museums of Canada, the University of Waterloo Research Foundation and Canada Council. Fieldwork among the Caribou Inuit was conducted by Burch in 1968 and by T.C. Correll in 1970 and 1971, under grants by Canada Council to Burch.

The purpose of the present paper is to reconsider the general subject of Chipewyan-Inuit relations in the light of previously unpublished information found in the Archives of the Hudson's Bay Company as well as data collected through fieldwork carried out among both the Chipewyan and the Inuit. In general, our findings support Janes' thesis. Despite uniform expressions of hostile *sentiment* on both sides of the ethnic boundary, the *content* of Chipewyan-Inuit relations was considerably more complex than the literature has indicated.

The geographic area dealt with in this paper is a huge area of north-central Canada west of Hudson Bay. Although the paper touches on the entire region between Hudson Bay and Great Bear Lake, the population of primary concern are the historic Caribou-Eater Chipewyan and Caribou Inuit [Eskimo].[5] For descriptive convenience the 350-odd year time span covered is divided into four parts: the early historic period, 1613–1715; the period of Hudson's Bay Company intervention, 1715–1782; the period of peaceful co-existence, 1782–1950; and the period of nucleated settlements, 1950–1977.

The Early Historic Period, 1613–1715

The historic period began on the west coast of Hudson Bay with the exploration of Thomas Button in 1613,[6] and ended with the journey of William Stewart or Stuart into Chipewyan country in 1715–1716.[7] Our knowledge of the natives for this period is scanty, but when the historical data are combined with those obtained through archaeological research there is enough information to establish at least a general ethnographic baseline for the region.

On the basis of archaeological research it can be said with some assurance that the ancestors of the historic Chipewyan (including Yellowknives) had lived along the forest-tundra ecotone for several hundred years prior to the seventeenth century. Sources on Chipewyan prehistory drawn on for this account include Campbell, Gordon, Minni, Nash, Noble and Wright.[8] Although the boundaries fluctuated to some extent over time, in general the Chipewyan and Yellowknives extended from the vicinity of the Coppermine River, Great Slave and Great Bear Lakes, on the west, to the Hudson Bay drainage, north of the Seal River, on the east. Toward the south, Chipewyan extended to the northern margin of the full boreal forest, while to the north they ventured far out onto the tundra; the extent of their territory in the latter direction remains uncertain at the time of this writing, but included the southern Keewatin, i.e., the region south of Chesterfield Inlet and Baker and Aberdeen Lakes.

The prehistoric Inuit, by contrast, occupied coastal districts only. Within the area of concern here, they are known archaeologically from two regions. Toward the northwest they were distributed along the shores of Coronation Gulf in the region later occupied by the historic Copper Eskimo.[9] Evidently Inuit arrived in the area in the last century of the first millennium A.D., and their descendants continued to inhabit it until historic times.[10] They are known to have impinged on the Chipewyan (including Yellowknife) only in the vicinity of the lower Coppermine River, a pattern that also persisted into historic times.

The second prehistoric Inuit population of relevance here was distributed along the west Hudson Bay coast south of Chesterfield Inlet, extending at least to Eskimo Point, and possibly as far south as the mouth of the Churchill River. Sources on the prehistory of the Inuit of the southern Keewatin include Clark, Gordon, Linnamae and Clark, Mathiasson, McCartney and Merbs.[11]

Although it seems certain that an Inuit population was in the area A.D. 1100, the details of its subsequent occupation remain unclear and are currently the subject of debate.[12] This particular prehistoric Inuit population occupied a portion of the coastal territory later inhabited by the historic Caribou Inuit.[13]

There is virtually no evidence concerning Chipewyan-Inuit relations during the prehistoric period, except that cultural or genetic diffusion is not evident from the available evidence. The few indirect references in the literature from the latter support the view that relations between the two groups were hostile. In 1689, for example, Henry Kelsey[14] had to abandon his attempts to find Indians along the west coast of Hudson Bay because the Chipewyan boy who accompanied him was too terrified of encountering Inuit to proceed north of the vicinity of Eskimo Point. Similarly vague references to hostilities are contained in some of the subsequent French accounts, although it is far from certain whether the "wars" referred to in those accounts implicate the Chipewyan or the Cree as the "enemies" of the Inuit.[15] To the extent that they refer to Chipewyan, it is also debatable whether the Inuit concerned were those living along the west coast of Hudson Bay or those living on the shores of Coronation Gulf, several hundred kilometers to the northwest.

The fragmentary direct evidence just cited suggests that the Chipewyan and Inuit of the early historic period were indeed engaged in the mutual hostilities so often attributed to them. The established fact that the Chipewyan were fighting with their Cree neighbours as well[16] suggests that they probably were fighting with *all* of their neighbours, however, regardless of ethnic background. As Birket-Smith[17] noted many years ago, though, "war and trade... do not of course exclude each other." The likelihood that the members of the two groups were at each others' throats—at least from time to time—therefore does not *preclude* the possibility of more peaceful encounters.[18]

The differential environmental adaptations of the two societies were undoubtedly of significance in limiting contacts, peaceful or hostile. The Inuit had the typical maritime-inland adjustment, based on exploitation of the sea mammals on the one hand, and fish, caribou and other animals on the other. The Chipewyan were dependent to an enormous degree upon the migratory and nomadic caribou that typically winter in their foraging ranges in the northern boreal forest and forage in the summer on the tundra. In their normal subsistence activities Chipewyan and Inuit *might* encounter one another while hunting caribou near the coast north of Churchill or near the mouth of the

Coppermine River, where both also exploited the raw copper resources. For the most part, vast areas of the Barrens ordinarily separated the two. Moreover, should they be in some proximity, the smoke of the Chipewyan fires would give the Inuit fair warning of potential trouble. One may speculate that the very ignorance of one another contributed to the pervasive sense of mutual fear and suspicion that existed at the onset of the period that followed, although modern world history hardly supports the hypothesis that neighbouring societies familiar with one another are characterized by friendly relations.

The Period of Intervention, 1715–1782

The period of intervention began with William Stuart's journey of 1715–1716 into the heart of Chipewyan country, and terminated with the French capture and destruction of Churchill in the summer of 1782. It has been identified by the label "intervention" because during the period the Hudson's Bay Company personnel based at York Factory and (after 1717) at Churchill, deliberately interfered in native affairs in the study region. Of particular concern here are their efforts to encourage the natives to trap furbearing animals, and to stop fighting one another. Both objectives were related to Company attempts to develop the fur trade over a vast region of the central Canadian Subarctic, as well as to humanitarian impulses.

1715–1739

The French apparently made attempts to make peace among the native peoples in the immediate hinterland of York Fort without success.[19] The intervention period effectively began in 1715 when William Stuart was sent into the unknown region west of Hudson Bay to locate the Chipewyan, to arrange a peace between them and the Cree and to bring them to trade.[20] He was moderately successful in this effort and in 1716 a few Chipewyan accompanied him back to York Factory, which was located well within Cree territory. When they were en route back to their own country in the spring of 1717, however, these Chipewyan were ambushed by a party identified by Knight as Inuit (although conceivably consisting of Cree) near the mouth of the Churchill River; six of the party of nine were killed.[21]

In the summer of 1717 the Company established a post at the mouth of the Churchill River for the specific purpose of trade with the Chipewyan.[22] Since the Churchill River was within Cree territory, however, and since Stuart's peace was tenuous at best, Richard Norton was sent to the western interior to reinforce it.[23] Norton was successful in achieving that goal, a result that both facilitated the fur trade, and freed the Chipewyan's southern boundary from serious threat.

The whereabouts of the Inuit between 1715 and 1717 are uncertain.[24] After 1717, however, it is known that they impinged on the Chipewyan territory only on the extreme northwest, at the mouth of the Coppermine River, and on the extreme southeast, along the west coast of Hudson Bay. The overall distribution of the two populations as of about 1718 is depicted in figure 1.

That Chipewyan-Inuit relations were relatively complex at the outset of the intervention period can be demonstrated by a number of passages contained in the Churchill post journals of the Hudson's Bay Company. On 8 June 1720, for example, 23 Chipewyan arrived at Churchill, and the journal reported the following:

> As for Copper and Other mettalls, they brought non, but tell me they was agoeing last Summer for Some, being a hungry forced 'em to the Sea Side for provisions, on a Sudden advanced near the Esquimoues who fell on them & Kill'd Severall, which I may believe in part fiction.[25]

In this particular instance even the journalist was not convinced of the accuracy of the report, knowing full well that the Chipewyan might have been using the Inuit as scapegoats for their own failure to provide items wanted by the trader. Also unclear is the whereabouts of the Inuit concerned, although the implication is that they may have been located near the mouth of the Coppermine River rather than along the Hudson Bay coast.

The factor was not entirely convinced that the Chipewyan report was false, either, and he encouraged the Chipewyan to be friendly with the Inuit. Thus, in the journal for 16 April 1721, he observed:

> I have been a Discoursing ye Northoran Indians againe. for to be brisk in Hunting & gotting of furrs by going into ye Woods up in ye Countrey & not to Keep by ye Sea Side and in ye barren plaines; and if they see any Esquimoues thay should not Meddle wth them thay being our friends, thay Reply'd yt Last Summer... had made a peace wth them; thay saying yt thay Traded togather thay giving them Knives and alls, ye other Returning small Copper Lances & arrow heads.[26]

Thus, according to the Chipewyan's own account, they had been fighting with Inuit one year and trading with them the next, both possibly in the Coppermine River area.

The nature of Chipewyan-Inuit relations was even more obscure just two years later. On 13 June 1725, 104 Chipewyan reported to the Churchill factor that:

> ye Ewquemoys had been to warr with them & had Murdered Severall of them. . . then they askt me whether they must Stand Still & be Knockt on the head Like Dogs or fight in their own Defence or now by Reason we had ordered them not to warr with any Natives.[27]

This passage, of course, supports the view that Chipewyan-Inuit relations were hostile. However, the extraordinary feature of this reported encounter is that it apparently took place on or near Marble Island, in the heart of Inuit country, and at least 150 kilometers farther to the northeast than Chipewyan were supposed to have ever gone during the historic period. The possibility that Chipewyan actually may have visited this sector of the study area rather frequently, however, is supported by the fact that, in 1722, the Chipewyan guides who accompanied John Scroggs on a coastal voyage to the north of Chesterfield Inlet reported at the entrance to Roe's Welcome Sound that they were only two to three days' walk from their own country.[28] One must conclude from this that both Chipewyan distribution and Chipewyan-Inuit relations were rather different in the very early postcontact years than generally has been supposed.

The 1740s

In the 1740s the situation with regard to both Chipewyan distribution and Chipewyan-Inuit relations was scarcely any clearer than it had been twenty years earlier. In the summer of 1742, for example, Christopher Middleton[29] conducted an exploration of the west coast of Hudson Bay, taking two Chipewyan along as guides. It was agreed in advance[30] that he would put them ashore within three or four days' journey of their homeland. The location where this condition was met turned out to be Marble Island.[31] Although Middleton's critics[32] suggested that the Chipewyan thought "they would be sacrificed to their Enemies the Eskimaux," who occupied the land around Marble Island, the fact remains that they survived without a hint of ill use at the hands of the Inuit.[33] How can one explain these phenomena in terms of a relationship of *total* enmity between Chipewyan and Inuit?

The one-sided view of Chipewyan-Inuit relations received more support a few years later in an account now attributed to Charles Swaine. He reported that warfare between Indians and Inuit was "now entirely laid aside, through the good management of the Governors at the [York] Factory." He also noted that:

> The *Indians* are inclineable to go to War; if there is a bad Season of hunting in the winter, or if any one of their People is missing, or that they have a Sickness amongst them, they must prepare in Spring to go out and seek out the *Eskemaux*, and make a Carnage of them; for they attribute to them the Cause of their Misfortunes. It is the *Eskemaux* that have killed their Friend; it is the *Eskemaux* have kept the Deer away; and the Sickness is occasion'd by a Charm or Witchery of the *Eskemaux*.

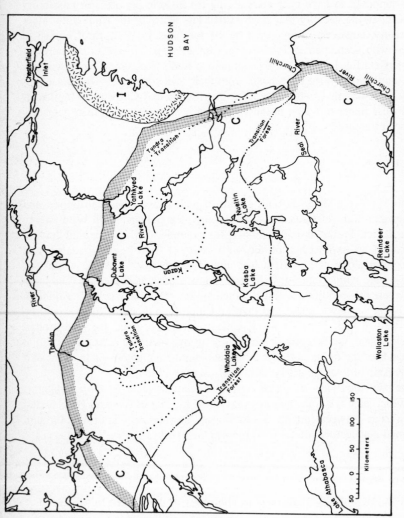

FIG. 1. Map of Central Canadian Subarctic Showing the Distribution of the Chipewyan (C), the Closely Related Yellowknife (Y) and the Inuit (I) Populations, ca. 1718.

While the above remarks seem straightforward enough, the authority on which they are based is open to question. In the first place, their author had spent only one winter (1746–1747) in the area, and that aboard a ship frozen in a river near York Factory—in the heart of Cree territory. He never visited Churchill, which was the only place he could have seen Chipewyan (except as noted below). He evidently had had first-hand experience only of Cree, and relatively little even of that. Even his second-hand knowledge must have been limited. The entire expedition of which he was a member had been sent in opposition to the Hudson's Bay Company. The Company's officers at York Factory, while civil to them, were scarcely encouraged to spend long hours divulging full and accurate information about native life.

On the basis of these considerations, we conclude that Swaine's account of Indian customs is of questionable accuracy, and that to the extent that it is correct, it probably refers more to Cree than to Chipewyan customs under the general heading of "Indians."

Swaine's account did, however, contain an eye-witness report of another interesting phenomenon which bears on the subject of Chipewyan-Inuit relations. In August of 1747, on board the *California* he was exploring the inner reaches of Wager Bay, some 900 kilometers north of Churchill. The explorers already had made contact with Inuit there, but on 3 August he saw a different kind of person. In Swaine's words:

> two Persons appeared on the Southern Shore [of Wager Bay], and on the *Eskemaux's* Return to the Boats, one of them came in one of the *Eskemaux* Canoes [Kayaks], but seemed to know little how to manage her; and there being a Swell, was very much frightened; returning ashore conducted between two other Canoes. These People were in Complexion and Manner, very different from the *Eskemaux*, although in the same Habits....[35]

Who could these people have been? We presume they must have been Chipewyan, but the capacity in which they were living among the Inuit is obscure. The explorers *assumed* that they were slaves and attempted to purchase them. The Inuit rejected the offer, and evidently were offended by it, suggesting that the strangers may not have been slaves after all. For us the significant point is the probability that here were two Chipewyan, alive and well and living with Inuit in some capacity or other, at least 300 kilometers to the northeast of the outer extremity of known Chipewyan territory. These observations, which have been in print for more than two centuries, have not been noted by writers on the Chipewyan-Inuit relations since they first appeared.

The 1750s

In 1750 the Hudson's Bay Company escalated its intervention in native affairs with the institution of an annual summer trading voyage along the west coast of Hudson Bay from Churchill to Marble Island for the purpose of trade with the Inuit.[36] James Walker, who commanded the 1750 voyage, was instructed to take two Chipewyan along with him, and to "Endeavor to contact a Friendship Between their Country Man and the Eskemaux."[37] When the sloop arrived at Knapp's Bay (Eskimo Point) Walker observed that the Inuit there "were Very Much Afraide of our to Northard Indians [Chipewyan] and would give them Any thing they had."[38]

The continuing efforts to make peace between Chipewyan and Inuit had some success, but the Chipewyan resented the preferential treatment given to the Inuit. The latter had a vessel sent right to their doorstep, as it were, while the Chipewyan were forced to walk at least 150 kilometers to Churchill to trade. Since Knapp's Bay (Eskimo Point), one of the sloop's regular stopping places, was very close to Chipewyan country, they felt they should be allowed to trade there as well, although the sloop's cargo was specifically chosen for the Inuit trade.

In 1755 matters came to a head. The sloop journal for 1756 relates how a group of Chipewyan had traded at Churchill in 1755, then proceeded to the north, where they killed a great number of caribou.[39] As the sloop passed them just south of Eskimo Point, they made a smoke signal to attract it. The captain ignored the signal and traded the next day with Inuit gathered at Knapp's Bay. Insulted by this treatment, the Chipewyan waited until the sloop had gone, then massacred 16 to 18 of the Inuit who had traded with the sloop. The Chipewyan explanation for this attack was as follows:

> that seeing the sloop in the offing they made that smoak for us to come on shore to trade it [caribou meat] with us and that when they saw we did not mind them they Reflected with these words that they obliged to carry there trade to the English for many miles and then trade on there conditions but that the usquemaes had it brought to there doors therefore says they let us go and kill our Rivals or to this purpose.[40]

Hearne provides another reason for the attack, however.[41] According to him, two leading Chipewyan had died during the winter of 1754–1755, the implication being that the Inuit had killed them by magical means. Since this incident has been a matter of some controversy, the full text of this portion of the sloop's journal is attached to this paper as Appendix I.

The Eskimo Point area, which was on the extreme southern border of Inuit country in the eighteenth century, was abandoned by them for several years after the massacre of 1755. In 1762, however, they were back.[42] In 1764 they met with Chipewyan, there, and effected a truce with them.[43] In 1765 the 30 to 40 Inuit who met the sloop at Eskimo Point were joined by nearly twice as many Chipewyan, again apparently without incident.[44] By 1767 relations between the two groups were so good that two Inuit families spent the winter (of 1767–1768) with Chipewyan about 250 kilometers northwest of Churchill.

In the spring of 1769 Chipewyan-Inuit relations apparently took a turn for the worse. On March 8 of that year three Chipewyan,

> Brought the disagreeable News that the Northern Indians thay left is a going to Kill the Usquemays, the reason thay gave for it thay have had Many of the Northern Indians died, and thay think the Usquemay have Cungered them to dith.[45]

However, when the sloop arrived at Eskimo Point on July 13 of that year, the commander learned that the threat had not been carried out.[46] More trouble was rumoured again the next year, but about 30 Inuit and more than 100 Chipewyan traded peacefully with the sloop at Eskimo Point that summer (1770).

1770–1782

The summer of 1771 saw the famous Chipewyan-Yellowknife massacre of Inuit at Bloody Falls, near the mouth of the Coppermine River. This dramatic event, so luridly described by the reluctant eye-witness Samuel Hearne,[47] has done more than all other events combined to contribute to the prevailing anthropological view of Indian–Inuit hostility in Northern Canada. The fact that many Chipewyan joined Hearne's party "with no intent other than to murder the Eskimo" has done nothing to alter the stereotype image of Chipewyan-Inuit relations.[48] In an apparently entirely overlooked note on his friend Matonabbee, Hearne wrote that a few years before, Matonabbee in company with I-do-lat-ze had visited the mouth of the Coppermine and had given gifts of valuable European trade goods to Inuit there, under the most amicable conditions.[49] The massacre, in other words, may have been an aberrancy.

Another fact that is not generally known is that quite literally while the Bloody Falls massacre was taking place, both Chipewyan and Inuit were meeting peacefully some 1300 kilometers to the southeast, having gathered at Eskimo Point to trade with the sloop. They continued to meet there without recorded incident in each of the seven years thereafter that the sloop visited the coast prior to the French capture of Churchill in 1782.

The Period of Peaceful Co-Existence, 1782–1950

The period of peaceful co-existence got off to a wrenching start, at least from the Chipewyan point of view. During 1782 three momentous events occurred: a smallpox epidemic that had devastated Indian populations farther south reached the Chipewyan in the winter of 1781–1782; the French captured and destroyed the Hudson's Bay Company fort at Churchill; and traders had begun operations in the region of Lake Athabasca in 1778 and thereafter. These developments had no known effect on the Inuit populations of concern here, but their impact on the Chipewyan and both immediate in application and longlasting in effect.[50] These events combined to reduce the size of the Chipewyan population by an undetermined but significant factor and to redirect the focus of their trading operations from Churchill toward the southwest. Both developments greatly reduced the number of Chipewyan likely to come into direct contact with Inuit. These demographic changes probably did more to reduce the level of Chipewyan-Inuit conflict than all the deliberate actions of the Hudson's Bay Company combined.

It is useful at this point to differentiate between the two areas of Chipewyan-Inuit contact, namely, the Hudson Bay littoral, on the southeast, and the lower Coppermine River on the northwest. The primary Athapaskan-speaking inhabitants of the latter area actually were Yellowknives, close social, cultural and linguistic relatives of the Chipewyan, but not Chipewyan "proper."[51] During the early and middle eighteenth century the Chipewyan had enjoyed a profitable middleman position vis-à-vis the Yellowknives and their neighbours, the Dogribs, since they controlled access to Fort Churchill.[52] The Yellowknives, too, had been able to act as middlemen between the Chipewyan, on the one hand, and the still more remote Athapaskan-speaking peoples of the Mackenzie drainage, on the other. With the establishment of inland posts by the North West Company and the Hudson's Bay Company in the final decades of the eighteenth century the privileged positions of the Chipewyan was lost. The Yellowknives retained an advantageous middleman position with the Dogribs (and perhaps other Athapaskans) that drew them primarily into the region between Great Bear and Great Slave Lakes, and away from the zone of potential conflict with the Inuit of the Coppermine River area. Indeed, the Yellowknife leader Akaitcho told Captain Franklin that they had last attacked the Inuit in 1811. Yellowknife domineering attitudes led in 1823 to a disastrous war with the Dogribs, followed by two severe epidemics.[53] Contacts between the Chipewyan (including Yellowknives) and the Inuit of the Coronation Gulf-Coppermine River region were effectively terminated by this series of events. Accordingly, the focus of this paper henceforth is exclusively on the eastern sector of the Chipewyan territory.

Many of the Chipewyan inhabiting the central and eastern portions of their range began moving south into former Cree territory in the northern boreal forest during the final decades of the eighteenth century. Some, who came to be known as "Caribou-Eaters" remained in their own lands, however, and continued to follow their ancient pattern of seasonal migration between the tundra and the northern transitional forest.[54] The Inuit, too, remained in their traditional territory along the west coast of Hudson Bay, although they evidently were increasing steadily in numbers within that territory. The approximate distribution of the two populations as of the second decade of the nineteenth century is shown in figure 2.

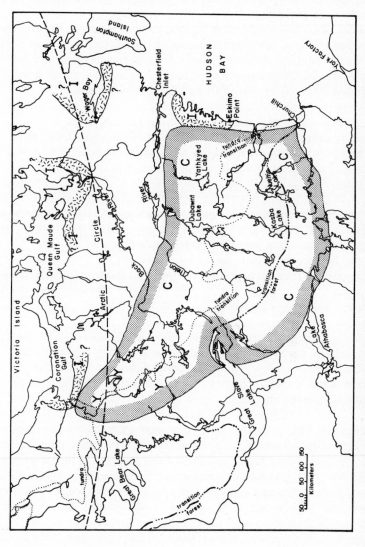

FIG. 2. Map of the West Hudson Bay Drainage Showing the Distribution of the Chipewyan (C) and Inuit (I) Populations within the Study Area, ca. 1815.

After trading voyages were resumed in 1785 both Chipewyan and Inuit continued to meet the sloop at Eskimo Point, and no unpleasant incidents were reported. The voyages were terminated permanently at the end of the 1790 season, however, which reduced even further the opportunities for contact between these two populations.[55]

A reduction is not equivalent to cessation of contact, however, and Chipewyan and Inuit continued to encounter one another both in their own lands and at Churchill. At Churchill, of course, all contact occurred under the watchful eyes of Company personnel, but their relations were often strained nonetheless. Thus, on 19 June 1807, the Churchill journal noted:

> Much jealousy subsists between these [the Eskimo] & the
> other natives indeed the 3 distinct tribes [Chipewyan, Cree] and
> Inuit] are excessively jealous of the least favour being shewn to
> any of the others so that it is with much difficulty we can please
> them.[56]

This passage indicates, once again, that while animosity between the Chipewyan and Inuit definitely existed, the activities of the Hudson's Bay Company traders were among the factors contributing to it.[57]

In the hinterlands, where the natives were left to their own devices, Chipewyan-Inuit relations apparently retained their more complex qualities of earlier years. For example, on 22 July 1818, the Churchill post journal reported:

> This evening a Northern Indian [Chipewyan] arrived with his
> family, in starvation, owing to the general scarcity of deer in the
> Chipewyan country. He says some of his party have been
> plundered of their property by the Esquimaux who left this place
> on the 20th Instant.[58]

However, just four years later, two other Inuit spent the winter among the same general population of Chipewyan. Although by spring they "and the North" Indians seemed to be quite tired of one another,"[59] the factor had to confess that "the circumstances of the two Esquimaux wintering with our Northern Indians of their own free will is what I little expected...."[60] It might not have been such a surprise, however, had the Company men investigated Chipewyan-Inuit relations more thoroughly. The Rev. John West who did inquire on the subject in 1823, learned that Inuit and Chipewyan were meeting *annually* at Chesterfield Inlet for purposes of trade.[61]

The Era of Inuit Expansion, 1820–1890

During the 1820s the Caribou Inuit began to expand their forays into the interior west of Hudson Bay. In so doing they were entering lands formerly within the traditional summer range of the Chipewyan. The latter now were too reduced in numbers in the barrens to mount an effective resistance to Inuit expansion, but there is no evidence that such was their intent in any case. On the contrary, by the early 1830s they were meeting *annually* with Inuit in the vicinity of Yath-kyed Lake,[62] and in 1838 parties of Inuit and Chipewyan passed the entire summer together along the lower Thelon River.[63] By 1841 relations between the two groups were so good that they were conspiring to fool the Hudson's Bay Company traders at Churchill:

> The Chipewyans had previously been forbidden to trade with the Esquimaux. Nevertheless the first party brought 12 white foxes and 9 wolves that we find were procured from the Esquimaux and which was not known till they left here. The last party brought 17 white foxes of the same kind and which were traded on the Esquimaux standard, as would the rest if known in time. However, we happen to know the parties and hereafter will make them pay the difference which is considerable, same time given them a lecture for their roguerry and sly tricks.[64]

During the 1840s and 1850s the Inuit began to live permanently in the interior of the southern Keewatin, expanding outward from their newly established base along the Kazan River just south of Yath-kyed Lake. By the 1860s the interior Barrens, once the land of the Chipewyan, had become even in Chipewyan eyes "the land of the Eskimos."[65] Despite the change, all or most of the Caribou-Eater Chipewyan still spent their summers on the Barrens, some of them venturing as far north as the shore of Dubawnt Lake. By 1870 Chipewyan and Inuit territories no longer were discrete even in theory, overlapping in an area of some 24 000 square kilometers near the southern margins of the tundra. The distribution of the two populations as of about 1870 is indicated in figure 3.

The Roman Catholic missionaries at the newly established outpost of Lac de Brochet knew of the Chipewyans' annual forays into the Barrens, and they also knew that the Indians frequently met Inuit during the course of those expeditions. In order to make contact with the latter, Father Alphonse Gasté[66] decided to accompany the Chipewyan on their trip north in the summer of 1868. The party went as far as the southern shore of Dubawnt Lake, meeting Inuit along the Kazan River on both the outward and return journeys. Several important points emerge from Gasté's account: the Chipewyan expected to be regularly in touch with the Inuit; some Chipewyan spoke Eskimo, although without great fluency; a ritual form of greeting had developed between Chipewyan and Inuit; trade played a prominent part in the relations between the two groups and the Inuit knew enough about Chipewyan food preferences to offer them sundried rather than half-rotten meat.[67] In short, despite the fact that mutual fear and suspicion evidently persisted at a covert level, the overt animosity that once had existed between the Chipewyan and Inuit seems to have disappeared entirely.

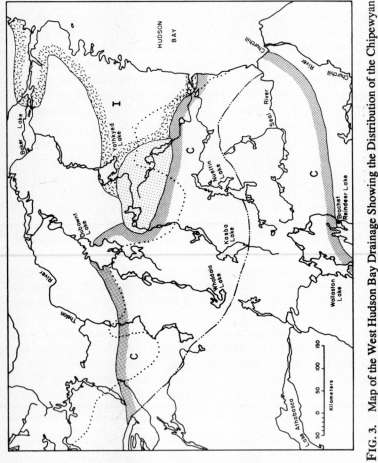

FIG. 3. Map of the West Hudson Bay Drainage Showing the Distribution of the Chipewyan (C) and Inuit (I) Populations within the Study Area, ca. 1870. The speckled area indicates the region occupied at least seasonally by members of both groups.

Father Gasté persuaded some of the Inuit to accompany his party back to Brochet. The good Father's intention, of course, was to induce the Inuit to visit his mission. Instead, they were attracted to the recently established (1859) trading post nearby, which they regarded as being more accessible to their home along the middle Kazan River than the one at Churchill.

By the fall of 1881, 217 Inuit were recorded as "belonging" to the Lac du Brochet post, as opposed to 386 Chipewyan and 29 Cree.[68] The comparable figures for the Churchill post that same fall are 515 (coastal) Inuit and 157 Chipewyan.[69] These figures, combined with the evidence for Inuit territorial expansion and the fact that several Chipewyan had learned to speak Eskimo but that almost no Inuit had learned Chipewyan, may indicate that the dominant position in Chipewyan-Inuit relations was now held by the latter— or that, as traders, the Chipewyan had to learn and had the opportunity to learn *inuktitut*, the language of their customers.

By the 1890s the Inuit had expanded over practically all of the tundra portion of southern Keewatin and they were even encroaching into the northern transitional forest zone. Chipewyan territory continued to contract, particularly along its northern margins. The result of these trends is indicated in figure 4, which shows the approximate distribution of the two populations as of 1890. As the map shows, the Chipewyan and Inuit territory continued to overlap near the tree line, but the number of Chipewyan venturing very far out on to the tundra had declined considerably during the preceding half century.

Territorial Stabilization, 1890–1950

The number of Chipewyan-Inuit contacts continued to decline during the final decades of the nineteenth century. A few Inuit continued to trade at Brochet and Churchill, although much of this trade was conducted through an emerging group of Inuit entrepreneurs who acted as middlemen for their own people. The bulk of the Inuit trade with Europeans still, however, took place along the Hudson Bay coast. Their contacts there were with American whalers, particularly after 1870,[70] and later with the Hudson's Bay Company sloops, whose annual trading voyages were resumed in the summer of 1882.[71] Toward the end of the nineteenth century, therefore, trade with Europeans began to pull Chipewyan and Inuit in opposite directions, whereas previously it had acted to bring them together.

From about 1885 on Chipewyan-Inuit contacts involved a steadily decreasing number of individuals from both populations, and they occurred at progressively fewer locations. One of these locations was the old trading post of Churchill. Observing representatives of both groups there in the summer of 1912, Christian Leden reported that,

> Nowadays there still remains a condition of enmity between Eskimos and Indians. To be sure, they don't kill each other any

more; but they don't like each other, and keep out of each other's way by mutual preference. The Eskimos who come to Churchill in the summer happily build their camp out by the shore, by the old fort, where they have 4.5 km and the police between themselves and the Indian camp.[72]

Leden also noted that the Chipewyan, Cree and Inuit at Churchill cooperated only in the unloading of ships.[73] A decade later Birket-Smith[74] echoed Leden's observations, adding that, when Inuit whaling boats arrived at Churchill, they were met by Chipewyan who begged for caribou hides and meat. To avoid that, the Inuit kept to themselves as much as possible.

A second location where Chipewyan-Inuit contacts continued to occur after 1885 was Brochet. Although the number of Inuit trading at Brochet declined toward the end of the nineteenth century, a few specialist traders regularly visited the post and other Inuit made the trip on occasion.[75] This pattern persisted into the second decade of the twentieth century, but declined thereafter.[76] Nevertheless, as recently as 1938, a band of starving Inuit arrived at Brochet and were given permission to camp and hunt in the vicinity of Reindeer Lake. The only documented case of intermarriage also occurred about this time. Unfortunately, both the husband and wife died immediately following the birth of their child, giving rise to the Chipewyan belief that it is impossible for them to breed successfully with Inuit, suggesting that the latter, in contrast to Cree and whites—with whom Chipewyan can breed successfully— must be something less than human.

Two additional zones of contact remained moderately active in the hinterlands between about 1885 and the 1920s, both being located some distance from European trading posts. One was the Ennadai Lake areas, on the upper Kazan River,[77] and the other was the northern shore of Nueltin Lake.[78] Inter-ethnic relations seemed to have been sporadic in both areas, and when it did occur it was focused primarily on trade. However, Chipewyan-Inuit relations in this particular district during this specific period may have been more harmonious than they were in any other place or at any other time covered in this paper.[79]

During the 1920s a boom in the fur trade led to the establishment of a number of new posts by the Hudson's Bay Company, the Revillon Frères, and various free traders, both north of the tree line and within the northern transitional forest zone. The locations of the major posts as of 1930 as well as the approximate distribution of the Chipewyan and Inuit populations within the study area at that time are indicated in figure 5.

Of primary interest here is a series of posts built and operated on or near the north shore of Nueltin Lake between about 1922 and 1950,[80] and a number of outposts that were operated intermittently in various locations in the general vicinity of the tree line. During the internal and competitive fur trade of the 1920s Chipewyan and Cree men were utilized as freighters between Brochet and these more northerly posts and outposts. A number of them established

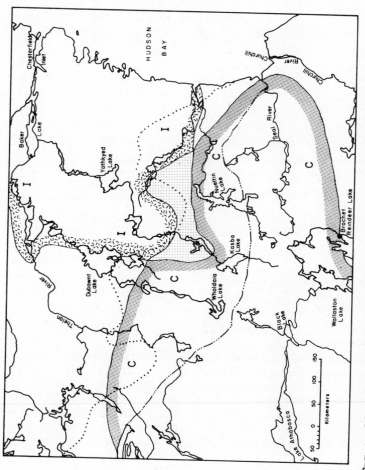

FIG. 4. Map of the West Hudson Bay Drainage Showing the Distribution of the Chipewyan (C) and Inuit (I) Populations within the Study Area, ca. 1890. The Speckled area indicates the region occupied at least seasonally by members of both groups.

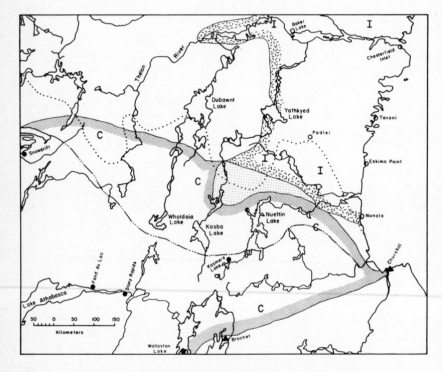

FIG. 5. Map of the West Hudson Bay Drainage Showing Distribution of the Chipewyan (C) and Inuit (I) Populations within the Study Area, ca. 1930. The speckled area indicates the region occupied at least seasonally by members of both groups. Open circles indicate trading posts with a predominantly Inuit clientele; closed circles are trading posts catering to the Chipewyan. The post near Nueltin Lake drew members of both groups, while the Churchill post attracted Chipewyan, Cree, Inuit, and Whites.

friendly relations with Inuit, and a few became reasonably competent speakers of the Eskimo language. According to informants a number of relatively stable partnerships were established during this period, and Chipewyan and Cree would regularly stop to visit their Inuit friends. While it may have been the intent of the traders to establish separate posts for Chipewyan and Inuit, both groups normally frequented the one most convenient to them. Inuit and Chipewyan informants assert that contacts were cordial at these posts, although members of both groups continued to tell tales of ancient atrocities committed against their people by members of the other group.

The Period of Nucleated Settlements, 1950–1977

During the depression and war years fur prices dropped steadily, and the number of trading posts declined accordingly. By the fall of 1950 the only ones left were situated in locations close to mission stations and/or government outposts of various kinds. During the decade that followed, famine conditions north of the tree line led the Canadian government to relocate many of the Caribou Inuit to those centers, and virtually all of the rest eventually moved in voluntarily. The result was a series of nucleated settlements inhabited by Inuit and whites distributed along the eastern and northern margins of the study area, and a similar group of Chipewyan-white communities (with some Cree) located along the southern and western margins. The locations of these communities as of 1970 are indicated in figure 6. Through this process of concentrating in fewer but larger settlements the Chipewyan and Inuit became separated from one another by an expanse of uninhabited territory some 750 kilometers wide at its narrowest point. From the early 1950s on, therefore, the only place where Chipewyan and Inuit could come into contact with one another was at Churchill.

Churchill, of course, had been established as a Hudson's Bay Company trading post in 1717, and had served as a locus of annual Chipewyan-Inuit contact since at least 1791. It had become a mission center in the latter part of the nineteenth century and had acquired an RCMP post in the first decade of the twentieth. The resident native population, consisting of a variable number of Caribou Inuit, Chipewyan, and an occasional Cree, never had numbered more than a few individuals throughout this period, however.

In 1929 the Canadian National Railroad was extended to Churchill, but even that development had relatively little impact except on the summer population of the area. In 1942 this began to change when the U.S. Army built a base at Fort Churchill, a few kilometers from the main town site. The construction and maintenance work drew a number of whites to the area, as well as several Cree and Cree-Métis. The whole tenor of life there changed considerably. After World War II the base was turned over to the Canadian government, which continued to operate it as a major research, transportation and communications center into the early 1970s.

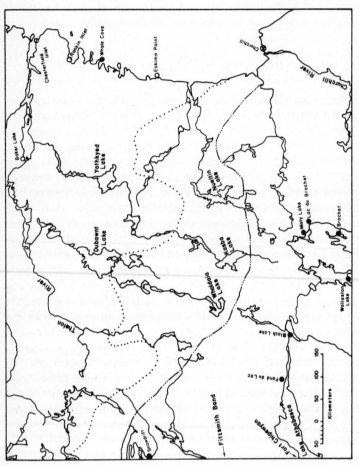

FIG. 6. Map of the West Hudson Bay Drainage Showing the Distribution of the Chipewyan (closed circle) and Inuit (open circle) Settlements Situated within the Study Area, ca. 1970. Churchill had an ethnically heterogeneous population.

Native emigration into Churchill involved several different groups and took place in several distinct movements. These are summarized in table 1.[81] As the table suggests, most of Inuit who moved to Churchill during this period were not Caribou Inuit, although the odd Caribou Inuit family did move to town for a relatively brief period from time to time. Accordingly, as far as the majority of the Inuit immigrants were concerned, neither they nor their ancestors had ever had any contact with Chipewyan before moving to Churchill. There was thus a fundamental break in the continuity of Chipewyan-Inuit relations within the study area between the period under review here, on the one hand, and all of the periods that preceded it, on the other.

The "settlement" of Churchill had become divided into a number of physically distinct and ethnically segregated neighbourhoods by the early 1960s.[82] The whole was, in Porter's terms, a miniature Canadian "vertical mosaic" of hierarchically ranked ethnic groups.[83] At the top of the hierarchy were government employees living at Fort Churchill, followed by Euro-Canadians living at the town site, all of whom were ranked internally according to military or civil service status, occupation, education and income. Below virtually all the whites were Inuit, Cree, Cree-Métis and Chipewyan, in that order. The low position of the Chipewyan may be inferred from a federal government report, broadcast by the Canadian Broadcasting Corporation, which stated that Churchill was Canada's worst slum, and the fact was that the Chipewyan occupied the worst part of it.

The Chipewyan had been relocated to Churchill with totally inadequate preparation. Very few spoke any English, and only those few who had attended residential schools in the south had had any experience living in reasonably although generally segregated communities. Their economic life was a disaster. Their trap lines were too remote to be used, hunting was poor near the town, firewood was lacking, and linguistic problems (as well as other cultural factors) prevented significant employment in either the townsite or Fort Churchill. In addition, they encountered the typical strong negative stereotype toward Indians common among the Euro-Canadian population.

The Inuit, on the other hand, enjoyed a comparatively strong and positive stereotype in the eyes of the local white population. They had a much higher level of employment and a much lower record of "troublemaking" than the Chipewyan. Just why these discrepancies should have existed is beyond the scope of the present paper. The pertinent point is that although Chipewyan and Inuit were geographic neighbours within the context of "greater Churchill," they were almost completely isolated socially from one another. Not only did these particular groups lack a tradition of contact in the past, they had no basis for interaction in the present. When the Chipewyan abandoned the Churchill area for their traditional homeland a few years ago, therefore, they changed virtually nothing as far as the Chipewyan-Inuit relations were concerned. There already had not been any active relations between the two groups within the study area for more than a generation. That general condition has persisted up to the time this paper was written.

TABLE 1 *Native Immigrants to the Churchill Area in the Twentieth Century*

Native Group	Period/Year	Moved From	Reason for Move
Cree and Cree-Métis	1920s–1930s	York Factory	Seek employment
Iglulik (Aivilik) Inuit	1950	Keewatin	Seek employment
Quebec Inuit	1953–1955	Fort Chimo	Government re-location
Cree and Cree-Métis	1956	York Factory	Y.F. trading post closed
Chipewyan	1956	Duck Lake	D.L. trading post closed; government re-location

In this paper we have presented a descriptive summary of the evidence concerning some three and a half centuries of Chipewyan-Inuit relations. We believe that the data—of which we have cited only a representative sample—show convincingly that enmity never has been the sole characteristic of relations between the two groups even though it has been a more or less permanent aspect of those relations. Even when hostilities were historically at their peak, between about 1715 and 1782, peaceful contacts between the two groups were also taking place.

On the basis of our review of the evidence several conclusions are in order. They are presented below under two headings, "empirical" and "methodological." The former focus attention on the data themselves, and basically summarize points that have been made already. The methodological conclusions, on the other hand, are concerned with how data on Chipewyan-Inuit relations typically have been collected and interpreted in the past.

Empirical Conclusions

One important reason why so many authors have reported hostile feelings between Chipewyan and Inuit is that such feelings did in fact exist in the past; to some extent they still do. On the Chipewyan side, at least, this animosity seems to have been rooted in a general world view that led them to interpret certain types of natural disaster as having been caused by human agents. For example, as Hearne noted nearly 200 years ago:

> When any of the principal Northern Indian [Chipewyan] die, it is generally believed that they are conjured to death, either by some of their own countrymen, by some of the southern Indians [Cree] or by some of the Esquimaux. Too frequently the suspicion falls on the latter tribe, which is the grand reason of their never being at peace with these poor and distressed people.[84]

Since prominent Chipewyan inevitably died, a basis for recurrent outbreaks of hostility toward members of neighbouring groups, including both Inuit and Cree, was inherent in the situation.

More recently, it has been noted by Bone and Müller-Wille,[85] among others, that the Chipewyan believe that caribou—their primary source of food and clothing—are continuously available in unlimited numbers unless offended by some human or other animate agent. Unfortunately, the number and distribution of caribou in fact change radically over time due to a variety of causes of which human action is probably one of the least significant.[86] No matter what the Inuit did, therefore, the number of caribou within Chipewyan territory were likely to fluctuate from one year to the next. Since the Inuit were among those most likely to be blamed for a poor hunting season, a basis for continuing Chipewyan hostility toward the Inuit was inherent in the situation from this point of view as well.

We are unaware of any beliefs among the Inuit directly comparable to those just described for the Chipewyan. However, the Inuit, like the Chipewyan, did have a highly institutionalized ethic of retaliation. Once hostilities had been started the Inuit were likely to perpetuate them. Futhermore, even a vague understanding of Chipewyan attitudes toward them would have provided a solid basis for reciprocal negative feelings.

Still another basis for mutual hostility in the seventeenth and early eighteenth centuries *might* have been competition for territory, at least along the west coast of Hudson Bay. There is reason to believe,[87] however, that the eastern portion of southern Keewatin was nearly devoid of human inhabitants between about 1540 and 1640. If that is true, then the Chipewyan and the Inuit both would have been in the process of reoccupying this region toward the end of the early historic period. The construction of the post at Churchill in 1717 would have hastened the eastward expansion of the Inuit, thus bringing them abruptly into contact in what is now the southeastern-most sector of Keewatin and the adjacent portion of northern Manitoba. If this had been their first contact in more than a century, then they probably lacked any means of even communicating with one another, to say nothing of any structured modes of peaceful interaction. Tension is all but inevitable in such a situation.

Another matter that we do not dispute is that the general state of enmity occasionally erupted into bloodshed. Hearne's account of the 1771 Bloody Falls massacre, for example, is scarcely open to question, as is the apparently similar event that took place near Eskimo Point in 1755. What we challenge is the view that overt hostility was the *only* form of interaction between the two groups at this time, yet it was greater during this period than at any other. There were *many* more documented instances of peaceful than of violent encounters between the Chipewyan and Inuit between 1755 and 1782. Even though we do not know just what transpired when Chipewyan and Inuit met peacefully, the failure to even mention that such contacts occurred has been a serious flaw in most of the literature.

A third point that we accept as correct is that Hudson's Bay Company personnel did act to reduce the level of overt hostility between Chipewyan and Inuit. That does not mean, however, that fighting was the only form of interethnic contact previously. It is also possible that the presence of Hudson's Bay

Company posts served to exacerbate tension between the two groups by giving them differential access to supplies of European goods. There is little question but that preferential treatment of the Inuit by the crew of the Company sloop contributed to the massacre of 1755, for example. Even though that was the only recorded instance of bloodshed related to that issue, it was by no means the only time that the Chipewyan expressed their resentment about more favourable treatment being accorded to the Inuit. In sum, we contend that Hudson's Bay Company intervention in native affairs served to simplify a previously complex relationship that involved *both* peaceful and hostile contacts. It did *not* function to replace a wholly hostile relationship with an entirely peaceful one.

Ironically, we have found little evidence to support the one negative influence on Chipewyan-Inuit relations that has been widely attributed to the Hudson's Bay Company.[88] According to the generally accepted view, the fact that the Chipewyan had guns from 1717 on, while the Inuit did not receive any until the 1770s, tipped the balance of power in favour of the former to such an extent that they became much more aggressive toward the Inuit than they ever had been before. A more realistic view, in our opinion, was expressed to Captain W. Coats by a Chipewyan early in the eighteenth century:

> The iron, he said, his countrymen valued most, and our guns they liked very well, but the want of powder and shot induced them to cut them up for knives and chizzells....[89]

Furthermore, the early trade musket was of a quality inferior to that of its military counterpart, and the Churchill journals are full of references to blown, broken and rusted guns being brought to the post for repairs. At least as important as the quality of the equipment and the supplies of powder and shot was the native approach to warfare. Both Inuit and Chipewyan tactics called exclusively for surprise attacks, preferably made in early morning at very close quarters. Eighteenth century muskets were worse than useless in such encounters.

Methodological Conclusions

The methodological issues we wish to consider arise out of the following question: if Chipewyan-Inuit relations actually included many more peaceful contacts than violently hostile ones, why has the literature been so highly biased in favour of the latter? The general answer to that question is straightforward: the literature has been characterized by a combination of sampling error and faulty reasoning. Since similar problems can affect research on ethnic relations in any part of the world, it is instructive to consider those problems in some detail.

The eighteenth century literature concerning peoples along the west coast of Hudson Bay was produced during an era when overt hostilities of a significant order actually were taking place. Since battles are much more dramatic than, say, trade relations, it is not unreasonable to suppose that native accounts would be highly biased in favour of the former. Since the Europeans acquired most of their information from the natives, their accounts naturally reflected that same bias.

Native reports were probably reinforced in European eyes by the assumption that warfare and any kind of peaceful contact are mutually exclusive categories. Given that assumption, of course, Europeans would have been persuaded to accept that native view uncritically; it never would have occurred to them to inquire about other types of encounters. This general bias was established in Hudson's Bay Company circles between 1714 and 1719 by Governor James Knight, and became an integral part of the world view of Company personnel during the decades that followed. The Bloody Falls massacre, which was actually witnessed by a Company employee (Hearne), proved—at least in the eyes of Company personnel—that the Chipewyan and Inuit would attempt to exterminate one another if left to their own devices.

The European's predisposition to accept native tales as true and to assume that warfare precluded other types of relationship led them to interpret a few extraordinary events—like the massacres of 1755 and 1771—as being representative of the prevailing state of affairs. The departures from that pattern, which were much more numerous but much more mundane, were simply ignored. We are indeed fortunate, therefore, to have access to the unpublished material in the Hudson's Bay Company Archives; without it, it would be all but impossible to correct the bias of the early published works.

In evaluating the archives or published literature, it is also necessary to consider the negative evidence. As in Sherlock Holmes' cases of "The Adventures of Silver Blaze" and "The Hound of the Baskervilles," it was the dog that did not bark that provided the clue to the resolution of the mysteries. In the case of Chipewyan and Inuit there are far more years in which no hostilities are recorded—this may mean years in which no contact occurred, or in which contacts were peaceful and thus not worthy of inclusion in the reports.

An analysis of the early published reports reveals yet another source of bias. Literally all the information they contain was acquired from the Chipewyan side of the Chipewyan-Inuit boundary. Not a single one of the eighteenth century authors had available to him any information on the Inuit view of the situation; indeed, Rev. John West, in 1823, was the first writer to seek Inuit opinion. We can state from personal experience that to collect all of one's information from one side exclusively is to introduce a serious distortion into one's findings. The Chipewyan, for example, still tell tales of past warfare with the Inuit. They use the term *otel'ena* ("enemy of the lowlands") when referring to Inuit, and they remark with horror that the Inuit eat raw meat, a custom showing Inuit to be less than human.[90] For their part, the Inuit recount instances of Chipewyan atrocities, and refer to them derisively as *itqiliit* ("louse eggs"). The only really effective way to overcome the biases inherent in such attitudes is to view the ethnic boundary from *both sides*, not from just one or the other. We presume that a similar caution is in order for *all* studies of ethnic relations.

The final methodological point we wish to make concerns the confusion of sentiment and content in the analysis of inter-ethnic relationships. Both must be taken into consideration, but they must be clearly distinguished. If one does not record the details of specific instances of contact between Chipewyan and Inuit, for example, one can be easily misled by expressions of suspicion, fear, and derision into believing that no kind of civil interaction would be possible. Conversely, observation of actual contact and nothing else can be equally misleading. Thus, as Birket-Smith noted, Chipewyan and Inuit meeting at Churchill in the early 1920s would converse politely with one another, and the Inuit would even address the Chipewyan as "my cousins."[91] As soon as Chipewyan's backs were turned, however, the Inuit would revert to the conventional appellation of "louse egg."

The literature on the particular region covered in this paper probably has done more to contribute to the prevailing view of generalized animosity between Indians and Eskimos than the literature from any other sector of the Indian-Eskimo interface. Hearne's account, in particular, seems to have contributed to that perspective. We have tried to show that, while the conventional picture does derive some substance from the data on Chipewyan-Inuit relations, so also does the exact opposite point of view. We hope that our analysis will contribute to the establishment of a more balanced understanding of the situation than has prevailed in the past.

Appendix I

Extract from Journal of the most material Occurrances on board the Churchill Sloop from 11 July to 23d Augst 1756 Kept by John McBean [Bain] Master[92]

In my [1755] journal the year Before my first voyage to the Nd you find on Saturday at 11 AM that I made a Remark of a smais made on the land which I took to be No Indians that made it for us to Come towards them But as there was no such thing mentioned in my Instructions and had no such comodities as they Trade for and the Coast at the same time being very shoall haveing then but 5 and 6 fathom 4 or 5 Leagues off I did not go near them but proceeded on of the cape [Eskimo] and got in that afternoon this smoak being about 5 Leagues to the southward of the cape these it seems happened to be No Indians and was filled with such jelousy because we took no notice of them that they went instantly to the cape where they know was our first randezvooes and they lay in ambush in sight of us all the time we lay there and saw all our actions with the native and the evening as we saild and it seems before we got out of there sight they went and fell on 4 tents of the Usquemaes that tented on a point that joynd to the main and murdered every soul of them men women and Childeren The men they shott as they took to there canoes and the women they sabt [sic] in the tents where they found them actcept one women which it seems some of them fancied and after being sometime there captive in baran place where there was neither bush nor brier to shelter when they were all fast a sleep she stole away and after walking and without dout runing as long as the night coverd her she found no place to hide her but a pond of watter where she went in and left no place out but her head to breath with but these crewell villons after making diligent search found her and shott her instantly in the watter the other 4 tents was on an isle about 3/4 of a mile so that they could not get at them of these that was destroyed there was about 16 or 18 of them young and old and very affable jocose people for I was in all there tents the day before they were destroyed all this I was quite ignorant off until the fall of the year in the November following viz. There there was a young fellow of a No Indean that was kept for the Factory as a hunter he was atenting as a partridge hunter on the track that the No Indeans comes to the fort And on there Return back from the fort they Related the whole affair to him being their countrymen and he ackuanted Moses Norton with it in the southern Indean language for he could speak it as well as the northern he likewise ackuanted him that these No Indeans that killed the Usquemase had bin a gang that was at the fort a few days before trading and on there Return to the No^d they came a thwart a herd of deer and killed great quantities of them and that seeing the the sloop in the offing they made that smoak for us to come on shore to trade it [caribou] with us and that when they saw we did not mind them they Reflected with these words that they were obliged to carry there trade to the English for many miles and then trade on there conditions but that the usquemaes had it brought to there doors therefore says they let us go kill our Rivals or to this purpose. There was several familys on the spot where this smoak was made and among the best one midleowns and they soliceted him to joyn them but it seems he would not but dissuaded them from it what he could telling them that the english was their frinds that it is of both the usquemaes and them selves and they would get nothing by it but the ill will of the English however the gang that proposed it first went and acted with the crewelty befor mentioned and accordingly this voyage when I came to Naps [Knapps] Bay at the cape as soon as I anchored the vessell I went on shore to the place where they tented to see if there was any proffe of what was Reported and indeed there was all the fatal proffe imaginable of it for where there tents was pitched there was all there aparall lying both of the men and the women all tore as I took it by the vile beasts that I supose tore them to get the carkases out of them such as bears wolfes and foxes Several of their bones lying about their tent poles and tents lying all in a heap by being as I supose blown down with the severity of the weather all their utensils lying about such as stone pots kits [?] bows arrows with all there canoes lying stove along shore & c with several other certain proffes.

Notes

1. Kaj Birket-Smith, *The Caribou Eskimos. Material and Social Life and Their Cultural Postion. I. Descriptive Part. Report of the Fifth Thule Expedition, 1921–24*, vol. 5, pt. 1 (Copenhagen, 1929), 163–65; Edward Chappel, *Narrative of a Voyage to Hudson's Bay in His Majesty's Ship 'Rosamund', Containing Some Account of the Northeastern Coast of America and of the Tribes Inhabiting that Remote Region* (London, 1817), 166; Henry Ellis, *A Voyage to Hudson's Bay by the 'Dobbs Galley' and 'California' in the Years 1746–1747* (London, 1748; reprint New York: S.R. Publishers Ltd. and Johnson Reprint Corp., 1967), 182; Jean Gabus, *Iglous, vie des Esquimaux-Caribou* (Neuchatel, 1941), 78, 216, 217; James Knight, Journal Kept at Churchill River 14 July to 13 September, 1717, in *The Founding of Churchill*, ed. J.F. Kenney (Toronto, 1932), 152–53; Knud Rasmussen, *Observations on the Intellectual Culture of the Caribou Eskimos. Report of the Fifth Thule Expedition, 1921–24*. vol. 7, pt.2 (Copenhagen, 1930), 13, 15, 32; Glyndwr Williams, ed., *Andrew Graham's Observations on Hudson's Bay 1767–1791*, Hudson's Bay Record Society, no. 27 (London, 1969), 174, 195.

2. Kaj Birket-Smith, *Contributions to Chipewyan Ethnology Report of the Fifth Thule Expedition, 1921–24*, vol. 6, pt. 3 (Copenhagen, 1930), 34; Alan Cooke, "The Eskimos and the Hudson's Bay Company," in *Le peuple Esquimau aujourd' hui et demain*, ed. Jean Malaurie (Paris, 1973), 212; John Rae, *Narrative of an Expedition to the Shores of the Arctic Sea in 1846 and 1847* (London, 1850), 190–91; Thomas Simpson, *Narrative of the Discoveries on the North Coast of America; Effected by the Officers of the Hudson's Bay Company During the Years 1836–39* (London, 1843), 71; Charles Swaine, *An Account of a Voyage for the Discovery of a Northwest Passage* 2 Vols. (London, 1748; reprint New York: S.R. Publishers Ltd. and Johnson Reprint Corp., 1968), 2:43–44.

3. Richard Glover, Introduction in *Andrew Graham's Observations on Hudson's Bay 1767–1791*, ed. G. Williams, Hudson's Bay Record Society, no. 27 (London, 1969), xiv.

4. Robert Janes, "Indian and Eskimo Contact in Southern Keewatin: An Ethnohistorical Approach," *Ethnohistory* 20, 1 (1973): 39–54.

5. James Smith, "Introduction: The Historical and Cultural Position of the Chipewyan," *Arctic Anthropology* 13, 1 (1976): 1–5; Birket-Smith, *The Caribou Eskimos*.

6. Thomas Rundall, *Narrative of Voyages Toward the North-West in Search of a Passage to Cathay and India, 1496 to 1631* (London: Hakluyt Society, 1849), 68–87.

7. The name is always spelt Stewart in Captain James Knight's post journal at York Fort, but Stuart in the Hudson's Bay Company's personnel records. Sylvia Van Kirk, "Thanadelthur," *The Beaver* 304, 1 (1974): 40–45; York Factory Journal for 1717, Hudson's Bay Company Archives (hereafter HBCA), B.239/a/2/passim, Public Archives of Manitoba, Winnipeg. Microfilm copies of this archival material from 1670–1870 are on deposit in the Public Archives of Canada (hereafter PAC), Ottawa.

8. John Campbell, "Current Research: Arctic," *American Antiquity* 29, 4 (1964): 535–39; John Campbell, "Current Research: Arctic," *American Antiquity* 31, 2 (1965): 290–95; Bryan Gordon, *Of Men and Herds in Barrenland Prehistory*, National Museum of Man, Mercury Series, Archeological Survey of Canada Paper 27 (Ottawa, 1975); Bryan Gordon, Chipewyan Prehistory (Paper presented to the Conference on Northern Athapaskans, University of Calgary, Archaeological

Association, 1976); Bryan Gordon, *Migod—8000 Years of Barrenland Prehistory*, National Museum of Man, Mercury Series, Archaeological Survey of Canada Paper 56 (Ottawa, 1976); Bryan Gordon, "Prehistoric Chipewyan Harvesting at a Barrenland Caribou Water Crossing," *Western Canadian Journal of Anthropology* 7, 1 (1977): 69–83; William Irving, "The Barren Grounds," in *Science, History and Hudson Bay*, ed. C.S. Beals (Ottawa, 1968), 1:26–54; Sheila Minni, *The Prehistoric Occupations of Black Lake, Northern Saskatchewan*, National Museum of Man, Mercury Series, Archaeological Survey of Canada Paper 53 (Ottawa, 1976); Ronald Nash, "The Prehistory of Northern Manitoba," in *Ten Thousand Years. Archaeology in Manitoba*, ed. W.M. Hlady (Altona: Manitoba Archaeological Society, 1970), 77–92; Ronald Nash, *Archaeological Investigations in the Transitional Forest Zone: Northern Manitoba, Southern Keewatin, NWT*, Manitoba Museum of Man and Nature (Winnipeg, 1975); William Noble, "Archaeological Surveys and Sequences in Central District Mackenzie, NWT," *Arctic Anthropology* 8, 1 (1971): 102–35; William Noble, "Applications of the Direct Historic Approach in Central District of Mackenzie, NWT," in *Proceedings: Northern Athapaskan Conference, 1971*, ed. A.M. Clark, National Museum of Man, Mercury Series, Canadian Ethnology Service Paper 27 (Ottawa, 1975), 2:759–85; James Wright, *The Aberdeen Site Keewatin District, NWT*, National Museum of Man, Mercury Series, Archaeological Survey of Canada Paper 2 (Ottawa, 1972); James Wright, *The Prehistory of Lake Athabasca: An Initial Statement*, National Museum of Man, Mercury Series, Archaeological Survey of Canada Paper 29 (Ottawa, 1975).

9. Diamond Jenness, *The Life of the Copper Eskimos. Report of the Canandian Arctic Expedition, 1913–18. Southern Party, 1913–16* (Ottawa, 1922).

10. Robert McGhee, *Copper Eskimo Prehistory*, National Museum of Man, Mercury Series, Publications in Archaeology, no. 2 (Ottawa, 1972); William Taylor Jr., "Interim Account of an Archaeological Survey in the Central Arctic 1963," Anthropological Papers of the University of Alaska 12, 1 (1964): 46–55; William Taylor Jr., "The Fragments of Eskimo Prehistory," *The Beaver* 295, 4 (Spring, 1965): 4–17; William Taylor Jr., "Summary of Archaeological Field Work on Banks and Victoria Islands, Arctic Canada, 1965," *Arctic Anthropology* 4, 1 (1967): 221–43; William Taylor Jr., *An Archaeological Survey between Cape Parry and Cambridge Bay, NWT, Canada, in 1963*, National Museum of Man, Mercury Series, Archaeological Survey of Canada Paper 1 (Ottawa, 1972).

11. Brenda Clark, *The Development of Caribou Eskimo Culture*, National Museum of Man, Mercury Series, Archaeological Survey of Canada Paper 59 (Ottawa, 1977); Brenda Clark, "The Thule Occupation of West Hudson Bay," in *Thule Eskimo Culture: An Archaeological Retrospective*, ed. A.P. McCartney, National Museum of Man, Mercury Series, Archaeological Survey of Canada Paper (Ottawa, 1979); Bryan Gordon, *1974 Thule Culture Investigations of Baker Lake, NWT*, Canadian Archaeological Association Bulletin 6 (1974): 218–24; Elmer Harp Jr., "Ecological Continuity on the Barren Grounds," *Polar Notes* 1 (1959): 48–56; Elmer Harp Jr., "The Moffatt Archaeological Collection from the Dubawnt Country, Canada," *American Antiquity* 24, 4 (1959): 412–22; Elmer Harp Jr., *The Archaeology of the Lower and Middle Thelon, Northwest Territories*, Arctic Institute of North America, Technical Paper 8 (Montreal, 1961); Elmer Harp Jr., "Archaeological Evidence Bearing on the Origin of the Caribou Eskimo," International Congress of Anthropological and Ethnological Sciences 1960, vol. 2 Comptes Rendus, pt. 1 Ethnologie (1963): 409–413; Urvé Linnamae and Brenda Clark, "Archaeology of Rankin Inlet, NWT," *Musk-Ox* 19 (1976): 37–73; Urve Linnamae and Brenda Clark, "The Archaeology of Rankin Inlet: A Report of the 1975 Season," MS, 1976; Therkel Mathiassen, *Archaeology of the Central Eskimos,*

I. Descriptive Part, Report of the Fifth Thule Expedition 1921–24, vol. 4, pt. 1 (Copenhagen, 1927); Therkel Mathiassen, *Archaeology of the Central Eskimos. II. The Thule Culture and Its Position within the Eskimos Culture. Report of the Fifth Thule Expedition 1921–24*, vol. 4, pt.2 (Cophenhagen, 1927); Allen McCartney, *Thule Eskimo Prehistory along Northwestern Hudson's Bay* (Ann Arbor, Michigan, 1971); Charles Merbs, "An Island of the Dead. Sir Thomas Rowe's Welcome," *The Beaver*, 301 (Spring 1971): 16–24; Charles Merbs, *An Archaeological Study of the Eskimo Thule Culture in the Northwest Hudson Bay Area*, National Geographic Society Research Reports, 1968 Projects (Washington, D.C., 1976), 247–65.

12. Ernest Burch Jr., "Caribou Eskimo Origins: An Old Problem Reconsidered," *Arctic Anthropology* 15, 1 (1978): 1–35; Ernest Burch Jr., "The Thule-Historic Eskimo Transition on the West Coast of Hudson Bay," in *Thule Eskimo Culture: An Archaeological Retrospective*, ed. A.P. McCartney, National Museum of Man, Archaeological Survey of Canada Paper (Ottawa, 1979); Clark, "Thule Occupation of West Hudson Bay"; McCartney, *Thule Eskimo Prehistory*.

13. Birket-Smith, *The Caribou Eskimos*.

14. Henry Kelsey, A Journal of a voyage and journey undertaken/ by Henry Kelsey to discover and endeavour to bring/ to a commerce ye northern Indians inhabiting to ye/ Northward of Churchill River and also ye dogside Nation/ June ye 17th. 1689, in *The Kelsey Papers*, ed. H.G. Doughty and C. Martin (Ottawa: 1929), 27–28.

15. Robert Douglas and J.N. Wallace, eds., *Twenty Years of York Factory, 1694–1714. Jeremie's Account of Hudson Strait and Bay* (Ottawa, 1926), 21; J. Burr Tyrell, ed., *Documents Relating to the Early History of Hudson Bay*, The Champlain Society (Toronto, 1931), 128, 258, 265. The possibility that Cree and not Chipewyan were in contact with the Inuit along the west coast of Hudson Bay during the seventeenth century is intriguing. It implies that either the Cree extended much farther north, or that the Inuit extended much farther south than has generally been supposed. It is perhaps not accidental that the Caribou Inuit word for Cree was *unaalit*, a term derived from an old base meaning "competitive" or "belligerent"; Thomas Correll, "Ungalaglingmuit: A Study in Language and Society" (Ph.D. diss., University of Minnesota, 1972), 107. During the period under review the Cree were anything but belligerent *vis-à-vis* the Caribou Inuit, with whom they had almost no direct contact.

16. Regarding Chipewyan-Cree hostilities around the end of the seventeenth century, see the following: K.G. Davies, ed., *Letters from Hudson Bay, 1703–1740*. Hudson Bay Record Society, no. 25 (London, 1965), 410 ff; Douglas and Wallace, eds., *Twenty Years of York Factory*, 20; Beryl Gillespie, "Territorial Expansion of the Chipewyan in the 18th Century," in *Proceedings: The Northern Athapaskan Conference, 1971*, ed. A.M. Clark, National Museum of Man, Mercury Series, Canadian Ethnology Service Paper 27 (Ottawa, 1975), 2:350–99; James Kenney, Introduction in *The Founding of Churchill, being the Journal of Captain James Knight, Governor-in-Chief in Hudson Bay from the 14th of July to the 13th of September, 1717*, ed. J.F. Kenney (Toronto, 1932), 51–52; Knight, Journal kept at Churchill River, 57; Tyrrell, ed., *Early History of Hudson Bay*, 20; Van Kirk, "Thanadelthur," 42.

17. Birket-Smith, *The Canadian Eskimos*, 165n.

18. See Ernest Burch and Thomas Carroll, "Alliance and Conflict: Inter-Regional Relations in North Alaska," in *Alliance in Eskimo Society, Proceedings of the American Ethnological Society, 1971, Supplement*, ed. D.L. Guemple (Seattle, 1972), 17–39.

19. Churchill Post Journal 1718–1721, HBCA, B.42/a/1/ fol. 29d.

20. Van Kirk, "Thanadelthur."

21. Kenney, Introduction, 59; York Factory Journal, 15 July 1717, HBCA, B.239/a/3.

22. Knight, Journal kept at Churchill River.

23. Richard Glover, Introduction, in *Letters from Hudson Bay 1703–1740*, ed. K.G. Davies, Hudson Bay Record Society, no. 25 (London, 1965), l–lv.

24. Burch, "Caribou Eskimo Origins."

25. Churchill Post Journal, 1718–1721, HBCA, B.42/a/1 fol. 80d.

26. Churchill Post Journal, 1718–1721, HBCA, B.42/a/1 fol. 127d.

27. Churchill Post Journal, 1718–1721, HBCA, B.42/a/5 fol. 24d.

28. Ellis, *A Voyage to Hudson's Bay*, 81; Swaine, *Account of a Voyage*, 2:176.

29. Christopher Middleton, *Journal of H.M.S. 'Furnace'*, 1742, TS, MG18, D4, vol. 4, PAC, Ottawa; Christopher Middleton, *A Vindication of the Conduct of Captain Christopher Middleton in a Late Voyage on His Majesty's Ship the 'Furnace'* ... (London, 1743; reprint New York: S.R. Publishers Ltd. and Johnson Reprint Corp., 1967); Christopher Middleton, Remarkable Observations on board Her Majesty's Ship *Furnace*, from Churchill towards Ne Ultra on a Discovery, in an Appendix to C. Middleton, *Vindication of the Conduct* (London, 1743; reprint New York: S.R. Publishers Ltd. and Johnson Reprint Corp., 1967).

30. Churchill Post Journal, 17 June 1742, HBCA, B.42/a/23.

31. Middleton, *Journal of H.M.S. 'Furnace'*, 105–6; Middleton, *Vindication of the Conduct*, 119.

32. Arthur Dobbs, *An Account of the Countries Adjoining to Hudson's Bay in the North-West Part of America* (London, 1744; reprint New York: S.R. Publishers Ltd. and Johnson Reprint Corp, 1967), 118.

33. Churchill Post Journal, 3 May 1743, HBCA, B.42/a/24.

34. Swaine, *Account of a Voyage*, 2:43–44.

35. Swaine, *Account of a Voyage*, 2:266; cf. Ellis, *Voyage to Hudson's Bay*, 260.

36. Trading vessels had been sent north on several occasions prior to 1750, but the voyage became regular only in 1750.

37. A Journal of Proceedings on Board the *Churchill* Sloop 1170...1750, HBCA, B.42/a/35 fol.1d.

38. A Journal of Proceedings, HBCA, B.42/a/35 fol. 11d.

39. A Journal on Board the *Churchill* Sloop...1756, HBCA, B.42/a/47 fol. 2,3.

40. A Journal on Board, HBCA, B.42/a/47 fol. 2d.

41. Samuel Hearne, *A Journey from Prince of Wales's Fort in Hudson's Bay to the Northern Ocean in the Years 1769, 1770, 1771, 1772* ed. Richard Glover (Toronto, 1958), 217.

42. A Journal ... in the Good Sloop *Churchill* and the *Strivewell* Cutter, 20 July 1762, HBCA, B.42/a/58.

43. Churchill Post Journal, 16 November 1764, HBCA, B.42/a/62.

44. *Churchill* Sloop Journal for 1764–1765, 19 July 1765, HBCA, B.42/a/63.

45. Churchill Post Journal 1768–1769, HBCA, B.42/a/74 fol. 29d.

46. Journal on Board the *Churchill* ... 1769, HBCA, B.42/a/75 fol. 30–34.

47. Hearne, *Journey from Prince of Wales's Fort*, 95–105.

48. Hearne, *Journey from Prince of Wales's Fort*, 73–74.

49. Hearne, *Journey from Prince of Wales's Fort*, 224n.

50. It is beyond the scope of this essay to evaluate in detail the effects on the Chipewyan. Beryl Gillespie, "Yellowknives: Quo Iverunt?" in *Migration and Anthropology Proceedings of the 1970 Annual Spring Meeting of the American Ethnological Society*, ed. R.F. Spencer (Seattle: Washington University Press, 1970), 61–71; Beryl Gillespie, "An Ethnohistory of the Yellowknives: Northern

Athapaskan Tribe," in *Contributions to Canadian Ethnology, 1975,* ed. D.B. Carlisle, National Museum of Man, Mercury Series, Canadian Ethnology Service Paper 31 (Ottawa, 1975), 191–246; Gillespie, "Territorial Expansion"; Beryl Gillespie, "Changes in Territory and Technology of the Chipewyan," *Arctic Anthropology* 13, 1 (1976): 6–11; Gillespie has discussed the impact of smallpox and the North West Company trade, and our data support her conclusions. No one, however, has commented on the direct effects on the Chipewyan of the closing of Fort Churchill. There is some reason to believe that this event alone had disastrous consequences for at least some of those groups attempting to trade there in the winter of 1782–1783; London Inward Correspondence; Letters from Churchill, 1774–1791, 12 October 1784, and 28 August 1785, HBCA, A. 11/15; Churchill Correspondence Book, 1783–1801, 14 August 1799, HBCA, B.42/b/44. According to Hearne, *Journey from Prince of Wales's Fort,* 228, the Chipewyan leader Matonabbee committed suicide—the only recorded case of Chipewyan self-destruction—on discovering the destruction of Fort Churchill.

51. Gillespie, "Ethnohistory of the Yellowknives."
52. Glover, Introduction, xxix–xxvi.
53. Gillespie, "Territory and Technology of the Chipewyan," 214–23.
54. James Smith, "The Ecological Basis of Chipewyan Socio-Territorial Organization," in *Proceedings: Northern Athapaskan Conference, 1971,* ed. A.M. Clark, National Museum of Man, Mercury Series, Canadian Ethnology Service Paper 27 (Ottawa, 1975), 2:389–461.
55. See Chappell, *Narrative of a Voyage,* 116.
56. Churchill Post Journal, 1805–1806, HBCA, B.42/a/132 fol. 18.
57. Churchill Post Journal, 1814–1815, HBCA, B.42/a/141 fol. 18d.
58. Churchill Post Journal, 1818–1819, HBCA, B.42/a/144 fol. 2.
59. Churchill Post Journal, 1821–1822, HBCA, B.42/a/147 fol. 26d.
60. Churchill Post Journal, 1821–1822, HBCA, B.42/a/147 fol. 18.
61. John West, *The Substance of a Journal During a Residence at the Red River Colony* (London, 1824; reprint New York: S.R. Publishers Ltd. and Johnson Reprint Corp., 1966), 183; cf. Churchill Post Journal, 1822–1823, HBCA, B.42/a/149 fol. 46.
62. Simpson, *Narrative of the Discoveries,* 71.
63. Simpson, *Narrative of the Discoveries,* 71.
64. Churchill Post Journal, 1841–1842, HBCA, B.43/a/175 fol. 13d.
65. Arsène Turquetil, Chronique histoire de la Mission Saint-Pierre du Lac Caribou, depuis 1846 jusqu'au nos jours, 1912, *Missions de la Congregation des Missionaires Oblats de Marie Immaculée* 40 (1912): 183.
66. Alphonse Gasté, "Father Gasté Meets the Inland Eskimos," *Eskimo* 57 (1960): 3–15.
67. Gasté, "Gasté Meets the Inland Eskimos," 3, 9, 6, 6–11, 9.
68. H. Belanger, Cumberland House District Report for 1885, HBCA, B.49/e/9 fol. 4.
69. Churchill Census, 1881, HBCA, B.42/2/2. Some Chipewyan and Inuit may have been recorded as belonging to both posts. On the other hand, some members of both populations probably were not counted at all.
70. W. Gillies Ross, *Whaling and Eskimos: Hudson Bay 1860–1915,* National Museum of Man, Publications in Ethnology, no. 10 (Ottawa, 1975).
71. George McTavish, *Behind the Palisades, An Autobiography* (Sidney, BC, 1963).
72. Christian Leden, *Uber Kiwatins Eisfelder. Drei Jahre unter Kanadischen Eskimos* (Leipzig, 1927), 26.

73. Leden, *Uber Kiwatins Eisfelder*, 30.
74. Birket-Smith, *The Caribou Eskimos*, 165.
75. J. McDougall, Inspecting Officer, Inspection Report, Lac du Brochet Post, Cumberland District, 1 January to 8 January 1894, HBCA, B.296/e/2 fol. 14; Arsene Turquetil, Première tentative d'apostolat chez les Esquimaux, *Missions de la Congregation des Oblats de Marie Immaculée* 45 (1907): 332.
76. Angus Buchanan, *Wildlife in Canada* (Toronto, 1920), 156–57.
77. Turquetil, Première tentative d'apostolat, 490; J. Burr Tyrrell, Report on the Doobaunt, Kazan and Ferguson Rivers, and the North-West Coast of Hudson Bay, and on Two Overland Routes from Hudson Bay to Lake Winnipeg, *Ninth Annual Report*, pt. F, Geographical Survey of Canada (Ottawa, 1897), 131–32.
78. Arsène Turquetil, Lac Caribou apostolat des Esquimaux - Premières tentatives, *Missions de la Congregation des Missionaries Oblats de Marie Immaculée* 42 (1904): 51.
79. Correll, "Ungalaglingmiut," 159; Valene Smith, "Eskimo and Caribou. The Padlimiuts of Hudson Bay," MS 1970, 213; Geert van de Steenhoven, Report to the Department of Northern Affairs and National Resources on a Field Research Journey for the Study of Legal Concepts Among the Eskimos in Some Parts of Keewatin District, NWT, in the Summer of 1955 (The Hague, 1956; mimeographed), 22; Geert van den Steenhoven, "Ennandai Lake People 1955," *The Beaver* 298, 4 (1968): 17.
80. Prentice Downes, *Sleeping Island* (Toronto, 1943), 211; Peter Usher, *Fur Trade Posts of the Northwest Territories 1870–1970*, Department of Indian Affairs and Northern Development, Northern Science Research Group 71–4, (Ottawa, 1971), 143.
81. This account of the ethnic situation at Churchill is based on the following sources: Lorraine Brandson, *The Chipewyan Dene Resource Manual*, Manitoba Museum of Man and Nature, Winnipeg [in press at time this article was first published, M.S. Egloff, "Cree-Métis and Other People on the Flats," in *Ethnographic Survey of Churchill* ed. John J. Honigmann, University of North Carolina Institute of Social and Economic Research (Chapel Hill, 1968); Peter Elias, *Metropolis and Hinterland in Northern Manitoba*, Manitoba Museum of Man and Nature (Winnipeg, 1975); William Koolage Jr., "Chipewyan Indians of Camp 10," in *Ethnographic Survey of Churchill*, ed. John Honigmann, University of North Carolina Institute of Social and Economic Research (Chapel Hill, 1968), 61–127; William Koolage Jr., "Relocation and Culture Change: A Canadian Subarctic Case Study," *Atti del XL Congresso Internazionale degli Americanisti* (Roma-Genova, 1972); William Koolage Jr., "Conceptual Negativism in Chipewyan Ethnology," *Anthropologica* 171 (1975): 45–60; William Koolage Jr., "Differential Adaptations of Athapaskans and Other Native Ethnic Groups to a Northern Town," *Arctic Anthropology* 12,1 (1976): 70–83; George Vranas, "Akudlik and Its Residents," in *Ethnographic Survey of Churchill*, ed. John Honigmann, University of North Carolina Institute of Social and Economic Research (Chapel Hill, 1968), 27–60.
82. For a map of Churchill see Elias, *Metropolis and Hinterland*, 14.
83. John Porter, *The Vertical Mosaic* (Toronto, 1965).
84. Hearne, *Journey from Prince of Wales's Fort*, 216–17.
85. Robert Bone et al., *The Chipewyan of the Stoney Rapids Region*, University of Saskatchewan Institute for Northern Studies, Mawdsley Memoir 1 (Saskatoon, 1973), 86–87; Ludger Müller-Wille, "Caribou Never Die. Modern Caribou Hunting Economy of the Dene (Chipewyan) of Fond du Lac, Saskatchewan and NWT," *Musk-ox* 14, 7 (1974): 7–19.
86. Ernest Burch Jr., "The Caribou/Wild Reindeer as a Human Resource,"

American Antiquity 34, 3 (1972): 339–68; James Smith, "Economic Uncertainty in an 'Original Affluent Society': Caribou and Caribou Eater Chipewyan Adaptive Strategies," *Arctic Anthropology* 15, 1 (1978): 71–75.

87. Burch, "Caribou Eskimo Origins."

88. For example in Williams, ed., *Andrew Graham's Observations*, 174; Joseph Robson, *An Account of Six Years Residence in Hudson's Bay, from 1733 to 1736, and 1744 to 1747* (London, 1752; reprint New York: S.R. Publishers Ltd. and Johnson Reprint Corp., 1965), 66.

89. John Barrow, ed. *The Geography of Hudson's Bay; Being the Remarks of Captain W. Coats in Many Voyages to that Locality between the Years 1727 and 1751* (London: Hakluyt Society, 1852), 33.

90. Henry Sharp, "Man: Wolf: Woman: Dog," *Arctic Anthropology* 13, 1 (1976): 31–32.

91. Birket-Smith, *The Caribou Eskimos*, 165.

92. A Journal on Board the *Churchill* Sloop...1750, HBCA, B.42/a/47 fol. 2,3.

WHALING, INUIT, AND THE ARCTIC ISLANDS*

W. GILLIES ROSS

Most of the century under consideration in this symposium [1880 to 1980] has been characterized by the absence of whaling,[1] rather than by its presence. By 1880 whaling was in decline throughout the world's oceans, and by the First World War the Arctic whaling industry was moribund, its capital equipment and techniques out of date, its markets captured by petroleum products, vegetable oils, and spring steel, its quarry the Greenland whale reduced to the threshold of survival. Nevertheless, the activities of whalemen during the nineteenth century and early twentieth century are worthy of consideration because they exerted a powerful influence upon the animal life, native population, and political status of the Arctic Islands.

The Expansion of Whaling Into the Arctic Islands

From the beginning of European and American whaling in the Davis Strait region during the seventeenth century the distribution of sea ice in summer strongly influenced the location and timing of whaling activities, and for a long while discouraged whalemen from reaching the Baffin Island coast. As one whaling surgeon expressed it:

> The quantity of floating ice on the west shore of Davis' Straits is so considerable, as to present an almost insurmountable obstacle towards approaching the land in that direction. This ice, which has from time immemorial occupied nearly the same situation, is termed the West Pack.[2]

*A Century of Canada's Arctic Islands, 1880–1980, ed. M. Zaslow (Ottawa: Royal Society of Canada, 1981), 33–50.

Although there were undoubtedly occasions during the seventeenth and eighteenth centuries on which ships were able to reach the southeastern part of Baffin Island,[3] the whaling operations of the Dutch, Germans, Americans, English, and Scottish were largely confined to the Greenland coast (the "East Land" or "East Side") for the better part of two centuries. It was therefore highly significant when the Northwest Passage expeditions of John Ross in 1818 and Edward Parry in 1819 demonstrated the feasibility of a high latitude crossing of Baffin Bay to the eastern fringe of what now constitute the Canadian Arctic Islands. Furthermore, in 1819 Parry effectively shattered the myth that Lancaster Sound was an inconsequential cul-de-sac by sailing clear through it to the threshold of the Beaufort Sea, putting onto the blank spaces of the existing charts the prominent headlands and openings from Baffin Bay to Melville and Banks Islands.

The new dimensions of geographical knowledge, and reports of whales on the "West Side," led quickly to a revolution in the itinerary of Davis Strait whalers. Instead of simply cruising off Hudson Strait (the "Southwest Fishery"), then ascending the Greenland coast towards Melville Bay (the icy, forbidding region that had constituted the frontier of European whaling until this time), and finally returning south by the same route, the ships in 1820 began to cross from Melville Bay to the mouth of Lancaster Sound, whale in this region during late July and early August, and return homeward either by sailing back to the familiar Greenland coast or by cruising southward along the coast of Baffin Island. Whaling was no longer confined to the East Side; the waters off the Canadian Arctic Islands were now the principal destination.

What were the geographical limits of whaling operations during the next century? The northern most extent of voyages was between Greenland and Ellesmere Island. When crossing to the West Side whaleman usually attempted to break through the dangerous pack ice of Melville Bay into the ice free area, or polynya, of northern Baffin Bay, which provided convenient access to the remarkable concentration of whales in the mouth of Lancaster Sound and off Pond Inlet. When the North Water (as they called this enigmatic feature) did not extend very far south, whaling masters had to resort to a more northerly course. In 1819 at least nine vessels sailed to 77°33'N but failed to get farther,[4] and two years later three whaling ships "looked into Sir Thomas Smith's Sound."[5] These waters, however, held no important whaling prospects; they were merely the route to the promised land.

Lancaster Sound itself was not neglected by the whalemen. Even before Parry's ships the *Hecla* and *Griper* had returned from their 1819–1820 winter at Melville Island whaling vessels had penetrated the sound to a distance of eighty miles,[6] and it appears likely that within a decade they had entered most of its adjacent bays. When the *Isabella* cruised for whales in Prince Regent Inlet in 1834, her logbook[7] gives no indication that the voyage was out of the ordinary; this region, by inference, was already familiar to British whalemen. The frequency of early voyages westward from Baffin Bay was probably not great, however, for sea ice and surface currents often restricted navigation in

Lancaster sound. In addition, whaling masters were usually reluctant to depart from known whaling grounds as long as the prospects of filling their ships were good, and whaling off the mouth of Pond Inlet—"our usual fishing ground" according to Captain Penny in 1847[8]—was normally excellent.

The east coast of Baffin Island from Pond Inlet to Cape Dyer came immediately within the range of whaling activities. Parry encountered three whaleships off Clyde Inlet in 1820,[9] and from this time onward it was customary for a number of vessels to cruise southeastward along this coast in August and September, prior to departing homeward. Farther south, between Cape Dyer and the mouth of Hudson Strait, however, whaling ships rarely ventured until 1840, when Cumberland Sound was first exploited for whales.[10] This deep indentation, almost as large as Lancaster Sound in the north, soon became the most important region for autumn whaling.

Thus, shortly after reaching the West Side in 1820 European whalemen were cruising northward to the entrance of Smith Sound (77°30′N), westward in Lancaster Sound to at least 90°W, south into Prince Regent Inlet, and southeastward along the Baffin Island coast to Cape Dyer (67°N) and, by 1840, Cumberland Sound.[11]

In subsequent decades there was little enlargement of the extreme limits of whaling activity in the Davis Strait whale fishery, for these limits were already more or less coincident with the periphery of bowhead whale occurrence, but the introduction of steam auxiliary power to the British fleet after 1857 probably made it easier to reach remote parts of the whaling ground. Prince Regent Inlet was described as "rarely visited" in 1865,[12] but whaling voyages to this region were evidently "quite commonplace" by 1874.[13] In that year at least nine vessels out of a fleet of sixteen cruised in Prince Regent Inlet, and for the first time they succeeded in getting south of Bellot Strait into the Gulf of Boothia.[14]

The western margin of the Canadian Arctic Islands remained beyond the sphere of whaling influence throughout nearly all of the nineteenth century. Not until 1889 did the American Bering Sea whale fishery expand past Point Barrow to the Canadian waters of the Beaufort Sea. Whales were found to be abundant off Herschel Island and the mouth of the Mackenzie River, and each subsequent season brought an eastward extension of the whaling grounds until by 1897 vessels had penetrated Amundsen Gulf to the mouth of Dolphin and Union Strait, and possibly beyond. In 1899 the steam whaler *Jeannette* ascended the entire west coast of Banks Island, entered M'Clure Strait, and almost reached Mercy Bay,[15] where the Franklin Search vessel *Investigator* had been abandoned in 1853. It is possible that the *Jeannette* also crossed M'Clure Strait to Crozier Channel, on the eastern margin of Prince Patrick Island.[16] Other whaleships cruised the waters off the west coast of Banks Island as well, but none is known to have duplicated the achievement of the *Jeannette*. On the east coast of the island the *Belvedere* cruised through Prince of Wales Strait to its northern extremity in 1905.[17] The extreme range of whaling cruises in the Western Arctic thus extended eastward to about 117°W, and northward to at least 74°30′N, and conceivably to 75°40′N.

Compared to the Davis Strait whale fishery among the eastern Canadian Arctic Islands (1820–1915), whaling in the Beaufort Sea and adjacent waters was of very short duration (1889 to approximately 1908), and affected a much smaller area.

The Biological Impact

Whaling was an uncertain venture in which returns fluctuated from year to year and often varied significantly among the various ships of the fleet. In some seasons few whales were seen and few killed, but at other times, especially in the early years of whaling in a new region, the killing was more akin to a wasteful slaughter, in which a great many whales of both sexes and all ages were harpooned and lanced, stripped of their blubber and ''bone'' (baleen), and their ''kreng'' (carcasses) cast loose to drift away, decompose, and sink. The carnage on 27 July 1823 off Pond Inlet, where more than forty British whaleships were cruising within sight of each other, was described as follows:

> Here and there along the floe edge lay the dead bodies of hundreds of flenshed whales, and the air for miles around was tainted with the foetor which arose from such masses of putridity. Towards evening the numbers come across were ever increasing, and the effluvia which then assailed our olfactories became almost intolerable.[18]

From 1820 to 1840 was the peak period of nineteenth-century whaling in the Davis Strait fishery (table 1). There were sometimes ninety or more vessels on the whaling grounds in one season, and in several years the catch of the fleet exceeded 1000 whales. More than 1400 were killed in 1823 (quotation above), and more than 1600 in 1833.[19]

The number of whalers operating in the Eastern Arctic decreased dramatically after the 1830s, but the Greenland whales were not granted a respite. The whalemen's employment of Baffin Island Inuit after about 1840, the initiation in 1853 of the practice of wintering on the whaling grounds, the general trend towards larger vessels with more whaleboats and greater oil capacity, the introduction of steam power after 1857, and the adoption of harpoon guns, bomb lances and darting guns—all these contributed to greater cruising and hunting effectiveness, and had the effect of maintaining intensive pressure upon the whales, even as the number of ships and the average yield per ship declined. By the end of the whaling period, early in this century, more than 18 000 bowhead whales had been killed since 1820 (table 1), and *Balaena mysticetus* had assumed the precarious status of an endangered species. It was accorded international protection from non-native whaling in 1931,[20] long after it was economically feasible for men and ships to pursue the whales. Almost seventy years have passed since the conclusion of commercial whaling, but the Davis Strait stock clearly has not recovered. Aerial and coastal surveys in 1976 and 1978 resulted in sightings of fewer than fifty whales migrating in and out of Lancaster Sound, where a century and a half ago the flensed carcasses would lie by the hundreds along the floe edge after a week or two of hunting. The total number of bowheads in this part of the Canadian Arctic is considered to be a few hundred at best, possibly less than a hundred.[21]

TABLE 1 *Davis Strait: Whaleships and Catch by Decade*

Decade	No. of ships	No. of whales caught	Average no. of whales per ship
1820–1829	752	8023	10.7
1830–1839	610	5361	8.8
1840–1849	158	1147	7.3
1850–1859	189	874	4.6
1860–1869	288	1054	3.7
1870–1879	175	998	5.7
1880–1889	116	434	3.7
1890–1899	58	140	2.4
1900–1909	60	90	1.5
1910–1919	12	12	1.0
Total	2418	18 133	4.9

SOURCE: W. Gillies Ross, "The Annual Catch of Greenland (Bowhead) Whales in Waters North of Canada 1719–1915: A Preliminary Compilation," *Arctic* 32, 2 (1979): 100–6, table 3.

In the Western Canadian Arctic, the Beaufort Sea whale fishery was brief but effective. Utilizing a number of large steam whalers, employing Eskimo labour, and frequently wintering at Herschel Island and other Arctic harbours for a succession of years,[22] American whalemen took approximately 800 whales in two decades (table 2). The termination of this fishery was probably due more to economic reasons than to whale depletion, and the current status of the stock is much more encouraging than that of the Davis Strait stock, despite a modest hunting pressure from Alaskan Eskimos since the cessation of commercial whaling early in this century. Observations in the spring of 1978 indicated that approximately 2300 bowheads migrated eastward past Point Barrow towards the Beaufort Sea.[23]

TABLE 2 *Beaufort Sea: Whaleships and Catch by Decade*

	No. of ships	No. of whales caught	Average no. of whales per ship
1889–1899	123	453	3.7
1899–1909	103	341	3.3
Total	226	794	3.5

SOURCE: W. Gillies Ross, "Annual Catch," 117, table 5.

Although whaling ultimately deprived the Inuit of an important resource species, or severely reduced its abundance, the first "boom" periods of whaling may have had the opposite effect. Whalemen discarded hundreds of carcasses close to land after removing bone and blubber. Some of these carcasses sank immediately, but many remained afloat. In addition, a considerable number of whales wounded by harpoon or shoulder gun but not secured by the ships later died. Internal putrefaction would keep these "stinkers" afloat for a considerable time. Thus whaling released into the marine environment many dead whales, some flensed and others not, which drifted with surface currents and often came to rest along the Arctic shores, providing a fortuitous supply of meat, blubber, and baleen to Eskimo coastal dwellers. In this way the initial years of whaling in each region probably increased the availability of whale products to native inhabitants. Subsequent depletion of the whale stocks, however, must have reduced not only the supply of drift whales but also the number of live targets for Eskimo hunters, until eventually whales were less available than they had been before the beginning of commercial whaling.

It seems almost axiomatic that the reduction of the bowhead population must have ultimately caused a critical decrease in food supply for the Eskimo inhabitants of the whaling regions, in the same way as the destruction of bison herds undermined the subsistence base of the Indian tribes on the Great Plains. This was probably not the case, however. The importance of the bowhead to the Inuit, although great in some regions, was generally less than that of the bison to the Plains tribes, having declined from the peak period of Thule culture several centuries before. Other animals were available and the Eskimo culture was flexible, quite capable of adapting to changing ecological conditions. Furthermore, the reduction of bowheads probably resulted in a surplus of planktonic krill, their usual food, which may have led to population increases in the fish and sea mammal species that depend either directly or indirectly on zooplanktonic food. This in turn could have improved the possibilities for Eskimo food procurement in other segments of the food chain.[24]

The most direct and enduring environmental consequence of whaling was the depletion of the bowhead whales themselves, but whalemen, and Eskimos working on their behalf, pursued a number of other animals as well. To supplement their shipboard, scurvy-prone diet, whaling crews consumed fish, the eggs and meat of several sorts of birds, and the meat of caribou, musk-oxen, Arctic hares, ringed seal, polar bears, and even mountain sheep (from the interior of the Yukon). Wintering crews were often equipped with clothing, footwear, and sleeping bags of robes, made by Eskimo women from the skins of caribou, ringed seal, bearded seal, arctic hare, wolverine, and wolf. A ship's crew could consume more than ten tons of caribou meat and wear out a few hundred pairs of skin mittens and boots in a winter. When a dozen or more vessels were together in one harbour, with a combined complement of several hundred men, the demand for wildlife products for food and clothing could be very large indeed.

Skins and furs were important in the commercial sense as well, especially in the declining years when whales were scarce. Arctic fox, musk-ox, arctic wolf, and walrus were the animals most sought after, but a few other species were taken as well. Whaling captains also collected the valuable tusks of walrus and narwhal, and occasionally captured live polar bears, walrus, and foxes for sale to zoos. In addition they obtained oil from the blubber of several marine mammals other than bowheads, in particular the white whale, which was hunted intensively in Prince Regent Inlet and Cumberland Sound.

The intensity of this non-native pressure upon animals that had once been important in traditional Eskimo life has never been investigated. If it altered the relative abundance of various species in certain regions it may have caused changes in native hunting emphasis, annual cycle, diet, and material culture.

The Human Impact

Whaling masters often had occasion to enter fiords, bays, and offshore island groups to take shelter from ice of wind-driven seas, to flense whales, or to procure fresh water and game ashore. Inevitably their recourse to protected anchorages brought them into unscheduled contact with Eskimo groups inhabiting the coastal regions. The earliest contact occurred along the coast of Baffin Island in 1820, the first season for which there is certain evidence of the presence of British whaleships on the West Side. In September of that year Captain Williamson of the Hull whaler *Lee* met Inuit at Clyde Inlet.[25]

At first the meetings served no practical purpose for the whalemen and conferred few benefits upon the native groups encountered, but by the 1840s economic relationships advantageous to both sides were evolving in certain localities where contact tended to be relatively frequent and prolonged. When the capabilities of Eskimo men as dog drivers, ice pilots, hunters, and whalemen were recognized, and the talents of Eskimo women as seamstresses were appreciated, whaling masters began to employ them in return for wages in kind. The Inuit, for their part, were quick to understand the usefulness of European weapons, tools, domestic implements, and materials, and were anxious to procure them through trade and employment. As soon as the mutual benefits of an exchange of commodities and services were clear to both parties the initial sporadic souvenir trade and gift-giving advanced to more regular and more formalized economic relationships. Systematic contacts tended to develop and persist in regions where native settlements, whales, and adequate ship harbours were found together. Such areas attracted whaling captains year after year, and encouraged both the wintering vessels and the establishment of shore bases.

In the complex and unknown geography of the Eastern Arctic the most favourable localities for whaling and Eskimo contact could not be immediately identified; it took a few decades of random and irregular whaling operations before a pattern of predetermined voyage itineraries and concentration of effort at a few distinct foci emerged. Cumberland Sound, with its advantageous whaling sites of Kekerten and Blacklead Island, was the most important region, but Pond Inlet, Clyde Inlet, Home Bay, Merchants Bay, Frobisher Bay, and other areas, also experienced a degree of localisation of whaling effort and Eskimo contact.

In the Western Arctic the configuration of the coasts was comparatively well known by the beginning of whaling in 1889, and the excellent harbour at Herschel Island presented itself directly to incoming vessels. Herschel Island remained dominant as a wintering harbour and whaling depot through the period, although ships occasionally wintered farther east, at the Baillie Islands, Langton Bay, Cape Parry and a few other places. No wintering harbours or shore stations developed on the coasts of Banks and Victoria Islands.

Contact between whalemen and Inuit could occur anywhere along the inhabited coasts of the whaling regions during the navigation seasons, but such sporadic encounters were too brief and irregular to contribute much to cultural change among the native population. At the whaling harbours and stations, however, whalemen were often present throughout the year for a succession of years, and their numbers could be great. These centres of non-native population with their depots of stores, whaling gear and trade goods, and with their dances, games, concerts, plays, and other interesting forms of entertainment, attracted Inuit off the land in search of the economic and social benefits available there, and it was at such whaling communities that cultural change proceeded most rapidly.

It is sometimes assumed that the influence of whaling was similar to that of the trading post system which followed it after the First World War, and it has even been implied that traders and whalemen both "were interested that the Inuit retain...a pattern of dispersed settlement."[26] But as soon as some whaling captains recognized the advantages of using Eskimo labour, as early as the 1840s, it became necessary to have prearranged "manpower centres," places where the Inuit would be available when the ships reached the whaling grounds, where contracts could be drawn up for employment, and where the natives could either be discharged at the end of the season or kept on as hunters and seamstresses for wintering vessels. The precontract pattern of dispersed settlement was an inconvenience to the whalemen; in order to utilize Inuit as an effective arm of the industry they had to alter the traditional dispersal of population and the nomadic annual cycle of food procurement. Demographic centralization was as essential to whaling in the nineteenth century as it has been to government services since the Second World War.

The corollary is that for those Inuit who sought to benefit from participation in whaling activities, a nomadic, dispersed pattern of settlement was equally inconvenient. A modification of traditional patterns of residence and livelihood was necessary to attain their goals; semi-permanent location at a whaling harbour was essential in order to develop a profitable relationship with the whalemen.

Of course, not all inhabitants of the whaling regions relocated to the centres of whaling activity. In this early period of Eskimo history there was a forerunner of a phenomenon which was observed along the west coast of Hudson Bay in the 1950s, namely a division of Eskimo society into two groups, the "kabloonamiut"—natives who were attracted to settlement life and employment among the whites—and the "nunamiut"—those who preferred to continue life on the land and retain the traditional pursuits and values.[27] The numbers of strict kabloonamiut were not large, perhaps two or three hundred individuals at each of several winter harbours and shore stations. Nevertheless, the demographic influence of whaling was of considerable importance. Not only were dispersal and nomadism reduced by the attraction of a proportion of the Eskimo population to whaling harbours, but the rigidity of territorial groupings within the Eskimo domain was relaxed. Adjacent groups, previously held apart by suspicion, hostility, or distance, mixed together at whaling centres, where the opportunities for employment and trade overcame isolation or longtime rivalry. This sort of process was most striking in the Western Arctic, where the whalemen-assisted immigration of Alaskan Eskimos virtually overwhelmed the native Mackenzie Inuit, numerically and ecologically.

Inuit attached to whaling harbours did not totally abandon traditional pursuits. Indeed, employment usually depended upon their considerable skills in hunting, winter travelling, and trapping. But new ideas, foods, weapons, implements, and materials available from the whalers exerted a strong influence upon their culture, and of course spread by intertribal barter far beyond the confines of the whaling harbours. By the turn of the twentieth century whaleboats, guns, steel traps, saws, hatchets, knives, files, European clothes, metal containers, and even sewing machines, sunglasses, accordians, and fiddles were present among the Inuit of the whaling regions. Most introduced items performed functions already carried out by traditional articles but they possessed some advantages. Rifles had greater accuracy, range, and killing power than bows; tin kettles and pots were far lighter than ones of stone; metal blades and points were sharper and more durable than ivory ones. The adoption of manufactured articles such as these often resulted in replacement or atrophy of the traditional, handmade items. Other introductions, such as the telescope, had no native equivalent; they were simply additions to the material culture. While the general effect of such introductions was to increase the survival capacity of the Eskimo people, this was not accomplished without a loss of independence, for the Inuit were bound to a continuing reliance upon outside sources of manufactured articles, through avenues of supply over which they had no control.

Close relationships between whalemen and Inuit at the winter harbours and shore stations inevitably resulted in the introduction of alien diseases, some of which ran through native communities with awful impact. Children of mixed blood were another legacy of whaling contact, the outcome of unions of Eskimo women with sailors from places as far apart as the Azores and the Hawaiian Islands. Changes in diet, clothing, and shelter may have played a role in undermining health, and certainly the whalemen's traffic in spirituous beverages in the Western Arctic was a severely disruptive force. On the other hand, employment on whaling vessels and at winter harbours brought a measure of food and medical security. Whaling captains customarily provided daily meals to the dependents of ships' natives, sometimes supported entire groups from ships' stores when game was scarce, and occasionally treated sick or injured Inuit.

If some whalemen were irresponsible, unfair, and even immoral in their dealings with the Eskimo people, it is well to remember that whaling was in some measure responsible also for the extension of missionary activity into the Arctic Islands. The oft-repeated pleas of the Scottish whaling captain William Penny persuaded the Moravian Church to send Brother Warmow to Baffin Island for a year in 1857, and it was Penny's vessel that bore him to and from Cumberland Sound. The establishment of an Anglican mission at Blacklead Island by the Reverend E.J. Peck in 1894 was facilitated by the Scottish whaling company of Crawford Noble, which transported personnel and stores free of charge. In the Western Arctic reports of the licentious behaviour of American whalemen among the Inuit demonstrated a need for missionary endeavour and encouraged the Anglican Church to extend its mission system northward to the Mackenzie Inuit. When the mission was established at Herschel Island in 1896 the whalemen assisted financially and in other ways in its operation.

Explorers, like whalemen, were agents of cultural change among the Inuit, and their activities began long before the frontier of whaling extended to Baffin Island in 1820. But one cannot escape the conclusion that the contact arising out of exploratory activities touched the culture of the native inhabitants of the Arctic Islands far more lightly than the relationships resulting from the operations of whalers. The number of whaling voyages greatly exceeded the number of discovery and search expeditions; the wintering of vessels and crews was much more frequent; whalemen were engaged in an economic partnership with the Inuit; whalemen/Inuit encounters tended to be more regular and predictable in space and time, and therefore more intense and meaningful. At whaling harbours, where several ships might be wintering together for ten months or so, there would be daily interpersonal contact between whalemen and native families. Constant interaction in a wide variety of activities both serious and frivolous, accompanied by a degree of bilingualism on both sides, and reinforced by the requirements of the employer–employee relationship, drew aside the veil of ignorance and mistrust that had previously separated native and non-native, and contributed to their mutual awareness and understanding. Of the two cultures, that of the Inuit experienced the most extensive and enduring alterations, but cultural influences moved in both directions, and it must be admitted that the whalemen were flexible enough to adopt certain Eskimo techniques, implements, clothing, and foods, that were demonstrably superior to their own in the demanding Arctic environment.

In the second half of the nineteenth century, well before whaling commenced in the Western Canadian Arctic, it had become economically marginal in the Eastern Arctic. After 1870 fewer than a half-dozen American vessels remained active, none of them equipped with steam power, and the British whaling industry which sent a maximum of seventeen ships to the Davis Strait fishery from that year on, was "sailing up a backwater as dangerous and ruinous as any in Baffin Bay."[28] As voyages became fewer and average yields dropped, the few British and American whaling firms remaining in business altered their methods in a way that had important consequences for the Eskimos. They adopted the technique of harvesting game resources from a few shore stations, using native labour supervised by a few whites. Once a year a supply ship would collect the catch and deliver the outfit for the next year. The expensive, time-consuming wintering of ships and crews was largely dispensed with, and consequently the extent of whaleman-Eskimo contact was significantly reduced. At the same time whaling firms diversified their operations, turning more and more to skins, furs, ivory, and other sources of oil, and consequently depriving Eskimos near the stations of most of the necessities of life. The whalemen demanded their seal oil (the usual fuel for heat, light, and cooking), seal skins (normally used in the making of footwear, dog traces, and harpoon lines), and caribou skins (their most important clothing material). Furthermore, the companies were not always able or willing to send out enough food, ammunition, equipment, and trade goods to satisfy the needs of the whites and natives at the remote outposts. Hardship and privation were often the result.

Captives of a declining alien economic system, the Inuit could not easily break free of these fetters and resume traditional life. "They have quite given up the use of their primitive weapons," wrote A.P. Low around the turn of this century, "and there is no doubt that a withdrawal of the whalers would lead to great hardship and many deaths among these people if the Government did not in some manner take their place and supply the Eskimos with the necessary guns and ammunition."[29] As it turned out, it was not government but the trading post system that filled the gap when whaling ceased. Whaling had already created a need among the Inuit for a variety of imported goods and had attracted them to localities which were accessible to ships, so it was relatively easy for free traders and the Hudson's Bay Company to move in and take up where the whalemen had left off. Insofar as it sought wildlife products through native labour, the fur trade system resembled whaling. But there was a fundamental difference. Inuit were not needed around the posts, and therefore the traders encouraged them to return to the land, spend their time trapping, and come in to the posts only occasionally to barter their furs. Thus the traders reversed the trends towards population centralization, sedentary life, fairly regular employment, and frequent cultural interaction with a large number of whites, all of which had characterized the whaling period. Trading interrupted, suspended, and even reversed some of the acculturative influences that had affected the native people of the Arctic Islands during the nineteenth century, and it was not until the Second World War that outside forces, this time more administrative than economic, attempted again to draw the native population off the land into the settlements as whaling had done, and thereby provide the choice of becoming "kabloonamiut."

The Political Dimension

The political status of the islands north of Rupert's Land and the Northwest Territory was not altogether clear during the nineteenth century. At the root of the problem was the fact that the geography of the Arctic Islands was imperfectly known. Although discovery and search expeditions were adding land to the charts with each decade, the work was slow and the task immense; a number of islands were to remain unknown until the twentieth century.

It would have been difficult to define and claim lands whose existence and location were uncertain, without recourse to some arbitrary, encompassing geometrical boundaries. Fortunately there did not appear to be any pressing need for the British government, or any other for that matter, to proclaim sovereignty over this remote region. Jurisdiction over other northern lands, such as Greenland and Spitsbergen, was also indefinite, and as whaling was primarily a pelagic industry, the voyages by whaling ships of several nations to the eastern margin of the North America Arctic were apparently not regarded as a threat to British or Canadian political rights or aspirations. But whaling on the Davis Strait grounds did not remain entirely pelagic, as we have seen, and when formal requests came forth for shore concessions on Baffin Island, the issue of sovereignty could no longer be ignored.

The potential importance of shore bases to whaling and exploration had been made clear little more than a decade after British whaleships first reached the West Land in 1820. The disastrous years of 1835–1837, in which unusually severe ice conditions resulted in a number of winter drifts, ship losses, and deaths, led to the suggestion that year-round settlements be established somewhere on the West Land, to provide refuges for distressed ships and crews, and facilitate whaling operations along the coast.[30] At first nothing came of this suggestion, but in 1852 Captain Penny applied to the British Colonial Office for a grant of land "in and about Northumberland Inlet" (Cumberland Sound).[31] Penny wanted all of a mythical "Cumberland Island"—the southern part of Baffin Island between Home Bay and Frobisher Bay, stretching from Davis Strait westward to Foxe Basin.

During ensuing discussions within the Colonial Office it was observed that such a grant would conflict, in its western portions, with the territory granted earlier to the Hudson's Bay Company,[32] an explicit admission that the sections of Baffin Island draining into Foxe Basin and Hudson Strait were included in Rupert's Land. More interesting and revealing was the comment that Penny's application "involves us in all the hitherto carefully avoided difficulties of fixing boundaries in those icy regions."[33]

The Colonial Office was inclined to grant a lease, if the Board of Trade would grant a charter to Penny's proposed company,[34] but before this could be done the government was defeated. Penny raised the matter with the new ministers, but in the face of petitions from several whaling ports opposing the granting of exclusive privileges to Penny, the Board of Trade refused a charter, and the question of a lease of land remained unresolved.

These events, however, did not prevent whaling vessels from wintering in Cumberland Sound, beginning in 1853, nor did they discourage Hull merchants from attempting to form a whaling settlement there in the same year, without success.

During the government's discussion of Penny's proposal the spectre of increasing American involvement in the Arctic Islands created considerable concern. Penny had initially pointed out in 1852 that an American whaling crew had already wintered ashore in Cumberland Sound, and that "unless anticipated by an English colony, American adventurers will next year make a settlement & establish a fishery in the Inlet."[35] In subsequent correspondence with the government and others he repeatedly emphasized the threat that the American presence posed to British territorial rights, remarking more than once that a certain American ship owner had predicted that the American flag would one day fly from the High Arctic to Tierra del Fuego.[36]

When a Colonial Office memorandum of 5 September 1853 concluded that on the basis of initial discovery and Hudson's Bay Company visitations "we may lay claim to territory in question as a British possession,"[37] the Foreign Office instructed the British ambassador in Washington to "take an opportunity of bringing this matter in a friendly manner under the consideration of the United States' Government," and to request that government to warn its citizens against trespassing on "Cumberland Island."[38] This appears to have been the first explicit declaration of British sovereignty over any part of the

Arctic Islands beyond the limits of Rupert's Land, and it arose directly out of whaling activity.

The British note to Washington appears to have had no effect on the activities of American whalemen. They wintered in Cumberland Sound on twenty-two occasions during the next decade and later established several shore stations in the Eastern Canadian Arctic, but no objections were raised by Britain.

The sovereignty issue, like an unwanted guest, came again before the British government in 1874. An American naval officer, Lieutenant Mintzer, who had visited mica deposits near the whaling harbour of Niantelik in 1873, applied for a land grant of 400 square miles in Cumberland Sound for mining purposes,[39] and an Englishman, Mr. Harvey, who claimed to have already been involved in whaling in the same region, stated his intention to erect temporary buildings there to facilitate whaling. Did Great Britain own "Cumberland," Harvey wanted to know, and if so was it administered by Canada?[40]

During the discussions that followed in the Colonial Office, Foreign Office, and Admiralty, and between Britain and Canada,[41] the 1854 memorandum to the American government proclaiming British sovereignty over "Cumberland Island" was never explicitly mentioned. When the Colonial Office spoke of the territories north of Canada that had been "taken possession of in the name of the country but not hitherto annexed to any Colony,"[42] it appears to have been referring to the individual acts of taking possession effected by explorers rather than to the 1854 warning to the United States government against trespass on a British "Cumberland Island." Could the government have lost sight of the fact that two decades earlier a firm stand had been taken on the matter of sovereignty in the Arctic Islands? Or was it simply that the 1854 memorandum, in retrospect, was not regarded as an adequate formal annexation of territory?

After prolonged negotiations, during which Harvey and Mintzer were not given the satisfaction of definite answers, the remaining British Arctic territories in North America (whatever they were) were transferred to Canada, in 1880.

The 1880 Transfer did not automatically render Canadian jurisdiction over the Arctic Islands secure. Foreign whalers and exploration parties continued to operate along the Arctic coasts without any regulation whatever, and the nature and extent of their activities was largely unknown down south. It was not until another two decades had passed that Canadians became fully aware of the foreign presence in the North. By the turn of the twentieth century there was considerable concern over the uncontrolled killing of whales and other animals, the unrestricted importation of trade goods, the unregulated commercial and social relationships with the Eskimo people, the flag-raising of explorers from other nations, and the political implications of such activity in remote territories where Canadian sovereignty rested on an insecure basis. This concern resulted in the establishment of police posts, the promulgation of Canadian laws, the imposition of whaling licenses, the taxation of imported trade goods, the prohibition on the killing of certain species, and the inauguration of a series of government voyages into Hudson Bay and the Arctic Islands. By these measures the government sought to advertise the Canadian presence, and to turn a vague paper sovereignty into secure territorial possession and effective administration.

Notes

1. Whaling here is taken to mean the commercial pursuit of the Greenland or bowhead whale (*Balaena mysticetus*) by non-native or Euro-American peoples. This paper does not discuss the commercial exploitation of small whales such as the white whale and narwhal, nor does it examine the native hunting of any of these species.

2. William Jameson, "Narrative of a Voyage to Davis' Straits in 1821," *Edinburgh Philosophical Journal* (October 1821), 312.

3. Jan Kupp and Simon Hart, "The Dutch in the Strait of Davis and Labrador during the 17th and 18th Centuries," *Man in the Northeast*, (1976), 3–20; W. Gillies Ross, "The Davis Strait Whale Fishery 1820–1860," Report submitted to the National Museum of Man (Ottawa, 1974), 3, 4.

4. Basil Lubbock, *The Arctic Whalers* (Glasgow, Brown, Son & Ferguson, 1955), 21.

5. Alexander Fisher, *A Journal of a Voyage of Discovery to the Arctic Regions, in His Majesty's Ships "Hecla" and "Griper," in the Years 1819 & 1820* (London, Longman, Hurst, Rees, Orme, and Brown, 1821), 271.

6. Newspaper report of whaling voyages of the *Cumbrian* and *Earl Fauconberg*, *Liverpool Mercury*, 6 October 1820.

7. Manuscript logbook of the *Isabella*, 3 August 1834, Scott Polar Research Institute, Cambridge, England.

8. Clive Holland, "William Penny, 1809–1892: Arctic Whaling Master," *Polar Record* 15, 94 (1970): 34.

9. William Edward Parry, *Journal of a Voyage for the Discovery of a North-West Passage...in the Years 1819–1820...* (London: John Murray, 1821), 276.

10. Alexander M'Donald, *A Narrative of Some Passages in the History of Eenoolooapik...* (Edinburgh: Fraser, 1841).

11. The last major advance of the whaling frontier in the Eastern Arctic occurred in 1860 when American vessels led the way through Hudson Strait into the northwestern reaches of Hudson Bay. The subsequent whaling operations, however, were in the Hudson's Bay Company's territory of Rupert's Land rather than in the region involved in the Transfer of 1880, and they are therefore not discussed in this paper. See W. Gillies Ross, *Whaling and Eskimos: Hudson Bay 1860–1915*, National Museum of Man, Publications in Ethnology, no. 10 (Ottawa, 1975); and A.P. Low, *Report on the Dominion Government Expedition to Hudson Bay and the Arctic Islands on Board the D.G.S. "Neptune," 1903–1904* (Ottawa: Government Printing Bureau, 1906).

12. E.P. Philpots, "An Account of the Land in the Vicinity of Cape Horsburgh, Lat. 74° 44′24″N., Long.79° W., and of the Island Discovered There," *Proceedings of the Royal Geographical Society*, Session 1868–1869, Old Series 13 (1869): 373.

13. Andrew Taylor, *Geographical Discovery and Exploration in the Queen Elizabeth Islands,* Department of Mines and Technical Surveys, Geographical Branch Memoir, no. 3 (Ottawa, 1955), 81.

14. Thomas Thornton Macklin, "Notes on a Whaling Voyage to Davis Straits in the S.S. *Narwhal* of Dundee," 6 August 1874, Copy of manuscript journal, Glenbow-Alberta Institute, Calgary.

15. John Bockstoce, "Contacts between American Whalemen and the Copper Eskimos," *Arctic* 28, 4 (1975): 299.

16. Reginald B. Hegarty, *Returns of Whaling Vessels Sailing from American Ports....1876–1928* (New Bedford, Mass.: Old Dartmouth Historical Society, 1959), 34.

17. John Bockstoce, "Contacts," 299.

18. Charles Edward Smith, ed., *From the Deep of the Sea...* (London: Harris, Black, 1922), 279.

19. W. Gillies Ross, "The Annual Catch of Greenland (Bowhead) Whales in Waters North of Canada 1719–1915: A Preliminary Compilation," *Arctic* 32, 2 (1979): 103, table 3.

20. Willman M. Marquette. "The 1977 Catch of Bowhead Whales (*Balaena mysticetus*) by Alaskan Eskimos," *Report of the International Whaling Commission,* 29, SC/30/Doc 35 (Cambridge, England: 1979), 281.

21. Rolph A. Davis and William R. Koski, "Recent Observations of the Bowhead Whale in the Eastern High Arctic," Report submitted to the International Whaling Commission, SC/31/Doc 57 (Toronto: LGL Limited, 1980), 16.

22. John R. Bockstoce, *Steam Whaling in the Western Arctic* (New Bedford, Mass: Old Dartmouth Historical Society, 1977).

23. Howard Braham et al., "Preliminary Report of the 1978 Spring Bowhead Whale Research Program Results," *Report of the International Whaling Commission,* no. 29, SC/30/Doc 36 (1979), 304.

24. In Antarctic waters the reduction of the baleen whale numbers during the last few decades has permitted an expansion of krill stocks, which in turn appears to have led to substantial increases in populations of Adelie and Chinstrap penguins, fur seals, and crabeater seals. See M.A. McWhinnie and C.J. Denys, *Antarctic Marine Living Resources with Special Reference to Krill, Euphausia Superba: Assessment of Adequacy of Present Knowledge,* Report submitted to the National Science Foundation (Washington, 1979), 4, 5.

25. Parry, *Journal of a Voyage,* 275.

26. Robert Paine, "The Path to Welfare Colonialism," chapter 2 in *The White Arctic: Anthropological Essays on Tutelage and Ethnicity,* St. John's Institute of Social and Economic Research, Memorial University, Newfoundland Social and Economics Papers, no. 7 (1977), 7.

27. F.G. Vallee, *Kabloona and Eskimo in the Central Keewatin* (Ottawa: Canadian Research Centre for Anthropology, Saint Paul University, 1967), 136ff.

28. Gordon Jackson, *The British Whaling Trade* (Hamden, CT: Archon Books, 1978), 143.

29. A.P. Low, *Report on Expedition to Hudson Bay and Arctic Islands, 1903–1904,* 271.

30. Alan Cooke and W. Gillies Ross, "The Drift of the Whaler *Viewforth* in Davis Strait, 1835–1836, from William Elder's Journal," *Polar Record* 14, 92 (1969): 590; Clive Holland, "William Penny," 26–28.

31. William Penny to Sir John Pakington, 20 November 1852, CO 42, vol. 588, 2930, fol. 144, Public Record Office (hereafter PRO), London.

32. Herman Merivale to the Earl of Desart, 7 December 1852, CO 42, vol. 588, 2930, fol. 158, PRO.

33. Merivale to Desart, 7 December 1852, CO42, vol. 588, 2930, fol. 158, PRO. Three decades later, in 1880, Britain used vague and ambiguous language to describe the area it was transferring to Canada, failing even to mention its Arctic location. This reluctance to specify precise limits for its Arctic possessions appears to have been a long-standing policy.

34. Sir John Pakington to William Penny, 14 December 1852, CO 42, vol. 588, 2930, fol. 160, PRO.

35. William Penny, "State of Facts in Support of Application to the Crown for a Grant of Lands & Fisheries in and about Northumberland Inlet...," CO 42, vol. 588, 2930, fol. 150, PRO.

36. William Penny to the Duke of Newcastle, 30 July 1853, CO 42, vol. 592, 3646, fol. 496d, PRO.

37. Seymour Thellusson, Foreign Office memorandum, FO 4915 (North America), 5 September 1853, CO 42, vol. 591, 2906, fol. 93, PRO.

38. Lord Clarendon to John F. Crampton, 9 January 1854, FO 115, vol. 136 X/K 551, fol. 22d, 23, PRO.

39. W.A. Mintzer to George Crump, 10 February 1874, vol. 732, 2810, fol. 178, PRO.

40. A.W. Harvey to Under Secretary of State for the Colonies, 3 January 1874, vol. 734, 2810, fol. 419, PRO.

41. For a detailed summary of these events see Gordon W. Smith, "The Transfer of Arctic Territories from Great Britain to Canada in 1880, and Some Related Matters, as Seen in Official Correspondence," *Arctic* 14, 1 (1961): 53–73.

42. Lord Carnarvon to Lord Dufferin, 30 April 1874, FO 115, vol. 731, fol. 59, PRO.

INUIT ECONOMIC RESPONSES TO EURO-AMERICAN CONTACTS: SOUTHEAST BAFFIN ISLAND, 1824–1940*

PHILIP GOLDRING

It is now generally recognized that native populations often affected the pace and direction of Euro-American penetration of British North America's resource frontier. The fur trade as a set of economic institutions[1] and Christian missions as ideological ones[2] have recently been studied as widely distributed agencies of change with distinct local and temporal variations. Incomers relied on natives for information, for indigenous technology for survival and travel, and for labour, before overseas investors made continuous commitments of men, capital, and goods to remote regions. Such partnerships, whether equal or not, allowed aboriginal societies in contact with Euro-Americans to retain essential elements of their ideology, social structure, and way of life even when superficially subordinated to a nonindigenous system of production.[3] Although these perspectives evolved with reference to the Subarctic fur trade, they are relevant to other fields of inquiry, including the contacts between Inuit and southerners before the advent of the fur trade.[4]

Historical Papers/Communications Historiques, Canadian Historical Association (1986): 146–72. This paper is based on research done for the Prairie and Northern Region Office, and the National Historic Parks and Sites Directorate of Environment Canada-Parks. Grateful acknowledgement is due to the Governor and Committee of the Hudson's Bay Company for permission to research in and quote from their Archives in the Provincial Archives of Manitoba, and to the Keeper of the HBCA and her staff for the help I received there. Acknowledgement is also due to Mystic Seaport Museum, to the New Bedford Free Public Library, to the Old Dartmouth Historical Society Whaling Museum Library in New Bedford (for their own holdings and those of the International Marine Archives); to the General Synod Archives of the Anglican Church of Canada; and to Doug Whyte of the Federal Archives Division, Public Archives of Canada. Marc Stevenson, the Rev. Dr. Gavin White and John R. Bennett kindly allowed me to read unpublished works before this paper was written, and provided helpful comments on the manuscript itself. The shortcomings that undoubtedly remain are my own.

The Inuit of southeast Baffin Island have a complex history, richly documented over nearly 160 years, but discussion of the region has only recently been drawn into the mainstream of Canadian historical writing. Southern penetration here lagged behind the western parts of Canada north of sixty degrees. Fur trade companies, for example, entered Baffin Island a century after they reached the Mackenzie valley. Granted, commercial fisheries began off Baffin Island in 1820, but serious scientific inquiry started in 1882, the first Christian mission was established in 1894, the Hudson's Bay Company arrived in 1911 and the RCMP followed in 1921. The little mineral exploitation undertaken was rarely a commercial success before 1975.[5] Historical interest, like economic development has been slow to take account of Baffin Island.

Baffin is one of the world's five largest islands, but it lies entirely north of sixty degrees and north of the tree line. Until the 1960s, most people in this region lived in multifamily hunting groups, depending for food, fuel, and shelter on marine mammals—chiefly the ringed seal— and on caribou. Loosely grouped as "tribes"[6] living around Cumberland Peninsula, the Inuit of southeast Baffin Island have linguistic and cultural affinities with other groups as far afield as Alaska, Siberia and northern Greenland. In 1981 the island had four thousand people in eight hamlets and settlements, and another twenty-three hundred in the one town, Frobisher Bay. Little has happened to draw Baffin Island into the broader story of Canadian development.

Historiography caught up with the northwest coast of Hudson Bay in the 1960s[7] and substantial advances have followed in the literature on Baffin Island. Alongside the indigenous traditions, most districts now have a century and a half of recorded contact with southerners.[8] The orientation of historical scholarship has also changed: less research is now focused on European exploration, and historical writing is coming to terms with a shortage of paradigmatic events with broad national implications. Led by historically minded social scientists, inquiry into Baffin Island's past reveals a story which invites comparisons with widely separated events elsewhere on the resource frontier, particularly in regard to exchanges between natives and incomers. Although general propositions about such exchanges have been offered, study is still at a stage where local case studies help advance a broader understanding.

A great deal of recent attention has been devoted to southeast Baffin, the area surrounding Pangnirtung and Broughton Island. Until fifteen years ago written accounts of this region's history relied heavily on government reports hastily compiled around 1900. Since 1970 geographers, ethnographers, and historians have uncovered a distinctive history and exposed rich veins of primary source material. Clive Holland,[9] W. Gillies Ross,[10] and local historian Kenn Harper[11] unearthed a considerable number of first-hand accounts of whaling in the area. Maija Lutz's work on musical traditions at Pangnirtung documented interaction between whalers and Inuit,[12] and the Rev. Dr. Gavin White expertly probed the region's distinctive trading patterns between 1900 and 1925.[13] R.G. Mayes provided an outline of the region's history to 1973.[14]

More recently, the centennial of Franz Boas's field work in southeast Baffin stimulated useful articles by historian Douglas Cole and geographer Ludger Müller-Wille.[15] Bibliographer Karen Evans described the Rev. Edmund Peck's contributions to syllabic literacy,[16] and archaeologist Marc Stevenson exploited old sources and, through excavation and interviews, virtually created new ones to study the last days of the whaling industry at Kekerten Island.[17] Parks Canada commissioned interviews with a dozen Pangnirtung elders in 1984[18] and a recent research paper by John Bennett sensitively linked oral and artistic sources to show the continued importance of the late whaling period in the way Pangnirtung elders perceive their past.[19]

Such works can all be supplemented or debated in detail, but they make events in Cumberland Sound reasonably accessible to students of the North. Abundant documentation on the whaling era, and a considerable body of later evidence which is less widely known, make it possible to go beyond local history and to consider the experience of this region and its people in light of interpretive frameworks devised to describe change elsewhere. Modern interpretations of the fur trade as an agency of contact have already been mentioned; relevant work has also been published on events north of the tree line. In a survey of Hudson Bay, David Damas in 1968 divided the postcontact experience of the Inuit into four periods, defined roughly by the importance of imported material culture and foodstuffs, and the frequency and nature of face-to-face encounters with southerners.

In the period Damas termed "aboriginal," Inuit met occasional parties of explorers but little trade occurred to bring European items into local use. In Hudson Bay this period ended in 1860, when American whalers began wintering. This ushered in a "transitional" stage marked by frequent direct trade, and by the transfer of rifles and whaleboats to Inuit as trade or wages. This phase in turn gave way between 1904 and 1920 to a "contact-traditional" era marked economically by trapping of the arctic fox, and socially by the archetypal northern white community of HBC trader, mounted policeman, and missionary. The hegemony of this trio was shattered in the 1950s and 1960s by government agencies: teachers and settlement managers urged Inuit to abandon the trapping camps. Damas called this the "centralized period."[20]

This periodization was generally endorsed by W. Gillies Ross in *Whaling and Eskimos*, with one important refinement. Ross saw change as cyclical: in the first and third periods the Inuit dispersed in small hunting groups. In the intervening whaling era and the modern, centralized period Inuit gathered in larger numbers for social and economic exchanges with southerners. Whaling was not part of a continuum from isolation to close contact, but an interruption in traditional relations between the people and the land.[21] In southeast Baffin Island, socioeconomic changes occurred in stages that are similar but not identical to the experience of northwest Hudson Bay.

Four Stages of Contact in Southeast Baffin Island

Baffin Island has always been marginal to the southern economic system that intermittently exploited it; therefore, the chronology of contact varied from one locale to another. Damas's four-stage model of contact can be applied to Baffin Island, but the dates differ, not only between Hudson Bay and Baffin Island, but among Pond Inlet, Cumberland Sound, and Hudson Strait.

The change from "aboriginal" to "transitional" conditions, which occurred early in the 1860s in Hudson Bay, was more diffused in Baffin Island. Whaling fleets made contact with Baffin Island Inuit in 1820, but until 1903 people around Pond Inlet had only intermittent contact with whalers in summer. Hudson Strait (south of Frobisher Bay) was so isolated from the whaling industry that American captains brought Inuit whalers from Cumberland Sound in the 1870s to hunt bowheads.[22] The people around Lake Harbour, in effect, remained at the "aboriginal" stage of contact until commercial whaling was near collapse. In southeast Baffin Island, the region north of Frobisher Bay and south of Cape Henry Kater, whalers first made contact in 1824 and were wintering ashore or in ice-bound vessels from 1851 onwards. The change was particularly rapid on the productive new whaling ground of Cumberland Sound, reached by British whalers in 1840 and the focus of wintering voyages thereafter (see table 1).

Although commercial whaling lasted around Cumberland Sound for a century, resource depletion brought substantial changes after roughly 1871 as fewer vessels visited, and the social environment changed when vessels stopped wintering after 1880. In some years no ships called at all, two or three white men staffed a couple of stations, and the local pidgin English fell into disuse.[23] From 1880 to 1920 the annual routine of spring and autumn whale hunts continued, but on average only one whale was caught each year (see table 2). Seal-skins, with blubber attached, became the staple trade of most of Cumberland Sound's three hundred Inuit by 1880. The period from 1851 to 1919 does correspond to the "transitional" stage of Damas's model, but it was in fact two sharply different phases. After twenty exuberant years of opportunity came forty years of difficult adjustment, when Inuit frequented large settlements where they had access to Euro-American manufactures, but had fewer face-to-face encounters with whites than before. The old whaling stations experienced a very brief revival after 1919 as centres for a briskly competitive fur and seal-oil trade. This competition was short-lived. Between 1923 and 1927 the Hudson's Bay Company bought out or outlasted all its competitors and the people settled down, somewhat reluctantly, to a "contact-traditional" period not unlike the similar stage in Hudson Bay.

TABLE 1 *Crews Wintering in Cumberland Sound, 1851–1852 to 1889–1890**

1851 – 1	1861 – 2	1871 – 4	1881 – 1
1852 – 0	1862 – 3	1872 – 2	1882 – 1
1853 – 4	1863 – 7	1873 – 1	1883 – 1
1854 – 0	1864 – 7	1874 – 1	1884 – 1
1855 – 3	1865 – 9	1875 – 2	1885 – 2
1856 – 3	1866 – 8	1876 – 2	1886 – 0
1857 – 5	1867 – 9	1877 – 5	1887 – 1
1858 – 2	1868 – 5	1878 – 3	1888 – 1
1859 – 4	1869 – 10	1879 – 1	1889 – 1
1860 –11	1870 – 6	1880 – 0	

*Covers winter harbours between Cape Edwards and Cape Mercy. Additional US vessels wintered near the mouth of Frobisher Bay between 1855 and 1862, and in Hudson Strait after 1876. Includes crews of tiny station schooners, wrecked vessels, and of the *McLellan* in 1851–1852. Crew size varied between five and fifty men.

PRINCIPAL SOURCES: Dennis Wood, "Abstracts of Whaling Voyages," MS in New Bedford Free Public Library; printed annual return of whaling voyages, Kinnes MSS, Dundee University Library; Alexander Starbuck, *History of Whaling Vessels Sailing from American Ports, 1876–1928* (New Bedford, 1959). Details may be consulted in the author's unpublished MS on file at the Canadian Parks Service in Hull, "Checklist of Whalers Making Wintering Voyages to Cumberland sound, 1853 to 1890."

TABLE 2 *Bowhead Whales Taken by Stations in Cumberland Sound, 1883–1914*

1883 – 1	1894 – 1	1905 – 0
1884 – *	1895 – 3	1906 —
1885 – 2	1896 – 3	1907 – 0
1886 – 2	1897 – 1	1908 – 0
1887 –	1898 – 2	1909 – 1
1888 – 0	1899 – 2	1910 – 1 (sucker)
1889 – 3	1900 – 1	1911 – 0
1890 – 0	1901 – 2	1912 – 0
1891 – 1	1902 – 0	1913 – 1 (sucker)
1892 – 1	1903 – 2	1914 – 1
1893 —	1904 – 0	

*The dash ("–") represents a year for which no report has been found. Years following a dash may include returns caught the previous year.

SOURCE: Kinnes lists, missionaries' journals, PAC Whaling Logs Collection, and logs and published journals of whaling and exploring ships.

Settlements at Pangnirtung and Broughton Island remained small until 1962, but centralization was swiftly achieved thereafter. Although local differences were experienced between the two populated coasts of Cumberland Peninsula, a general exchange of population prevailed across the peninsula during the whaling and fur-trading eras, and the choices of individuals were influenced, in succession, by whaling ships, whaling stations, trading posts, and government agencies. The chronology of these developments is accessible in outline through the secondary literature. The focus in this paper is therefore on the transitions between the first three stages of contact.[24]

Enduring Features of Life around Cumberland Sound

Although the postcontact history of southeast Baffin Island may be divided coherently into stages of conflict, enduring ecological and social facets of that life can be examined by themselves. Inuit have lived in the region for many centuries; they displaced or merged with the Tunit or "Dorset" people who, though distinct in the artifacts they have left behind, were probably similar in culture and even language. The Eskimos or Inuit are the postcontact descendants of the people archaeologists call "Thule."[25]

The Thule culture is distinguished by its technique for hunting and using the bowhead whale, *Balaena mysticetus* but, like other cultures above the tree line, the people depended mainly on other marine mammals. The most important of those in Cumberland Sound has been the ringed or jar seal, *Phoca hispida*.[26] Apart from offering a balanced diet almost without supplement, the ringed seal provided heat and light from its blubber and clothing from its skin. It has therefore been consistently harvested for centuries. The skins of harp seals, beared seals, and caribou all had important specialized uses for clothing, shelter, and boats, but the ringed seal was the dietary mainstay except during the late summer caribou hunt. In the 1850s and 1860s additional pressure was put on ringed seal stocks as the Inuit hunted fresh meat for the whaling crews, who understood its value as an antiscorbutic and, unlike their counterparts in Hudson Bay evidently consumed little caribou meat.[27] In the 1870s seals became an export commodity, their skins dried or salted, and their blubber scraped from the skin and boiled at the underemployed try-works of the whaling stations.

In 1877 German-American naturalist Ludwig Kumlein denounced what he saw as overhunting of seals, but his concern was misplaced.[28] Conditions in Cumberland Sound are ideal for ringed seals, and in most years, for those who hunt them. Bad weather or ice conditions wrought severe hardship in exceptional years such as 1846, 1847,[29] 1894, 1899, and 1903.[30] Franz Boas was severely critical of much of Kumlein's research: he believed that there was no biological shortage of animals. Bad hunts were due to ice or storms, and hardship was worse when religious beliefs prevented hunting after a recent death.[31] In 1922 a trader estimated, "the number of seals of all kinds killed yearly in Cumberland Gulf at 5000 to 6000, and the supply does not appear to be affected, as this has been going on for many years."[32] Seal-hunting gradually began to change. On the establishment of the Hudson's Bay Company post at Pangnirtung in 1921 blubber skins continued to be traded, but they were not very profitable and the commercial seal hunt (as distinct from the meat hunt) shifted to newborn "white-coats" and yearling "silver jars." Under this pressure the Inuit in 1946 began to report a shortage of seals, probably due to the annual killing of two thousand to twenty-five hundred whitecoats.[33] Despite this scarcity stocks held up, and in the 1960s ringed seal skins were again as big a part of the local economy as they had been from 1880 to 1920.[34]

Gillies Ross has identified population change as one of the central but most intractable issues in the historical literature on whaling. American whaling contributed to the virtual disappearance of the original Mackenzie Delta Eskimos before 1915, and it sometimes loosely assumed that the same occurred in the eastern Arctic as well. Ross noted that contemporary observations were unsystematic and he emphasized how whaling stimulated group migrations, which further confuse attempts to measure net population changes.[35] In southeast Baffin during the whaling era, people migrated frequently across the Cumberland Peninsula, and between Cumberland Sound and the mouth of Frobisher Bay. In the contact-traditional period, free movement continued between Davis Strait and Cumberland Sound. Disease was a persistent problem in the whaling era: as late as 1898–1899 epidemics carried off 10 percent of the people of Cumberland Sound.[36] Population was probably at its lowest ebb in 1883–1884 when Franz Boas counted 245 Inuit in eight winter camps around the Sound. Families were remarkably small. Kumlein reported in 1879 that infanticide was no longer practised, but his ship-mate George Tyson remarked that very few women had three children still living.[37] Boas noted seventy-seven married couples with only sixty-six children—a low ratio even if many couples had grown children. Infertility, infant mortality, or both must have been prevalent during the 1870s and 1880s.[38]

Imprecise though they are, the early demographic data all point in the same direction: in 1840 up to one thousand Inuit lived around Cumberland Sound. Starvation in the mid-1840s and diseases introduced by whalers in the mid-1850s cut that figure perhaps as low as 350 people by 1857. Deaths exceeded live births by at least one hundred in the next twenty-five years. Later reports consistently showed 250 to 300 in the sound,[39] although people followed the Anglican missionaries between 1911 and 1914 to Lake Harbour, where communications with Britain were better.[40] Despite losses by out-migration, a reliable census in 1925 showed a population that was about equal to Boas's report (see table 3). It grew steadily thereafter and now, with the northeast side of Cumberland Peninsula, may exceed fifteen hundred—about the number some observers thought were present when the whalers first made contact in 1824.

TABLE 3 *Population of Cumberland Sound, 1924*

Less than one year old-	11
1–5	40
5–10	26
10–15	43
15–20	18
20–25	17
25–30	21
30–40	21
40–50	22
50–60	17
60–70	14
70–80	4
80 and up	1
Total	255

SOURCE: Burwash to Finnie, 3 March 1925, RG85/64, file 164–1(1) PAC.

A third enduring factor was native leadership. In the earliest contacts individual Inuit took the lead in exchanges with southerners; not all of these people were necessarily hunting leaders or shamans, but many were. Commercial whaling gave added prominence to men whose skills lay, specifically, in hunting bowhead whales. Certain names recur in the whaling narratives; Tesuwin negotiated for about two dozen Inuit whalers at Kekerten Harbour in 1859, and in 1877 conducted a middlemen trade at Niantilik for vessels wintering one hundred kilometers away.[41] In the same year an American captain came to terms with the noted hunter and whaler Nepekin, and remarked in passing, "of course his boat's crew will do as he tells them."[42] This is apparently an early prototype of the "Eskimo boss" of the contact-traditional era, the hunting and trapping leader who acted as intermediary between incomers and Inuit, and gave direction in hunting matters as well.[43] An RCMP corporal, reporting on the free traders in the 1920s, described their methods as "the old whaler system of trading, whereby a few were overpaid at the expense of the many."[44] The success of the most skilled and knowledgeable hunters was vital to the whole group and these leaders, by common consent, controlled the use of scarce tools, especially whaleboats.[45] This was not essentially a class distinction, nor was it unique to the whaling period.

Some southern observers thought that the authority of the best hunters could extend to an unequal distribution of food and material things generally. Marc

Stevenson's analysis of Kekerten site, and his interviews with Etuangat Aksayook, link the size and elaboration of dwellings to their owners' status in the whale hunt.[46] In the early twentieth century several known traders or camp leaders were first-rate hunters or religious leaders (shamans or catechists) or both. The Inuit who dealt closely with Scottish station managers in the early twentieth century apparently grew accustomed to some hierarchical notions and practices. This was facilitated by the fact that the stations, the mission, and later the government-commercial complex of Pangnirtung gradually took over part of the responsibility for sharing out food or its near-equivalent, ammunition.[47] By the 1930s a new balance was achieved, with the settlement carrying out redistributive functions for people who were too old or disabled to live in camps, and the camp leaders taking care of the rest. As one observer reported, "In these camps there were good hunters and poor hunters, there were natives that were provident and those that were not and I found that those who had food and fuel were sharing with those who had not."[48]

The effect of contact on native social structure is obviously important, but the ambiguity of precontact patterns obstructs clear analysis. So does the flexibility of Inuit social organization in the contact era: "Inuit community organization has varied from... small flexible bands without clearly marked leadership, to stable camps with quite powerful leaders, to settlement living without long-term leadership."[49] The Inuit of Cumberland Sound weathered successive upheavals in their social and economic relations with whalers and fur traders, continuing to make choices under the guidance of indigenous leaders.

Early Contact, 1824–1851

Inuit in southeast Baffin had brief encounters with Frobisher in 1575–1577, missed or avoided meeting John Davis a decade later, and had no further contact with southerners until July 1824, when six people in Merchants Bay visited the Anglo-Scottish whaling fleet. The fleet followed declining whale stocks into increasingly perilous waters, and had never before touched Baffin Island so far south. Early contacts were marked by suspicion, some shows of force on each side, but no recorded casualties. The mate of the Scottish whaler *Ellen* went ashore hunting in 1825 and was surrounded by Inuit who tried to take his gun. They aimed the "bows and darts" at him but the mate frightened them off by shooting a dog.[50]

Incidents like this became uncommon, and by 1830 visits of whalers had become predictable enough that some Inuit migrated from Cumberland Sound to live around Durban Harbour. Others migrated seasonally. For the most part Inuit conducted exchanges with caution and reserve, and the British were slow to learn to communicate; the whalers' traditional counterclockwise circuit of Baffin Bay brought them late in the season to Cumberland Peninsula and few chances arose to pursue the natives' reports that whales were abundant in Cumberland Sound, just 250 kilometers south of Durban Harbour.[51] These rumours were given substance in 1837 when Inuit went overland in five days to fetch baleen to trade with two Scottish captains. Two years later at Durban Harbour a number of Inuit boarded the *Neptune* to help her captain produce a tolerably accurate map of potential whaling grounds to the southwest. One of these Inuit, Inuluapik, visited Britain with Captain William Penny and piloted Penny into Cumberland Sound in 1840. Repeated Inuit attempts had at last drawn the hesitant whalers into uncharted waters.[52] Cumberland Sound's productivity may have attracted enough whalers in the 1840s to check the flow of population northward across Cumberland Peninsula. Inuluapik's safe return from his visit to Britain probably reinforced trust between Inuit and whalers and such visits, though never routine, persisted into the twentieth century.

One consequence of this exchange was that Inuit began to incorporate the whalers into their own systems of sharing resources to minimize the risks of Arctic living. Initial interest centred on tools: Europeans traded or gave away files, nails, needles, and knives, as well as bread and molasses. In the short term commercial whaling gave Inuit access to stranded carcasses from which only baleen and blubber had been stripped. In this early stage of exchange the Inuit traded baleen from their own hunts, traded weapons and implements as souvenirs, hunted seals for wintering whalers, and admitted Europeans and Americans to the system of wife-exchange even though incomers could not reciprocate directly.

Inuit were also anxious to increase their contacts, because of the mobility and reserves of food that whaling fleets represented. Two consecutive winters of poor sealing occurred in 1846 and 1847. When Captain Parker reached Niantilik in 1848 he found twenty of the 160 people at the settlement had died of hunger in the preceding winter, "of whom several, horrible to relate, had gnawed the flesh from their own arms"—or so British press reported. On Parker's departure a young couple asked to be taken to England where "food was to be had at all times, and people did not die of hunger." The wife died on the return trip but her husband, Memmiadluk, chose to return to his birthplace at Durban Harbour. He contended that food was more abundant there than in Cumberland Sound. This was not always the case, but may have been temporarily true because of imbalances caused by Inuit migrations in response to the whalers. Parker reported in 1848 that "many more natives than usual were in Northumberland Inlet [Cumberland Sound] this autumn in the expectation of meeting with whalers and obtaining useful articles from them." Only the *Truelove* arrived, and many were disappointed.[53]

In these circumstances the Inuit in the 1840s had two courses open: to write the whalers off as unreliable contacts and make little effort to meet them, or to encourage the whalers to visit more regularly. Cumberland Sound was still only visited late in the season by vessels with cargo space to spare. The Inuit repeatedly informed the whalers that bowheads were most numerous in spring at the floe edge, where they could only be reached by parties who wintered in the sound. At length this advice was heeded by the one American master in the whaling fleet.[54] Following a poor hunt in 1851 the *McLellan* left two boats' crews to winter at Kingmiksok, a large settlement near Niantilik. The Americans "had to learn the Esquimaux way of eating and cooking," and could not have sustained themselves without "the help of the friendly Esquimaux." The floe edge was well up the gulf in 1852 and with native help (or, more likely, under native guidance) the Americans took seventeen whales. "Had we been more experienced, we could have captured many more," wrote George Tyson afterwards, "but this was the first season that any whalemen had passed the winter in that region, and we had everything to learn."[55]

Intensive Whaling, 1852–1880

This American success disappointed Captain Penny of Aberdeen, for it stirred interest in other British whaling ports, and ruined Penny's slender change of getting a monopoly licence and land grant to carry out a gradual harvest of whales. Penny was more successful in the short run than his rivals in Hull: their supply vessels scattered, their land station was vandalized by Americans and they did not winter over. Penny, on the other hand, wintered successfully with two ships in 1853–1854 and in 1855–1856, and with ships and two land stations in 1857–1858.

Penny's stations were an important innovation because they relied primarily on native whale-hunters; his wintering vessels also depended partly on Inuit. Penny engaged fifty Inuit at Niantilik in 1853, presumably to hunt seals for his men and whales for his Scottish backers; this they did, despite a midwinter epidemic which carried off a "chief" and seven of his relatives. The successful spring hunt depended almost entirely on Inuit: whales were encountered nearly twenty miles from the ship and the Scottish crewmen at first refused to "enter on the fishery." They ultimately took part, but it was Inuit who carried the fifty sledge-loads of blubber and baleen from seventeen whales over the ice to the boiling-house on Nuvujen Island. Penny in the *Lady Franklin* returned to Aberdeen with this cargo early in 1854. The *Sophia* stayed until the end of the season, her crew of fourteen men, with Inuit, catching a further dozen whales.[56] The success of Penny and the two American whalers attracted international attention, ensuring that this whaling ground, like any other, became popular for a time but was quickly depleted.

For the people of Cumberland Sound, this activity stimulated competition for their services as whale-hunters. Cumberland Sound, apart from Repulse Bay, was the last place in the eastern Arctic where the Inuit had a regularly successful whale hunt when the Europeans arrived; eight to twelve whales were being taken yearly at the head of the sound.[57] Skilled in handling small craft and knowledgeable in the ways of whales, the Inuit were probably better whalers than the incoming crews, who always included many green hands.

Inuit apparently contracted as crews to hunt for the southerners, with one or more leaders in each party. The well-known hunter Tesuwin was reported in 1859 to have travelled across the Sound at the end of May "with three or four boats and crews" to offer to help hunt for the *Emma* of Hull. Cryptic notes in a seaman's journal suggest that Tesuwin negotiated with Penny's station as well as the nearby *Emma* before going to work for the vessel, and that separate disposal of the blubber and bone were included in the terms of negotiation. At the floe edge, native and English crews took turns manning the same boats in shifts.[58] When the *Lady Franklin* arrived in Niantilik in 1857 she found only a blind man and some women and children on hand; the men had all gone further up the sound with the ships.

A minority clung to the old ways: one old hunter from the head of the sound refused to work for Europeans, though they "had promised him much, if he would work for them, he had always kept at a distance from them, and had therefore remained a real Esquimaux, making use of bows and arrows, while some of the others obtained fire arms—though not a few, alas, possessed neither the one nor the other." This missionary's assumption that a man without traditional weapons was not a "real Esquimaux" became commonplace among visiting whites. It does not seem to have troubled any Inuit.[59]

This old man must have been quite atypical by 1858. There is episodic evidence of the reluctance of small bands or individuals to deal with whites, and one anecdote from 1870 points to the fact that the reciprocity involved in wife-sharing sometimes broke down.[60] Yet on the whole, as long as whales were plentiful, the whalers were welcome and the terms of exchange did not appear onerous to Inuit. The natives were handling American-built whaleboats as early as 1852[61] and the references to Tesuwin, cited above, suggest that in 1859 one Inuk controlled four whaleboats and bargained on behalf of his crews for division of the hunt.[62] This was similar to the way in which whalers, particularly Americans, paid their crews, but with one difference. The whaleboats themselves could be part of the bargain, remaining in the hands of the natives as wages at the end of the season. This practice is known to have started by 1858 at Frobisher Bay and 1867 at Repulse Bay.[63] It probably occurred quite early in Cumberland Sound, though recorded instances are later. Nepekin received a boat from the *Isabella* in 1876, and another from the *Florence* in 1878.[64] When the *Mattapoisett* set sail for New Bedford on 8 July 1879, her native boatheader Toawadle received a boat and oars, with a rifle and six hundred rounds of ammunition; he had also been drawing clothing, tobacco, small tools, and cooking utensils all winter. Boatsteerer "Jim Brown" received the usual winter rations plus an E. Allen rifle and five hundred rounds at the end of the season. Six other crewman received less, though all got ammunition.[65]

The intensity of disruption in the 1860s may be surmised from the state of affairs when the *Florence* arrived to winter in 1877. She was only the fifth vessel into the sound but found that the Kekerten stations and four steamers had come to terms with virtually the whole population from Blacklead to Kekerten for the winter. Tyson, the *Florence*'s master, was well acquainted with the local natives but had to winter at Anarnitung near the head of the sound. There he could trade for meat and skins with the prosperous camps near Netilling Fiord, but was barred by ice from the spring whaling.

According to Euro-American accounts, it was during this period that the Inuit virtually lost their aboriginal hunting skills through trade with the whalers. Matthias Warmow noted reprovingly in 1857 that many Inuit had firearms—he forgot, perhaps, that guns had been delivered free by philanthropic Englishmen in response to tales of native destitution. Kumlein was of Warmow's persuasion; he believed that the "Cumberland Eskimo of today, with his breech-loading rifle, steel knives, [and] cotton jackets...is worse clad, lives poorer, and gets less to eat than did his forefathers." Although the hand harpoon was still used for sealing, the bow and arrow was little more than a child's toy; caribou hunters used rifles.[66] Franz Boas, without moralizing, noted similar changes in 1883.[67] Successive visitors painted progressively bleaker pictures. Canadian mariner William Wakeham reported in 1898 that "in the neighbourhood of the whaling stations the natives are fast ceasing to be expert in the use of their old fashioned weapons, such as spears, small harpoons, bows and arrows...and there can be little doubt that those who have been brought up about the stations would be badly off if these were closed."[68] The leader of the next Canadian expedition was more emphatic: "The natives...have quite given up the use of primitive weapons, and there is no doubt that a withdrawal of the whalers would lead to great hardship, and many deaths among these people" unless the government intervened.[69] Traditional weapons were still prized for competitive, recreational uses,[70] but the Inuit of Cumberland Sound had seized the chance to hunt more efficiently. Indigenous hunting skills were as necessary as ever but, by the end of the century, imported weapons were thoroughly integrated into the hunting economy.

This change took place against a background of shrinking personal contact between Inuit and whites. For five of the ten years from 1860 to 1869 whaling crews probably outnumbered the Inuit in Cumberland Sound; in 1861 gatherings of two hundred people—natives and sailors—attended theatrical events on board the *Antelope* north of Kekerten Harbour.[71] The whalers' original land-base at Nuvujen was abandoned by the mid-1860s; the Blacklead Island station was only intermittently manned between 1870 and the late 1880s; skeleton staffs kept trade going at Kekerten. After 1880 the sound rarely saw two vessels or a dozen white men, from November to July.

Marginal Whaling and the Seal-Skin Trade, 1880–1919

The virtual withdrawal of whites and the depletion of bowhead whales did not send the people quietly back to their original way of life. Just as the bowhead had been converted from a subsistence item to a commodity, surplus ringed seal skins were sold to the stations, blubber attached, so that supply vessels need not go home empty. From 1883 to 1903 the average trade was thirty-seven hundred skins a year, which helped carry the stations through the years (of which there were at least eight between 1883 and 1914) when no whales were caught. In 1883 the stations sent sledges "from one settlement to another to exchange tobacco, matches, coffee, bread, &c. for skins and the spare blubber which the Eskimo have carefully saved up," while the Inuit themselves took skins and blubber to the stations to trade for heavier durable goods like cooking pots.[72]

Even the Americans' withdrawal from Cumberland Sound in 1892 barely saved the Scottish stations. When their owners' supply vessel sank in 1902, she was succeeded by chartered vessels which were too small, inexpertly commanded, and often unseaworthy: some sank. Whaling vessels rarely called, and no bowhead was caught by a pelagic whaler in Cumberland Sound after 1880.[73] A two-man Anglican mission after 1894 was an alternative source of employment and provisions; if the Scottish station owners were quite willing to let the mission issue relief, they nonetheless controlled the missionaries' access to the labour of Inuit living around the stations.[74] A few beluga-hunting whalers,[75] government expeditions, and gentlemen-adventurers arrived between 1895 and 1910 to create momentary price fluctuations for skins, handicrafts, and casual labour, but the hard-pressed Scottish stations set the terms of trade most of the time. Relations between Scots and "station natives" or "sailors" in this period were as close to a system of personal labour relations as this region ever experienced. Traders dealt with their "sailors" on preferential terms, and there was a formal ritual for engaging men each autumn, with the phrase "You are going to be my sailor."[76] It is mainly this social context that makes it possible to describe the years from 1880 to 1919 as "transitional" rather than "contact-traditional."

Visitors and missionaries almost invariably described the population as concentrated at the two stations, Blacklead and Kekerten. Some allowance must be made for distorted perceptions during ship-time but most Inuit were considerably more closely linked to the stations after 1880 than they had previously been to any one ship or whaling company. Traditional life continued during the floe-edge and breathing-hole sealing seasons, and during the late summer caribou hunt.[77] For the rest of the year Inuit gathered at the stations as a seasonal reserve of labour for resident and visiting southerners.

Through all this the Inuit continued going down to the floe edge after whales in the spring and onto the stormy waters in autumn, and the whalers continued advancing them provisions and equipment to do so. Because of overhunting before 1880 this would not thereafter have been a profitable routine using carcasses for traditional purposes, but the survival of the whaling stations assured access to international markets, and for the Inuit the hunt was worth pursing even if it failed. Kekerten station in 1883 mustered five whaleboats and Blacklead about as many; together they caught one whale all year (see table 2). Although bowhead stocks were virtually exhausted, the Inuit persisted in the whale-hunting routine and continued to think of themselves as a whale-hunting people. Markosie Pitseolak recalled his youth many years later: "Then the white whaler chose his men to go out on the next whale hunt with him. They had to let you know a few months ahead before they went out whaling. Even if it was hard work, I really wanted to go, and when I was chosen to go I was so happy."[78] Life at the floe edge was reasonably secure. Rations were issued to whalers, the abundant seals could be hunted when whales were not actually being chased, and dependents were provisioned back at the stations. The social life of the floe edge was distinctive too; the early Christian convert Tulugajuak honed his teaching skills when camped for the whaling, and the whaling was followed by baptisms in 1904.[79] The presence of the whaler-traders allowed Inuit men to continue a socially valued routine even though its economic value was questionable.

Intermittently after 1880, southern visitors predicted the complete collapse of the whaling industry and a great deal of resulting misery for the Inuit. Contact was saved by the trade in seal oil and skins, by a market for walrus products arising about 1900, and by growing international interest after 1900 in the pelts of the white fox and polar bear. Despite the new market for these "scraps" or "Arctic produce" Cumberland Sound very nearly was cut off from the outside world during the First World War; to survive the war, the lone white man in the sound depended on the charity of the Inuit but he had nothing left to trade.[80] The Dundee syndicate which bought the stations in 1914 was unable to send a vessel in 1915 or 1918, and resupplied the posts but lost the returning vessel and produce in 1916.[81] When a chartered schooner got through in 1919, her success was reported in the London *Daily Mail*. The schooner had received "a most joyous welcome from the Esquimaux...[whose] ammunition has run out and they had had a severe struggle to sustain themselves. For a couple of years they had only seal meat to eat, and their clothing made wholly of the skins was very dilapidated. The influenza epidemic had extended to the gulf, but only four deaths occurred."[82] If this account is literally true the Inuit had, as earlier observers foretold, lost the capacity to kill caribou with bows and arrows. Although total dependence on the seal was no great hardship in the short run, the people of southeast Baffin Island apparently needed their international contacts in order for their hunting economy to remain viable.

The White Fox Era, 1920–1940

The transition from whaling to the fur trade followed a distinctive course in Baffin Island, particularly in the southeast. Pangnirtung so quickly became the focus of white activity over a large area that it is surprising to note the recollection of Mim Kilabuk in 1976, of a time when "there were only Eskimo leaders to lead the people. Before, they used to have white men coming by ship."[83]   Martha Kakee in 1984 also referred to the time when Kaneaku was leader at Nauleeniaqvik, "when they only had Inuit leaders not the white men."[84]   These recollections are almost perfectly accurate; for a decade after 1916 even the Anglican mission was kept in operation by the catechist Peter Tulugajuak, without white intervention.[85]   As whaling collapsed the number of trading stations actually increased: British speculators put tiny depots at most of the places where Inuit had previously gathered to meet the ships. Crawford Noble and Company sold the Blacklead and Kekerten stations in 1914 to a Dundee syndicate headed by whaling agent Robert Kinnes.[86]   Kinnes kept the stations open, though they were unsupplied during several war years. Noble's former employee James Mutch made annual visits to direct operations for the Sabellum Trading Company. This small London-based concern stayed out of Cumberland Sound, but set up seven posts from Frobisher Bay to Cape Henry Kater, showing enterprise and invention in testing supplies of various exportable commodities, but making most of their precarious profits on the white fox furs which Inuit were learning to trap in earnest after 1912. The strangely named Arctic Gold Exploration Syndicate (AGES) had one dependable German-American employee whom they moved around as opportunities offered. Before 1914 he was on Durban Harbour and after 1920 he was near the head of Cumberland Sound at Usualuk.

The trading picture in the region around 1920 was roughly this: in Frobisher Bay and nearby Cape Haven, a new post and an old whaling station were managed by Godiliak and Michiman for the Sabellum Company. On Blacklead Island in Cumberland Sound, Kinnes' station was run by Paul Roche, the elderly native son of an American whaler-trader. The mission house was occupied by Tulugajuak. Nearby, Kinnes' Kekerten station was run by Angmalik, and his relatives formed much of the island's greatly reduced population. (His wife had been housekeeper to one of the last Scottish traders.)[87]   The Usualuk post was run for AGES by William Duval, nearing the end of his fifty years among the Inuit. At the mouth of Cumberland Sound Kanaker (Kaneaku), a long-time Sabellum contact, managed two small stations. Overland at Cape Durban "Harry" Kingoodlee, who had organized trade there during the whaling era, managed a small depot. At Kivitoo, north of Broughton Island, a noted hunter named Niaqutiaq was rounding out a decade's work for the Sabellum Company at the old whaling haven of Hooper Harbour. A shell-shocked Englishman, Hector Pitchforth, kept the small Sabellum post near Cape Henry Kater.[88]   This system worked for a short time because of the reliability of the native traders and because the Inuit trusted the itinerant Mutch, the acculturated Duval, and the inexperienced Kinnes Company. Veteran whalers and native managers were essential to the new trading companies, and ties between the companies and Inuit were personal as well as economic. When Kinnes sold out in 1924 the agents received substantial gifts.[89]

These distinctive arrangements were upset by powerful competition. In September 1921 the Bay Chimo established a Hudson's Bay Company post in

Pangnirtung Fiord. Tough competition and bad luck drove Kinnes and AGES out of the region within two years, and central mismanagement and James Mutch's retirement undid the work of the Sabellum Company's native managers. The HBC had no effective opposition after 1924. Initially the outlook was not so clear, and the first two years' post journals by the HBC's J.W. Nichols reveal a good deal about the economy and social organization of Cumberland Sound during the last stage of transition.

Within his first month at the post Nichols engaged a boat's crew of Inuit—six of seven men under a leader, probably Veevee—to help haul goods, hunt seals and caribou, and begin trapping foxes. Visiting Inuit invariably expected to be fed, though not all accepted advances to trap for the HBC. "These people are evidently used to the custom of changing masters every year and cannot be depended to stick by any one Company," the trader remarked.[90] Initial fox returns disappointed Nichols, who recorded an ingenious excuse offered by the Inuit, that they were inexpert trappers because the whalers "had always taken every [pound] of fat & oil these natives would get and would never allow them to keep any for themselves. Consequently instead of hunting foxes in winter they have to hunt seals."[91] The reverse was actually true. Seal meat was always in demand for people and for dogs, but their skins were used, traded, or discarded. The whalers had taken on the task of distributing blubber skins in winter to people who needed oil, since the fat was not processed until May. Nichols himself, the Inuit thought, demanded too many skins in trade, and the story about excessive demands may have been invented as a warning which he failed to understand.[92]

Because the native station-keepers travelled a good deal, in the tradition of successful Inuit hunters and of wintering captains in the past, Nichols could size up his opposition. "Both Angmalie [of Kekerten] & Kanaka [of Cape Mercy] seem to have a wonderful hold on the natives with them and it means a lot of hard labour long pow wows and a great deal in the expense line to break their hold."[93] Nichols seems to have encountered the tradition of men engaging to work in parties of six or seven under a leader who handled relations with the white man. Kinship could cement the tie: "it seems that most of them are brothers or Brother-in-Laws to the man in charge [Angmalik] and do not want to leave him until the place [Kekerten] is sold to us," at which time, Nichols fulminated in his diary, they should be broken like dogs.[94] Nichols had never encountered such opposition elsewhere. Duval, Angmalik, Roche, and Kanaker all treated their trappers as "servants,"[95] issuing their rations in advance and then bartering for their skins.

Nichols made another note on this relationship, though it seems likely the natives were taking advantage of his ignorance: when two prominent hunters left the Blacklead station to work for the HBC, they told Nichols they had been forced to surrender their rifles, presumably to Roche. It meant, wrote Nichols, "that we have to give them a new outfit."[96] Nonetheless, by the end of the winter thirty-three hunters had attached themselves to the HBC and many others paid intermittent visits, either to barter their pelts directly (making no promise of future trade) or simply to accept the free rations that Nichols did not dare refuse them.

Not only was Nichols an outsider in a trading system governed by tradition and kinship, he was also up against men who could better his prices. Nichols attributed this in part to the fact that he was supplied from Montreal while the British free traders dodged Canadian customs duties. When Nichols' terms of trade failed to come up to what the natives thought right (for example, a pocket knife for a blubber skin), they accused him of cheating them. Nichols, for his part, thought Kanaka must be trading at a far more generous standard than Mutch had authorized, "but in any Case it knocks the price of our Rifles all to hell[.][I]t seems that all his other goods...is priced in proportion to his Rifles and Gramophones," which were trading at two white foxes and five white foxes respectively.[97] These rates in fact were not out of line with prewar prices[98] and it is likely the HBC had simply underestimated the savings to be made by companies using native staff in the country and "unwanted ships and unwanted men"[99] on the North Atlantic. Had the HBC understood just how complex a situation existed in Cumberland Sound it might never have sent in a man like Nichols, tactless and unfit for winter travel.[100] He was not left in place long enough to enjoy the results of his early stumbling efforts.

Nichols had urged Inuit to join him by saying that the HBC would soon buy out Kinnes and AGES, and in fact in this region the HBC was uncharacteristically willing to buy out opposition. While the Sabellum Company folded under the weight of its own inefficiency, Kinnes and AGES sold out well below their owners' initial optimistic valuation. Early in 1922 the Kinnes Company offered its Baffin assets to the HBC for £20 000. Unfortunately its schooner burned to the water-line at Kekerten Island, erasing the advantage gained when the HBC's supply ship failed to penetrate Cumberland Sound.[101] Nichols' trappers had to take fox skins to Kekerten to buy molasses and biscuits from Angmalik for the HBC post.[102] The Scottish firm's advantage was short-lived; the investors decided not to replace the burnt schooner, offered all capital assets to the HBC for £5000, and accepted £2000 a month later. The managers admitted reluctance to "forego the result of 50 years of difficult labour and organization" but their anxiety to cut their losses is obvious: the HBC would have paid up to £5000 to avoid even larger losses to win over "the natives who have been regularly employed by Kinnes for many years past."[103]

This left the HBC with only Henry Toke Munn's Arctic Gold Exploration Syndicate to contend with in Cumberland Sound. In addition to the Usualuk post near Pangnirtung, AGES had a serviceable little schooner and an established trade at Pond Inlet. Early in 1923 Mann offered £8000 for the Hudson Bay Company Pond Inlet and Cumberland Sound stations, or would sell the syndicate's own assets for £12 000. Munn was bluffing. After rapid negotiations in London and Montreal, AGES sold all its shares for $28 000, about half Munn's original offer. The Sabellum Company failed to resupply its posts after 1925, so the HBC had no serious opposition in southeast Baffin Island for the remainder of the "white fox" era.

Superficially the transition was complete: Kinnes and Munn withdrew; Duval and Roche became HBC employees; the old shaman Kanaker died at his station in 1926, still managing property for the Sabellum Company which would never return. In Cumberland Sound a white missionary was placed over Tulugajuak in 1925; he and Angmalik became leaders of the two largest trapping camps in Cumberland Sound. The centre of population probably shifted somewhat to the north and west, not in response to the position of Pangnirtung but because good fox trapping was discovered in what had always been the best seal and caribou district, the mouth of Netilling Fiord. No longer was it necessary to gather in spring at the stations, to go down to the floe to try to catch the great bowhead whale.

In this period, too, occurred something like a division Frank Vallee has described elsewhere,[104] of people into "nunamiut" and "kabloonamiut" (people of the land and people of the white man). Each of several white institutions—HBC, hospital, RCMP, and so forth—hired one or more Inuit as hunters, dog-drivers, and general assistants and these men, with their families and with the chronically ill or aged, formed the nucleus of the settlement of Pangnirtung while the majority of the people, under the best of hunting leaders, remained for most of the year in camps.[105] This was in contrast to the whaling era, when most people lived around ships or stations for much of the year.

Whaling of a sort continued, but it was beluga whaling, using small boats and loud noises to strand white whales behind a reef on a falling tide. This drive operated continuously from 1923 to 1937 and resumed intermittently thereafter. The oil and hides of beluga whales were luxury items that did not always show a profit, but the local HBC management valued them as a means of demonstrating that local resources were being harvested for the benefit of the natives. The company view was that the natives' profit on the whale drive outfitted the families completely for the autumn caribou hunt. The inquisitive Dr. Bildfell noticed something else about the whale drive: "it appears to me that the Native benefits very little from this materially," he wrote in 1934, "but it appears to be a routine which he enjoys."[106]

From the white incomers' point of view, one of the challenges of working in Cumberland South was the contentment of the Inuit. The Anglican missionary at Lake Harbour found his charges there "more active and industrious than those of the Pangnirtung area... due to the fact that the former have to go long distances to get food and clothing."[107] When Pangnirtung's Blacklead outpost closed as a cost-cutting measure early in the Great Depression, trapping declined: "they are more or less content to hunt seals, and the fur hunt is becoming of secondary importance. They appear to have little ambition to secure anything but ammunition and tobacco."[108] Nearer Pangnirtung this may have been less of a consideration. The sealskin returns of Outfits 252 to 266 (table 4) confirm the local conformity to a general northern pattern: in good fox years seal returns were lower, not because fewer seals were killed but because of "the disinclination of the natives to clean and bring in the skins while they can obtain their requirements much more easily with fox skins."[109]

TABLE 4 *Sealskins Traded at Pangnirtung Post, 1922–1936**

Year	Common Jar	White Coat	Silver Jar	Total
1922	520	–	–	520
1923	920	41	–	961
1924	1969	200	–	2169
1925	2195	1142	–	3337
1926	3672	907	–	4579
1927	1239	530	27	1796
1928	732	721	870	1523
1929	1238	1424	350	3012
1930	1050	930	583	2563
1931	224	872	756	1852
1932	240	663	692	1595
1933	675	1875	1803	4353
1934	55	750	952	1757
1935	81	2638	1486	4205
1936	454	1801	932	3187

*The "jar" or ringed seal has white fur for a few weeks after birth in March or April, and silver hair until it has spent a winter in the water.

SOURCE: Unclassified manuscript graph in Hudson's Bay Company Archives.

By the end of the 1930s, the Cumberland Sound natives' economic strategy was well understood and accepted with resignation by the HBC's managers. The Inuit lived comfortably on seals until they wanted coffee and biscuits, then trapped a few foxes to warrant a trip into Pangnirtung. The traders imagined that the Inuit were unusually stoical or passive. "He is also essentially a whaler type of native brought up entirely on the whaling tradition. This symptom was noted in the early days at the Hudson Strait Posts but fortunately has since almost disappeared. We have no doubt however that in time the Cumberland Sound natives will become better 'Hudson's Bay men'." Meantime, the local Inuk was a "pretty fair sealer and whaler but a very poor trapper."[110] Though these remarks were meant to be mildly derogatory, there is a delicate irony in them. From 1857 onward, missionaries, scientists, and even whalers deplored the influence of the whaling industry on the Inuit of Cumberland Sound and predicted that the people would become corrupt and dependent. "Lofty" Stewart's complaint suggests, on the contrary, that a distinctive environment and the whaling tradition helped the Inuit of Cumberland Sound retain a stubborn detachment from the values and preferences of the HBC post manager.

Conclusion

Inuit in southeast Baffin Island responded to commercial whaling in much the way Subarctic Indians responded to the fur trade. They informed British and American whalers of the best opportunities to hunt and provided essential logistical and social support to the whaler's initial faltering efforts to winter over. Inuit admitted southerners into the local system of sharing resources, and during intermittent periods of hardship they made heavy demands on the whalers (and later on missionaries and the Canadian government). They also made significant efforts and sacrifices, especially in hard years, when they hunted for the southerners.

Inuit also paid heavily for these exchanges through exposure to European diseases, but the winters of 1846–1848 appear to have been the last instance of widespread starvation caused solely by shortage of seal-meat. In this sense the adoption of Europeans into Inuit economic systems, and their own response to Euro-American commercial contacts, met the basic objective of increasing security for the indigenous groups.

Inuit also adjusted to the changing character and demands of subsequent groups of incomers. These strategies could not prevent destruction of bowhead whale stocks, and exposed the Inuit to the various international markets for Arctic produce. They were in no position either to control the movement of external prices, or to reap the full benefit when markets were most favourable for their commodities—whale oil and baleen, sealskins, or arctic fox. None the less, changes in the culture of southeast Baffin Island after 1824 embodied the choice made by Inuit to participate, as far as their own cultural values and their local resources allowed, in international commerce.

Notes

1.   Useful modern reviews include A. Tanner, "The End of Fur Trade History," *Queen's Quarterly* 90, 1 (Spring 1983): 176–91; J. Peterson and J. Afinson, "The Indian and the Fur Trade: A Review of Recent Literature," *Manitoba History* 10 (Autumn 1985): 10–18; and B.G. Trigger, "The Historians' Indian: Native Americans in Canadian Historical Writing from Charlevoix to Present," *Canadian Historical Review* 67, 3 (September 1986): 315–42.

2.   J.W. Grant, *The Moon of Wintertime: Missionaries and the Indians of Canada in Encounter Since 1534* (Toronto, 1984).

3.   A. Tanner, *Bringing Home Animals: Religious Ideology and Mode of Production of the Mistassini Cree Hunters* (St. John's, 1979).

4.   See also further publications of Memorial University's Institute of Social and Economic Research, both edited by R. Paine, *Patrons and Brokers in the Eastern Arctic* (St. John's, 1971), and *The White Arctic: Anthropological Essays on Tutelage*

and Ethnicity (St. John's, 1979).

5. Frobisher thought he had mined gold in Frobisher Bay; lead and zinc are mined at Nanisivik, as was mica at Lake Harbour ca. 1900–1910; coal was mined for local use at Pond Inlet. Mica (ca. 1875–1876) and graphite (1926) in Cumberland Sound were always commercial failures.

6. W. Kemp, "Baffinland Eskimo" in *Handbook of North American Indians, Vol. V: Arctic* ed. D. Damas, (Washington, 1984), 463–75.

7. D. Damas, "The Eskimo," in *Science, History and Hudson Bay*, ed. C.S. Beals and D.S. Shenstone (Ottawa, 1968), 141–71; W. Gillies Ross's 1969 Cambridge Ph.D. thesis was published as *Whaling and Eskimos: Hudson Bay 1860–1915* (Ottawa, 1975).

8. For precontact conditions, see A.P. McCartney, ed., *Thule Eskimo Culture: An Anthropological Retrospective*, Museum of Man Mercury Series (Archaeology), no. 88 (Ottawa, 1979).

9. "William Penny, 1809–92: Arctic Whaling Master," *Polar Record* 15, 94 (1970): 25–43.

10. Most recently in *Arctic Whalers, Icy Seas: Narrative of the Davis Strait Whale Fishery* (Toronto, 1985).

11. K. Harper, "Historical Survey, Baffin Island National Park," MSS, Contract No. 74–140, Environment Canada (Parks), Prairie and Northern Region Office Library; also "The Moravian Mission at Cumberland Sound," *The Beaver* (Summer 1981): 43–45; and "Profile" of William Duval in *Arctic* 38, 1 (March 1985): 74–75.

12. M. Lutz, *The Effects of Acculturation on Eskimo Music of Cumberland Peninsula*, Museum of Man Mercury Series (Ethnology), no. 4 (Ottawa, 1978).

13. I am indebted to Dr. White for letting me read his unpublished manuscript, "The Far Shores of Baffin." His published work includes "Scottish Traders to Baffin Island, 1910–1930," *Maritime History* 5, 1 (Spring 1977): 34–50; "Captain W.J. Jackson of Baffin Island," *Polar Record* 17, 109 (1975): 375–81; and biographical profiles of Henry Toke Munn and Hector Pitchforth in *Arctic* 37, 1 (March 1984): 74–75, and 38, 1 (March 1985): 78–79.

14. R.G. Mayes, "The Creation of a Dependent People: The Inuit of Cumberland Sound, Northwest Territories" (Ph.D. diss., McGill, 1978).

15. Notably D. Cole and L. Müller-Wille, "Franz Boas' Expedition to Baffin Island 1883–1884," Études/Inuit/Studies 8, 1 (1984): 37–63.

16. K. Evans, "Edmund James Peck: His Contribution to Eskimo Literacy and Publishing," *Journal of the Canadian Church Historical Society* 26, 2 (1984): 58–68.

17. M.G. Stevenson, "Kekerten: Preliminary Archaeology of an Arctic Whaling Station," MSS, Prince of Wales Northern Heritage Centre, Yellowknife, NWT.

18. Jaypeetee Akpalialuk, interviewer, "Oral History Interviews; Pangnirtung and Auyuittuq," MSS, Prairie and Northern Region Office, Environment Canada - Parks; cited hereafter as "Auyuittuq Interviews."

19. J.R. Bennett, "Whalers, Missionaries, and Inuit in Cumberland Sound" (M.A. research paper, Carleton University, 1985).

20. Damas, "The Eskimo," 142.

21. Ross, *Whaling and Eskimos*, 137–38.

22. F. Boas, "Baffin-Land," in *A. Petterman's Mitteilungen* (Gotha, 1885), 34; W. Wakeham, *Report of the Expedition to Hudson Bay and Cumberland Gulf in the Steamship 'Diana' ... 1897* (Ottawa, 1898), 59–60. Yale University Library has a log of this voyage of the *Era*.

23. D. Cole and L. Müller-Wille, "Boas' Expedition to Baffin Island," 54; Hector Pitchforth found it remarkable that the octogenarian "Jimmy Alexander"

(Netyape) knew a few words of English "and certainly a few he didn't ought to know." Pitchforth Journal, 30 March 1924, MG28 I198, Public Archives of Canada (hereafter PAC).

24. For the period 1953–1973, see Mayes, "Dependent People."

25. P. Schledermann, "History of Human Occupation," in *The Land that Never Melts: Auyuittuq National Park*, ed. R. Wilson (Toronto, 1975).

26. A.W.F. Banfield, *The Mammals of Canada* (Toronto, 1975), 372–75.

27. This observation is based on log-books and journals; see particularly the account of the *Florence* in 1877–1878; she wintered much nearer the caribou-hunting grounds than was customary, but may have used as few as three caribou carcasses all winter to supplement regular rations of fresh seal meat. See H. Howgate, ed., *The Cruise of the Florence, or Extracts from the Journal of the Preliminary Arctic Expedition of 1877–78* (Washington, 1879).

28. L. Kumlein, *Contributions to the Natural History of Arctic America Made in Connection with the Howgate Polar Expedition, 1877–78* (Washington, 1879), 60.

29. *Periodical Accounts of Work of the Moravian Missions* 19 (London, 1849): 19–23.

30. Mayers, "Dependent People," 99.

31. Franz Boas, "The Central Eskimo," in *Sixth Annual Report of the Bureau of American Ethnology 1884–85* (Washington, 1888).

32. H.T. Munn, "The Economic Life of the Baffin Island Eskimo," *Geographical Journal* 59, 4 (June 1922): 269.

33. Eastern Arctic Patrol Journal by J.G. Wright, 21–25 September 1946, RG85, Interim Accession 84–85/554, PAC.

34. Mayes, "Dependent People," 103; see also the important work by A.A. Haller in *Baffin Island - East Coast: An Area Economic Survey*, ed. G. Anders (Ottawa, 1966); Haller notes (35, 98) a local belief that Cumberland Sound seal stocks may be recruited annually by seals drifting in from Davis Strait.

35. W.G. Ross, "Whaling and the Decline of Native Populations," *Arctic Anthropology* 14, 2 (1977): 1–8.

36. Peck, circular 30 September 1899, Church Missionary Society MSS, MG17–B2 C1/0 item 1899–102; and Sampson, circular 20 September 1899, Church Missionary Society MSS, MG17 B2 C1/0 item 1899–104, PAC.

37. Kumlein, *Natural History of Arctic America*, 15; Howgate, ed., *Cruise of the 'Florence,'* 69.

38. Boas, *Central Eskimos*, 426.

39. E.G. W. Wakeham, *Report of the Expedition to Hudson bay and Cumberland Gulf in the Steamship 'Diana'* (Ottawa, 1898), 24.

40. Fleming to Peck, 5 September 1914, Peck MSS iv-1, Anglican Church Archives.

41. W.G. Ross, *Arctic Whalers, Icy Seas*, 169; Howgate, ed., *Cruise of the 'Florence,'* 25, 30, 119.

42. Howgate, ed., *Cruise of the 'Florence,'* 27.

43. The Parks Canada Auyuittuq interviews included a question on leadership; the rich variety in the answers suggests that informants understood the question in different ways. Most agree that leadership devolved upon those who best knew when and how to hunt.

44. Petty to O/C HQ Div., 30 June 1928, RG85/775, file 5648 PAC.

45. In the Auyuittuq interviews two Pangnirtung elders mentioned ownership or control of whaleboats as an attribute of leadership; Shaimaiyuk Simon (10) and Koagak Akulukjuk (11).

46. For the distribution of food, see Howgate, ed., *Cruise of the 'Florence,'* 113;

this observation does not suggest a class system, for it placed women and children generally in the bottom rank. See also Stevenson, "Kekerten: Preliminary Archaeology." Stevenson has argued that "Inuit society at whaling stations was divided into two distinct classes: the *privileged* and the *proletariat.*" See M.G. Stevenson, "The Emergence of Class Structure at an Arctic Whaling Station" (Paper presented to the 19th annual meeting of the Canadian Archaeological Association, 26 April 1986). Stevenson quotes several passages from Bernhard Hantzsch's journal in L.H. Neatby, trans. and ed., *My Life Among the Eskimos; Baffinland Journeys in the Years 1909 to 1911* (Saskatoon, 1977).

47. Ammunition was commonly given as relief to the blind: it let them contribute tangibly to the hunt. See, for example, relief invoices RG85/106, file 253–2, PAC.

48. Dr. MacKinnon to McKeand, 6 April 1935 and to J.L. Turner, 31 August 1935, RG85/815, file 6954(2), PAC.

49. P. Lange, "Some Qualities of Inuit Social Interaction," in *White Arctic*, ed. Paine, 108.

50. Journal of Thomas Scoresby, 24 September 1825, Collection 55, vol. 54 (*Alexander*, 1825), Mystic Seaport Museum Library.

51. Other important surviving manuscript logs and journals include *Brunswick*, 1824 MG24 H69, PAC and *Abram*, 1839, MG11 A7, Provincial Archives of Manitoba.

52. Printed sources for the period before 1850 include the *Nautical Magazine* 6 (London, 1837): 165–67; and 9 (1840): 98–103; *Periodical Accounts* (1849, 1851–1858); and A. M'Donald, *A Narrative of Some Passages in the Life of Eenoolooapik* (Edinburgh, 1841).

53. *Periodical Accounts* 19 (1849): 19–23.

54. P. Goldring, "Last Voyage of the *McLellan*," *The Beaver* 66, 1 (January/February 1986): 39–44.

55. E.V. Blake, *Arctic Experiences; Containing Capt. George E. Tyson's Wonderful Drift on the Ice-Floe* (New York, 1874), 89–90.

56. *Times* (London), 1 September 1854, reprinted in part in *Whaleman's Shipping List*, 3 October 1854.

57. Alexander M'Donald, *Some Passages*, 118.

58. W.G. Ross, *Arctic Whalers, Icy Seas*, 167–69.

59. *Periodical Accounts* 23 (1858): 131.

60. Relations with the Nugumiut seem to have been especially strained, but see J.P. Faulkner, *Eighteen Months in a Greenland Whaler* (New York, 1878), 203–06, for a tale of a Niantilik man who attacked sailors from a vessel which his wife visited regularly.

61. W. Barron, *An Apprentice's Reminiscences of Whaling in Davis Strait...1848 to 1854* (Hull, 1890), 40–42.

62. Tesuwin or "Tes-e-wane" was considered "a very useful man" by whalers until partly disabled in a hunting accident about 1875; Howgate, ed., *Cruise of the 'Florence,'* 24.

63. Dr. Susan Rowley, personal communication, re. whaleboat given by Buddington to Cudlargo in 1858; for Repulse Bay, see W.G. Ross, *Whaling and Eskimos*, 93.

64. Howgate, ed., *Cruise of the 'Florence,'* 29, 176.

65. *Mattapoisett* Account Book, 1878–1879, International Marine Archives, MSS no. 310, Old Dartmouth Historical Society, Whaling Museum Library.

66. Kumlein, *Natural History of Arctic America*, 14, 34–35.

67. Boas, *Central Eskimo*, 466–68.

68. W. Wakeham, *Report of the Expedition*, 75.

69. A.P. Low, *The Cruise of the 'Neptune,'* 271.

70. W.G. Ross, *Arctic Whalers, Icy Seas,* 238.

71. *Antelope,* 1860–1861, 22 January/February 1861, Log no. 771, Old Dartmouth Historical Society, Whaling Museum Library.

72. Boas, *Central Eskimo,* 467; also Howgate, ed., *Cruise of the 'Florence,'* 91 for similar trips five years earlier.

73. Clippings, MG29 A5, vol. 8, file 6, PAC.

74. Bilby to CMS, 12 July 1905, Church Missionary Society MSS, MG17 B2 C 1/P item 1905-32, PAC.

75. R. Reeves and E. Mitchell, "White Whale Hunting in Cumberland Sound," *The Beaver* 312, 3 (Winter 1981): 42–49.

76. See Inventory of Process, Second Division, Lord Salveson, Part 1 Ordinary, Wrightington and Co. against O.C. Forsyth Grant, Scottish Record Office, C.S. 241/W/25/8, 100. I am indebted to the Rev. Dr. White for this reference. Other aspects of this relationship in summer are documented in the logs of the *Erme* (1912–16) in the Stefansson Collection, Baker Library, Dartmouth College.

77. In 1899 the whaling crews were paid off on 25 July, and immediately began preparing for the caribou hunt. Extracts from J.W. Bilby's Journal, CMS, MG17 B2 C.1./0/ item 1899–114, PAC.

78. *Stories from Pangnirtung* (Edmonton, 1976), 25.

79. Journal, 30 April, 24 July 1904, Peck MSS, xxxv, no. 4, Anglican Church Archives.

80. *Stories from Pangnirtung,* 35–36 (Jim Kilabuk) and 75 (Malaya Akulujuk); and Ross, *Arctic Whalers, Icy Seas,* 227–39.

81. Voyage information in Kinnes to HBC, 28 April 1922, Hudson's Bay Company Archives (HBCA), A.92/212/1.; partly corrected by reference to *Erme,* 1916.

82. *Daily Mail* (London), 21 October 1919.

83. *Stories from Pangnirtung,* 35.

84. Auyuittuq Interviews, Martha Kakee (2).

85. *Proceedings of the Church Missionary Society* (London, annually), and *The Year Book and Clergy List of the Church of England in the Dominion of Canada* (Toronto, annually).

86. See Kinnes to Secretary, 28 April 1922, HBCA, A.92/212/1, for transfer date. Records connected with the dissolution of the Cumberland Gulf Trade Company are preserved in the Scottish Record Office, BT2/11549.

87. Auyuittuq Interviews, Katchoo Evik (13), Etuangat Aksayook (22).

88. Major sources on the free trade era include the work of Gavin White and the following unpublished sources: AGES, RG85/568, file 0049, PAC; Sebellum, RG 85/775, file 5648; Duval, RG85/762, file 4958; Pitchforth, RG85/763, file 4999; the Stefansson Collection in the Baker Library, Dartmouth College contains a number of important logbooks. See also Kinnes, HBCA, A.92/212/1 and AGES, HBCA A.92/179/1.

89. Kinnes to HBC, 16 May, 1924, HBCA, A.92/212/1.

90. 12 November 1923, HBCA, B.455/a/3, 12.

91. 9 December 1921, HBCA, B.455/a/1.

92. See Greenshield to Finnie, 5 March 1923, RG85/610, file 2712, PAC.

93. 6 February 1922, HBCA, B.455/a/1.

94. 13 February 1922 and a/2, 18 December 1921, HBCA, B.455/a/1.

95. Nichols used "servants" in the Scottish sense, implying moderate status and considerable security; 6 February 1922, HBCA, B.455/a/1.

96. 22 February 1922, HBCA, B.455/a/1; it is most improbable that as powerful a

man as Tulugajuak did not own his own rifle by 1922.

97.   6 February 1922, HBCA, B.455/a/1.

98.   Log of the *Erme*, 1913, Stefansson Collection, Baker Library, Dartmouth College.

99.   Gavin White's splendid phrase, in "Scottish Traders," 46.

100.   Nichols' travel journals in HBCA, B.455/a/2, contain such expressions as "Now god knows where between Padley and Pangnatoot" (12–18 March 1922) and after aborting a trip to Cape Haven, "d—glad to once again get under a wooden roof." (26 January–5 February 1922).

101.   15 September 1922, HBCA, B.455/a/3, 11.

102.   15 January 1923, HBCA, B.455/a/3, 15.

103.   Correspondence from and concerning Robert Kinnes and Sons, HBCA, A.92/212/1.

104.   F.G. Vallee, *Kabloona and Eskimo in the Central Keewatin* (Ottawa, 1967), 132–40. Vallee was careful to explain that his terms were not distinct opposite types but the ends of a spectrum. He also acknowledged that the settlements attracted, in bad hunting seasons, many people who were still basically oriented towards the land.

105.   Much of the best social commentary on Pangnirtung in the "white fox" era is in the reports of medical officers at St. Luke's Hospital; though marred by amateur ethnography and outdated racial views, the reports of Drs. Livingstone, Stuart, Bildfell and Mackinnon repay study, Pangnirtung Health Reports, 1925–51.

106.   "Medical Report, 1934," 17, RG85/815, file 6954(2), PAC.

107.   Memo by D.L. McKeand, 14 November 1939, RG85/1045, file 540–3(3–C), PAC.

108.   Annual report, Outfit 264 (1933–34), HBCA, DFTR/27.

109.   Enclosure, Commissioner to Manager of St. Lawrence-Ungava District, 6 February 1935, HBCA, DFTR/27.

110.   S.J. Stewart, 28 July 1939, Ungava Annual Reports, HBCA.

SECTION 6

THE MODERN NORTH

THE POLITICS OF HEALTH IN THE FOURTH WORLD: A NORTHERN CANADIAN EXAMPLE*

JOHN D. O'NEIL

Anthropological interest in primary health care began with Paul's benchmark volume on public responses to health programs in developing countries.[1] Paul's basic thesis that successful primary health care programs must take into account the concerns and priorities of people in the communities has guided the research objectives of several decades of anthropological work.[2] However, as Baer and others have argued, much of this work has failed to include a political economic perspective in the analysis of problems and failures at the community level.[3] When projects designed to foster "health by the people" fail, anthropologists have tended to isolate local cultural and social factors rather than look for macrostructural conditions which generate inconsistencies and contradictions at the community level.[4]

At the same time, however, proponents of the political economy perspective have tended to explain poor public health achievements in developing countries solely in terms of *national* political economies. As Segall argues, critics of both socialist and capitalist systems exploit contradictions and inconsistencies from an empiricist (conservative) or idealist (socialist) bias in order to either undermine or overdetermine theoretical linkages between

*_Human Organization_ 45, 2 (1986): 119–28. The research was supported by the National Health Research and Development Program, Health and Welfare, Canada and the Arctic Institute of North America. The author wishes to acknowledge the contributions of the people of Gjoa Haven, Northwest Territories, and particularly Peter Akkikungark, Raymond Kamookak, Peter Ookpik, Agnes Porter and Tuppittia Qitsualik; health services staff including Leslie Knight, Kristine Robinson, Peter Sarsfield, Otto Schaefer, Rosemary Proulx, Patrick Brown, Brian Postl and Michael Moffatt; and Peter Emerk and Thomas Suluk of the Keewatin Inuit Association and the Parliament of Canada, respectively. He is also grateful for the editorial advice of Peter New, Joseph Kaufert, David Fish, Peter Sarsfield, Charlene Ball and several anonymous _Human Organization_ reviewers. Errors in interpretation are solely the responsibility of the author.

structural and ideological factors, and health care practices.[5] Segall goes on to argue that, rather than engaging in scholastic debates about the theoretical fit between national political economies and health care systems, a political economic perspective should focus instead on the way in which macro social economic and political factors affect: 1) the causes of disease, 2) the capacity of people to undertake health-related activities, and 3) the professional control of health care services and their distribution. Such an analysis should also be grounded in the everyday realities of community life.

This middle-range approach is well-suited for anthropologists struggling to incorporate a broader structural perspective into their analyses of local-level attempts to improve health status as several recent efforts have shown.[6] Interested primarily in factors which limit or enhance community involvement in health care services, a fundamental factor in successful PHC, anthropologists have much to gain, and to contribute, by examining and comparing political and economic factors which interact with local-level cultural and social realities to produce effective community-based primary health care services.

While most anthropological interest in primary health care is concentrated in Third World developing countries, Fourth World situations offer a somewhat different problem for analysis. Structured as internal colonies in relation to the larger nation-state, Fourth World situations exist within First (e.g., American Indians and Australian Aboriginals), Second (e.g., indigenous peoples in northern U.S.S.R.) and Third World contexts (e.g., Indians in Central America). These situations are better characterized as Fourth World, rather than as ethnic minorities, because the populations involved are the original inhabitants of the area, whose lands have been expropriated and who have become subordinate politically and economically to an immigrant population.[7] Fourth World peoples generally inhabit marginal geographic regions relative to central metropolitan areas, and their resources have historically been exploited by the dominant group without local consultation. While it could be argued that overt colonialism no longer characterizes relations among most independent nation-states, Fourth World situations continue to be structured by colonial policies.[8] Most importantly, Fourth World peoples are often aggressively involved in ethnonationalist movements. These movements sometimes generate regional political ideologies of a distinctly socialist character which must compete with capitalist/conservative national political ideologies.[9]

Although ''socialist'' and ''capitalist/conservative'' are used contrastingly in this paper to describe, in part, the political ideologies of ethnonationalist organizations and nation-states, they are used in a definitional rather than a strictly political sense. Socialist refers to an ideological orientation which ''advocates that community as a whole should own and control the means of production, distribution, and exchange.''[10] Given that the central issue for almost all Fourth World peoples is community control over the land base— without doubt the major means of production, distribution and exchange—there is little question that this ideology should be interpreted as socialist. Indeed, there has been considerable resistance among indigenous peoples, generally, to any suggestion that land should be owned by individuals as a means toward economic development. Such an orientation would be considered capitalist, a "system in which private capital or wealth is used in production and distribution of goods."[11]

"Conservative" is also used appropriately in this paper in conjunction with capitalist to describe the general tenor of a national political ideology which "is disposed to maintain existing institutions and promote individual enterprise."[12] This philosophy is fundamentally different from the articulation of social philosophy characteristic of indigenous organizations where the emphasis is on creating radically new governmental structures based on consensualism.[13]

Primary Health Care in Northern Canada

In the Canadian context of the Fourth World, the primary health care services appear, on the surface at least, to be among the best in the world. In terms of per capita government expenditures, aboriginal peoples in northern Canada are well serviced. For example, Young estimates conservatively that medical services expenditures in northern Canada are approximately $1000 per capita, as compared to $230 per capita in Tanzania in the late 1970s.[14]

Isolated communities with populations between two hundred and one thousand are serviced by health clinics staffed by one to three nurses who often have advanced clinical or public health training. These clinics provide a combination of preventive, curative, and public health services, free of charge, to all sectors of the population. They, in turn, are supported by a comprehensive and free referral and transportation system to hospitals and specialists in southern urban centers. Regionally situated physicians are responsible for up to five smaller communities and make regular monthly visits. Various specialists from tertiary centers also visit communities at least once per year.

However, despite laudable achievements in reducing mortality due to infectious disease, Inuit and Indian populations continue to exhibit morbidity and mortality rates in some dimensions in excess of even the poorest Third World countries. Deaths due to accidents and violence are of epidemic proportions. According to Young:

> Both in terms of crude mortality and proportionate mortality rates
> the accident statistics for the northern Natives are among the worst
> in the world. They surpass even the highly developed countries
> and are far in excess of the lower rates from predominantly rural
> Third World countries.[15]

Furthermore, deaths due to accidents and violence show little indication of improving, while deaths due to other causes such as cancer are increasing and approaching national averages, as table 1 illustrates.

TABLE 1 *Mortality Trends in Northwest Territories Compared with Canadian Standards[a]*

	NWT 1976[b]	NWT 1983[c]	Canada 1977[d]
Accidents, injuries, violence and poisonings	33.6%	29.6%	9.5%
Neoplasms	13.9	17.9	21.7
Diseases of circulatory system	17.4	15.6	48.6
Diseases of the respiratory system	N/A	12.9	6.5

[a] Figures expressed as percentage of total deaths but selected indicators do not add up to 100 percent.

[b] SOURCE: Report on Health Conditions in the Northwest Territories, 1976.

[c] SOURCE: Report on Health Conditions in the Northwest Territories, 1983.

[d] SOURCE: Perspectives Canada III; 1980.

Suicides, particularly among young adults, and alcohol-related injuries and deaths comprise a large proportion of the accident statistics and are indicators of profound mental health problems. Perhaps most distressing, infant health indicators which had been gradually improving to Canadian national standards, once again show signs of deteriorating to the levels of many Third World countries, as indicated in table 2.

TABLE 2 *Inuit Infant Health Indicators*

	1973	1978	1983
Low birthweight infants[a]	10.96	5.50	8.70
Perinatal mortality rates[b]	26.84	19.00	22.00
Neonatal deaths[b]	13.42	13.40	19.00
Post-neonatal mortality rate[b]	31.32	7.60	20.50
Infant mortality rate[b]	44.74	21.00	39.50

[a] Per hundred live births.
[b] Per thousand live births.

SOURCE: Report on Health Conditions in the Northwest Territories, 1983.

In light of this evidence, it seems obvious that expensive primary care services are not a simple answer for health problems in remote areas. A broader understanding of the primary care services in the context of community development is necessary in order to address the problems identified. Efforts in this direction are affected not only by local social and cultural factors often described by anthropologists, but also by the tensions and conflicts which flow from local and national political economies.

This paper will examine the issue of community involvement in primary health care services in northern Canada. It will delineate macro-political and economic factors which constrain efforts by northern communities to become involved in the pursuit of their own well-being. It will discuss the impact that an "internal colonial" health care system has on northern peoples' ability to respond effectively to changing patterns of excessive morbidity and mortality.

The data for this paper are drawn from nearly a decade of research on health issues in the Canadian North. This research has involved two years of intensive field research in an Inuit village, combined with extensive interviews of health care providers, health scientists and administrators who are responsible for northern health policy and practice.

Historical Background

An interpretation of northern history based on a model of internal colonialism argues that from the moment northern native people were first contacted by Europeans looking for cheap natural resources, their ability to determine their own livelihood was made problematic. Decisions as to the respective values of northern commodities were made without regard for the priorities of northern peoples, and these new economic relationships determined a massive reorganization of northern social life. New settlements sprang up around trading posts, and later mining enterprises, and once independent nomadic hunters became dependent almost overnight on whatever surplus value their labour could elicit from the colonial system. As their ecology changed, so did their epidemiology, and massive epidemics of previously unknown diseases added to their growing dependency on external foreign markets and agents for survival. From this perspective, the contemporary independence movement based on the emergence of ethnonationalist organizations is the natural product of a century of struggling to maintain some sense of independence and autonomy, rather than reflecting a growing familiarity with southern institutional systems.[16]

This struggle is being waged on both local and regional levels and has been directed at each new institution separately. It began with the co-operative movement to lessen dependence on colonial traders and continued with the establishment of native churches where traditional ideas could be re-expressed. It has culminated in the formation of local councils and regional and national associations to exert greater influence on the development of village-level infrastructure such as housing, sanitation and water supply, and to negotiate control over natural resources and land rights with various levels of government.[17] The last institutions to be wrestled with are education and health care and, significantly, education has been a priority during the past five years. Health care remains essentially in the hands of a southern urban bureaucracy and is still unaccountable at the community level.

In order to understand the practical effects that result from the ideological tensions implicit in Fourth World contexts, a case example of an Inuit leader's co-optation is presented. In the recent 1984 Canadian federal election, Inuit in the Northwest Territories contributed to the Conservative landslide victory by electing Mr. Thomas Suluk, an Inuk who was the Progressive Conservative candidate in the Nunatsiaq riding—which is the largest electoral district in Canada with the smallest population density. This election was significant on several levels: native societies in Canada (both Indian and Inuit) have historically elected representatives with distinctly socialist principles to regional and national political bodies. Identification with cultural issues and aboriginal rights movements has also usually meant a strong socialist commitment. Indeed, Mr. Suluk is the past president of the Tungavik Federation—the land claims negotiating agency of the Inuit—and was executive director of the Inuit Cultural Institute—an organization committed to protecting traditional culture—at the time of his nomination for the federal election.

Mr. Suluk's decision to seek federal office within a conservative political framework is symbolic of the major structural tension that exists in internal colonies where local socialist ideology must compete aggressively with the conservative ideology explicit in a national capitalist political economy. The consequences of this tension are complex. The issues of political and cultural self-determination become clouded with conservative rhetoric about free enterprise and individual autonomy. Economic independence is confused with overcoming welfare dependency by reducing budgets for social programs. Community development issues are localized and disaggregated from larger structural factors in the interests of dismantling "big government," but this tactic also facilitates further economic exploitation. Thus, an Inuit leader committed to the principle of asserting aboriginal rights and protecting cultural traditions can become convinced that the best way to iterate these views is from a capitalist/conservative perspective which rhetorically advocates individual freedom from state control. The hidden agenda that is sometimes overlooked by these populist leaders is the implicit conservative commitment to maintaining a colonial relationship with a northern workforce as a means to encourage capital investment in frontier extractive industries.

Development of Health Services in Inuit Communities

The colonially introduced onslaught of epidemic infectious diseases (including diphtheria, smallpox, measles, influenza and tuberculosis) in the first half of this century killed between 10 and 50 percent of most Inuit communities.[18]

Since the traditional shamanistic medical system was equipped to deal primarily with "psychosomatic" illnesses, these new epidemics forced Inuit to seek assistance from southern white traders and missionaries who offered access to new medical resources, at least implicitly, in exchange for economic and ideological dependence. Traditional Inuit medicine operated on the principle that every individual was responsible for his own and his family's well-being through the fulfillment of basic social obligations. Good health depended on the personal pursuit of moral, spiritual and social ideals, and healers were called upon to advise people when their behaviour was contrary to group expectations. In this light, individual and community health was a collective responsibility.[19]

In the 1940s and 1950s, Catholic and Anglican missions responded to the devastating impact of the new infectious diseases by building a series of cottage hospitals at various locations throughout the Canadian North. Hospitals were sometimes built in the same location, as the two religious missions competed for converts, and each attracted a growing sedentary population. They were staffed by southern-trained physicians, and indeed a Dr. Livingstone, hailed as somewhat of a radical in northern health history, was outspokenly critical of religious rivalry changing the nomadic ecology and hence disease epidemiology of Inuit peoples. He advocated a system of widely dispersed health stations staffed by local paraprofessionals, and argued that health improvements would only occur in the context of economic development.[20] Instead, government policy determined that these cottage hospitals functioned as way stations for increasing numbers of Inuit being sent south for periods of several months to several years for treatment and recuperation.

The consequence of this change was that Inuit went suddenly from a system where each individual had been involved in all dimensions of health care, to a system where health resources were controlled by outsiders. From a system where social relationships and health were understood in a fundamentally integrated manner, the colonization of mind, body and community in the Canadian North resulted in a situation where people became alienated from their own well-being. The outcome was a system of massive evacuation and relocation of the sick to southern centers where Inuit were isolated as individuals and made physically and emotionally dependent on outsiders.[21]

This external domination of health and health care was intensified when the federal government assumed direct control over health services. In 1955 the Indian and Northern Health Service, a division of the federal Department of Health and Welfare, was given the mandate to provide all health services in the two northern Canadian territories. They immediately began a construction program to provide a health clinic in all northern communities where a mission and/or trading post already existed and where a growing population of Inuit were living permanently on a year-round basis. By 1960 there were seven clinics in the major settlements, and by 1970 most communities with a population over a hundred people had a fully equipped Nursing Station.[22]

These Nursing Stations were staffed by southern-trained non-Inuit nurses who were permanent residents in the community and who were employed by the federal government. The Nursing Stations are out-patient health clinics which are supported by a highly developed system of referral to secondary and tertiary level care centres in southern Canada. Geographic distances between these levels average more than five hundred miles and transportation is exclusively by air.

In the 1960s and 1970s, when the nurse-based primary care system was being developed in the North, many British-trained nurses were hired because of their advanced clinical skills in areas such as midwifery. These nurses sometimes brought a "going to the colonies" attitude with them and often adopted a materialistic relationship with their community. Although they provided excellent primary health services, they continued to foster a situation where Inuit remained dependent on their services for all aspects of their well-being. Elsewhere I have argued that this relationship often resulted in the medicalization of community life as local nurses monitored the everyday well-being of people in the community as if they were all patients on a hospital ward.[23]

The following case illustrates the way in which community nurses reinforced Inuit dependency on their services.

Although shamanism as a distinct cultural expression was driven underground by earlier missionary activity, there is evidence that some shamans have been able to create new roles for themselves as senior members of the emergent Christian churches. In situations where the church is administered locally by a lay preacher and elders from the community, with minimal non-Inuit involvement, these local religious leaders often include people who once were practicing shamans. Their impact on contemporary religious expression has been to integrate traditional ideas about the personal and family responsibility for well-being that characterized relationships with the supernatural. These ideas essentially suggest that a person's moral behaviour is evaluated in supernatural terms and misfortune is a consequence of immoral behaviour which angers the spirit(s). In this case an elder in the church, who had practised shamanism as a young man, was injured one day in a road construction accident. Although apparently unhurt externally, he went home complaining of abdominal pains and nausea. His wife encouraged him to see the nurse, but he refused, insisting he had more faith in prayer than the nurse's medications. He arranged for the lay preacher in the church to pray for him, and stayed at home, reading his Bible and singing religious hymns.

The nurse learned of this accident indirectly through one of the support staff at the Nursing Station (who she had trained to report any gossip related to accidents or illnesses), and went to visit the injured man. He refused to allow her to examine him and was uncommunicative about describing the accident or the symptoms he was experiencing.

The injured man's wife was very upset, reporting that he was experiencing severe abdominal pain and an inability to have bowel movements. She implored the nurse to prescribe medication and requested that her husband be flown out to a southern hospital for further tests.

After considerable negotiation through a young woman who worked full-time at the Nursing Station as an interpreter, the injured man agreed to take a mild painkiller and a laxative. Neither of these medications was absolutely necessary, but their administration was an important symbolic statement of the nurse's power to intervene in people's lives.

Subsequently, the injured man became quite ill and his wife called the nurse back for another visit. She begged the nurse to send her husband south for better treatment, but the nurse refused, indicating that she would visit every day to monitor his condition. The injured man claimed that the medications were making him sick; he stated that he had never taken any medicine before in his life and believed they were poison designed by whites to make Inuit weak and dependent. Rumours spread through the community that he was dying, and that the nurse was refusing to send him out in order to demonstrate her power to him and break his independence.

Over the course of several interviews, I learned that the injured man felt he was being punished by God for a marital indiscretion his wife had committed after consuming alcohol. During this time period the village had experienced several traumatic, alcohol-related, accidental deaths and there was considerable pressure, particularly from the elders in the church, to prohibit alcohol from the community. The injured man was one of the main forces behind the move towards prohibition. In addition to his stature in the church, he was also a prominent member of the recently formed settlement council, and he was pushing that organization to petition the Territorial government to pass a prohibition by-law.

The anti-alcohol lobby in both the churches and council had a strong moral message, couched in traditional ideology. Alcohol caused people to lose their reason, to act like children, to ignore codes for appropriate behaviour between spouses and family members. The future of the "community" was at stake; if the principle of consensualism was to be maintained and traditional social control mechanisms sustained, people must stop drinking.

Clearly, the injury and "illness" of the shaman/elder was an important dramaturgical event in the life of a community attempting to articulate a culturally relevant vision of community health. The intrusion of the nurse into this event, and her attempt to control it without understanding its broader significance, was typical of the approach most northern nurses in the 1960s and 1970s had towards the communities in which they worked. They generally felt that Inuit had little understanding of health or illness and consequently felt responsible for all aspects of community health.

This materialistic structure is changing, due in part to a recent increase in the proportion of Canadian-trained nurses hired to work in the North. Canadian-trained nurses also tend to be younger, and hence lack the maturity and confidence to "control" the community to the same extent. Their training also has less emphasis on advanced clinical skills, which tends to make them less independent and more reliant on secondary and tertiary level physicians and specialists. Although there are exceptions, fewer Canadian-trained nurses develop a long-term commitment to their northern communities. Most indicate they would prefer to return to southern Canada to develop their careers, an option which was not always available to British-trained nurses for reasons of credentialling and immigration regulations.

While I am not arguing that nurses' nationality has a significant impact on the structure of their interaction with Inuit communities, there is considerable anecdotal evidence available to support the observation that Canadian-trained nurses bring a different professional and personal attitude to their work than their British-trained counterparts. In a previous paper I described a case that occurred in the mid-1970s in one Inuit village where the Nursing Station was staffed by a British-trained nurse-midwife and a Canadian-trained general duty nurse.[24] The British nurse-midwife adopted a comprehensive "healer" role and maintained an intimate knowledge of everyone in the community, which allowed her to intervene in their lives on all levels and in all circumstances. The Canadian nurse, on the other hand, saw herself more as a technician, who had professional tasks to perform as requested by clients, but who maintained a personal life separate from her clients.

In interviews, the Canadian nurse expressed dissatisfaction with an approach to community health which encouraged greater client dependency on the nurses' services. She felt that people needed to take greater responsibility themselves for health maintenance, and argued that the comprehensive involvement of the nurse in people's lives was counterproductive to the emergence of this attitude. From the community's perspective, the Canadian-trained nurse was behaving in an unacceptable manner. Her attempts to force clients to manage their own health status, which often entailed reprimands during clinical visits made outside regular hours, were interpreted by clients as simply rude and insensitive behaviour.

These two approaches to primary care services conflicted over issues such as policy regarding clinic hours and appropriate responses to client demands made outside of regular hours. These conflicts were serious enough that personal relations between the nurses deteriorated to the extent that the Canadian-trained nurse eventually resigned her position.

The northern primary care system has undergone recent changes for other reasons as well. Despite a steady increase in the technical capacity of primary care services available at the community level, and a steady decrease in morbidity, along most dimensions, medical evacuations to southern hospitals for both diagnostic and therapeutic procedures have been steadily increasing. Although as yet undocumented, many northern medical practitioners are aware of the trend towards southern referral for procedures once carried out locally in Nursing Stations. This concern was reflected in a recent, internally requested review of consultant services provided by the University of Manitoba to regions of northern Manitoba and the Northwest Territories. This review set terms of reference which included an assessment of unnecessary referrals stemming from specialist visits to remote communities.

This has been particularly true in obstetric care. In the mid-1970s, approximately 70 percent of deliveries were done in the communities, and there were cases where nurse-midwives had developed local systems where lay midwives from the community assisted in childbirth and infant care. This situation has changed dramatically. All Inuit women are now evacuated to southern transient centers up to six weeks prior to parturition, and local involvement of lay midwives has essentially disappeared.[25] Although a definitive study of the impact of this change in policy remains to be done, table 2 above suggests that there has been only minor improvements in perinatal mortality.

Inuit paraprofessional involvement in health care services has been on the decline in other areas as well. In the 1960s many smaller communities were served by Inuit "lay dispensers." These individuals were Inuit without any previous health care experience, of either a traditional or cosmopolitan orientation, who were given six weeks of intensive instruction in basic medicine, and left with the responsibility of basic diagnostic and medication procedures in small communities. They were in radio contact with nurses and/or physicians in larger communities and sometimes had the local support of resident white traders and missionaries.

When the construction of Nursing Stations in all Inuit communities was completed in the early 1970s, lay dispensers were no longer necessary and there was no attempt to upgrade their positions within the new health care system. Although some continued to work as interpreters or custodial workers in the newly constructed Nursing Stations, most were able to use the general experience of working for medical services to secure better paid and more responsible positions in the evolving municipal administrative structures.

Nonetheless, the new Nursing Stations offered positions for interpreters and other support staff (e.g., custodial workers) that were still economically attractive in situations where wage opportunities were scarce. Occasionally this resulted in prominent members of the community (i.e., men and women who belonged to large powerful families and who dominated locally elected councils which allocated employment opportunities) becoming interpreters or support staff in Nursing Stations. Since nurses in the 1970s were generally more independent and self-sufficient in terms of their relationship with the health care system, their relationship with their Inuit employees was often somewhat symbiotic and characterized by mutual respect. There are a number of cases in the North where prominent Inuit worked for up to ten years for the Nursing Stations and established a primary care role in the community that, while recognized and supported by the local nurse, was often ignored by the bureaucracy. These interpreters sometimes became part of the triage system; examining people after clinic hours to determine whether their complaint warranted attention from the nurses.[26]

However, Inuit involvement in health care delivery at even this most fundamental level has decreased. Support staff positions in Nursing Stations are no longer considered attractive employment opportunities. Other institutional sectors of community life such as education, housing and municipal services are territorial rather than Federal responsibilities. Although still somewhat hierarchical and ideologically removed from local interest, territorial services are significantly more accountable at the local level. Remuneration is generally better and the positions allow greater flexibility for incumbents to accommodate a land-based lifestyle. As a consequence, contemporary Inuit tend to be more interest in pursuing career employment opportunities in territorial and municipal institutions. Even the role of interpreters in health care is declining; not because there is less demand for language services, but because the positions are less attractive financially to people with the capabilities to potentially function in a more expanded health service role. Whereas medical interpreters were once mature and respected men and women in the community, they are increasingly younger and inexperienced, and indeed often have questionable linguistic abilities. Not only can older experienced men and women earn more money elsewhere, but there are few indications of either a structural or ideological nature that efforts by Inuit to build a paraprofessional primary care role within the health care institution will be rewarded.

Inuit involvement in primary health care in other than support roles has also been problematic. Although northern Medical Services have encouraged the development of local Health Committees and the training of Community Health Representatives (CHRs), and these efforts have been praised elsewhere in the literature,[27] I would contend there is little cause for celebration.

Health Committees, where they exist, are composed of seven or eight locally elected Inuit who function as an advisory board to the Nursing Station. Their role is to identify local health needs and communicate these needs to the nurses. They are expected to develop public health programs in response to identified problems, and to exert pressure on responsible agencies when particular public health hazards exist. However, most Health Committees disbanded several years after they were formed. Where they continue to meet intermittently, they function usually as personal complaint committees, relaying dissatisfactions with medical services to the nurses. While this is a potentially important function as well, it has tended to undermine the credibility of the Health Committees because nurses view them as ineffectual and unfairly critical.

In order to understand this failure, it is important to understand something of the local political structure and its relation to the regional and national political economy. Self-determination in other institutional sectors has come about as locally elected organizations struggled to assume fiscal responsibility in their respective areas. Typically, each Inuit village has a Hamlet Council, Education Society, Housing Association, and Co-op Board of Directors whose members are elected from a relatively circumscribed pool of prominent, middle-aged men and women in each village. These organizations were formed in the 1960s and 1970s initially as advisory bodies to various government departments who provide the bulk of external financial resources on which each community depends. Health Committees were formed in the same context and with similar objectives. However, these other local organizations have gradually assumed greater fiscal responsibility in controlling the administration of funds in each institutional sector (i.e., they set wage levels, hire and fire employees, construct yearly budgets, and, as happened recently with one Hamlet Council, donate money to Ethiopia out of a feeling of historical empathy with starving children).

Health Committees, by contrast, remain strictly advisory. While it is beyond the scope of the present paper to examine northern political evolution in detail, it is significant that at the community level, Medical Services remains one of two *federal* bureaucracies (the other being the Royal Canadian Mounted Police), while each of the other institutional sectors is territorially administered. While health care is administered from Ottawa almost exclusively by non-Inuit, the other services are centered closer to home in Yellowknife, where native people are increasingly well-represented in both the legislative bodies and bureaucracies.[28]

The impact of this political structure at the community level has meant that Health Committees are largely perceived as ineffectual by local political activists. Prominent men and women who are regularly elected to the other local organizations usually refuse nomination to the Health Committees. Membership is generally recruited from people with considerable experience in health care, which sometimes translates as the chronically ill and hypochondriachal.[29]

CHRs have also had variable success due to the political climate in which they must define their roles. While there are successful cases where CHRs have played a vital role in health education, health communication, and health advocacy, most of the Inuit CHRs trained in the 1970s are no longer working in the health field. Discussions of the role problems they have experienced generally focus on family and community level social and cultural factors.[30] From the perspective of this analysis, it is important to note that despite recommendations in earlier evaluations (mentioned above) that the CHRs needed to be structurally aligned with the local political organizations rather than with the federal bureaucracy, this has not occurred with any degree of success. Medical Services continues to provide the training curriculum. CHRs are socialized into accepting a role definition as a health service worker, which means their principal role support comes from resident local nurses rather than the Inuit sector of the community. The successful cases mentioned above usually arise, again, when an individual medical practitioner has an exceptional interest in community development.

Medicalization of Social Problems

The medicalization of social problems in Inuit communities has become a central facet of northern health ideology in the past five to ten years. As the primary care system brought morbidity from communicable diseases under control, problems associated with the stress of social change began to appear in Medical Services' annual reports as the leading causes of morbidity and mortality. Alcohol-related accidents and suicides are now considered the primary "medical" problems in northern Canadian communities. These problems are generally explained as "lifestyle" diseases which, in essence, "blames" individuals for failing to cope effectively with a changing social environment.[31] The medical response is to promote healthier lifestyles through problem-focused health education (i.e., alcohol education programs in the schools) or to provide more specialized health care practitioners such as mental health technicians or youth counsellors.[32]

The extent to which northern health ideology incorporates a commitment to community development in this regard is difficult to describe succinctly. On the one hand, Inuit paraprofessional workers, such as youth counsellors and alcohol educators, are socialized by non-Inuit health and social service personnel into a professional perspective which defines individual problems within the context of family and community. Family dynamics are usually considered in assessing the causes of an individual's drinking or mental health problems and the usual explanation offered is of a cultural nature. In families where there is apparent discontinuity between traditional and modern cultural interest, the conflict is considered the major dynamic in "coping failures." The health workers' task becomes one of "counselling" the family in order to ease the apparent cultural conflict.

This approach unfortunately overlooks the real source of cultural discontinuity which is related to the frontier capitalistic system. From the Inuit perspective, both traditional and modern subsistence strategies must be maintained within an extended family structure. The construction of social and cultural arrangements necessary to make those strategies successful is an essential survival strategy in a boom/bust economy where the larger economic system requires a flexible and mobile labour force. Conflict arises when either the family, or an individual member, finds himself no longer able to successfully exploit all subsistence avenues. For example, older men in a family may rely on younger men for the capital necessary to purchase the expensive technology which is now considered necessary for hunting and trapping. If the capital is unavailable, hunting success may decrease and the entire extended family suffers.[33]

However, northern health ideology maintains a strong separation between health issues and community development activities designed to address the economic problems described above. Even Inuit who are deeply involved in progressive political and economic movements find it difficult to see how their efforts relate to the health arena. In discussions with Inuit leaders in the land claims movement and Nunavut political forum (which are self-determination strategies designed to fundamentally restructure northern society), most could see little relevance in their work to improvements in health. Health care is still considered the responsibility of health care professionals who remain outside the developmental forum because of their symbolic power and formally bounded ideology. As social problems become increasingly medicalized, this distinction is potentially dangerous to the well-being of residents in northern communities.

Recent Trends and Future Developments

This trend towards desocializing health has been challenged in the past few years by several Inuit organizations that have begun to identify health care as a target for change. These organizations are usually the wellspring of socialist ideology in the North and stand outside the official administrative structure.[34] They are organizations dedicated to developing alternatives to the kind of government-sponsored tutelary social programs that are well described in the northern literature.[35]

For example, the Kitikmeot Inuit Association, which represents the interests of Inuit in the central Arctic region, has created a position for a Health Liaison Officer (HLO) whose primary objective is to generate interest in health issues at the community level. Superficially, her job description is similar to the CHRs described above. However, as a member of an organization dedicated to bringing about political and economic change within a culturally defined framework (i.e., establishing new forms of decision-making institutions that are more a reflection of traditional patterns of social organization than they are carbon copies of southern institutions), the HLO has the opportunity to provide a catalytic focus to new community health initiatives.

The principal obstacle to her success is the political struggle which the "socialist" Inuit organizations must wage within the "capitalist" political economy. While Inuit organizations are respected in the villages for their work in protecting the Inuit cultural heritage and pursuing land rights, they are still in the process of defining their mandate for holistic community development which would include health care and education. Since these activities are already the responsibilities of firmly entrenched territorial and federal bureaucracies that also control the fiscal infrastructure in the villages, this new "socialist" health ideology must struggle for political and economic legitimacy. Inuit in the communities are unlikely to find this initiative credible if these new health workers are practically excluded from the health care decision-making process and the allocation of health resources.

This same argument is relevant to several other initiatives that have occurred in the past few years. In one northern community, the Hamlet Council has petitioned Medical Services for the right to assume administrative control over the Nursing Station. This particular community and its representative political organizations are strongly collective in ideological orientation and express socialist principles (albeit in a "traditionalist" framework) in their efforts for community development. However, this "traditionalism" seems to have been interpreted by the bureaucracy as evidence for a lack of sophistication in administrative skills, and the petition has been refused.

In another case, the Keewatin Inuit Association, which is the regional counterpart of the Kitikmeot Inuit Association described above, is asking for a thorough review of all health services with an agenda of moving towards greater local responsibility in the health policy process. At issue is the technical capacity of village health clinics and the professional qualifications of local practitioners: one consequence of the impact of medicalization ideology on Inuit health dialogues is that many northern Inuit representatives are seeking the same level of health service available in southern urban centers for their own communities. They are insisting that hospitals and specialists are required before health status will improve. Behind this demand is a strong anti-colonial sentiment and a sense that community development (and health improvements) begin with political action.

Important to each of the above cases is the emerging role of contemporary health care providers with a commitment to the creation of a "socialist health system"—a system which empowers people to develop locally appropriate programs and interventions. At all levels of the health care system—community nurses, regional physicians, administrators and university-based specialists—there are health care professionals dedicated to restructuring the prevailing colonial model of health services. In each of the cases described there are individual health professionals who have worked with Inuit representatives in an attempt to accomplish shared objectives. In the case of the Kitikmeot Inuit Association, the regional physician has acted as an advisor to their program development and has lobbied on their behalf to different levels of government. In the case of the community petitioning for transfer of control, the local nurses documented gaps in health services available and made this report available to Hamlet Council to support their claim. In the case of the Keewatin Inuit Association's desire for a policy review, the university-based medical consulting group has advised and lobbied with Ottawa on their behalf.

These cases indicate that the struggle for *real* community development in northern health services has perhaps just begun. Previous initiatives, generated from within colonial frameworks, have failed largely because of structural factors outside the influence of Inuit villages. However, these new negotiations are also being conducted in a political climate where socialist orientations are in a difficult struggle for survival. The national political economy has, and will continue to confuse ideological issues in Fourth World contexts in order to perpetuate the economic dependency of frontier regions on the metropolis. Medical ideology and the health policy process have been negotiated in this context with unexpected outcomes. Colonial medical bureaucracies *appear* to have been fostering local involvement in health services through the establishment of health committees and liaison workers, and Inuit political organizations *appear* to be demanding a typically urban, high technology, doctor-dominated and hospital-based form of medical care. Since both initiatives are produced according to implicit agendas which are part of larger ideological struggles—on the one hand to maintain control over medical change, and on the other to decolonize the northern health care system—the dialectic is not yet a dialogue.

Discussion

In this paper I have outlined the major structural and historical dimensions of health ideology and praxis in the context of northern Canadian society. I have addressed specifically the fundamental contradictions that exist where a very expensive primary care system is maintained with little input from the clients of the service, and is increasingly ineffective in the face of a changing epidemiological picture where health problems are linked directly to broader community development issues. I have argued that these contradictions can be at best partially understood as a product of an internal colonial economic and political system where an indigenous socialist ideology must compete for existence within the national capitalist political economy. I would conclude that the greatest danger posed by this struggle is the increasing extent to which northern social life is medicalized and health is divorced from fundamental community development issues. We are already seeing evidence that health services are failing to meet the challenge that the changing epidemiological picture in the North has created. And thus we have the ultimate paradox where a rural primary health care system, which by most standards could be a model for the rest of the world, is failing because it continues to exclude its clients from a fundamental involvement in its structure.

Notes

1. B. Paul, *Health, Culture and Community* (New York: Russell Sage, 1955).
2. A.L. Bloom and J. Reid, eds., "Anthropology and Primary Health Care in Developing Countries," *Social Science and Medicine* 19, 3 (1984).
3. Hans Baer, "On the Political Economy of Health," *Medical Anthropology Newsletter* 14, 1 (1982): 1–2, 13–17.
4. Oscar Gish, "The Political Economy of Primary Health Care and 'Health by the People': An Historical Exploration," *Social Science and Medicine* 13C (1979): 203–11; Ronald Frankenberg, "Medical Anthropology and Development: A Theoretical Perspective," *Social Science and Medicine* 14B (1980): 197–207.
5. Malcolm Segall, "On the Question of a Socialist Health System: A Question of Marxist Epidemiology," *International Journal of Health Services* 13, 2 (1983): 221–25.

6. H.K. Heggenhougen, "Will Primary Health Care Efforts Be Allowed to Succeed?" *Social Science and Medicine* 19, 3 (1984): 217–25; J.J. Marchione, "Evaluating Primary Health Care and Nutrition Programs in the Context of National Development," *Social Science and Medicine* 19, 3 (1984): 225–37; Setha Low, *Culture, Politics and Medicine in Costa Rica* (Salem, N.Y.: Redgrave Publishing, 1984).

7. Nelson H. Graburn, "1, 2, 3, 4...Anthropology and the Fourth World," *Culture* 1, 1 (1981): 66–70.

8. Gurston Dacks, *A Choice of Futures: Politics in the Canadian North* (Toronto: Methuen Publications); M. Hechter, *Internal Colonialism: The Celtic Fringe in British National Development, 1536–1966* (London: Routledge and Kegan Paul, 1975).

9. Alternative constellations are also possible. Local and regional capitalist/conservative indigenous ideologies within national socialist political economies (e.g., aboriginal peoples in the Soviet Union) or aligned regional/national political economies could, and probably do, occur. Analysis of local-level health practices in these situations, if they exist, would provide a comparative framework for understanding the situation described in this paper. I would contend, however, that the particular constellation described here is probably the predominant model in most Fourth World contexts.

10. J.B. Sykes, ed., *The Concise Oxford Dictionary of Current English* (Oxford: Clarendon Press, 1982), 1006.

11. Sykes, ed., *Concise Oxford Dictionary*, 136.

12. Sykes, ed., *Concise Oxford Dictionary*, 200.

13. Michael Asch, *Home and Native Land: Aboriginal Rights and the Canadian Constitution* (Toronto: Methuen, 1984).

14. T.K. Young, "The Canadian North and the Third World: Is the Analogy Appropriate?" *Canadian Journal of Public Health* 74 (1983): 239–41.

15. Young, "Canadian North and the Third World," 240.

16. Hugh Brody, *The People's Land: Eskimos and Whites in the Eastern Arctic* (Middlesex, England: Penguin Books, 1975); Dacks, *A Choice of Futures*. One reviewer of this paper argued that local, regional and national Inuit political organizations are little more than "artifacts of a pseudo-democratic colonial system," show little ideological or structural continuity with traditional culture, and do not seem to be particularly socialist in character. Although rarely expressed in print, this critique is representative of a "cynical/romanticist" interpretation of the political development of indigenous peoples which is evident among some anthropologists in Canada. Although an important debate, it is beyond the scope of the present paper to engage in a detailed discussion of the political evolution of indigenous peoples. I would contend, however, that the "cynical/romanticist" argument suffers from the same limitations in analytical perspective that I outlined at the beginning of the paper. To condemn indigenous leaders as political opportunists alienated from their culture and without social vision, ignores the fact that these leaders must work within powerful sociopolitical structures whose interests are sustained if the credibility of indigenous leaders is compromised.

17. Anne McElroy, "Inuit Alliance Movements in the Canadian Arctic," in *Political Organizations of Native North Americans*, ed. E.L. Schusky (Washington, D.C.: University of Washington Press, 1980), 121–45.

18. D. Jenness, *Eskimo Administration: II, Canada* Arctic Institute of North America Technical Paper 14 (Washington, 1964), Robert G. Williamson, *Eskimo Underground: Sociocultural Change in the Canadian Central Arctic* (Uppsala, Sweden: University of Uppsala Press, 1974).

19. G. Wenzel, "Inuit Health and the Health Care System: Change and Status Quo," *Etudes/Inuit/Studies* 5, 1 (1981): 7–17.

20. G. Graham-Cumming, "Northern Health Services," *Canadian Medical Association Journal* 100 (1969): 526–31.

21. Corinne Hodgson, "The Social and Political Implications of Tuberculosis among Native Canadians," *Canadian Review of Sociology and Anthropology* 19, 4 (1982): 502–12.

22. B.H. Brett, "A Synopsis of Northern Medical History," *Canadian Medical Association Journal* 100 (1969): 521–26.

23. John D. O'Neil, "Observations on the Medicalization of Inuit Social Life," in *Circumpolar Health '84*, ed. R. Fortuine (Seattle: University of Washington Press, 1985), 436–43.

24. John D. O'Neil, "Health Care in a Canadian Arctic Village: Continuities and Change," in *Health and Canadian Society*, ed. D. Coburn et al. (Toronto: Fitzhenry and Whiteside, 1981), 123–42.

25. L. Guse, "Maternal Evacuation: A Study of the Experiences of Northern Manitoba Native Women," University College Ethnology Papers (Winnipeg, 1982).

26. O'Neil, "Health Care in a Canadian Arctic Village."

27. Hope Spencer, "Native Community Health Auxiliaries: Developments in Northern Canada, 1973–4,"in *Circumpolar Health*, ed. R.J. Shepard and S. Hoh (Toronto: University of Toronto Press, 1976): 588–91; A.K. Smith, "Indian and Eskimo Health Auxiliaries: Developments in Northern Canada," in *Circumpolar Health*, 591–96.

28. Dacks discusses the implications of these differences in *A Choice of Futures*. He argues that although northern politics are still colonial in general character, the increasing native representation, and particularly the somewhat radical and socialist representation that is part of the land claims and aboriginal rights movement, means that the territorial government is increasingly aligned with the communities rather than, as it was previously, functioning as token representation for Ottawa.

29. There are, of course, exceptions to these generalizations and I do not mean to belittle those occasions where Health committees have been active and successful in the field of public health and/or community development. However, when these exceptions occur, there is often a local individual or a medical practitioner with a particularly profound commitment to community health who provides the catalyst for Health Committee development.

30. Task Force on Community Health Auxiliaries, *Community Health Auxiliaries* (Ottawa: Health and Welfare Canada, 1973).

31. C.F.R. Love, D. Coburn, and J.M. Kaufert, "Beyond Individual Accountability: Public Policy Perspectives," in *Community Health Action*, ed. D. Paul Lumsden (Ottawa: Canadian Public Health Association, 1984).

32. John D. O'Neil, "Is It Cool to Be an Eskimo? A Study of Stress, Identity, Coping and Health among Inuit Young Adult Men" (Ph.D. diss., University of California, San Francisco-Berkeley, 1984).

33. O'Neil, "Is It Cool to Be an Eskimo?"

34. Questions have been raised in the review of this paper concerning the accuracy of describing Inuit ethnonationalist organizations as socialist. These questions in fact highlight the heart of Segall's argument in "On the Question of a Socialist Health System," outlined in the introduction to this paper that controversy of this type is misdirected. Obviously, Inuit organizations cannot be empirically demonstrated to be a pure form of socialist ideology. Indeed, where contradictions in rhetoric or praxis exist, these contradictions should be understood as a symptom of the overwhelming co-opting power of a national capitalist/conservative political

economy, rather than intrinsic structural faults in Inuit organizations themselves. Although Inuit organizations vary in the extent to which they publicly iterate policy of a distinctly socialist character, I maintain that the basic commitment to achieving communal ownership of land and a consensual sociopolitical structure is sufficient evidence to justify the argument presented here.

35.   Robert Parne, ed., *The White Arctic: Anthropological Essays on Tutelage and Ethnicity*, Newfoundland Social and Economic Papers, no. 7 (Institute of Social and Economic Research, Memorial University of Newfoundland, 1977); Brody, *The People's Land.*

Capital and Economic Development: A Critical Appraisal of the Recommendations of the Mackenzie Valley Pipeline Commission*

MICHAEL I. ASCH

To those concerned only with the Mackenzie Valley gas pipeline debate, an article criticizing the findings of Mr. Justice Berger's Mackenzie Valley Gas Pipeline Inquiry (popularly known as the Berger Inquiry) might appear to be trivial or at best of purely academic interest. In fact, nothing could be further from the truth. In finding against the construction of the pipeline in the near future, Justice Berger made specific recommendations for the future development of the Mackenzie River Valley. These recommendations now are finding support among influential northern researchers, administrators, and government planners. Indeed, it appears that even the Government of the Northwest Territories (which once labelled Berger's report as "racist") is now looking with favour on them. In other words, Berger's findings, far from being only of historic interest, are of extreme moment for they may well become the blueprint for the economic future of the North. As such, they deserve continued critical scrutiny.

Although it urgently needs doing, a complete critique and appraisal of the Report is beyond the scope of this contribution. Rather, here I will narrow my focus to one critical issue: the practicality of Berger's recommendations to achieve one goal: the maintenance of the Dene traditional way of life, or as Berger styles it "the native economy"[1] within the context of a modern northern economy.

* *Culture* 2, 3 (1982): 3–9. An earlier version of this paper was presented to the Second International Conference on Hunting-Gathering Societies, Quebec City, September 1980.

To this end, I will first briefly outline Berger's plan for northern development. Then, after exploring some of the main theoretical bases for this plan,
I will proceed to evaluate its usefulness in achieving the stated objective.
While I will provide much more detail below, at heart my critique is that
Berger's plan is founded upon an improper assessment of the native economy
and that this results in his recommending a plan which will have an effect opposite to that which he intends. That is, if faithfully followed, his plan will
lead to the destruction of the native economy and its replacement by a renewable resource sector based on the imperatives of the capitalist mode of production. Therefore, his program is not useful and ought to be rejected. Then in my
conclusion I will offer an alternative introduced to the Inquiry but rejected by
Mr. Justice Berger.[2] It is the plan advanced by the Dene themselves, the nub
of which is the demand for political and economic self-determination by
northern natives within Confederation. It is this proposal which I will argue is
the only one which stands any chance of success to attain the goal Berger
seeks.

Berger's Plan for Northern Development

In the view of the proponents of Mackenzie Valley gas pipeline, the political
economy of the Mackenzie River Valley can be described as in a period of
transition from a form based on the traditional economic pursuits of hunting,
fishing, and trapping to an industrial one based on wage labour and the
market. At the moment, their argument goes, there is a "dual economy" in
the region. This consists of one "backward" sector which exploits traditional
resources and one "modern" one which mainly exploits non-renewable
resources. As time goes on, however, the inherent superiority of the rational
industrial economy is such that it will inevitably replace the backward and ir-
rational one. The pipeline is merely one further step in that inexorable
process.

The view that the "traditional" or "native" economy is virtually moribund
and would soon wither away was strongly and successfully refuted by the testimony of expert witnesses speaking on behalf of native organizations and by
native witnesses themselves. Rather, they showed a viable and dynamic
economic sector which still provided much material, as well as spiritual sustenance for native people.[3] This was the view of the native economy accepted
by Justice Berger and it is his acceptance of this view that forms the basis of
his proposal.

Thus, in volume 1, Berger specifically rejects the "dual economy" position
and asserts rather that the traditional sector is a viable entity which forms,
along with the virtually independent and equally viable "modern" sector, a
unity which Berger calls "the mixed economy." The unity of this mixed
economy is created by the economic activities of native people so that "in the

north today, the lives of many native families were based on an intricate economic mix. At certain times of the year, they hunt and fish; at other times they work for wages, sometimes for government, sometimes on highway construction, sometimes for the oil and gas industry."[4]

Further, it is in their ability to synthesize two vastly different economic sectors into a single economic round that Berger finds one unique characteristic of the native people and of the northern political economy itself.[5] And it is to the end of preserving a "mixed economy" with two viable but virtually independent sectors that Berger's proposals on northern development are dedicated. That is, as he asserts, "The objective of Northern development should be parallel economic sectors—large scale industrial activity where and when appropriate, co-existing with continuing development of the native economy and the renewable resources sector."[6]

At the moment, according to Berger, the main problem in the realization of this goal is that the native economy is unable under present economic conditions to provide sufficient capital and employment opportunities for native people. As a result, many native people who might not otherwise do so, must seek wage employment outside the native economy. Such a process would be accelerated by the presence of a large-scale non-renewable resource-based project such as the proposed Mackenzie Valley gas pipeline and indeed could well completely undermine the native economy. Therefore, Berger urges that the goal of northern development of at least the next decade should be to strengthen the native economy so that it can compete successfully with the non-renewable resource-based sector for capital and labour.

To this end Berger specifically recommends the following. First, primary production of renewable resources traditionally associated with the native economy should be modernized and expanded so that production is increased to maximum sustainable yields. Second, to increase employment in the native economy, new industries based on the exploitation of these resources should be created. Among others, these could include fur farming and tanning. Finally, Berger recommends the expansion of the economy into new but allied fields such as tourism.[7]

Once the infrastructure needed to run such a modernized renewable resource-based economy is in place, Berger believes it will generate enough capital and employment opportunities to compete successfully for native labour with the job opportunities available on major one-time non-renewable resource-based projects such as the proposed Mackenzie Valley gas pipeline. In other words, at this point a strong and independent native economy will have been constructed and thus Berger's main development objective will have been realized.

Of course, before such an infrastructure can be created, much capital will be required. This capital, native organizations argue, could come from rents, royalties, taxes, and other monies generated by non-renewable resource activities on their lands. However, Berger specifically rejected this idea and instead proposed that, until the renewable resource-based sector in the north is able to generate its own capital, government could make funds available as a matter of public policy pursuant to such programs as the Western Northlands, established under the Department of Regional Economic Expansion (DREE), or pursuant to the Agriculture Rural Development Act (ARDA).[8]

At the heart of the matter it is Berger's position on this crucial point that is at issue.

Critique of Berger's Program

Broadly speaking, I am in complete agreement with Justice Berger's characterization of the contemporary "native economy." That is, I would assert that it is viable but weak. Furthermore, we both agree that a basic goal of northern development must be the strengthening of that economy. Where we disagree fundamentally is on the remedies necessary to attain that goal. Ultimately, the basis for this disagreement can be found to lie in our theoretical stance in general and in particular how we each would define "economy."

To Berger, an economy is defined primarily on the basis of the technical factors of production. Of these, the most important to him are the productive processes associated with the exploitation of a particular staple. In this, Berger is following his own reading of Harold Innis's staples theory and especially the following passage from *Empire and Communication*, cited in his text:

> Concentration on the production of staples for export to more highly industrialized areas in Europe and later in the United States had broad implications for the Canadian economic, political, and social structure. Each staple in turn left its stamp, and the shift to new staples invariably produced periods of crises in which adjustments in the old structure were painfully made and a new pattern created in relation to a new staple.[9]

Using this framework, Berger defines the "native economy" as a unified entity for it consists of a complementary set of small scale productive activities oriented around certain traditional bush staples. The weakness in this economy today, then, is attributed to the stamp of a new staple (oil, gas and minerals) on the lives of native people and the period of crises and adjustment which must inevitably accompany it.[10] This crisis is reflected in the relative lack of capital and job opportunities in the native economy vis-à-vis the sector devoted to the exploitation of the newly dominant staple. The problem and the solution, then, to Berger is attributable to technical factors alone.

In my estimation, Berger is partially correct in this analysis, for, indeed, the lack of capital and job opportunities are significant reasons for the weakness of the "native economy." Yet, this analysis is incomplete for there are urgent social and political problems tied directly to the technical ones which must be attended to with equal urgency. These can easily be seen if we switch our conceptual framework away from Berger's so as to include within our definition of economy the institutional framework of production: that is, if we move from a "staples approach" to a "mode of production" one.[11]

Although when examined from Berger's perspective the native economy can be defined as a unity, when institutional parameters are added, such is no longer the case. Rather, what emerges is that contained within the native economy are two modes of production.

On the one hand, there is what I have called the bush subsistence mode of production.[12] From it, the Dene provide for themselves through locally produced and finished goods many of their subsistence needs. This is done within a framework in which co-operative labour, collective economic responsibility, communal land tenure and the mutual sharing of surpluses are valued and institutionalized. It is a mode, it must be emphasized, which is not used to produce cash.

To obtain cash and/or trade goods, native people participate in another mode of production: capitalism. During the fur trade era, they did this primarily in the role of small-scale commodity producers who, like the family farmer, traded a cash crop for essential goods produced by the industrialized world. Through this involvement with the fur trade native people came into contact with the institutional framework of capitalism with its attendant institutions and values that stress private ownership of property, individual accumulation of goods, and individual economic responsibility.

In the fur trade era, the economy operated such that the capitalist institutional framework remained subordinate in the daily life of the Dene, so that they lived primarily under the influence of institutions and values associated with the traditional bush subsistence mode of production. How this was achieved is an important concern which I describe elsewhere.[13] However, the important point here is that with the collapse of fur prices and the concomitant inflation in the price of trade goods in the period since the end of the second World War, native people have had to seek cash from sources other than furs. This has resulted in a very marked increase in the impingement of capitalist institutions and values on their daily lives.

That this is the case for those for whom wage labour has become the principal means of obtaining cash should be self-evident. However, for most native people cash income is still not derived in this way. Rather, it comes in forms such as transfer payments which do not require labour input. Yet, it does not follow that such income is therefore free from the influence of capitalist values and institutions. Indeed, rather the contrary is the case. As in other capitalist transactions, these payments are made directly to individuals or nuclear family heads. Thus, they emphasize the separateness of these units and individualize ownership of property. As a result, these payments conflict with those institutions and values generated by the traditional mode of production in which emphasis is placed on the community as an indivisible economic unit and on the collectivity of property ownership. The case is particularly striking with respect to welfare. The payment of welfare to individuals and nuclear families isolated poverty and created a division between "rich" and "poor." Thus, it not only relieves the community of its traditional responsibility to share mutually, it actually provides the context for the penetration of its antithetical tendency, characteristic of the capitalist mode of production: social differentiation based on relative wealth.

In other words the weakness in the native economy today is not merely that it lacks capital and job opportunities but equally that its traditional institutions and values are being eroded by the very means native people must use to obtain essential cash. Today, the bush subsistence mode is still dominant in the daily lives of most native people but, even without the presence of large-scale non-renewable resource developments, is steadily losing this position as the need for cash drives native people further and further into the institutional sphere of capitalism.

Thus, in order for northern development to work, what is required is that the program adopted not only provide capital and jobs for the native economy, but that it does so in such a way that the impact of capitalist institutions decreases in the daily lives of native people. Berger's plan, then, is inadequate because he fails to attend to this very real concern. As a result, it can be expected that if his plan is adopted, traditional institutions and values will continue to lose their dominant place in the life of native people. Furthermore, Berger's program itself may well act to accelerate the pace of erosion. Large-scale government grants, it should be clear, differ little from small-scale ones such as transfer payments in their institutional implications; that is, like small-scale ones, they were formulated within an economic context that assumes the institutions and values of capitalism. In the case of large grants such as those made by DREE, this fact will be reflected in the very assumptions upon which grants are given: assumptions such as, that the grantee follow "standard business practices" or that the operation will be constructed so that it will ultimately show a "profit." As a result, it is not hard to imagine that in order to obtain funding native people will be forced to develop their renewable resources within a capitalist institutional framework. In other words, in the process of developing it, native people may well be forced to transform the native economy into a renewable resource sector of the local capitalist economy: a result which is antithetical to Berger's own stated objective.

Application to the Dene

The problem, then, of northern development is to provide sufficient capital to create an infrastructure for a modern renewable resource economy in a manner that promotes traditional institutions and values rather than capitalist ones. Such a problem admits of no easy or certain solution. In fact, in my opinion, there is only one approach which stands any chance of success. It is the proposal presented to the Berger Inquiry by the native northerners themselves: the power to determine for themselves their political and economic future within Confederation, including, among other powers, the right to control and tax all economic developments undertaken in the traditional homelands of these people.

The advantages of such a solution are two-fold. In the first place, it is a practical means for raising capital sufficient to meet all the economic needs of native northerners. For example, as Dr. Arvin Jelliss pointed out in evidence presented to the Inquiry, proper and equitable taxation of non-renewable resource operations now in place on Dene lands alone would yield a sum of approximately $51 million per annum (in 1974 dollars).[14] Such an income provided each year would easily provide the Dene with sufficient capital to service their total trade good needs, to develop within perhaps a decade the infrastructure necessary to operate the kind of economy outlined by Berger, and to provide a cash cushion to secure the long-term sustained operation of this economy.[15]

Secondly, this form of capital accumulation attends well to the problem of the continued penetration of capitalist institutions. To begin with, it does not require that native people participate in their daily lives or even orient any of their economic activities to capitalist institutions, for cash is generated without labour input. Furthermore, unlike government grants, these funds will be controlled and administered solely by native people. Thus, provided the native people can create such a development plant, these funds could easily be dispersed in a manner which promotes institutions and values of the bush subsistence mode of production. Finally, it is important to note that capital generated in this manner would be controlled by the native community as a whole and thus would remain consistent with their traditional framework which emphasized communal ownership of resources.

This, of course, is not to say that the solution proposed by the native people is perfect, far from it. Indeed, there are many major problems associated with it. Among these are the following. First, and perhaps most importantly, given the contemporary political situation in this country and particularly the specific rejection of this proposal by the Federal Government, it is highly unlikely that such powers could be quickly or easily obtained. Furthermore, even if these powers were granted, there is no certainty that a modern resource economy based on traditional institutions and values could be constructed. For example, it may not be possible to maintain a traditional form of egalitarianism as the division of labour shifts from its simple form in which everyone does just about the same thing, as is characteristic of the bush subsistence mode of production to a complex form with a high degree of specialization which modernization would entail. As well, the process of development itself may lead to class divisions as some native people gain the sophisticated knowledge necessary to oversee non-renewable resource industries and thus become alienated from the life-style of other native northerners.

Finally there is the ever present danger that the form of articulation with capitalist institutions envisioned in this proposal may itself act to undermine the ultimate goal. For example, it is a fact that the renewable resource sector will be dependent for a time for its capital on an economic component that is not necessarily compatible with it. As a result, native people may be manoeuvered into a situation where their long-term objectives must be sacrificed in the interests of obtaining immediate capital. This concern is particularly real in the North for the industry with which native northerners must negotiate is, to say the least, not known for its sensitivity to the environmental and economic interests of local inhabitants. Also, there is the ever-present concern that, when confronted with the option, native people may voluntarily choose short-term cash benefits rather than forego these gains to create the capital base necessary to construct the kind of economy they say they want and thus to ensure in the process that such an economy is never built.

In the past year, these issues have started to come into sharper focus among the Dene. This is due in the main to the Government of Canada's approval for the construction of a $20 million oil pipeline south along the Mackenzie River Valley from Norman Wells and the restart of negotiations over the outstanding aboriginal rights claim.

The Dene have responded to the challenges by beginning to flesh out in much more detail how their institutional arrangements might be adapted to a modern policy and economy. To date, most of the work has been undertaken in the political area. It has resulted in a proposal known as *Denendeh* which calls for consensus government in the Valley based on a traditional band model which nonetheless allows within its domain provision for non-native active participants (as equal band members) in the decision-making process once they have learned Dene culture.[16]

Although less work has been done in the economic area, it is significant to note that the Dene have not limited their concerns in this area to obtaining capital alone. Rather, Dene groups at both the national and local levels have started to work on how they might shape economic institutions in a manner consistent with decision-making principles found in the *Denendeh* document. In particular, interest is being shown in the area of ascertaining how a Dene-controlled enterprise might handle such issues as hiring, firing, wages, profits, management—labour relations, and the relationship of such enterprises to the community they serve.

Clearly, to create such an institutional setting will be a long process. However the fact that it is being worked on seems a clear indication that the Dene are seriously considering the option that will maximize the chance that their way of decision-making and their value orientation will not be lost as development begins in earnest.

Conclusions

The nub of the problem for renewable resource development in the North is two-fold. First, it is necessary to find large sources of capital to fund the new infrastructure essential to the economic well-being of the sector. The second problem, is to find a source of funds which allow maximum flexibility for the native group to promote in the development of this infrastructure the kinds of traditional institutions and values they wish to assert.

At the Berger hearings two proposals for obtaining these funds were put forward. The first, initiated by the Dene, called for a method which relied on obtaining rents and royalties on lands recognized under their jurisdiction. It is a solution which is rejected explicitly by Mr. Justice Berger when he states:

> The various native claims proposals include provisions for the transfer of capital to native control, chiefly through royalties on non-renewable resource development. Evidence from Alaska suggests that this is not without problems: it can create rather than reduce dependence on externally controlled development. Capital transfers will not, in themselves, assure the appropriate financing of renewable resource development unless specific provisions for that purpose are incorporated in native claims settlements.[17]

In short, he rejects it for he fears that the Dene may not be able to withstand pressures to use the funds for other purposes.

As an alternative, Berger proposes the second possibility: that the Dene and other northern native groups obtain funding through Federal Government grants. This solution, I have argued here, must be rejected on the grounds that such funding carries with it a set of capitalist institutional appendages which will inexorably lead the native economy away from a traditional institutional and value framework. Failure to discuss this potential eventuality I traced in part to Mr. Justice Berger's adopting the staples theory as his analytic stance.

Myself, I see no third option. On the one hand, the capital can come directly from government either in the form suggested by Berger or through direct cash payments as in the case of the James Bay corporations. Or, on the other hand, it must come indirectly through rents and royalties on lands controlled by the native society. I share with Justice Berger the concern that the latter option may well prove problematic as the opportunity to obtain these funds and hence use them to other ends becomes more real. It is a concern which I believe remains valid, but should be tempered by the experience of the past year.

At heart, though, I feel there is no other option. Rents and royalties may provide temptations, but they are better than any other form of potential cash flow in that: they come in a form which is "collective"; they do not require significant labour input; and they are obtained on a continuing rather than a one-time basis. Each of these, I have argued, is a prerequisite if the form capital takes is to allow maximum flexibility to initiate institutional innovations. It is for these reasons that I believe it is necessary to conclude that only the kind of proposal which the Dene have put forward offers any practical hope to ensure that a native economy consistent with Dene traditional institutions and values can become a reality.

Notes

1. Mr. Justice Thomas Berger, *Northern Frontier, Northern Homeland: The Report of the Mackenzie Valley Pipeline Inquiry*, 2 vols. (Ottawa: The Queen's Printer, 1978), 1:122.

2. Berger, *Northern Frontier, Northern Homeland*, 2:41.

3. This view has recently been supported by experts at the hearings into the Norman Wells pipeline application.

4. Berger, *Northern Frontier, Northern Homeland*, 1:122.

5. Berger, *Northern Frontier, Northern Homeland*, 1: 121.

6. Berger, *Northern Frontier, Northern Homeland*, 2:4.

7. Berger, *Northern Frontier, Northern Homeland*, 2: chapter 2.

8. Berger, *Northern Frontier, Northern Homeland*, 2: 41.

9. Berger, *Northern Frontier, Northern Homeland*, from Harold Innis, *Empire and Communications* (Toronto: Uptown Press, 1950).

10. Berger, *Northern Frontier, Northern Homeland*, 1:118.

11. Michael Asch, "The Ecological-Evolutionary Model and the Concept of Mode of Production," in *Challenging Anthropology*, ed. D. Turner and G. Smith (Toronto: McGraw-Hill Ryerson, 1979), 81–99.

12. Michael Asch, "The Economics of Dene Self-Determination," in *Challenging Anthropology*, 339–52.

13. Asch, "The Economics of Dene Self-Determination."

14. Arvin Jelliss, "Economic Rents," in *Dene Nation: The Colony Within*, ed. M. Watkins (Toronto: University of Toronto Press, 1977).

15. Asch, "The Economics of Dene Self-Determination."

16. Dene National Office, *Public Government for the People of the North* (Yellowknife: Dene Nation, 1981).

17. Berger, *Northern Frontier, Northern Homeland*, 2:42.

CANADIAN CONTRADICTIONS: FORTY YEARS OF NORTHERN POLITICAL DEVELOPMENT*

FRANCES ABELE

A sympathetic friend from France asked a very simple question this summer: Why does Canada exist? As an economist aware of the powerful tug of the United States economy, and as a citizen of a nation with much more cultural coherence, he meant: How does Canada survive?

His question prompted an hour of increasingly involved and perhaps not very persuasive explanation from the Canadians present. We were not surprised that explanation was so difficult. Canadians are accustomed to this problem.

In this essay, I propose that one account of Canada's survival is to be found in a careful reading of the recent political history of Canada's two northern territories. When the question of Canadian identity arises, it has been traditional for politicians (like John Diefenbaker) and writers (like Pierre Berton and Farley Mowat) to invoke northern imagery. Recent northern political history has revealed, however, that the old northern images are mere romance. Native peoples' political mobilization, their communication of their own interpretation of northern reality and their plans for the North's future have fundamentally changed the way in which the North is comprehended.

This change has only increased the importance of understanding northern political and economic issues; "the North" continues to be evocative. This is so because recent northern political development has been a compressed reiteration of earlier national struggles and dilemmas, and because current outstanding issues in the North crystallize major national concerns.

To make this case, I must rely upon some undefended generalizations about the characteristic patterns of Canadian development. These generalizations

* Arctic 40, 4 (December 1987): 310–20. The author would like to thank John Crump, Gurston Dacks, Mark Dickerson, Katherine Graham, David Hawkes, Graham Rowley, and Margaret McGee.

are not universally accepted, but neither are they idiosyncratic. They are developed from the works cited in the next section of the paper. The generalizations frame a narrative overview of the major phases in northern political history, with emphasis upon the last forty years.

Considering the recent period in this way exposes its continuity with the rest of Canadian development. The continuity is related to contradictions in Canadian conceptions of the role of the state and the nature of democracy and to the persistence of the "National Policy" economic development strategy. When the similarities are exposed, differences become more obvious. The most important of these is that, in contrast to the situation in the rest of the country, the foundations of northern constitutional practice have not solidified, nor has the economy of the North fully taken shape. Very great national issues still hang in the balance.

Colonial Dominion: Patterns of Canadian Development

Canada as a politically independent nation has known a protracted gestation. It was over fifty years after Confederation in 1867 before Canadian representatives spoke for Canada internationally without British sponsorship. The written constitution was patriated over a century after Confederation, and we are still completing the long collective labour to agree upon a written text.

There are good reasons for the difficult birth. We began with a hybrid form, a federal structure grafted to the parliamentary model that evolved in tiny, unitary, imperial England. From the beginning, compromise has been important. The presence of Quebec, and of francophones in other provinces, has compelled recognition of difference. There have been repeated attempts to accommodate the goal of equal treatment to the reality of cultural differences.[1]

Compromise has also been difficult. Colonial patterns of government prevailed through small-holder rebellions in Upper and Lower Canada in the 1830s, during the negotiations that produced Confederation, and after 1867 during the consolidation of Dominion control over the lands north and west of Ontario.[2] The old written constitution, the British North America Act (now the Constitution [1867]) soberly divides jurisdiction and revenue opportunities between two levels of government and carefully delineates the extent of religious and educational expression for francophone, Roman Catholic Quebec. The machinery of government is outlined as a function of executive prerogative, not as an expression of the citizens' will. To the extent that systematic expression of the will of the people was considered at Confederation, it is clear that all drafters assumed that Canadian practice would follow the British parliamentary model and that practices in Canada would evolve here as conditions dictated. This assumption persists as the "unwritten" part of our constitution. Thus the Constitution (1867) lacks the inspiring revolutionary rhetoric of, for example, the American constitution, as well as any reference to responsible government (control of the budget by elected officials) or to individual rights.

Constitutions record the balance of social forces in the nations for which they are written. The British North America Act was drafted by a fractious colonial elite who conceived the Canadian state as a solution to various problems of markets and capitalization created by American protectionism and expansionism and the waning of commercial privileges granted to British colonies.[3] These conditions determined that the state would play from the beginning an active role in creating a domestic economy. The Fathers of Confederation used the new Canadian state to borrow the capital needed to build a transcontinental transportation system, to displace western indigenous peoples with no more than the necessary level of coercion, to import a labour force, and to raise tariff barriers that protected central Canadian manufacturing from U.S. competition. This was the National Policy of 1878–1879, a program that worked reasonably well for fifty years. In a favourable international market setting, a national economy was created in which western farmers produced wheat for export while providing a captive market for manufactured goods from central Canada. Capital drained steadily from the old commercial centres of the Maritimes to central Canada.[4]

The state that achieved these feats cannot be seen as *laissez-faire*. A *laissez-faire* state is minimalist, an umpire restrained from active intervention in the economy except where it is necessary to enforce the rules of fair competition by protecting the rights of individual economic and political actors.[5] Early Canadian conceptions of the role of the state were "Tory," the old form of British conservatism elaborated by Edmund Burke and by Canada's pre-Confederation colonial administrators.[6] In the Tory conception, the state is seen as an instrument for promoting capitalist development by pragmatic intervention were market forces fail or are absent.

In Canada, the Tory conception of the role of the state has always contained contradictory tendencies. First, there has been the expectation that sooner or later the time would come for the state to withdraw. After the motor of capitalist development had been started, the state was expected to become more *laissez-faire*, more appropriate to a "normal" capitalist liberal democracy. Canada's geography and the federal system, among other factors, have inhibited realization of this goal. The federal state remained important for "regional development" and other forms of capital redistribution and for protection of sovereignty on the frontiers. Entrepreneurs located outside the centre of power have pressed alternately for Tory interventions more suited to their needs and for liberation from the heavy hand of state policy.

There have also been countervailing pressures "from below," in the form of resistance to the top-down Tory administrative style. The state, used so unself-consciously by merchants and landholders to create a national economy, was pressed to provide the preconditions of better lives to the rest of the population. In often isolated battles all over the country, workers, native peoples, farmers, women, and religious dissenters fought for political, economic, and social rights. These struggles generated political movements and political ideas with a strong "regional" flavour. They all challenged the commercial alliance and Tory philosophy through which Canada was born. The Métis revolt in the late nineteenth century, native resistance elsewhere in the country, the prairie farmers' movement, the Social Gospel movement, women's struggles for the vote, and socialist labour organizations all attacked in different ways the economic and political terms of Confederation.

Warfare, conquest, coercion, evacuation, civil disobedience, resistance, and great struggles have transformed Canadian life. In this process, we did not forge a national mythology of revolutionary achievement, as similar events have done in, for example, the United States or France. This aspect of our legacy is instead a tradition of gradual, piecemeal, unremarked reform worked painfully through the Byzantine architecture of federalism.

The entire history of federal northern administration reflects these national patterns. The northern territories were administered for decades as colonies of the South, at first lackadaisically and then, after World War II, with sudden energy. The National Policy strategy, which had opened the West, was revived for the North, like a recurring dream, whenever it appeared that northern resource development was possible. Repeatedly, the dream faded when geography and changes in the world economy frustrated development.[7]

In the last forty years, northern challenges to colonial administration, the National Policy development strategy, and the traditionally halting pace of Canadian constitutional change have occupied centre stage. Because the territorial North is home to distinct, self-conscious, and proportionately numerous native societies, as well as to a settler population, northerners confront the familiar questions of ethnic particularity and equal participation.

Early Dominion Administration

The Dominion government purchased "Rupert's Land and the North-West" from the Hudson's Bay Company in 1870; in 1880, Great Britain transferred to Canada jurisdiction over the Arctic Islands. For decades after, however, the federal state was preoccupied with national consolidation south of the sixtieth parallel. Relations with indigenous and migrant northerners were conducted almost absent-mindedly, on a crisis basis. Attention was drawn northward episodically, by the threat of American annexation of Canadian lands and by short-lived concentrations of non-native settlement that attended mineral developments.

Mineral "discoveries" by migrants provoked brief spurts of enthusiasm in the south for northern development. Where these discoveries led to production (in the Yukon after 1898 and at Norman Wells after 1921), Dominion regulations were duly drafted, following principles similar to those used to encourage mineral development in the rest of the country.[8] As was the practice in the south, treaties were sought with northern native societies only where open conflict threatened between migrants and indigenous people. No treaty was ever signed with Yukon Indians or with the Inuit of the Arctic. Treaty Eight (1898) and Treaty Eleven (1921) were negotiated hastily with the indigenous peoples of northern Alberta and Saskatchewan and with the Dene of the Mackenzie Valley when fortune seekers invaded these lands and disrupted native land use.[9]

The Yukon Territory was created in 1898 in response to the Klondike gold rush. The gold rush drew a large and heterogeneous population of non-natives to an area barely within the reach of Dominion authority. Eventually, the presence of these migrants and fears in Ottawa of American annexation led to the creation of the Yukon Territory and the establishment of a territorial government in the Yukon. While the migrant population remained large, there was some experimentation with intermediary forms of responsible government, but these were abandoned in favour of a contracted and less democratic territorial state structure during the 1920s, as gold fever and the migrant population both ebbed.[10]

The current boundaries of the Northwest Territories (NWT) delineate the land that remained after the staged extension of provincial boundaries northward and the creation of the Yukon Territory and the new provinces of Saskatchewan and Alberta. The Northwest Territories Act (1905) established a fairly broad legislative framework for the self-government of the NWT, including jurisdiction in many areas of provincial authority. Until the 1950s, however, the powers listed in the act were exercised by a small group of Dominion civil servants resident in Ottawa.

The human population of the territorial North was left largely in a "state of nature." Social services were provided by non-state institutions (principally the fur-trading companies and the churches) and in different ways by the indigenous peoples and the settlers for themselves. The only permanent state representatives were the Royal North-West Mounted Police, whose presence was used both to maintain sovereignty and to keep the peace. While Dominion policy towards native people in southern Canada had the official objective of making them "good, industrious and useful citizens" by settling them on reserves and replacing the hunt with agriculture, it was felt that *northern* native people ought best "to follow their natural mode of living and not...depend upon white men's food and clothing which are unsuited to their needs."[11]

The New Approach: A Problem of Development?

Early federal interest in northern Canada was sporadic and slight. The Dominion government was preoccupied with western development, intervening in the North only when mineral discoveries suggested that there was opportunity for economic development or threats to Canadian sovereignty. The Second World War and the global changes that followed completely transformed the federal stance.

With Japan's attack on Pearl Harbour in 1941, the western continental Arctic became an area of potential strategic importance. American military personnel rapidly constructed the Alaska Highway, a winter road from the Mackenzie Valley to Alberta, The Canol pipeline, and an oil refinery in Whitehorse, all in anticipation of the need to defend against an invasion from the Pacific.[12] The U.S. military effort had a major impact. David Judd has estimated that between 1941 and 1946, the American military population in northern Canada outnumbered Canadian residents three to one.[13]

The advent of the Cold War immediately after the defeat of Germany and Japan sustained northern military activity. Military personnel in reduced numbers remained in several locations, and in the 1950s weather and radar systems were constructed, while scientific research and military training exercises continued.

All of this activity created powerful incentives for the development of a new federal approach to northern administration. The American military presence in the North raised concerns for Canadian sovereignty. Concern for sovereignty provoked some delicate diplomatic manoeuvring. It also created interest in establishing a more effective state presence in the North.[14]

Reinforcing this interest were two other factors. First, military activity in the North had begun to create the technology and infrastructure that promised to render northern resource development practical, while global markets for these resources were forming. As a part of the war effort, a new office was created within the Department of Mines and Resources in 1943 to gather information about northern geography, resources, and population. This office produced a report, *Canada's New Northwest* (1947), which treated the region as an economic unit of potential importance to the national economy. Both Liberal and Progressive Conservative governments in the decades following incorporated the same reasoning in their national economic policies.

The Liberal government of Louis St. Laurent recognized in the expanding American economy opportunities to market northern resources and found in the strong state instruments developed during the war the means to promote northern resources development. Later, Prime Minister John Diefenbaker gave vivid political expression to the same economic strategy.

In Diefenbaker's "Northern Vision," the North was to be opened by means of a "new National Policy."[15] The North, like the West fifty years earlier, would provide staple export commodities. Northern minerals, like western wheat in an earlier period, would fuel the engine of the national economy by providing export credits, jobs, and investment opportunities. The role of the federal state would be to facilitate resource development. A Territorial Roads program and a "Roads to Resources" policy were announced, a railway was constructed to Pine Point, and new oil and gas regulations were drafted to promote exploration.

Increased penetration of the North by southerners had a second effect. It created a much greater awareness in southern Canada of the circumstances of northern indigenous people. Native northerners were suffering economic hardships as a result of a sharp decline in world fur prices, and they were exposed to new diseases from the South. There were well-publicized reports of starvation. In a period of national expansion of social welfare services and continued federal presence in the North, it was impossible to sustain the old "state of nature" policy.

The state response to this imperative was compatible in certain aspects with northern resource development. It also represented the extension of full-scale colonial administration to the territorial North. The full administrative apparatus was established very quickly.

Low-rent housing was provided in settlements, to which the nomadic and scattered native societies were induced and persuaded to relocate. The population was brought together to facilitate delivery of educational, medical, and social services. Also for this purpose, the Inuit were assigned "disc numbers" to make record-keeping possible for southerners unfamiliar with Inuit naming customs and language. As early as 1949, efforts were begun to bring native children into the school system. Over a few years, the old church-run hostel schools were taken over and new primary and post-primary schools constructed. Church-run hospitals were also absorbed into a new public health system, which incorporated a system of nursing stations in small communities and provision of advanced treatment at larger facilities in the south.

Family allowance payments were introduced in the North soon after their 1945 introduction in the south. By the early 1960s, virtually all native and non-native northerners were receiving the full panoply of social welfare transfer payments, including old age pension, social assistance, disabled and blind person's allowances and, for waged workers, unemployment insurance.

During 1949–1953, individual and group trap line registration was introduced in both territories to regulate game harvesting. Programs were begun "to encourage natives to develop agricultural activities where this seemed possible, to stimulate the growth of home and handicraft industries, to instruct and interest natives in the economical management of fur, fish and other wildlife resources, and even to operate retail stores."[16] There were even programs to teach native women "housekeeping" skills.

In all of these measures, it is possible to discern a new federal interpretation of the situation of native people.[17] Their hardships were understood as a consequence of "disadvantage." Besides emergency measures to deal with immediate problems, there was another, longer term strategy to overcome native peoples' disadvantaged circumstances by ensuring their full and equal participation as *Canadian citizens* in both the wage economy and the formal political process. In retrospect, the striking thing about the new approach was the extent to which it was developed without consulting with the people to whom it was directed. But retrospective judgments are too easily made: in this period, only a handful of people in Canada had any level of knowledge about northern native societies, communication with and among these societies was inhibited by linguistic, technological, and geographical barriers, and there were powerful economic and social welfare incentives for proceeding quickly.

Further, there were measures designed to improve the political representation of northerners and attempts to prepare native northerners for political participation. Like the social welfare and economic development measures, most of these attempts were coloured by non-native assumptions about appropriate pace and means and by a reluctance in Ottawa to devolve power. In this period, little was done to improve the political representation of Yukoners; instead, steps were taken to bring the Northwest Territories to the level of self-government already long established in Yukon.

Yukoners who were not status Indians had elected a representative to the federal Parliament since 1902. In 1947, the Yukon constituency was extended to include the western Northwest Territories, and then in 1952, in response to regional protest, a separate constituency was established for the Mackenzie District. In 1954, provisions were made for the Inuit of the Eastern Arctic to vote. Status Indians across the country were given the right to vote in federal elections finally in 1960.[18]

In stages beginning in 1951, the NWT Territorial Council gained gradually a greater proportion of elected members. A federal Commission of Inquiry led by A.W.R. Carrothers resulted in the relocation of the seat of NWT government from Ottawa to Yellowknife in 1967 and over the next few years transferred administrative responsibilities to the NWT. Appointed members remained on the council until 1975, and the commissioner retained a seat in the executive council until 1984. Until very recently in both territories, the commissioners remained very powerful. They were responsible to the federal cabinet, and the federal government retained the power to disallow territorial legislation and to alter territorial budgets.[19]

In the 1950s, there were attempts also to stimulate municipal government participation in northern communities. Most communities were provided with a federal administrator, the Northern Service Officer (NSO), who established in his or her assigned community a settlement council of elected representatives to deal with matters of municipal concern. The intention of these initiatives was apparently to train northern native people in the forms of liberal democratic self-government, but in this respect the early local government efforts were largely unsuccessful. The language barrier for community adults and their unfamiliarity with representative majority decision-making procedures discouraged native participation, as did a marked power imbalance expressed in the position of the NSO.

It was the NSO's role to relay the expressed needs of the communities to headquarters in Ottawa and to relay Ottawa's decisions back to the community. Because little power and no budgetary control were devolved to the communities, the NSO was frequently in the position of representing Ottawa more effectively locally than he or she was able to represent the community in Ottawa. There was thus relatively little incentive for native residents to overcome the other barriers to their participation in settlement councils.[20] Many Inuit found it more effective to write directly to Ottawa, in syllabics, with specific requests.[21]

More meaningful opportunities for participation were provided by some civil servants responsible for social program delivery. For example, housing programs in the NWT and the Arctic Co-operatives program across the territorial North were administered in a fashion intended to evolve towards local control. Community-based housing and co-operatives associations were established, and community members were trained for administration and service delivery. These initiatives provided native people with an opportunity to develop the skills for dealing with state-provided programs and for taking control in their new life circumstances.

This trend, however, was offset and sometimes subverted by an overall consolidation of federal control. Implementation of the new programs brought major changes to the structure of northern administration in Ottawa. The Advisory Committee on Northern Development was created in 1948 as a mechanism for interdepartmental co-ordination of northern policies and programs. In 1954, the Department of Resources and Development was recast as the Department of Northern Affairs and National Resources (DNANR), to emphasize that "the centre of gravity of the department [was] being moved north."[22] In 1965, major responsibility for national Indian affairs was added to the portfolio, which was renamed Indian Affairs and Northern Development in 1966. Expanding budgets and administrative consolidation in Ottawa far outstripped progress towards democratization in communities and in the territorial legislative branches.

There is practical consistency in the overall postwar federal approach. The aspirations of federal politicians regarding exploitation of northern resources were compatible with the need to address the hardships being endured by northern native people. The difficult circumstances of northern natives appeared to southern civil servants as a consequence of native people's unpreparedness for wage employment and the absence of viable economic opportunities; the remedy was federal programs to develop a native labour force and to create business and employment opportunities. Jobs were to be provided, ultimately, in the mineral extraction projects stimulated by the new National Policy.

The postwar federal approach also displays the two contradictory strands in Canadian political ideology and practice. The interpretation of the circumstances of northern native people as a result of individual disadvantage is fundamentally liberal, as is the solution implied by this interpretation. In addition, all of the postwar state initiatives bore the stamp of Canada's Tory beginnings. The northern National Policy, the new social welfare programs, and even the forms of democratic self-government were introduced from the top down. Administrators retained decision-making authority; political control was devolved very gradually.

As it turned out, neither the economic development strategy nor the programs to ameliorate native people's "disadvantaged" position succeeded in their longer term objectives. The "Roads to Resources" were built, but the North did not become a new cornucopia of exportable commodities. Health, education, and social welfare programs were introduced effectively, but northerners remained in a disadvantaged position with respect to both the waged workforce and the political process. The explanation for the short-term administrative success and longer term political failure of these federal designs did not become clear until the native people's version of northern history was revealed in the 1970s, when they found a means to make themselves heard.

The Changing Balance of Power in the 1970s

The dramatic events of the 1970s can be understood as the cumulative effect of "the new National Policy" and the new federal approach to northern native administration. Both sets of policies had the unforeseen and apparently paradoxical effect of creating resistance to further state intervention. The paradox dissolves, however, when native people's experience of the policies is taken into account.

Wartime and postwar interventions in the territorial North brought mixed blessings. The material circumstances of native northerners improved over the hard years, when trapping had ceased to provide a good living and when epidemic diseases and occasionally famine visited. The new health care facilities, infusions of cash in the form of social welfare payments, improved communications systems, and government-provided houses alleviated many hardships.

On the other hand, the new life in the settlements brought social problems. The new settlements concentrated populations at unprecedented levels, straining the old authority patterns and kin-based sharing relationships. In some cases, people were relocated far from their traditional hunting and trapping areas, and for others there were powerful influences to hunt and trap less: social welfare payments became a regular source of supplementary income in many households. The educational programs separated children from their parents physically, as they were attending school, and ultimately psychologically, as they absorbed a non-traditional education while missing the traditional lessons of their elders in the communities. A sense of dislocation from traditional life and the lack of local control over the distribution of the new benefits made dealing with these problems difficult for many individuals. Some opportunities for local control were created, but the success of these only underlined the fundamental lack of local and regional control over other aspects of public life.

"Province-like" control remained in Ottawa with the Department of Indian Affairs and Northern Development [DIAND], which was reaching the zenith of its power at the end of the 1960s. Fattened on the rapid expansion of federal northern programs, buoyed by the government's political commitment to northern resource development, the Ministry of Indian Affairs and Northern Development was a strong second-string influence in cabinet during this period. Since the 1950s the northern department had used regulatory changes and other forms of encouragement to support exploration for northern petroleum resources, but in two decades of exploration, very little oil or gas had been found. Finally in 1968, when a United States exploration company discovered commercial quantities of oil in Prudhoe Bay, Alaska, it even appeared that the long search for northern petroleum resources was coming to an end, and that the dream of economic growth based on a National Policy for the North would be realized.

The prospect of oil and gas development in the North raised for Ottawa a complex web of intersecting sovereignty, environmental, and economic considerations. These were confronted with varying degrees of creativity, but no new model of economic development was proposed.[23] Federal officials began to plan the construction of a transportation corridor in the Mackenzie Valley for Alaskan oil, in anticipation of eventual Canadian discoveries. Prime Minister Pierre Trudeau explained federal objectives by comparing the proposed Mackenzie Valley pipeline to the Canadian Pacific Railway, which had opened the West for settlement and wheat production in the nineteenth century. The pipeline corridor would open the North to a new wave of development and prosperity.

This time around, however, the federal "Northern Vision" encountered organized regional resistance. The late 1960s were a period of national mobilization for the native movement, provoked by the 1969 white paper on Indian policy. The white paper announced a new direction for Indian policy that was consistent with much of federal behaviour in the postwar period but inconsistent with the wishes of Indian people: it closed the book on the past, including existing treaties and outstanding disputes, and proposed instead the assimilation of Indians into the mainstream of Canadian society.[24]

The white paper galvanized native protest across the country. In the optimistic mood of the early Trudeau years, the federal response to native protest was similar to the response to other social movements of the period. Funding was provided for organizations to represent activist youth and poor people, as well as for native organizations at the provincial, territorial, and national levels, on the official premise that the solution to the problems identified by these groups was "participatory democracy."[25]

During 1969–1973, native people across the territorial North formed organizations, through which to struggle for their collective interests. The Council for Yukon Indians (CYI) represented status and non-status Indians in the Yukon Territory. The Committee for Original Peoples' Entitlement (COPE), the Indian Brotherhood of the NWT (IBNWT), and the Métis Association of the NWT represented the Inuvialuit, Dene, and Métis of the western NWT. The Inuit Tapirisat of Canada (ITC) was organized by the Inuit of the Eastern Arctic. All of these organizations eventually received federal funding. The status Indian organizations were funded by Indian Affairs; the others were funded by the Department of the Secretary of State as part of that department's responsibility to promote "citizen participation."

The existence of the aboriginal organizations introduced a new factor in territorial political life. In the NWT, leaders of the IBNWT (later the Dene Nation) reacted quickly to the news that a major pipeline project was intended for their territory. Believing that the disruptions that would attend this development were uncontrollable and potentially very dangerous, they commenced court action to freeze development on the land through which the pipeline was to pass. In 1973 they received a favourable decision in the Supreme Court of the NWT.[26] To further strengthen their position, the native leaders successfully sought support from the churches, southern environmental groups, and academics.

In the end, there was sufficient pressure to cause the minority Liberal government in Ottawa to appoint a commission of inquiry to investigate "the terms and conditions" under which a pipeline could be constructed in the Mackenzie Valley. Thomas Berger, a former New Democratic Party politician, native rights lawyer, and British Columbia Supreme Court Justice, was appointed to conduct the inquiry.

Berger led a wide-ranging and well-publicized inquiry during 1974–1976. He heard testimony from hundreds of northerners, including an unprecedented number of native northerners whose participation was facilitated by the use of translators and a culturally appropriate hearing format. The Berger Inquiry was significant for many reasons: it became the forum for a cathartic national debate about the assumptions underlying economic growth; the innovative procedures for social and environmental impact assessment developed during the inquiry set a precedent in northern decision making; the inquiry process itself delayed a federal decision about pipeline construction until it became clear that the project was inadvisable; and perhaps most important, participation in the inquiry provided native people in the Mackenzie Valley with a unique opportunity for political participation and consolidation, while northern native organizations in general gained new national recognition.[27]

As the inquiry proceeded, regional native organizations in both territories were engaged in a process of political development. Part of this development took place through participation in inquiries and hearings (such as the Berger Inquiry and the Lysyk Inquiry on the proposed Alaska Highway Pipeline in Yukon). A great deal of the political mobilization, however, was the result of grass-roots and community-building work undertaken by native people themselves, in southern Canada as well as in the North.

The Nishga [Indians] of British Columbia took the issue of their land rights to the Supreme Court. They lost the case on a legal technicality but achieved a decision that acknowledged that native peoples who had not signed treaties did have a form of aboriginal entitlement. Native political mobilization and this ruling prompted a formal reversal of federal policy. In 1973, the federal government announced its willingness to negotiate aboriginal land claims for those areas of Canada not covered by treaties.

By 1975, all of the northern native organizations had submitted "land claims proposals" to the federal government that claimed far more than real estate; each called for a fundamental readjustment in their relationship to the federal state, based upon native peoples' interpretation of their own situation and proposing new models of self-government that blended traditional governing forms with liberal democratic principles. Their goal was to establish regional governments through which they could have sufficient control to ensure their survival as collectivities.[28]

The initial federal response to the first wave of claims proposals was negative. There were panicky references to the undesirability of "ethnic governments" from federal politicians who clearly had one eye on the progress of the Parti Québécois and the impending referendum on sovereignty association in Quebec, which would have placed Quebec in a semiautonomous position in the Canadian federation. By the early 1980s, however, it was clear that the native organizations had gained considerable ground.

First, federal policy had recognized in 1973 the legitimacy of "comprehensive" native land claims, completely reversing the 1969 policy that promoted the eradication of all "special rights" for aboriginal people. Procedures for negotiation and a system for funding claims research by loans against an eventual settlement were in place. While federal claims policy excluded negotiation for native governments, in the negotiation process itself some para-governmental structures were contemplated.

Second, all of the organizations had developed strategies for working towards greater self-government outside the claims process. The CYI had decided to work towards improving existing Yukon government programs where possible, rather than to attempt to develop a totally separate system of services for their memberships. The NWT native organizations were participating in territorial electoral politics and were using this forum to advance their political goals, and the Inuit had implemented a system of regional councils within their territory to promote broadly based participation.

Third, through their national federations, native organizations from across the country waged a successful campaign to entrench "existing " aboriginal rights in the constitution as well as a five-year process to specify the meaning of aboriginal rights at a series of First Ministers' Conferences (meetings of the prime minister and the provincial premiers). Some progress had been made towards entrenching collective rights for aboriginal people.

Fourth, across the North, the native organizations were recognized as legitimate representatives of their memberships on native issues, and it had become a regular governmental practice to consult both the organizations and native people in general when decisions were being made that might affect them.

Fifth, as a result of native participation in the well-publicized Berger hearings, Berger's widely read final report, and political initiatives of the native organizations, the official analytical framework regarding northern development had been expanded. It was no longer possible for attentive observers to sustain an interpretation in which native people were seen simply as "disadvantaged" Canadians. The title of Berger's report, *Northern Frontier*,

Northern Homeland, concisely expressed the new image of North, which recognized that there were both native and non-native versions of northern history, leading to two visions of the future.

All of these changes were felt sharply in both territories, where the local balance of political power had shifted decisively. The native organizations provided a means for native people to express their views. The change was perhaps most rapid in the NWT. In 1975, the Territorial Council was dominated by non-natives hostile to native political goals and strongly supporting the Mackenzie Valley pipeline; just four years later, NWT voters elected a new legislature composed of a native majority and non-native representatives who were determined to respond to native concerns.

In the Yukon, a similar electoral adjustment came more slowly. In 1979, Yukoners introduced party politics in territorial elections and almost immediately were granted responsible government by the short-lived federal Conservative government led by Joe Clark. (The same provision was not made for the NWT, where parties did not then and still do not participate in territorial elections.)

The Progressive Conservatives, who formed the first Yukon government after the introduction of party politics, elected only one native member, but in 1985 the next territorial election returned a New Democrat majority. In this government, native people were represented proportionately to their numbers in the territory. The new government in Yukon, like the post-1979 Legislative Assembly in the NWT, included also non-native members who had concluded that it was in their interest to understand and to accommodate the native position on key political issues, because the extreme political polarization of the 1970s had led to stalemate in both territories.[29]

A New Political Landscape

The 1970s represented a period of dramatic confrontation and radical realignment of the balance of political forces in the North. In the 1980s, northerners faced a new political landscape, in which more room—though no one was clear how *much* more room—was available for aboriginal and regional self-government.

Certainly, DIAND's monopoly on northern policy was shattered. In part this was a consequence of greater involvement of other, more powerful ministries in northern development. The chaos in world energy relations during the 1970s drew cabinet attention to the development of a national energy policy, with the result that the Department of Energy, Mines and Resources assumed much greater responsibility for northern oil and gas development.[30] Other departments had developed relationships with northerners, as in the case of Secretary of State funding for some native organizations.

DIAND's influence was eroded from ''below'' as well: native people now dealt with the federal state from a much stronger position, through organizations capable of sustained political activity, and both territorial governments were representing northern interests with greater legitimacy and persistence. Although both northern governments still resembled colonies in their legal position, administered through federal legislation, in practice both had moved much closer to "province-like" authority during the 1970s.

These developments indicated a shift in political initiative to the North, but not to a permanent transfer of power. Constitutionally and legally, control remained in Ottawa, constrained only by the energy and solidarity with which northerners exploited their *de facto* political advantage.

Contrary Trends in the 1980s

Federal government practices in the territorial North were transformed during the 1970s through the political mobilization of northern native people and their new alliance with non-native northerners. Some political power was devolved, as consultation about major projects and funding for representative native organizations became routine and as the territorial governments moved towards more province-like behaviour. Federal economic intervention in the North was obstructed partially by these forces. Further, some basis was laid for an ideological and constitutional accommodation of native objectives for collective self-determination in the elaboration of processes for negotiation of comprehensive claims and with the recognition of "existing aboriginal rights' in the new constitution.

In the 1980s, the contradictions inherent in these changes became more apparent. Federal action in two areas underlined the limits to northern influence over northern affairs. The imperatives of national energy policy brought a boom and then a bust to the territorial economies, and the resolution of the national constitutional process through the Meech Lake Accord produced significant setbacks for all northerners and for native northerners in particular. At the same time, in the North, two processes were launched that provided an alternative model for decision making on constitutional and economic development. In the 1980s, the federal government exercised executive authority in the secret negotiations, while political leaders in the territories created broadly based, broadly democratic deliberative forums.

Two Federal Initiatives

The federal legislation establishing the framework of government in the two territories grants to the territorial governments province-like legislative powers, with one major exception. As was the case for Alberta and Saskatchewan before 1930, jurisdiction over "Crown land" is retained by the federal level of the state. Thus the territories lack the economic power exercised by provinces in taxing and regulating non-renewable resource development.

The world energy "crisis" that began in 1973 created a situation in which federal control of northern resources gained new importance. The crisis prompted major revision of Canadian energy policy, culminating in the announcement of the National Energy Policy (NEP) in January 1980. The NEP was promoted as a program to achieve the dual goals of "Canadianization" of a significant portion of the foreign-controlled energy sector and national self-sufficiency in energy supply. Principal mechanisms for achieving self-sufficiency in energy were various kinds of subsidies to encourage exploration and development of petroleum reserves in the federally controlled land in the two territories (referred to in the NEP as "Canada Lands").

The NEP was developed by a relatively small group of senior federal officials, without consultation with northerners or, in fact, with the Department of Indian Affairs and Northern Development.[31] Implementation of the NEP produced an energy boom in the western NWT and significantly increased activity elsewhere in the NWT and in Yukon. Especially in the NWT, the boom was boosted by another project, to expand the oil production system at Norman Wells and construct a small diameter pipeline along the Mackenzie Valley south from Norman Wells to Alberta. The smaller Norman Wells project was approved by the federal government just four years after Berger's recommendation that there be a ten-year moratorium on pipeline construction. There was ongoing opposition by native organizations.

With the completion of the construction phase of the Norman Wells project, and the withdrawal of the NEP by the new Conservative government after 1984, northerners faced a sudden collapse of petroleum industry employment opportunities. Both the boom and the bust were economic events of major consequence over which northern residents had no control.

More effective participation was possible in the process through which the Canadian constitution was patriated, but in the end insufficient opportunities for participation were permitted. Northern native people joined the successful campaign by native people from across the country to entrench affirmation of "existing aboriginal and treaty rights" in the new constitution. It was evident that federal, provincial and native representatives held widely diverging views about what these rights entailed. Accordingly, to the section affirming aboriginal rights was added another that provided for a series of conferences of first ministers and national native leaders to determine what was meant by this phrase.[32] Representatives of territorial governments attended the patriation meetings but were not parties to the agreement. Both the territorial governments and national native organizations participated in the First Ministers Conferences (FMCs) on aboriginal and treaty rights.

In 1987, the constitutionally required First Ministers Conferences concluded without agreement on the meaning of "existing aboriginal rights," leaving open the question of when or how this fundamental issue will be decided. Just one month after the failure of the last FMC on aboriginal rights, another First Ministers Conference reached an accord among the provincial premiers and the prime minister on the terms by which Quebec would enter the new Canadian constitution. This Meech Lake Accord included an agreement to revise the constitutional amendment process. If the accord is ratified, the establishment of new provincial boundaries, formation of new provinces, and reform of federal institutions will require agreement of the federal government and all ten provinces. In the 1982 version of the constitution, these changes required only the agreement of the federal government and seven of ten provinces, representing 50 percent of the Canadian population.

Neither the territorial governments nor the national native organizations were invited to attend the meetings that produced the Meech Lake Accord. Native leaders reacted angrily to the accord, not because they opposed resolution of Quebec's constitutional position, but because their own distinct societies had so recently been disappointed by the same assembly of provincial and federal leaders. Inuit leader John Amagoalik commented in a television interview: "If Quebec is a distinct society, what are we? Chopped liver?"

The accord's amending formula is another source of concern for both native leaders and the territorial governments. It seems clear that provincial status for the territories will be much more difficult to achieve, and changes to northern representation—in, for example, the Senate—could be effected without territorial agreement. While no northern leader expects or demands provincial status for either territory in the near future, all are concerned about the long-term implications of the Meech Lake Accord.

Two Territorial Initiatives

Independently of the federally led national initiatives in energy policy and constitutional development, the territorial governments addressed fundamental regional economic and constitutional questions during the 1980s. In each territory, processes were established that stand in remarkable contrast to those at the national level.

Since early 1980, residents of the NWT have been participating in a process of territorial constitution-building. The process was born in the new spirit of accommodation and co-operation attending the 1979 territorial election. The Legislative Assembly created a "Constitutional Alliance" to bring members of the Legislative Assembly together with leaders of territorial native organizations in a forum to promote discussion of future territorial government structures. Two public conferences were held for this purpose.

Then, in 1982, Inuit members of the Legislative Assembly asked the Assembly to hold a plebiscite on division of the NWT. They argued that division would provide more democratic government of their constituents in the Eastern Arctic by bringing the seat of government closer than Yellowknife, which is hundreds of kilometers away from any Inuit communities, and by bringing territorial boundaries into line with the area expected to be included in the Inuit land claim.

The Inuit proposal was supported by other members of the Assembly. In 1983, the plebiscite was held, and division was supported by 85 percent of the (predominantly Inuit) residents of the eastern NWT and by 56 percent of territorial voters overall. In light of this result, the Constitutional Alliance divided into the Western Constitutional Forum (WCF) and the Nunavut Constitutional Forum (NCF), so that northerners' constitutional discussions could be focused upon development of separate constitutions for two new territories.

Each forum launched a process of constitutional discussion that included repeated visits to northern communities, research, and the publication of background papers, working documents, pamphlets, and newsletters in English and native languages. Forum representatives met frequently in joint session, often publicly. The NCF reached consensus on a constitution for the proposed new eastern territory, to be called Nunavut, while the WCF, working with a much more heterogeneous population in the western NWT, made considerable progress.

None of this activity, however, could actually produce new territorial constitutions. Legally, division of the NWT is a federal prerogative. Nine months after the plebiscite, the then Minister of Indian Affairs and Northern Development, John Munro, agreed to accept the plebiscite decision, but he attached a number of rather stringent and imprecise conditions that would have to be fulfilled before division could proceed.[33] These conditions have been relaxed somewhat by later ministers. There has been a complicated period of negotiation among northerners about division, and most recently about the exact location of the new boundary that will divide the two territories. Many different interests must be satisfied in an extremely unstable political setting; in the meantime, the issue remains unresolved.

In the Yukon, the political landscape is quite different. Constitutional questions were resolved for the short term with the introduction of party politics and the achievement of responsible government in 1979. Territorial politics are complex and often heated, and large questions about the economic future of the territory remain.

As in the NWT, perhaps the greatest political divide in Yukon has been between some non-native business interests strongly favourable to non-renewable resource development and native people working through the claims and other processes to gain control over the pace and direction of economic and political change. Yukon Indians, who constitute just one-third of the Yukon population, came very close to concluding a comprehensive claims agreement in 1984. They have participated in electoral politics through all three political parties. Non-natives are a diverse group, including a local economic elite, many of whom are second-or third-generation Yukoners, independent placer miners, and a growing number of permanently resident professionals, artists, and white collar workers. All have different, although sometimes intersecting, economic interests.

Yukon economic health depends upon a few mines, government expenditures, and an associated service sector. The volatility of the heavily subsidized mining sector has meant wild fluctuations in levels of unemployment and frequent infusions of federal "emergency" capital to prevent mine closures.[34]

In 1985, the new Yukon government introduced a number of measures intended to repair the wide breaches dividing the Yukon electorate. Probably the most innovative new measure is Yukon 2000, a participatory planning process intended to produce a long-term economic development strategy. The process is designed to unfold over several years, incorporating conferences in which participants representing various strands of opinion work through small groups to achieve consensus, supported by wide-ranging research papers. It is too early to comment upon the outcome of this process, but to date all sectors of Yukon society have worked successfully through the early phases of consensus building.

Summary

These examples of federal and territorial behaviour highlight some salient trends. On the federal side are two major initiatives—one economic, the other constitutional—that conform in some respects to the patterns of Canadian development identified earlier. The National Energy Program treated the territorial North as an internal colony. Developed without northern consultation, the NEP deployed northern energy resources "in the national interest" using regulations and subsidies to implement a particular economic strategy. The territorial governments and aboriginal organizations were excluded from the secret negotiations that produced the Meech Lake Accord and thus lacked the means to defend their interests at a crucial stage in the development of the new constitution.

Clearly, the old patterns have not been abandoned: development proceeded despite outstanding native claims, while the penultimate national constitutional agreement ignored the interest of both native people and northerners. Yet in federal behaviour there are contradictory elements. The NEP's "Canada Lands" are the same lands that are considered by northern native societies to be *their* lands. That the native societies have some claim to the land has been acknowledged in federal policy, which includes provisions for working out a practical resolution of conflicting federal and native interests. Although the territorial economies are still controlled by Ottawa, the Department of Indian Affairs and Northern Development has continued to devolve other governing responsibilities to the territorial level. And while the Meech Lake part of the constitutional process excluded both native and territorial participation, their participation was both permitted and effective at earlier stages. It is still possible, too, that their interests will be recognized before the accord

is ratified. Further, it was, after all, federal funding that enabled the two northern deliberative processes to take place, and in the case of the constitutional
development process, at least, federal policy has had to respond to the results.

Conclusions

This essay began with the claim that recent northern political history is evocative for Canadians because it compresses into sharp focus basic national issues
and fundamental patterns of Canadian development. Specifically, four areas of
congruence have been identified.

First, northern constitutional development bears the mark of Canada's
colonial heritage. The Tory conception of the role of the state recognizes that
market forces alone cannot be relied upon to build a national economy or to
keep it functioning; nothing could have been clearer to the representatives of
the four colonies who conceived Confederation. The same imperatives that led
them to confederate led also to the creation of the Yukon and Northwest Territories. The same tradition of colonial domination shaped federal administration of these territories and permitted their exclusion from a crucial stage in
the renegotiation of the terms of federation, which is now nearly completed.

Second, it is clear that the strategy for national economic development formulated by the fathers of Confederation, the National Policy implemented by
Prime Minister John A. MacDonald, persists. The dream of a northern version
of the National Policy recurred repeatedly during the twentieth century, and
dreamlike, it evaporated again in the cold light of economic reality.

Third, like the westward-looking National Policy of the nineteenth century,
the northern version eventually provoked regional resistance. The resistance
included the broad mobilization of previously excluded populations, and it
was manifested in a broadly democratic and participatory format contrasting
sharply with the undemocratic federal policies that gave it birth.

Fourth, northern political development helped to place on the national
agenda unfinished business related to the rights of the original inhabitants of
Canada, of the real founding nations who were not included in the "two
nations" compromise of the British North America Act. Accommodation of
cultural particularity and collective rights with respect to native people has
proven quite indigestible, constitutionally and ideologically, but mysteriously
amenable to some progress at the practical level.

The original pragmatic Tory compromise with Quebec was buried in the
BNA Act references to "denominational schools" and rules for the use of
French in certain legislatures. It required 120 years for explicit constitutional
recognition of Quebec as "a distinct society" to occur. The spectre of more
"distinct" societies haunted those federal politicians who reacted with horror
to native demands for governments that permitted the survival of their collectivities. In the long gestation of Canada, though, the particularity of Quebec
was finally recognized. A precedent is established that may prove useful in the

long term for aboriginal people.

The parallels between northern constitutional and economic development and other national processes are on reflection perhaps not very surprising. More interesting, I think, are the differences. History never really repeats itself, because what has gone before limits and shapes the changes that come after, and because human beings are capable of acting in awareness of their history.

Sometimes, of course, people act as if they were unconscious of prior experience: this is the lesson of the recurring National Policy dream. In varying world economic settings, both Liberal and Conservative politicians have expended large amounts of public money in attempts to replicate a probably unique national feat. The Canadian experience with the northern version of the National Policy and the evidence from other nations suggest that a development strategy based upon commodity exports is insufficient, if only because commodity prices and world markets fluctuate uncontrollably and disappear unpredictably.

Not all northern history has been lived unconsciously, however. Native people's consciousness of their own history has shaped and strengthened their political project to decolonize and to protect their collectivities. In turn, these actions expose a fundamental tension in Canadian political ideology. It is the tension between the liberal understanding of a state founded upon the political and economic rights of the individual and the Tory constitutional practice of compromise, accommodation, and state intervention.

Native people and northerners have reacted against both the liberal and Tory elements of Canadian government. Liberal ideology was expressed most baldly in the 1969 white paper on Indian policy, and generally in the redefinition of native people as "disadvantaged" Canadians who required the removal of barriers to their individual participation in the mainstream. This view clearly misunderstood the strength of native collectivities and the importance to them of their collective rights. On the other hand, northerners—both native and non-native—have resisted the heavy hand of Tory colonialism. They demand the same level of self-determination as other Canadians, as well as, for native people, collective rights.

Paradoxically, both strands in the Canadian constitutional tradition, as they have confronted Quebec nationalism and regional differences, have created a notably open-ended political setting in which the terms of the federation are frequently renegotiated. Native people have entered these negotiations now, taking advantage of both ideological tendencies. The liberal strand in Canadian politics requires that citizens have equal rights to participation, and so funding is provided to eliminate differences in citizens' capacities to contribute. Tory pragmatism and willingness to compromise with particularity makes constitutional recognition of "distinct societies" with special rights within Canada both comprehensible and possible.

Perhaps the most ironic legacy of Canada's Tory beginnings lies in the propensity of this state-led development strategy to provoke an insistently democratic form of resistance. Here native people and northerners joined the ranks of other Canadians who resisted imposition of the designs of governing elite. There are particularly northern reasons for the democratic pattern of northern politics: the population is small, and the traditions of aboriginal societies are directly democratic. To understand, however, the tenacity with which northern practice and northern demands have focused on the question of self-government, it is necessary also to recall their vivid experience of colonialism. Northerners seek to implement just what is denied by colonial administration.

So how *does* Canada survive? As the northern case illustrates, we survive amidst ideological contradictions and we struggle over issues that may appear to be arcane, particularistic, or "just regional." Regional issues, however, are also national. They continue to be the basic issues of Canadian political life, and they are the source of the Canadian compromise and innovation.

Notes

1. P. Russell, "The Dene Nation and Confederation," in *Dene Nation: The Colony Within*, ed. M. Watkins (Toronto: University of Toronto Press, 1977), 163–73; E. Forsey, "Canada: Two Nations or One?" *Canadian Journal of Economics and Political Science* 28,4 (1962): 485–501.

2. L.H. Thomas, *The Struggle for Responsible Government in the North-West Territories 1870–97*, 2d ed. (Toronto: University of Toronto Press, 1978); R. Whitaker, "Images of the State in Canada," *The Canadian State: Political Economy and Political Power*, ed. L. Pavitch (Toronto: University of Toronto Press, 1977), 28–68.

3. R. MacG. Dawson, *The Government of Canada*, 5th ed. (Toronto: University of Toronto Press, 1970).

4. V.C. Fowke, *The National Policy and the Wheat Economy* (Toronto: University of Toronto Press, 1973); G. Paquet, "Some Views on the Pattern of Canadian Economic Development," in *Growth and the Canadian Economy*, ed. T.N. Brewis (Toronto: University of Toronto Press, 1968), 34–64.

5. K. J. Rea, *The Political Economy of the Canadian North* (Toronto: University of Toronto Press, 1968).

6. Whitaker, "Images of the State"; C. Goodwin, *Canadian Economic Thought* (Durham: Duke University Press, 1961).

7. Paquet, "Some Views on the Pattern of Canadian Economic Development," 41–42.

8. M. Zaslow, *The Opening of the Canadian North 1870–1914* (Toronto: McClelland and Stewart, 1973); C. Martin, *"Dominion Lands" Policy* (Ottawa: Carleton University Press, 1968).

9. R. Fumoleau, *As Long as This Land Shall Last: A History of Treaty 8 and Treaty 11, 1880–1939* (Toronto: McClelland and Stewart, 1973); Thomas, *The Struggle for Responsible Government*.

10. K. Coates, *Canada's Colonies: A History of the Yukon and Northwest Territories* (Toronto: James Lorimer and Company, 1985); D. Morrison, *The Politics of the Yukon Territory* (Toronto: University of Toronto Press, 1968).

11. Fumoleau, *As Long as This Land Shall Last*; D. Judd, "Canada's Northern Policy: Retrospect and Prospect," *The Polar Record* 14, 92 (1969): 593–602.

12. Coates, *Canada's Colonies*.

13. D. Judd, "Seventy-Five Years of Resource Administration in Northern Canada," *The Polar Record* 14, 93 (1969): 791–806.

14. T. Armstrong, G. Rogers, and G. Rowley, *The Circumpolar North* (Toronto: Methuen, 1978); Judd, "Seventy-Five Years of Resource Administration."

15. Coates, *Canada's Colonies*; Rea, *Political Economy of the Canadian North*.

16. Rea, *Political Economy of the Canadian North*, 37–39.

17. See D. Jenness, *Eskimo Administration: V Analysis and Reflections* (Montreal: Arctic Institute of North America, 1968); G. Robertson, "Administration for Development in Northern Canada: The Growth and Evolution of Government," *Canadian Public Administration* 3, 7 (1960): 354–62.

18. Rea, *Political Economy of the Canadian North*, 43–45.

19. G. Dacks, *A Choice of Futures: Politics in the Canadian North* (Toronto: Methuen, 1981).

20. H. Brody, *The People's Land: Eskimos and Whites in the Canadian Arctic* (London: Penguin Books, 1975); W. Bean, "Colonialism in the Communities," in *Dene Nation: The Colony Within*, ed. M. Watkins (Toronto: University of Toronto Press, 1977), 130–41.

21. G. Rowley, personal communication, 1987.

22. Rea, *Political Economy of the Canadian North*, 47.

23. E.J. Dosman, *The National Interest: The Politics of Northern Development* (Toronto: McClelland and Stewart, 1975); F. Bregha, *Bob Blair's Pipeline* (Toronto: James Lorimer and Company, 1979).

24. S.M. Weaver, *Making Canadian Indian Policy: The Hidden Agenda 1968–1970* (Toronto: University of Toronto Press, 1981).

25. Weaver, *Making Canadian Indian Policy*; M. Loney "A Political Economy of Citizen Participation," in *The Canadian State: Political Economy and Political Power*, ed. L. Panitch, 446–72.

26. Dosman, *The National Interest*.

27. T.R. Berger, *Northern Frontier, Northern Homeland: The Report of the Mackenzie Valley Pipeline Inquiry*, 2 vols. (Ottawa: Department of Indian Affairs and Northern Development, 1977); R. Page, *Northern Development: The Canadian Dilemma* (Toronto: McClelland and Stewart, 1986); E.J. Dosman, "The Mackenzie Valley Pipeline Inquiry: The Politics of Catharsis," *Canadian Ethnic Studies* 10, 1 (1978): 135–41; Bregha, *Bob Blair's Pipeline*.

28. Dacks, *A Choice of Futures*; Page, *Northern Development*; M. Watkins, ed., *Dene Nation: The Colony Within* (Toronto: University of Toronto Press, 1977).

29. Dacks, *A Choice of Futures*; M. Whittington, "Political and Constitutional Development in the Northwest Territories and Yukon: The Issues and the Interests," in *The North*, ed. M. Whittington, Collected Research Studies of the Royal Commission on the Economic Union and Development Prospects for Canada vol. 72 (Toronto: University of Toronto Press, 1985), 53–108.

30. Bregha, *Bob Blair's Pipeline*; G.B. Doern and G. Toner, *The Politics of Energy: The Development and Implementation of the National Energy Program* (Toronto: Methuen, 1985).

31.   Doern and Toner, *The Politics of Energy*; L. Pratt, "The Roots of National Policy," *Studies in Political Economy* 7 (1982): 27–59.

32.   Constitution, 1982, Sec. 35, 37.

33.   F. Abele and M. Dickerson, "The Plebiscite on Division of the Northwest Territories," *Canadian Public Policy* 9, 1 (1985): 1–15.

34.   Coates, *Canada's Colonies*.

FURTHER READING

Though there is an immense literature on the Canadian North, there are few general histories of the region north of the sixtieth parallel. An attempt at a synthesis from the northern point of view is K.S. Coates, *Canada's Colonies* (Toronto, 1985) and K.S. Coates and Judith Powell, *The Modern North* (Toronto, 1989). One history of the Yukon Territory has been published— K.S. Coates and W.R. Morrison, *Land of the Midnight Sun: A History of the Yukon* (Edmonton, 1988). Morris Zaslow, ed., *A Century of Canada's Arctic Islands 1880–1980* (Ottawa, 1981) contains a variety of useful studies of the High Arctic. Keith J. Crowe, *A History of the Original Peoples of Northern Canada* (Montreal, 1974), is a good introduction to the subject, and Kenneth Rea, *The Political Economy of the Canadian North* (Toronto, 1968) provides an overview of northern economic development. Morris Zaslow's two-volume history of northern Canada, *The Opening of the Canadian North, 1870–1914* (Toronto, 1971) and *The Northward Expansion of Canada, 1914–1967* (Toronto, 1988) is a wide-ranging study which concentrates on the early period of government intervention in the region.

Until fairly recently, most of the books published on the North dealt with exploration or with personal reminiscences. Dozens of books by and about men such as Frobisher, Franklin, Stefansson, Amundsen, Parry, and a host of others have been written to satisfy a seemingly insatiable public taste for tales of adventure and hardship from the Far North. A good introduction to this aspect of northern history is Daniel Francis, *Discovery of the North: the Exploration of Canada's Arctic* (Edmonton, 1986). An encyclopedic treatment is Alan Cooke and Clive Holland, *The Exploration of Northern Canada: 500 to 1920, a Chronology* (Toronto, 1978). The *Dictionary of Canadian Biography* is another excellent source of information on the lives of northern explorers. Probably the most readable account of the early explorers is Samuel Eliot Morison, *The European Discovery of America: The Northern Voyages, AD 500–1600* (New York, 1971). H. Wallace, *The Navy, the Company and Richard King* (Montreal, 1980) is also a valuable work on this subject.

Section One: Images of the Canadian North. A notable attempt to assess the northern nature of Canada is L.-E. Hamelin, *Canadian Nordicity: It's Your North Too*, trans. W. Barr (Montreal, 1978); also of value is P.J. Usher, "The North: Metropolitan Frontier, Native Homeland?" in L.D. McCann, ed., *Heartland and Hinterland* (Scarborough, 1982). On the wider subject of Canadian regionalism, see J.M.S. Careless, "Limited Identities—Ten Years Later," *Manitoba History* 1981/1, and William Westfall, "On the Concept of Region in Canadian History and Literature," *Journal of Canadian Studies* 15, 2 (1980). For an overview of northern historiography, see K.S. Coates and

W.R. Morrison, "Northern Visions: Recent Historical Writing on the Canadian North," *Manitoba History* (Fall 1985).

Section Two: Indians and the Advance of Europe. A basic work is Shepherd Krech III, ed., *The Subarctic Fur Trade: Native Economic and Social Adaptations* (Vancouver, 1984). Alice Kehoe, *North American Indians: A Comprehensive Account* (Englewood Cliffs, NJ, 1981) has a useful section on the Canadian North. For the general background to the northern fur trade, see H. Innis, *The Fur Trade in Canada* (Toronto, 1975), E.E. Rich, *The Fur Trade and the Northwest to 1857* (Toronto, 1976) and T. Karamanski *Fur Trade and Exploration* (Vancouver, 1984). A recent account of the history of the Indians of the Yukon from the perspective of an anthropologist is Catherine McClellan's *Part of the Land, Part of the Water: A History of the Yukon Indians* (Vancouver, 1987). See also June Helm, *Handbook of North American Indians, Vol. 6: Subarctic Indians.* (Washington, 1981). The literature on the subject in the academic journals is much too extensive to be fully covered here; recent scholarship includes W. Sloan, "The Native Response to the Extension of the European Traders into the Athabasca and Mackenzie Basin, 1770–1814," *Canadian Historical Review* 60, 3 (1979); J.C. Yerbury, "The Nahanny Indians and the Fur Trade, 1800–1840," *Musk-ox* 28 (1981); K. Coates, "Furs Along the Yukon: Hudson's Bay Company—Native Trade in the Yukon River Valley, 1840–1893," *BC Studies* no. 55 (Autumn 1982). Most of the biographies of northern missionaries are hagiographic; more analytical accounts include F. Peake, "Fur Traders and Missionaries: Some Reflections on the Attitudes of the Hudson's Bay Company towards Missionary Work among the Indians," *Western Canadian Journal of Anthropology* 3, 1 (1977). Also of value is J.W. Grant, *The Moon of Wintertime* (Toronto, 1984).

Section Three: The Gold Mining Frontier. On the history of mining in the Yukon before the gold rush, see Melody Webb, *The Last Frontier* (Albuquerque, 1985), and A.A. Wright, *Prelude to Bonanza* (Sidney, BC, 1976). A contemporary account is William Ogilvie, *Early Days on the Yukon* (London, 1913). Two articles by Thomas Stone, "The Mounties as Vigilantes: Reflections on Community and the Transformation of Law in the Yukon, 1885–1897," *Law and Society Review* 4, 1 (1974), and "Atomistic Order and Frontier Violence: Miners and Whalemen in the Nineteenth Century Yukon," *Ethnology* 30 (1983), further develop the theme contained in the selection by him in this volume. W.R. Morrison, *Showing the Flag: The Mounted Police and Canadian Sovereignty in the North, 1894–1925* (Vancouver, 1985) is a study of the role of the police in the establishment of government authority in the Yukon and Northwest Territories. R. Stewart, *Sam Steele: Lion of the Frontier* (Toronto, 1979) is a popular biography of the NWMP's most famous officer. There is a huge popular literature on the gold rush; the most readable account is Pierre Berton, *Klondike Fever* (New York, 1958).

Section Four: After the Gold Rush. The last five chapters of Coates and Morrison, *Land of the Midnight Sun* deal with the Yukon after the rush. An account of mining in the Yukon after 1900 is Lewis Green, *The Gold Hustlers* (Anchorage, 1976). D. Hall, *Clifford Sifton,* 2 vols. (Vancouver, 1982 and 1984), chronicles the waxing and waning of government interest in the mining frontier. Robert Bothwell's *Eldorado* (Toronto, 1984), is an account of the development of Port Radium. Two excellent memoirs are indispensible for this period: Laura Berton, *I Married the Klondike* (Toronto, 1954), and Martha Black, *My Seventy Years* (London, 1938). K.S. Coates, "Best Left as Indians: Government-Native Relations in the Yukon Territory, 1894–1950," *Canadian Journal of Native Studies* (Fall, 1984), illuminates this neglected aspect of the post-gold rush Yukon. See also Gordon Bennett, *Yukon Transportation: A History* (Ottawa, 1978).

Section Five: The Inuit. The standard work on the Inuit from an anthropological perspective is Diamond Jenness, *Eskimo Administration: II. Canada* (Montreal, 1964), now partly superseded by more recent scholarship. A good introduction to the history of Canada's Inuit is Hugh Brody, *The People's Land: Eskimos and Whites in the Eastern Arctic* (Don Mills, 1975); see also his *Maps and Dreams* (Vancouver, 1981) and his *Living Arctic: Hunters of the Canadian North* (Vancouver, 1987). Case studies of relations between the Inuit and whalers are W.G. Ross, ed. *An Arctic Whaling Diary: the Journal of Captain George Comer in Hudson Bay, 1903–1905* (Ottawa, 1975), Thomas Stone, "Whalers and Missionaries at Herschel Island," *Ethnohistory* (1981), and J.R. Bockstoce, *Steam Whaling in the Western Arctic* (New Bedford, Mass., 1977). Richard Diubaldo's *Stefansson and the Canadian Arctic* (Montreal, 1978) is a source of material on the Inuit of the western Arctic as well as the best biography of the North's most controversial explorer.

Section Six: The Modern North. There is a vast literature on numerous aspects of the contemporary North. An overview of the north's position in continental defence is R.J. Diubaldo and S.J. Scheinberg, *A Study of Canadian-American Defence Policy* (Ottawa, 1976). The basic work on Canadian-American northern wartime projects is S.W. Dzubian, *Military Relations Between the United States and Canada, 1939–1945* (Washington, 1959). A study of various aspects of the construction of the Alaska Highway is K.S. Coates, ed., *The Alaska Highway* (Vancouver, 1985). W.R. Morrison, *A Survey of the History and Claims of the Native Peoples of Northern Canada,* 2d ed. (Ottawa, 1985) is an introduction to the subject of native land claims. The "Berger Report"—Thomas R. Berger, *Northern Frontier, Northern Homeland: The Report of the Mackenzie Valley Pipeline Inquiry, 2* vols. (Toronto, 1977) is essential for an understanding of native-government relations as is Réné Fumoleau, *As Long as This Land Shall Last, A History of Treaty 8 and Treaty 11, 1870—1939* (Toronto, 1973). D.H. Pimlott, et al., eds., *Arctic Alternatives*

(Ottawa, 1973), is another useful work. Also of value are H. and K. Mc-Cullum, *This Land is Not for Sale* (Toronto, 1975), P. Cumming, *Canada: Native Land Rights and Northern Development* (Copenhagen, 1977), and M. Watkins, ed., *Dene Nation—the Colony Within* (Toronto, 1977).

Other useful works on contemporary northern economic and political development are Edgar Dosman, ed., *The Arctic in Question* (Toronto, 1976), Edgar Dosman, *The National Interest: the Politics of Northern Development, 1968–1978* (Toronto, 1978), M. O'Malley, *The Past and Future Land* (Toronto, 1976), G. Dacks, *A Choice of Futures* (Toronto, 1981), Sam Hall, *The Fourth World: The Heritage of the Arctic and Its Destruction* (New York, 1988), Kevin McMahon, *Arctic Twilight: Reflections on the Destiny of Canada's Northern Land and People* (Toronto, 1988), John Honderich, *Arctic Imperative* (Toronto, 1987), Barry Lopez, *Arctic Dreams* (New York, 1986), Ulli Stetler, *Inuit: The North in Transition* (Vancouver, 1985), R.Q. Duffy, *The Road to Nunavut* (Kingston, 1988), J.T. Jockel, *No Boundaries Upstairs: Canada, the United States and the Origins of North American Air Defence, 1945–1958* (Vancouver, 1987), and Robert Page, *Northern Development: The Canadian Dilemma* (Toronto, 1986).

L.-E. Hamelin, "Images of the North," In *Canadian Nordicity: It's Your North Too* (Montreal: Harvest House, 1979), 1–13. Reprinted by permission of Harvest House Ltd.

I.S. Maclaren, "The Aesthetic Map of the North, 1845–1959," *Arctic 38*, 2 (June 1985): 89–103. Reprinted by permission of The Arctic Institute of North America, University of Calgary.

Shepard Krech III, "On the Aboriginal Population of the Kutchin," *Arctic Anthropology* 15, 1 (1978): 89–104. Reprinted by permission of Wisconsin Press.

Kerry Abel, "Of Two Minds: Dene Response to the Mackenzie Missions, 1852–1902," (University of Manitoba, 1987). Printed by permission of the author.

Arthur J. Ray, "Periodic Shortages, Native Welfare, and the Hudson's Bay Company, 1670–1930," in *The Subarctic Fur Trade*, ed. S. Krech III (Vancouver: University of British Columbia Press, 1984), 1–20. Reprinted by permission of the University of British Columbia Press.

Thomas Stone, "Flux and Authority in a Subarctic Society: The Yukon Miners in the Nineteenth Century," *Ethnohistory* 30, 4 (1983): 203–16. Reprinted by permission of the author.

Morris Zaslow, "The Yukon: Northern Development in a Canadian-American Context," in *Regionalism in the Canadian Community 1867–1967,* ed. M. Wade (Toronto: University of Toronto Press, 1969), 180–97. Reprinted by permission of the University of Toronto Press.

Kenneth Coates, "Betwixt and Between: The Anglican Church and the Children of the Carcross (Chooutla) Residential School, 1911–1954," *BC Studies* no. 64 (Winter 1984–1985), 27–47. Reprinted by permission of *BC Studies*.

William R. Morrison, "Eagle Over the Arctic: Americans in the Canadian North, 1867–1985," *Canadian Review of American Studies* (Spring 1987), 61–75. Reprinted by permission of the journal.

K.S. Coates and W.R. Morrison, "Transiency in the Far Northwest after the Gold Rush: The Case of the *Princess Sophia*" (University of Victoria, 1988). Printed by permission of the authors.

James G.E. Smith and Ernest S. Burch, Jr. "Chipewyan and Inuit in the Central Canadian Subarctic, 1673–1977," *Arctic Anthropology* 16, 2 (1979): 76–101. Reprinted by permission of the University of Wisconsin Press.

W. Gillies Ross, "Whaling, Inuit, and the Arctic Islands," In *A Century of Canada's Arctic Islands, 1880–1980*, ed. M. Zaslow (Ottawa: Royal Society of

Canada, 1981), 33–50. Reprinted by permission of the Royal Society of Canada and the author.

Philip Goldring, "Inuit Economic Responses to Euro-American Contacts: Southeast Baffin Island, 1824–1940," *Historical Papers* (Ottawa: Canadian Historical Association, 1986), 146–72. Reprinted by permission of the Canadian Historical Association and the author.

John D. O'Neil, "The Politics of Health in the Fourth World: A Northern Canadian Example," *Human Organization* 45 (Summer 1985): 119–28. Reprinted by permission of The Society for Applied Anthropology and the author.

Michael I. Asch, "Capital and Economic Development: A Critical Reappraisal of the Recommendations of the Mackenzie Valley Pipeline Commission," *Culture* 2, 3 (1982): 3–9. Reprinted by permission of *Culture*.

Frances Abele, "Canadian Contradictions: Forty Years of Northern Political Development," *Arctic* 40, 4 (December 1987): 310–20. Reprinted by permission of The Arctic Institute of North America, University of Calgary.

1   2   3   4   5   4782-4   93   92   91   90   89